MONEY FREE AND UNFREE

MONEY FREE AND UN-FREE

GEORGE SELGIN

CATO INSTITUTE
Center for Monetary and Financial Alternatives
WASHINGTON, D.C.

eBook ISBN: 978-1-944424-30-5
Print ISBN: 978-1-944424-29-9

Library of Congress Cataloging-in-Publication Data available.

Cover design: Faceout Studio.
Printed in the United States of America.

CATO INSTITUTE
1000 Massachusetts Avenue, N.W.
Washington, D.C. 20001
www.cato.org

Contents

Figures and Tables

INTRODUCTION

If one institution can be said to exercise a greater influence than any other on the economic well-being of the world's citizens, that institution must surely be the Federal Reserve System. Through its influence on the supply of money and credit in the United States and, indirectly, in other parts of the world, and also through its role in regulating the U.S. financial market, the Fed directly influences both the long-run behavior of spending and prices and the short-run behavior of real interest rates, real output, and unemployment. Occasionally—such as during the so-called Great Moderation roughly coinciding with Alan Greenspan's tenure (1987–2006) as Fed chairman—its conduct has been tolerable, if not beneficial. At other times its policies have been at best controversial and at worst widely condemned.

Despite the Fed's spotted record, most people, economists included, continue to regard it and, more particularly, its governing and monetary-policymaking bodies, the Federal Reserve Board and the Federal Open Market Committee, as the best of all possible means for managing the U.S. dollar, and for indirectly regulating interest rates, prices, unemployment, and countless other macro- and microeconomic variables.

On what evidence or arguments does this consensus rest? Most non-experts who take part in it do so, presumably, out of deference to (most) experts. And the experts themselves? It's only natural to suppose that their own consensus rests upon a careful comparison of the Fed's performance with that of other arrangements, including ones already tested in the United States or elsewhere, and as-yet untested ones that might be put into practice. People who defer to expert opinion presumably do so owing to this natural supposition.

Yet the surprising truth is that most economists, including most champions of the monetary status quo (or something not far from it), are only vaguely familiar with alternative arrangements, assuming that they are aware of them at all. Ask a monetary economist to compare the Fed's record to that of the pre-Fed National Currency System, for example, and he or she is likely to declare confidently that, since World War II at least, the price level has become more predictable, output much more stable, and business contractions much less frequent and protracted, than was the case before 1913. In fact, none of these claims is true. Although the Fed was established in response to a series of severe economic crises, in most respects its performance has been even worse than that of the admittedly flawed system it replaced.

Likewise, although most economists are quick to pronounce the gold standard an unstable, if not barbaric, arrangement, few appreciate the crucial difference between the pre-1914 "classical" gold standard, which actually worked remarkably well, and the interwar "gold exchange standard," which did not. Many also tend to blame the (classical) gold standard for pre-Fed financial and economic instability that was actually the fault of ancillary banking and currency legislation—a mistake that's easy enough to avoid if one compares the United States' classical gold-standard experience with that of some other gold-standard countries.

Not surprisingly, most U.S. economists know even less about the monetary histories of other countries than they do about U.S. monetary history. Take, for example, Canada's experience prior to 1935, when the Bank of Canada was established. Few know that even though it also lacked a central bank, Canada avoided not only the crises that shook the United States before 1914, but also those by which it was afflicted after 1929. In fact, not a single Canadian bank failed throughout the entire 1930s, while thousands of U.S. banks went under. Still less is it likely that our economist knows that the Scottish banking system was almost crisis free for a century prior to 1845, while England suffered from crisis after crisis—despite the fact that Scottish banks had no central bank to turn to, and despite the relative lack of banking regulations north of the Tweed. Instead of knowing about the actual record of past, decentralized monetary systems, most economists today simply take for granted that no country can avoid financial crises except by resort to substantial government regulation, including laws establishing a central bank capable of regulating its money supply and serving as a "lender of last resort."

Given that so many economists today are unfamiliar with the non-central-bank-based monetary arrangements of the past, and so are convinced, in their ignorance, that such systems couldn't have worked well, it should come as no surprise that few have bothered to seriously consider how other, still experimental alternatives, might also prove more conducive to financial and monetary stability than the Fed and other central banks.

Of the many misunderstandings that lack of familiarity with past and hypothetical monetary alternatives can be said to have bred, one is of paramount importance: the failure to distinguish both weaknesses in financial arrangements and fluctuations in money and credit attributable to market-based forces and institutions from ones attributable to government interference with such market-based forces and institutions. It is owing to this paramount misunderstanding that experts, instead of appreciating the harm done by past and present government interference with market-based monetary and banking arrangements, continue, despite failure after failure, to cling to the vain hope that lasting stability might be achieved by adding still more layers of government control to those already in place.

Economists' general lack of awareness of, and interest in, alternative monetary arrangements—and decentralized alternatives especially—is partly due to the tremendous influence exerted by central banks themselves, and partly a reflection of the state of modern economics graduate programs.* Most of the latter programs have dispensed with classes on either economic history or the history of economic thought—subjects once considered indispensable—so as to make room for more courses on mathematical modeling and econometrics. Courses on monetary theory and macroeconomics have at the same time become increasingly abstract—so much so, indeed, that many of them hardly refer to "money" at all! Faced with such a curriculum, graduate students are left to their own devices when it comes to learning anything at all about existing U.S. monetary institutions, let alone foreign or historical ones, or others that have been proposed but never tried.

My own exposure to such alternatives has been due mainly to a series of lucky accidents. First, the beginning of my graduate studies happened

* Concerning the Fed's influence, see White (2005).

to coincide with the height of the post-1970s inflation, which sparked my interest in monetary economics. Second, I was, at the time, enrolled in an MA program in resource economics. Consequently, I had no expert (and, given the time, presumably Keynesian) professors to "train me" on the topic, and so had to avail myself of the university library. Third, after reading scores of very bad books on money, I finally got to Ludwig von Mises' *Theory of Money and Credit*, which at last gave me what felt like a firm foothold on the topic. Von Mises in turn led me to F. A. Hayek, whose *Denationalization of Money* sparked my interest in market-based, competitive currency systems. My pursuit of that interest led me to Lawrence White, then himself a graduate student at the University of California, Los Angeles, who shared with me his work on the Scottish banking system. That encounter, finally, led to my becoming Larry's first graduate student when he joined the faculty at New York University and to my pursuit there and since of my own research on free banking and other, alternative monetary arrangements.

The essays reproduced here, with minor changes, represent a sample of that research, with an emphasis on my writings pertaining to U.S. experience. For convenience, I've divided the volume into three parts. The essays in Part I, "Regulatory Sources of Financial Instability," trace financial and monetary instability to government interference with monetary systems' free (and competitive) development, and explain how that interference has itself often been aimed not at securing monetary and financial stability, but at securing government revenue.

Part II, "Before the Fed," begins with two papers examining the harmful long-run consequences of the Civil War monetary reforms inspired by the Northern government's desperate search for wartime revenue, and ends with a revisionist account of the reform efforts that resulted in the passage of the Federal Reserve Act.

Part III, "The Federal Reserve Era," begins with an overview of the rise and fall of the gold standard, which was supposed to constrain the Fed's powers of money creation, but which was instead gradually dismantled following the Fed's establishment. This overview is followed by a chapter assessing the Fed's record during its first century, and another reviewing Fed officials' tendency to misrepresent that record. The section ends with a paper that argues for streamlining the Federal Reserve's operating system, while making it work equally well both in normal times and during crises, by dispensing with both the primary dealer system and discount window lending, while having the Fed purchase private as well as government securities by means of auctions open to numerous bank and nonbank counterparties.

$ $ $

The essays gathered here were written over a time span just shy of three decades. Consequently, I cannot hope to recall, much less to properly acknowledge, my debts to all the people who assisted me in writing them. I cannot possibly overlook, on the other hand, my indebtedness to several persons, starting with Larry White who, besides having been my mentor in graduate school and my colleague at the University of Georgia, is also the coauthor of several of the papers collected here. Bill Lastrapes, another of my Georgia colleagues and the best darn time-series econometrician I know, also collaborated on one of those papers. Finally, this volume would not be before you were it not for the efforts of my Cato colleagues Tom Clougherty, who edited the manuscript, and John Samples, who has seen it into print. Finally, I am extremely grateful to John Allison, Cato's former president and CEO, who turned my dream of directing a Center for Monetary and Financial Alternatives into reality.

PART I

REGULATORY SOURCES OF FINANCIAL INSTABILITY

1

A FISCAL THEORY OF GOVERNMENT'S ROLE IN MONEY*

WITH LAWRENCE H. WHITE

> Economic policy has, up to the turn of the century, been motivated primarily by fiscal considerations. . . . [F]iscal measures have created and destroyed industries . . . even where this was not their intent, and have in this manner contributed directly to the construction (and distortion) of the edifice of the modern economy.
>
> —JOSEPH SCHUMPETER ([1918] 1954: 7)

WHY DO GOVERNMENTS play the roles they do in the monetary system? In particular, why have national governments almost universally taken over the business of issuing coins and paper currency, and replaced precious metals with fiat money as the base supporting bank-issued money? Why have they not (in developed countries, at least) also nationalized the production of checking accounts, choosing instead to tax and regulate private banks?

* Originally published in *Economic Inquiry* 37, no. 1 (January 1999): 154–65. The authors received helpful comments from John Lott, David Glasner, seminar participants at George Mason University and North Carolina State University, and session participants at American Economic Association and Southern Economic Association meetings. Lawrence H. White is a professor of economics at George Mason University and a senior fellow of the Cato Institute.

Standard answers to these questions refer to market failures (natural monopolies, externalities, or information asymmetries) that might render unregulated private production of money inefficient or unstable or infeasible. Market-failure explanations assume that governments shape monetary institutions to serve money holders, by providing a more efficient and stable payments system than would exist under laissez faire. Thus, private competition is not allowed in currency issue because markets inherently would fail (or historically did fail) there, and the legal restrictions we see on deposit banking are ones needed to prevent market failures in that industry.

Recent research supplies three reasons for doubting the adequacy of the market-failure approach for explaining monetary arrangements. First, economic historians have found that the actual forms taken by money and banking regulations, and the timing of their adoption, often have little apparent connection to alleged market failures. Observed regulations (e.g., reserve requirements that freeze rather than enhance liquidity) are ill designed to remedy the suboptimalities that are supposed to have motivated them. Second, monetary historians have found that systems close to laissez faire have (by and large) been at least as successful as more restricted systems. Finally, monetary theorists have pointed out weaknesses in theoretical arguments for market failure in money.[1]

If the market-failure explanation is doubtful, how else can one explain government's role in money? Charles Kindleberger (1994: xi) poses the challenge squarely: the economist who doubts the market-failure approach "has to explain why there seems to be a strong revealed preference in history for a sole issuer." We propose a *fiscal* hypothesis: governments have come to supply currency, and to restrict the private supply of currency and deposits, not to remedy market failures, but to provide themselves with seigniorage and loans on favorable terms. Government currency monopolies and bank regulations can thus be understood as part of the tax system. The "strong revealed preference in history for a sole issuer" is, fundamentally, the preference of fiscal authorities, not of consumers.[2]

Economic historians have, of course, often recognized fiscal motives behind specific monetary arrangements, especially those of ancient and medieval autocracies. Analysts of developing countries today have recognized that policies of "financial repression" aim at fostering "financial institutions and financial instruments from which government can expropriate significant seigniorage" (Fry 1988: 14; Giovanni and de Melo 1993). We go further in arguing that fiscal forces have *typically* shaped the industrial organization of money production, throughout history and across countries, and account for its major institutional features even in advanced democracies today. Such observed legal restrictions as statutory reserve requirements, interest rate ceilings, foreign exchange controls, and monopoly issue of currency impede efficiency but raise revenue.

A RATIONAL DICTATOR MODEL

To develop our hypothesis, we adopt a method found in the writings of the Italian fiscal theorists, especially Amilcare Puviani. According to James Buchanan (1960: 64), Puviani tried to account for overall government tax arrangements by asking "two simple questions." First, what sort of tax system would a "rational dictator" put in place if his aim were "to exploit the taxpaying public to the greatest possible degree," gaining the greatest revenue consistent with a given threshold of public resistance? Second, to what extent do actual tax arrangements conform with those predicted by such a rational dictator (or "Leviathan") model? Puviani found a high degree of correspondence between actual tax arrangements in postunification Italy and ones predicted by his model.[3] We argue that a fiscal approach also accounts for monetary arrangements.

To avoid misunderstanding, we are not proposing that governments have consciously designed all monetary arrangements, from scratch, to achieve purely fiscal ends. Such a view would be at odds with the gradual and piecemeal historical development of governments' monetary roles. Instead, as we discuss in more detail below, revenue-seeking governments have opportunistically modified private-market arrangements as they developed.[4] Revenue-enhancing modifications tend to survive, while others are more likely to be discarded. The resulting arrangements thus look *as if* they were designed from scratch to generate government revenue. The "rational dictator" model of monetary arrangements should be understood in this as-if fashion.

SEIGNIORAGE-ENHANCING INSTITUTIONS

An extensive literature analyzes the revenue-raising device known as seigniorage or inflationary finance. The basic concept is straightforward: a government reaps profit by producing new base money at an expense less than the value of the money produced. The government finances expenditures by spending the new units of base money into circulation.[5] Such expansion of the monetary base implicitly taxes base money holders by diluting the value of existing money balances. For the most part, the literature treats the base-money expansion rate (or the associated price inflation rate) as the government's choice variable, taking monetary institutions as given. The focus lies on the rate that maximizes seigniorage, or alternatively minimizes the deadweight burden of taxation subject to a revenue constraint. In contrast, we inquire here into what sorts of monetary *institutions* enhance seigniorage.

WHY COLLECT SEIGNIORAGE AT ALL?

Several features make seigniorage an attractive option for raising revenue. First, a tax on money balances might be consistent with the Ramsey rule for minimizing the deadweight burden of raising a given amount of overall government revenue. Several theorists have argued, however, that when money is regarded as an intermediate good, any positive inflation tax is inefficient, even given a positive revenue constraint. The optimal inflation tax is then zero (Banaian et al. 1994; Correia and Teles 1996). If so, the collection of seigniorage, and the shaping of monetary institutions to that end, cannot be justified on the grounds of fiscal efficiency.[6]

Second, seigniorage is a relatively hidden tax. If the public blames inflation on causes other than the government's monetary policy, the political resistance provoked by an inflation tax may be lower, for a given amount of revenue, than that of more obvious taxes. A rational dictator concerned with maximizing his survival in power, extracting seigniorage to the point where the marginal political resistance incurred per dollar of revenue is equal to that of alternative taxes, will then exploit the inflation tax even beyond the point where its marginal deadweight burden equals that of other taxes.

Finally, to the extent that changes in the nominal stock of base money can be made unexpectedly, they impose an ex post capital levy on holders of the state's unindexed nominal liabilities, including base money. Such a levy may yield substantial revenue rapidly, making seigniorage an especially valuable fiscal resource during an emergency that threatens the state's survival, such as an insurrection or external military threat (Glasner 1997). Its unique revenue-raising speed helps to explain why state monopoly of base money survives into modern times, long after state monopolies of other goods like salt have given way to taxation of private producers. We later discuss surprise inflation and the time-consistency issue it poses.

SEIGNIORAGE FROM COMMODITY MONEY

What sort of outside-money regime would a rational dictator prefer for fiscal purposes? Precious metals offer the potential for seigniorage extraction through debasement. By adding base metal, 100 silver coins can be remade into 105 (or 150 or 200) apparently similar coins. Coins entirely composed of base metal, by contrast, cannot be further debased. A cowrie shell or a peppercorn, being a naturally occurring unit, cannot be easily remade or redenominated. Putting aside fiat money for now, fiscal considerations would incline a rational dictator to favor the precious metals over other commodity monies.

Although the earliest known coins appear to have been privately produced, ancient rulers seeking a new source of revenue (and propaganda, by putting the ruler's name or face on the coins) soon granted themselves legal monopolies in minting (Burns 1965). A monopoly mint extracts seigniorage from the metal it coins, subject to the accounting identity

$$M = PQ + C + S,$$

where M is the nominal value assigned to a batch of coins (e.g., 100 "shillings"), P is the nominal price paid by the mint per ounce of precious metal,

Q is the number of ounces of precious metal embodied in the batch of coins, C is the remaining average cost of minting, and S is the nominal seigniorage. Out of every M's worth of shillings coined, PQ is paid to individuals who brought in precious metal, C covers other mint expenses, and S is retained as profit for the mint owner. Total seigniorage per year depends on how many batches of coins are produced per year.

Greater nominal seigniorage per batch is earned by *debasement* when Q is reduced for a given M. When reducing silver content, medieval governments typically added base metal, reducing the *fineness* rather than the size of coins. Minting costs were lower because coin dies did not need to be resized, and the new coins would circulate more readily because they closely resembled the old. The reduction in metallic content might even go undetected for a time, enhancing short-run real revenues. Alternately, each new shilling could simply be declared to have a higher nominal value, increasing M for a given Q.[7] Greater seigniorage per batch can also be earned without debasement by reducing P, that is, putting as much silver into each shilling but paying fewer shillings per batch back to the provider of silver.

As an excess profit or rent in coin production, seigniorage cannot persist without legal restrictions on entry. The fiscal motive thus accounts for state-enforced coinage monopolies. In a competitive minting industry with constant returns to scale, competition would enforce the condition of price equal to marginal and average cost, $M = PQ + C$. Every mint, including the monarch's, would earn zero seigniorage if competing mints could be established side by side, bullion owners were free to choose where to take their bullion to be coined, and no steps were taken to restrict the circulation of nongovernmental coins so that all coins were valued by precious metal content. The few historical cases where competing private mints were allowed (e.g., gold-rush California) do not exhibit the sort of market failures—fraud, or lack of standardization—that are sometimes hypothesized to provide an efficiency-enhancing role for the state in coinage.[8]

The efficiency theory of government coinage predicts that coinage systems will vary in geographic scope only in response to changing economies of scale in coin production. The fiscal hypothesis, by contrast, predicts that coinage systems will have exclusive territories that expand and contract with sovereign realms. The history of medieval coinage supports the fiscal hypothesis. European monarchs of the Middle Ages insisted that the right to mint coins belonged exclusively to the sovereign (thus Thomas Bisson [1979] speaks of "the proprietary coinage"), even when diseconomies of plant scale led them to delegate actual coin production to local moneyers. During the early Middle Ages kings and princes had trouble enforcing their laws against independent coinages. This "fragmentation of monetary rights" was not due to changing economies of scale in coin production but "corresponded to the multiplication of territorial powers" (Bisson 1979: 3). When kings regained power over the nobility, one of their first objectives "was to reclaim control over the coinage" (Glasner 1997: 27).

Many rulers also enforced legal restrictions that were designed to secure the profit from issuing debased coins accepted at face value. Marie-Thérèse Boyer-Xambeu and others (1994: 49–59) note, "Until the sixteenth century princes in most countries prohibited the weighing of coins and made people accept them all, even when used up, simply in view of their imprints and inscriptions." Even when weighing was later allowed (to encourage the return of worn coins to the mint), the practice of valuing coins in exchange by bullion weight rather than by tale was "expressly forbidden." Payments in metal other than the prince's coin, and contracts specifying payments by bullion weight, were outlawed. The practice of culling good coin and passing on bad was a crime that "systematically carried the death sentence." It is hard to imagine an efficiency-enhancing rationale for such restrictions.

Two reasons consistent with the fiscal hypothesis suggest why past monarchs preferred owning monopoly mints to taxing private mints. First, as the modern theory of vertical integration suggests, monitoring and enforcement problems would likely be lower with vertically integrated (state-owned) mints. Second, increases in the seigniorage rate might be accomplished at lower cost than equivalent increases in the rate of mint taxation, in part because the incidence of an increased mint tax would be more transparent, more concentrated, and therefore likely to meet with more political resistance than a debasement. Both considerations become especially relevant during a fiscal emergency, when revenue needs to be raised immediately. Peter

Spufford's (1988) figures indicate that, in times of war, mint-owning medieval rulers raised as much as 60 percent to 92 percent of their total revenues through debasement.

The value of the ability to meet a fiscal emergency also explains why an insecure rational dictator would prefer owning a monopoly mint to the alternative of selling or leasing monopoly franchises to private bidders. Franchising substitutes fixed advance payments for what would otherwise be a variable flow, but rules out recourse to surprise inflation and corresponding emergency capital levies. Accordingly, we observe that central governments have typically retained operational control over mints.

LOCAL VERSUS INTERNATIONAL COIN

A government that seeks seigniorage from the monopoly production of coin may act as a *discriminating* monopolist when the elasticity of demand with respect to their depreciation rates varies across coins: the revenue-maximizing rate is lower for coins facing relatively elastic demand. During the early Middle Ages in Europe, low-value or "petty" silver coin from local mints circulated almost exclusively in local exchange. Higher-value coin from the same mints was mainly used in international markets (Cipolla 1956), where it competed head-on with foreign coin.[9] Because the demand for high-value coins was much more elastic, a rational dictator would subject high-value coins to lower rates of seigniorage (less frequent debasement).

Medieval European governments accordingly extracted less seigniorage from gold coin than from silver, and debasement of silver coins was much less frequent for large denominations than for small.[10] Mints went to great lengths to preserve the quality of their "international" monies (*monete grosse*) even while ruthlessly debasing the locally used petty coins. The Spanish government, for example, took pains to preserve the metallic content of its silver coin, which by the late 15th century had become Europe's (and the New World's) most stable and coveted, while actively debasing the petty copper coinage that it produced as a local monopoly (Motomura 1994). The English government debased some small-denomination coins, but carefully protected the international reputation of larger coins, especially sterling (Mayhew 1992).

FIAT VERSUS COMMODITY MONEY

The seigniorage motive favors fiat over commodity money in three respects. First, government captures a one-shot profit from replacing the existing stock of monetary metal with fiat money.[11] Second, issuing fiat money is a cheaper way to capture an ongoing flow of seigniorage revenues each year. Finally, the demand for a fiat money is less elastic, because users encounter greater costs in trying to employ any foreign money in its place. We elaborate on these last two points in turn.

Seigniorage flow is most profitably captured with a money that can be produced (in nominal units) at zero resource cost, and whose nominal stock can be expanded at whatever rate desired. In principle, nominal units of money can be created under a silver standard without incurring mining costs, and the nominal money growth rate can be controlled, by continual debasement (i.e., by continually redefining the unit of account to equal progressively fewer grams of pure silver). A mint that wants to earn a large annual profit from debasement, however, must recoin a large part of the outstanding money stock. In practice, it is much more costly to expand the nominal stock of coins by 5 percent through recoinage than it is to expand the nominal stock of a fiat money by 5 percent, which requires only the expansion of ledger entries and the printing of more identical paper notes.

The process of debasement also invites substantial public resistance. Compulsion, no lighter and no more popular than that necessary to exact ordinary taxes, is needed to prevent market participants from exchanging and valuing new (debased) coins by weight rather than face value, and thus to encourage them to treat both old domestic coin and foreign coin as mere raw material to be taken to the mint. The tax imposed by recoinage is fairly obvious once the reduced precious metal content of the new coins becomes known. Seigniorage flow can be extracted more easily and less obviously with a fiat money, whose nominal quantity can be increased merely by spending new units into circulation that are identical to existing units, obviating the need to recall or devalue the old currency. No one objects to accepting the newly issued units at a value equal to the old—since they are identical in (zero) commodity content and interchangeable—so no obvious compulsion is needed.

Fiat money also offers the public smaller opportunities for switching to alternative base monies. Under a silver standard, alternative coins can always be evaluated (even if not legally) by weight, making the substitution of foreign for domestic money a relatively simple matter of measuring both in terms of silver content (measured in a fixed reference weight unit, a so-called "ghost money" unit). If domestic money is being frequently debased, traders quoting prices in weight units would naturally favor more stable foreign coins—less frequently requiring weighing and assaying—as their medium of exchange. By contrast, traders who consider switching from a domestic to an alternative *fiat* currency as a medium of exchange find that there is no simple common metric. A network effect associated with using the common unit of account protects the incumbent currency by imposing high transactions costs on those who would switch first (Selgin 2003). Acceptance of an alternative currency in transactions presupposes familiarity with its exchange value, but until its acceptance is widespread, or at least until the domestic unit has become thoroughly unreliable as a unit of account (as in a high inflation), there is scant individual incentive to track the exchange rate between the incumbent and alternative currencies. Inflation thus usually has to become quite severe before "dollarization" of domestic transactions occurs.

Because currency substitution and the elasticity of demand for domestic base money are reduced under fiat currency, the fiscal hypothesis predicts higher inflation rates under fiat standards than under metallic standards (which allow inflationary finance via debasement). This prediction is borne out historically in a comparison of commodity-money and fiat-money episodes after 1600 (Rolnick and Weber 1994).

FIAT-MONEY MONOPOLY

Why does a revenue-seeking government itself issue fiat currency monopolistically, instead of taxing private issuers? The reasons for thinking that a seigniorage-seeking government would prefer a mint monopoly to taxation of private mints apply again. In the case of fiat money, a more fundamental reason exists as well: open competition in the production of fiat currency is, to date, a purely hypothetical possibility, and one that might not be sustainable in practice. If "competitive supply" of fiat money meant free entry into the production of fiat dollar notes—the equivalent of legalized counterfeiting—each counterfeiter would produce notes until even the highest denomination note was worth no more than the paper and ink it contained. If there were no upper bound on denominations, profits from producing dollars would persist until the dollar became worthless (Friedman 1960). Alternatively, with trademark protection, perfectly competing firms might issue distinct irredeemable monies, bearing identifiable brand names but perfect substitutes for one another (Klein 1974; Taub 1985). The result would again be an equilibrium without economic profit, either (in the case where an enforceable infinite-horizon precommitment is feasible) with positive-valued money paying a competitive rate of return, or (in the case where time-inconsistency or "cheating" cannot be prevented) with the same worthless-money outcome as the legalized counterfeiting case (Selgin and White 1994).

Monopoly revenues from the production of fiat money could in principle be obtained by a group of fiat-money issuing institutions whose aggregate currency issue is set at the monopolist's revenue-maximizing level. The principle drawback of this arrangement is that it requires costly monitoring to avoid cheating (issues in excess of allotments) by individual cartel members. Italy in the late 19th century offers a case in which the cartel approach proved unsustainable. Following the Risorgimento, the new national Italian government, having failed in its early attempts to establish a single bank of issue, awarded legal tender status to the (then irredeemable) notes of six established banks in return for their funding of government debt. The system broke down because one cartel member—the Bank of Rome—was discovered to have cheated on the cartel, secretly exceeding its note allotment by issuing notes with duplicate serial numbers (Sannucci 1989).

RESTRICTIONS ON SUBSTITUTES

The ability of a national fiat-money producer to earn seigniorage is, like that of a national mint, limited by the availability of substitutes for domestic base money. Potential substitutes include foreign currencies. As noted above in the contrast between local and international coin in medieval Europe, opportunities for substitution into foreign currency increase the elasticity of demand for domestic money. They thereby reduce the maximum steady-state real seigniorage, and raise the inflation rate associated with achieving any target level of real seigniorage. A rational dictator would take steps to limit currency substitution, and could do so using such means as exchange controls and legal tender laws (Nichols 1974). Nations threatened by loss of seigniorage due to currency substitution, because they have for other reasons committed to dismantle barriers to free capital flows, might try to form a cartel—a multinational central bank—and share its seigniorage. The movement for a European central bank can thus be given a fiscal interpretation.

A second set of close substitutes for domestic base money consists of private financial assets, including redeemable private bank notes and deposits, that function as exchange media. Here again, a rational dictator would take steps to suppress the substitutes, either by prohibiting them altogether (as has been commonly done with private bank notes), by capping their interest yield (as has sometimes been done with bank deposits), or by otherwise restricting their availability or attractiveness.

Alternatively, bank liabilities can simply be taxed—for example, by reserve requirements. Unlike competitive private issue of commodity or fiat base money, private banking does not deprive the government of the ability to manipulate the rate of inflation. When bank notes and deposits are redeemable claims to fiat money, their rate of expansion ultimately depends on the rate at which the stock of fiat money expands. It follows that, in allowing private firms to issue redeemable substitutes for (fiat) base money, a rational dictator would not deprive himself of the ability to increase short-run seigniorage via a surprise inflation.

Gerald Dwyer and Thomas Saving (1986) show that, if bank deposits and currency are perfect substitutes, and if government is as efficient as private firms in producing money, then government can obtain the same maximum steady-state revenue by imposing a positive reserve ratio or other form of tax "licensing fee" on a private banking industry as it would by suppressing private banking altogether. Historically, governments have typically chosen to suppress private bank notes, while allowing checkable private bank deposits to coexist along with fiat money. A straightforward explanation for this, consistent with the rational dictator model, is that the public treats reputable bank notes as very close substitutes for base money. In historical cases where private note issuance was relatively unrestricted, as in Scotland and Canada, commercial bank notes displaced coin (and, in Canada, government-issued "Dominion" notes) almost entirely where their denominations overlapped. The government therefore enhances its seigniorage tax base by suppressing private notes.[12]

Bank deposits, by contrast, are *not* such close substitutes for base money, and competing private banks can typically produce deposits and other banking services more efficiently than government can.[13] Taxes on private banks are likely to bring in more revenue than a ban on private banking that enhances seigniorage only slightly. In consequence, as David Glasner (1989: 33) notes, for fiscal reasons, "most governments have preferred allowing banks to operate and exploiting them as a source of credit to suppressing them or to operating banks of their own."

Fiscal considerations can thus account for governments allowing competitive deposit-taking (subject to statutory reserve requirements and other devices aimed at directly or indirectly taxing bank deposits) while suppressing redeemable private bank notes.

MONETARY REPUDIATION AND THE TIME-INCONSISTENCY PROBLEM

Governments, as we have noted above, may sometimes seek revenue through a surprise inflation that acts as a "capital levy" on money. The capital levy is imposed by a deliberate short-run burst of money creation. Holders of cash balances experience a loss of real wealth as the price level jumps more than expected. Such a capital levy makes it possible to generate more real revenue in the short run, but at the cost of smaller steady-state seigniorage once the public recognizes the risk of a high-inflation period occurring and therefore holds less real base money at any given nonpeak inflation rate than it would hold if the inflation rate were viewed as stable.

The rational dictator would find inflationary capital levies most worthwhile during emergencies (especially wars) that put present revenues at a large premium over future revenues by threatening his reign (Glasner 1989).

A capital levy is attractive to a government that attaches a high discount rate to revenues obtained in the future, or one that expects to be short lived without the levy. Consistent with this view is the finding of Alex Cukierman and others (1992) that inflation rates and reliance upon seigniorage revenue are positively correlated with political instability and polarization. In countries with more unstable and polarized political systems, established governments are more willing to sacrifice their long-run inflation tax base to remain in power, because such a strategy will either preserve the particular government that resorts to it, or will at least serve to "constrain the behavior of future governments . . . with which they disagree" (Cukierman et al. 1992: 538). In general, a rational dictator could not exclude the possibility of confronting a fiscal emergency at some future date, and so would value a monetary arrangement that allows him to resort to an inflationary capital levy even if in ordinary times he collects little seigniorage (Glasner 1997).

However, a capital levy strategy is time inconsistent: it yields more revenue (in present value terms) than steady inflation only if levies are greater than expected. A capital levy that appears "optimal" for each rational dictator, considered in isolation from his predecessors and successors, may be suboptimal for all successive rulers together. If the public fears that the government will expropriate much of their monetary wealth, they will hold smaller real balances, reducing (to zero, in the limiting case where total expropriation is expected) the maximum yield to all successive governments from a steady-state inflation tax.

The time-inconsistency problem associated with monetary repudiation supplies a rational dictator with a motive for trying to convince the public that monetary policy would be based upon a long time horizon, beyond the term of any particular ruler. In other words, the rational dictator would want to be able to resort to surprise inflation, but would also want the public to believe that he would probably not resort to it.

If the dictator were well entrenched, faced few external military threats, and had credibly arranged for a line of successors who would maintain his policies indefinitely, then the public might recognize that he had more to lose than to gain by repudiating the currency. On the other hand, short-lived dictators (and rulers in democratic regimes) are typically unable to make such arrangements, and so must seek a different solution. One historical solution was retention of a fixed-parity metallic standard, modified to allow for the suspension of central bank convertibility during fiscal emergencies.[14] Drawbacks of this arrangement included its inability to yield much seigniorage during noncrisis times, and the high cost of sustaining (via postcrisis deflation) the public's confidence in the promise to preserve the ancient and honorable parity.

Another solution, where rival parties are not severely polarized (and so are willing to cooperate to attain mutually desired ends) is the establishment of an "independent" monetary authority that is supposed, like a business corporation, to operate with a time horizon much longer than its current directors' terms. The decision to form an independent monetary authority is most likely to be made when rival political parties have little to lose by cooperating to restore a depressed inflation-tax base, such as immediately following an inflation-based capital levy that has greatly increased the public's estimate of the likelihood of future high inflation.

Historically, then, central banks are most likely to be given independence by democratic governments in the wake of relatively severe inflations. The Reichsbank, for example, gained independence at the end of the German hyperinflation. In the United States, the "accord" giving the Federal Reserve greater independence from the Treasury came in the wake of the post–World War II inflation. Cross-sectionally, our argument predicts that independent central banks—serving the need for a commitment device—should be found more commonly in pluralistic democracies than in autocratic states where a ruling lineage has secure tenure. This prediction is broadly consistent with evidence from the 1980s. In Cukierman's (1992) ranking of 46 central banks, the 14 most independent were found in liberal democracies, with the sole exception of Hungary's. Of the remaining 32 less-independent banks, 16 were in countries that were authoritarian for the entire 1980s, and 6 more were in countries that were authoritarian at the start of the decade.[15]

The fiscal hypothesis suggests that central bank independence is unlikely to be absolute, and predicts that independence is most likely to be withdrawn during periods of heavy fiscal demand. Consistent with that prediction, the Reichsbank lost its independence during Adolf Hitler's rearmament program, and the Federal Reserve System lost its during both world wars (Sylla 1988).

THE EVOLUTION OF MONETARY ARRANGEMENTS

On the face of it, present-day monetary institutions display several striking similarities to those predicted by the rational dictator model. Practically everywhere, base money *does* take the form of fiat paper or deposit credits issued by a central bank.[16] These central banks enjoy exclusive monopoly privileges granted to them by their governments, returning the bulk of their seigniorage revenues to the sponsor governments. Currency areas correspond to national political boundaries rather than to the criteria suggested by the theory of optimal currency areas. Typically, no statute or rule limits the rate at which the central bank may expand the monetary base. Private firms are typically prohibited from issuing redeemable bank notes. Banks are, on the other hand, typically allowed to supply checkable deposits, subject to reserve requirements and other taxes.

Just how is it that monetary institutions came to take a form so well suited for meeting governments' fiscal ends? An answer based on continuous seigniorage maximization, in which governments are portrayed as designing monetary arrangements from scratch purely to achieve fiscal ends, would be far from adequate. Fiscal motives, we have argued, do directly explain why various rulers monopolized coinage, providing a precedent for later state monopolization of paper money. But fiscal motives by themselves do not account for the gradualness and seeming haphazardness with which revenue-enhancing reforms arrived, culminating in monopoly issue of fiat money.

In modern times, especially, the governments of industrial democracies do not continuously act to maximize seigniorage: inflation rates would be much higher if they did. Yet monetary institutions capable of extracting maximum seigniorage from the public have emerged and have persisted. Indeed, the single most effective means for extracting seigniorage—monopoly issue of fiat money—became a permanent feature of monetary systems only during the 20th century.

Our explanation for the gradual and uneven development of seigniorage-enhancing monetary institutions consists of three parts. The first is that government monetary institutions represent to a large extent piecemeal and opportunistic modifications of private-market developments, including the growth of banking and substitution of paper notes and checking accounts for gold and silver coins. The more genuinely "Leviathan-like" governments of preindustrial times were simply unable to take advantage of such technological developments, and so had to settle for relatively limited seigniorage revenues obtainable through mint monopolies. Eventually, as explained above, increased opportunities for foreign currency substitution made the exploitation of mint monopolies for revenue unprofitable, causing governments to look elsewhere for sources of revenue, and emergency revenue especially. One such source was the banking industry, originally perceived not as a device for earning seigniorage, but as a source of loans on favorable terms. Such loans were typically obtained in exchange for awards of monopoly privileges, especially in note issuance (Smith 1936). The harnessing of monopoly banks of issue—central banks—as sources of substantial seigniorage came later, with the discovery that such banks (unlike competing banks of issue) could suspend payments with relative impunity, opening the way to the emergence of fiat money.

We hypothesize that the seigniorage motive did not produce fiat money before the 20th century[17] because (redeemable) bank notes had not yet become commonly accepted in areas of lesser financial sophistication; thus, those areas could not be subjected to a capital levy by the government's monopolizing the issue of bank notes and permanently suspending redemption of government notes. As Gabriel Ardant (1975: 192) puts it, "a developed economy was the prerequisite. It was necessary that bank bills be common in all circles and that the state could pay its soldiers, its functionaries, even its peasants in paper money. . . . France in the seventeenth century did not have the conditions for a successful state manipulation of the money supply." During the Restriction period of 1797–1821, even while the rest of the United Kingdom operated on a Bank of England–note standard, Northern Ireland's continued adherence to a gold coin standard indicated that bank notes did not yet commonly circulate there. California likewise remained on a gold coin standard during the American Civil War, accepting "greenback dollars" only at a discount, and thus remained immune from seigniorage taxation through the issue of greenbacks.

The second part is that governments, and democratic ones especially, are most anxious to obtain seigniorage revenues, and to alter monetary arrangements in ways that generate more seigniorage, during fiscal emergencies, especially wars. Such emergencies act as fiscal catalysts for seigniorage-enhancing innovations that public resistance might otherwise preclude. Thus, the fiscal hypothesis explains the observation that the move from commodity to fiat money typically occurred in steps corresponding to fiscal emergencies.[18] The first step away from the gold or silver standard in many countries, as already noted, was the establishment of a government-sponsored bank. The Bank of England, the Bank of France, and the Swedish Riksbank are well-known examples of government-sponsored banks established to play the fiscal role of lending the government funds on favorable terms. Over time, with the aid of further legislation that granted it a note-issuing monopoly, the privileged bank's liabilities became high-powered money. In many European countries this step was reached by end of the 19th century. Fiat money could then be established by the suspensions of central bank liabilities prompted by the fiscal emergency of World War I.[19] In the United States, where central bank liabilities achieved high-powered status somewhat later, the establishment of fiat money awaited the fiscal emergency of the Great Depression. The leading alternative to the fiscal hypothesis, the view that government's purpose in establishing fiat money is to remedy a market failure to converge to a more efficient monetary standard, offers no explanation for the historical timing of the steps toward fiat money.

The third and final part of our explanation is that, once a revenue-generating reform is in place, it is more likely to survive than other arrangements even when it proves to be a source of disorder. Glasner (1997: 36) argues that early states with access to seigniorage "improved their chances of survival in military competition." During peacetime also, fiscally advantageous innovations prove especially durable, in part because they enjoy the support of powerful interest groups: the recipients of state spending, and the fiscal authorities and regulators themselves. The result is a gradual accretion of revenue-enhancing changes, culminating in arrangements that look remarkably as if they were designed from scratch to maximize government revenue.

Together these arguments imply that seigniorage-enhancing institutional arrangements will be observed emerging later in countries that face fewer fiscal crises, and especially those facing fewer external military threats. Thus, central banking came early to belligerent nations of Europe and only later to Switzerland, North America, Australia, and New Zealand.

CONCLUSION

Fiscal considerations explain the main contours of government's roles in money and their evolution through the centuries. To say this is not to claim that the fiscal hypothesis accounts for every organizational detail of past or present arrangements, or that alternative accounts are universally invalid, but rather that the fiscal hypothesis provides a useful "default rule." It fits the overall historical pattern of facts better than its leading competitor, the market-failure hypothesis. Researchers seeking to explain particular government roles in the monetary system should therefore "follow the money": they should not fail to consider the fiscal implications.

2

CENTRAL BANKS AS SOURCES OF FINANCIAL INSTABILITY*

THE RECENT FINANCIAL crisis has set in bold relief the Jekyll and Hyde nature of contemporary central banks. It has made apparent both our utter dependence on such banks as instruments for assuring the continuous flow of credit in the aftermath of a financial bust, and the same institutions' capacity to fuel the financial booms that make severe busts possible in the first place.

Yet theoretical treatments of central banking place almost exclusive emphasis on its stabilizing capacity—that is, on central banks' role in managing the growth of national monetary aggregates and in supplying last-resort loans to troubled financial (and sometimes nonfinancial) firms in times of financial distress. This one-sided treatment of central banking reflects both the normative nature of much theoretical work on the subject, by which I mean its tendency to focus on ideal rather than actual central bank conduct, and the (usually tacit) assumption that however much central banks might depart in practice from ideal, financially stabilizing policies, they at least succeed in limiting the amplitude of booms and busts, compared to what would occur in the absence of centralized monetary control.

---

* This chapter is based on a lecture given at the conference "Free Currency: The Future of Money," sponsored by the Friedrich Naumann Foundation, Potsdam, Germany (April 24, 2009). It was originally published in *The Independent Review* 14, no. 4 (Spring 2010): 485–96.

I propose to challenge this conventional treatment of central banking by arguing that central banks are fundamentally *destabilizing*—that financial systems are more unstable with them than they would be without them. To make this argument, I must delve into the history of central banking and explain both why governments favored the establishment of destabilizing institutions in the first place and why there is a modern tendency to regard central banks as sources of financial stability. I hope to show that the modern view of central banks as sources of monetary stability is, in essence, a historical myth.

THE ORIGINS OF CENTRAL BANKING

An objective understanding of the macroeconomic and financial consequences of central banking requires, first of all, a value-free definition of the term "central bank"—that is, a definition that does not presuppose any particular sort of conduct, whether beneficial or malign. Common textbook definitions of central banks as institutions devoted to combating inflation, dampening business cycles, and serving as lenders of last resort must thus be rejected, both because they involve a tacit counterfactual whose validity is open to doubt, and because they are flagrantly inconsistent with the actual conduct of many real-world central banks.

So what, really, is a central bank? It is fundamentally a bank that possesses a national monopoly or something approaching a national monopoly on the right to issue circulating paper currency. Although outright monopolies are most common today, in a few instances—for example, in the United Kingdom, Ireland, and China—other (commercial) banks also enjoy highly circumscribed currency-issuing privileges.

The privilege of issuing paper currency was not always so limited, however. On the contrary, it was once enjoyed by practically all banks, which depended on it as a means of extending credit when the custom of transferring deposits by means of checks was not yet developed. Although the earliest central banks began as "public" banks that typically enjoyed a monopoly on the banking business of their sponsoring governments only, while sharing with other banks—at least to a limited extent—the right to issue currency, they gradually acquired currency monopolies as well. Indeed, the transition to central banking in its modern guise tended to follow public banks' consolidation of currency-issuing privileges, for reasons to be made clear in due course.

Nevertheless, the first steps toward modern currency monopolies long predated modern notions of central banking with their emphasis on central banks' stabilizing role. Instead, the public banks that later became full-fledged central banks were established solely for the purpose of catering to their sponsoring governments' fiscal needs—by managing their deposits, administering their debt, and, especially, accommodating their short-run credit needs. Despite their close relationships with the national governments that helped to establish them, these proto-central banks were profit-maximizing firms, and as such were managed solely in their owners' interest rather than in the interest of the broader financial community. The notion that public banks' privileges obliged them to promote general economic stability came only in the aftermath of numerous financial crises—crises which, I intend to show, the public banks themselves helped to bring about.

Although the Bank of England was not the first major public bank (the Swedish Riksbank preceded it by a quarter-century), it was to become the prototype "modern" central bank, having been the earliest to acknowledge, at first tacitly and grudgingly but at length officially, its duty to rescue other financial firms by serving as a lender of last resort during periods of financial distress. The Bank of England's fiscal origins, and its founders' corresponding unconcern for any broad macroeconomic consequences its creation might entail, are evident in the 1694 "Tonnage" Act (5 and 6 Will. & Mar. c 20) granting it its original charter, an act "for securing certain Recompences and Advantages . . . to such persons as shall voluntarily advance the sum of Fifteen hundred thousand Pounds towards carrying on the War against France."

Other early central banks had similar beginnings. Napoleon established the Bank of France, for example, for the express purpose of buying up French government securities, for which there was no other market at the time; and Germany's Reichsbank, predecessor of the present Bundesbank, grew out of the former Royal Bank of Berlin, founded by Frederick the Great for the purpose of managing the funds of the Prussian state. Yet the fiscal origins of early-modern central banks are often overlooked, especially by their proponents, including central bankers themselves.[1]

The fact that the first central banks evolved from public banks established for purely fiscal reasons suggests that any stabilizing potential they harbored was unanticipated by their founders. That fact might simply mean that by a sheer stroke of good luck, institutions originally designed to serve governments' narrow fiscal ends just happened to be ideally suited, given appropriate constitutional modifications, for scientific crisis management. I shall argue, however, that the public banks themselves were sources of instability, and that their vaunted stabilizing potential was at bottom little more than a potential for self-discipline, and a rather limited one at that.

THE PRINCIPLE OF ADVERSE CLEARINGS

To explore the possibility that central banks' unique privileges may themselves have contributed to financial instability, we must consider precisely how these privileges alter the scope for credit expansion. Doing so requires that we consider the limits to such expansion in a competitive or "free" banking system, meaning one in which numerous banks enjoy equal rights to issue their own distinct brands of circulating notes.[2] In keeping with circumstances surrounding the early development of central banking, I assume that banks, whether enjoying exclusive privileges or not, are obliged to redeem their notes on demand in specie—that is, in gold or silver coin.

In a free-banking system, banks treat rival banks' notes much as they treat checks drawn on rival banks today: they routinely return them to their sources for redemption. Indeed, the modern practice of "clearing" checks daily, with net dues settled by transfer of base money, usually on a central bank's books, grew out of the pre–central banking practice of regular note exchange, with banks returning rivals' notes directly to them or to central clearinghouses and settling accounts in specie.

This routine note-exchange and settlement process imposes strict limits on credit expansion by individual note-issuing banks and, hence, by the banking system as a whole, creating a tight connection between those limits and the available supply of specie reserves. Domestic monetary equilibrium in such a system can be understood as a state in which individual banks' lending policies are consistent with zero long-run or expected net-reserve drains, and bank reserve ratios just suffice to guarantee an optimally low probability of default owing to random variations of net-reserve drains around their zero mean. Starting from such an equilibrium, and assuming an unchanging demand for money balances, any bank that further expands its balance sheet independently of its rivals will face a corresponding absolute and relative increase in the return flow of its notes (or checks) through the clearing system, and a corresponding net loss of reserves, which will leave it with an inadequate reserve cover, if it does not default outright. Banks in a free-banking system may thus be likened to prisoners in a chain gang: escape is impossible for any single prisoner acting alone, and also for the group as a whole because of the difficulty its members will encounter in trying to coordinate their steps. The greater the size of the gang, the more difficult escape becomes.

I have referred elsewhere (Selgin 1988) to this competitive check against overissuance of bank money as the principle of adverse clearings. Because of it, the total volume of money and credit in a free-banking system cannot easily expand beyond limits consistent with a stable overall volume of payments. Once banks have expanded to the point at which their reserve cushions have fallen to some minimal, prudent level, they can expand further only if the demand to hold their notes or deposits increases—that is, if the value of the flow of their outstanding liabilities through the clearing system, whether notes or checks drawn against deposits, declines.

It follows that, for the system as a whole, if we assume that all payments are conducted with bank money rather than with specie itself, the demand for (precautionary) reserves can be understood as increasing, though perhaps less than proportionately, with the volume of payments, MV, where M is the stock of bank liabilities, including outstanding notes and demand deposits, and V is the velocity of circulation of that stock, or its rate of turnover. It also follows that for any given domestic stock (supply) of specie reserves and real rate of interest (the latter influencing the demand for precautionary reserves), there will be a unique level of spending, $(MV)^*$, at which reserve demand and supply (R^D and R^S) are equal. Should a change in the public's demand for real money balances, as manifested in a change in V, result in a level of spending no longer consistent with such an equilibrium, the banks will respond by expanding or contracting credit until equilibrium is restored. An increase in V, for example, will result in an excess demand for reserves, prompting banks to reduce their lending and thereby to reduce their outstanding liabilities, whereas a decline in V will have the opposite effect. These implications of the principle of adverse clearings are summarized in Figure 2.1.[3]

Figure 2.1: Reserve and Spending Equilibrium under Free Banking

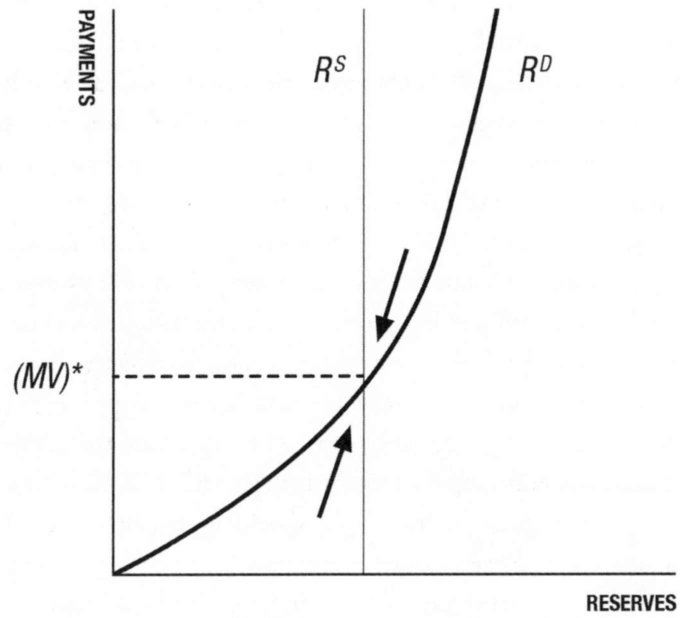

The tendency of a free-banking system to stabilize total spending has the obvious macroeconomic advantages of helping to maintain "natural" values of employment, interest rates, and real output. It also serves to prevent changes in the general price level, apart from ones reflecting shifts in an economy's long-run supply schedule.

INTERNATIONAL MONETARY EQUILIBRIUM

The "tight" nature of domestic monetary equilibrium under free banking also has implications for the preservation of international monetary equilibrium.

In the context of an international specie standard—let us say gold—the condition for such an equilibrium, that of "purchasing power parity," implies that a given sum of gold bullion should purchase approximately the same bundle of tradable goods in all gold-standard countries: "approximately" because prices can differ persistently by amounts that reflect the costs of importing goods from abroad, including transport costs and duties. Should the bundle's price in any one country vary from its price elsewhere beyond upper and lower boundaries known as "gold points," consistent with the aforementioned costs, the difference will cause more goods to be imported into and fewer to be exported from the country where prices are higher, with gold flows serving to finance the increased trade deficit. This Humean price-specie-flow mechanism will eventually restore purchasing power parity by promoting, on the one hand, monetary contraction in the country where goods are more expensive and, on the other, monetary expansion where goods have been less expensive.

A virtue of free banking is that it limits the occasions in which the Humean mechanism must operate by checking a domestic overexpansion of money and credit *before* it has a chance to drive domestic prices higher than their values consistent with the international purchasing power equilibrium. That this virtue is considerable will become apparent when we examine the workings of a central banking system, where the preservation of international monetary equilibrium is far more likely to depend on long-run corrections based on international specie movements. International gold flows would of course also occur in a world with only national free-banking systems: national shares of the world supply of gold reserves would alter for reasons analogous to those that can alter individual banks' market shares within a particular country. But such flows would not be evidence of a prior substantial disturbance of international equilibrium brought about by the arbitrary overexpansion of credit in any one nation.

CENTRAL BANKS: PIED PIPERS OF CREDIT

What happens if, instead of allowing all or at least many banks to issue circulating notes, authorities grant that privilege to a single bank? For domestic exchanges, paper notes are generally more convenient than gold and silver coins, and so the notes will typically be preferred to the coins. Banks that are denied the right to issue their own notes will consequently stock and reissue notes from the privileged bank. They themselves will, in other words, tend to treat those notes as a superior substitute for specie reserves. Two important consequences follow from this fact: first, the less-privileged (henceforth "commercial") banks will tend to send their specie to the privileged (henceforth "central") bank, which will consequently become the sole custodian of the nation's specie reserves. Second, the central bank will be exempt from the principle of adverse clearings. The central bank therefore can operate on a very slim cushion of specie reserves, with a correspondingly greater leveraging of central bank capital. It will also be able to expand credit, and thereby to increase the effective supply of commercial banks' reserves, without having to fear any immediate internal drain of precious metal from its own coffers.

These last observations account for the perceived fiscal advantages of central banking, and thus for government's ability to secure generous fiscal support from central banks in return for the monopoly rights granted to them. The fiscal advantages, however, come at the cost of greater potential macroeconomic and financial instability, because the privileges on which they are based also make it far more likely that domestic credit expansion will proceed beyond sustainable limits, with equilibrium being restored in the long run by means of an external drain of specie. Central banking, in other words, set the stage for the classical 19th-century business cycle.

To see this connection, imagine a typical central bank of the early 19th century, pressed by its sponsoring government to supply the government with additional credits. Because the central bank is exempt from adverse clearings, it has no certain way of ascertaining, in the short run, when it has expanded too far. If it only rarely faced unexpected (if modest) changes in the balance of payments, it might even be tempted to lend its entire specie reserve. Nor can it easily determine whether domestic prices are approaching levels that must trigger an external drain of specie because available price statistics, both domestic and international, are limited and crude and because a general discrepancy may not be apparent in price indexes constructed for any particular bundle of goods.

Although commercial banks themselves remain constrained, like so many members of a chain gang, the central bank's own exemption from adverse clearings allows it to lead them all, Pied Piper fashion, in a general overexpansion by adding to the effective, aggregate supply of their reserves. Figure 2.1 shows that, as the central bank expands, the reserve-supply schedule shifts to the right, and the equilibrium volume of aggregate spending (*MV*) increases accordingly. If given aggregate (goods) supply schedules are assumed, prices will be bid up, eventually triggering an external drain of specie from the central bank. The central bank, finding itself in danger of imminent default, proceeds to save itself by aggressively contracting credit. The contraction reduces commercial banks' reserves, forcing them to contract as well, triggering a general credit crunch.

FROM VILLAINS TO HEROES: THE ORIGINS OF THE CLASSICAL LENDER OF LAST RESORT

If central banks are in fact sources of financial instability, how have they come to be regarded as just the opposite? The explanation resides partly in modern economists' limited understanding of the workings of competitive currency arrangements, which causes them to assume that such arrangements must necessarily be less stable (because less subject to central control) than monopolistic ones, and partly in their failure to appreciate the origins of the idea that monetary systems require a lender of last resort.

The Bank of England was the first central bank to assume the role of last-resort lender. During the crises of 1857 and 1866, it did so informally and reluctantly. At length, however, and under public pressure, it came to acknowledge a duty to rescue other banks threatened by cash shortages, though otherwise solvent.

The chief architect of this newfound understanding was Walter Bagehot, best known today as the second and most illustrious editor of *The Economist*. In *Lombard Street*, Bagehot (1873) outlined what is now known as the classical lender-of-last-resort doctrine, according to which central banks, during times of financial distress, ought to continue to lend freely, though at high rates aimed at attracting capital from abroad and at discouraging borrowing by insolvent (as opposed to merely illiquid) banks.

Although many economists are aware of Bagehot's role in developing the modern lender-of-last-resort doctrine, few appreciate his position as one of the foremost *critics* of central banking. Indeed, some even imagine that Bagehot, in recommending that the Bank of England be held responsible for last-resort lending, actually meant to endorse its monopoly privileges and (at least implicitly) to recommend that all nations create similar institutions. In fact, as even a casual perusal of *Lombard Street* will attest, nothing could be farther from the truth. On the contrary, Bagehot believed that central banks were financially destabilizing, and hence undesirable institutions, and that it would have been far better had England never created one. He offered his lender-of-last-resort formula not as an ideal, but as a first aid to what was, in his view, a fundamentally unhealthy arrangement, the healthy alternative to which was free banking, with numerous banks issuing their own notes and maintaining their own reserves, as in the pre-1845 Scottish banking system.[4] England needed a lender of last resort not to rescue it from crises inherent in competitive banking, but to limit the severity of crises that were inevitable consequences of the monopolization of currency.

Here is Bagehot's own apology from the closing pages of *Lombard Street:*

> I know it will be said that in this work I have pointed out a deep malady, and only suggested a superficial remedy. I have tediously insisted that the natural system of banking is that of many banks keeping their own cash [i.e., specie] reserve, with the penalty of failure before them if they neglect it. I have shown that our system is that of a single bank keeping the whole reserve under no effectual penalty of failure. And yet I propose to retain that system, and only attempt to mend and palliate it.
>
> I can only reply that I propose to retain this system because I am quite sure that it is of no manner of use proposing to alter it. . . . You might as well, or better, try to alter the English monarchy and substitute a republic. (Bagehot 1873: 329)

Today, indeed, it appears that a proposal to do away with the English monarchy would meet with far less opposition than one to do away with the Bank of England's monopoly of paper currency!

Despite Bagehot's explicit disavowal of the Bank of England, posterity has managed to treat him, not as an opponent of central banking, but rather as one of its high priests—a fate that must surely have him spinning furiously in his grave. Generations of monetary economists have consequently been taught, quite wrongly in my opinion, that central banks are absolutely indispensable tools for financial stabilization. Even so, central bankers themselves, having thus come to be lionized, do little justice to the man who was their (admittedly inadvertent) champion, honoring his last-resort lending rules mainly in the breach.

THE U.S. CASE

According to my stylized history of central banking, the concentration of currency-issuing privileges in favored public banks was an important cause of financial crises, which then supplied a rationale for reinforcing and enhancing public banks' monopoly privileges while assigning them a public duty to serve as last-resort lenders.

However, financial crises have not been limited to those nations in which currency-issuing privileges are concentrated in a single bank. The United States, in particular, endured a series of severe crises—in 1873, 1884, 1893, and 1907—prior to its decision to embrace central banking in the form of the Federal Reserve System, which was created in 1913. The U.S. case therefore appears to contradict my claim that central banks are properly regarded as destabilizing rather than stabilizing institutions.

The contradiction, however, is more apparent than real. First, by almost any measure, the major financial crises of the Federal Reserve era—those of 1920–21, 1929–33, 1937–38, 1980–82, and, most recently, 2007–09—have been more rather than less severe than most of those experienced between the Civil War and World War I, even overlooking outbreaks of relatively severe inflation from 1917 to 1920 and from 1973 to 1980. More importantly, the pre-Fed crises can themselves be shown to have been exacerbated, if not caused, by regulations originally aimed at easing the Union government's fiscal burden. The U.S. case therefore represents a special instance of the general pattern according to which central banking emerged as an unintended by-product of fiscally motivated government interference with the free development of national financial institutions.

The interference in the U.S. case consisted, in part, of Civil War legislation that limited commercial banks' ability to issue their own bank notes.[5] The new "national" (that is, federally authorized) banks were allowed to issue their own notes only if every dollar of such notes was backed by $1.10 in federal government bonds. State-chartered banks were in turn forced to withdraw altogether from the currency business by a prohibitive tax assessed against their outstanding circulation beginning in August 1866. The result of these combined interventions was an aggregate stock of paper currency geared to the available supply of government securities. From the late 1870s onward, as the government took advantage of regular budget surpluses to reduce its outstanding debt, the supply of eligible backing for national bank notes dwindled, and the total stock of such notes also dwindled until, by 1891, the latter stock was only half as great in value terms as it had been a decade earlier. Regulations also prevented the stock of currency from adjusting along with seasonal increases in currency demand. Yet the U.S. economy was growing, and the seasonal demand for currency tended to rise sharply during the harvest season—that is, between August and November of each year. In the circumstances, it is hardly surprising that the United States endured frequent crises, and that they all involved more-or-less severe shortages of paper currency.

Canada's experience, in contrast, gives the lie to the claim that the United States could put an end to crises only by means of more complete centralization of its currency system. Canadian banks, unlike their U.S. counterparts, were free to issue notes on the same general assets that supported their deposit liabilities. They were as a result perfectly capable of accommodating both secular and seasonal changes in the demand for currency. Figure 2.2 displays the course of Canada's well-behaved bank-note currency, regulated solely by unfettered market forces, alongside the course of regulation-bound national bank notes in the United States for the years from 1880 to 1909. To anyone the least bit conversant with 19th-century patterns of currency demand, the superiority of the less-regulated arrangement ought to be obvious. If we consider both Canada's highly successful arrangement, which avoided all of the antebellum crises to which the U.S. economy had been subject, and the Fed's own performance, to characterize the U.S. turn to central banking in 1913 as a second-best solution is perhaps being overly generous.[6]

Figure 2.2: Bank Notes in Circulation, 1880–1909, Monthly

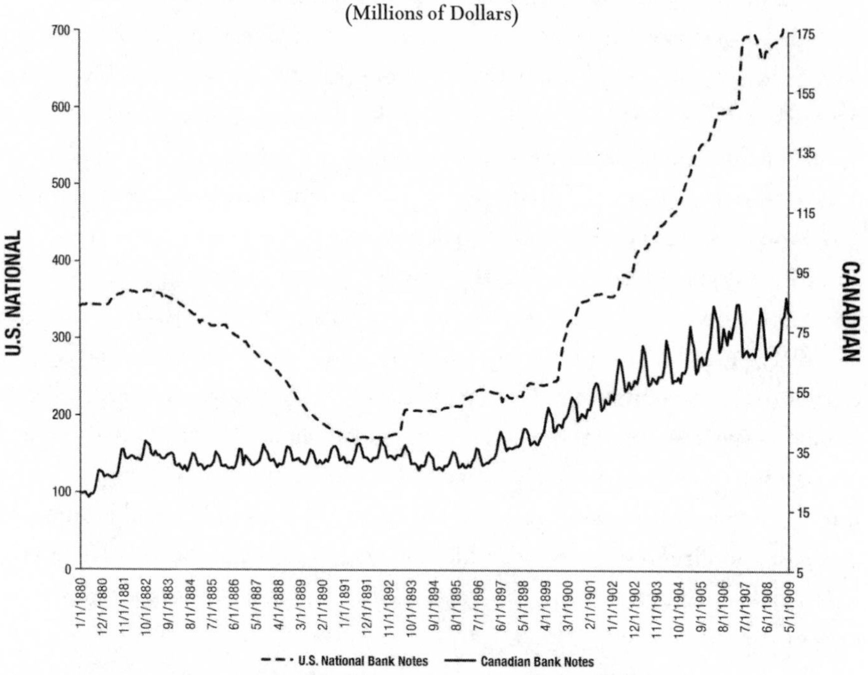

SOURCES: Data for Canadian bank notes are from Curtis (1931: 20). Data for U.S. national bank notes are from Comptroller of the Currency, *Annual Report* (various dates).

THE PATH TO FIAT MONEY

Understood as a means for preventing crises and preserving the international gold standard, Bagehot's lender-of-last-resort solution was a failure. Crises continued, and even worsened, in part because the rules for last-resort lending were often disobeyed, but also because such lending alone could limit but not eliminate altogether violent changes in credit conditions and associated disruptions of gold payments that stemmed from prior central bank misconduct. It eventually became evident that the international gold standard and central banking were incompatible arrangements, one of which had to go (Redish 1993).

The dismantlement of the international gold standard, temporarily at the outbreak of World War I, and permanently in the course of the Great Depression, marked the end of classical financial crises: no longer was there a Humean price-specie-flow mechanism to snap back to equilibrium the national monetary systems that had temporarily escaped beyond its confines. Fiat (that is, inconvertible) money instead allowed central banks to expand without any clear constraints, on a permanent basis and with impunity, though at the cost of persistent inflation. Yet these new circumstances did not bring an end to financial crises or even reduce their severity. They merely altered the nature of the crises. The former Humean denouement, in which central banks were forced to retrench by an external drain of reserves, was replaced by a more subtle turning-point mechanism consisting of the tendency of factor prices, caught behind other prices during booms, to catch up, thus raising interest rates, eliminating inflation-based profits, and exposing and bursting related asset-price bubbles. Such postclassical crises are today no less frequent than their classical counterparts were during the 19th century, and are equally attributable to central banks' mismanagement of money.

Although the advent of fiat money has not rendered central banks any less capable of generating booms and busts, it has considerably complicated the possibility of fundamental reform, because a fiat standard, unlike a gold or silver standard, *must* be monopolistically administered if fiat currency is to retain any value, and because allowing commercial banks the right to issue notes that are themselves redeemable in fiat money, whatever advantages such a policy may have, will not by itself deprive fiat-money-issuing authorities of their crisis-making capacity.

It is important that people recognize the route by which we came to the present impasse, so that they might shed their essentially romantic notion of central banking and instead approach it, as Walter Bagehot once did, as a fundamentally dangerous institution—one even more in need of confinement and taming today than it was in Bagehot's own day.

3

LEGAL RESTRICTIONS, FINANCIAL WEAKENING, AND THE LENDER OF LAST RESORT*

> It is not unlikely that the bolstering up of banking systems by their Governments is a factor which makes for instability.
>
> —VERA SMITH (1936: 5)

A POPULAR DEFENSE of central banks and fiat money claims that they are needed to protect the payments system against the peril of financial crises. A central bank can act as a "lender of last resort" to other banks, assuring depositors that they need never fear a general banking collapse; fiat money in turn guarantees that the lender of last resort itself will never go broke.[1]

A crucial assumption behind the lender-of-last-resort argument is that fractional-reserve banking is inherently "fragile" and crisis prone—that central banking and fiat money are an unavoidable response to market failure. According to Hyman Minsky (1982: 17), "conditions conducive to financial crises emerge from the normal functioning of a capitalist economy." In a free market, says Minsky, such conditions will occasionally produce "wide and spreading bankruptcies" that could, however, be prevented by "an alert lender of last resort" (Minsky 1982: 13).[2]

---

* Originally published in the *Cato Journal* 9, No. 2 (Fall 1989): 429–59. The author thanks Thomas M. Humphrey and William A. Niskanen for their comments.

In this chapter I take issue with the lender-of-last-resort argument by showing that its underlying assumption is false: fractional-reserve banking systems are *not* inherently weak or unstable. They are weak and unstable because legal restrictions have made them that way. The collapse of a fully deregulated banking system would be highly improbable if not impossible. It follows that central banks and fiat money are at most second-best solutions to problems peculiar to regulated banking.

The chapter proceeds in two parts. The first concerns the role of more familiar legal restrictions in fostering financial fragility and crises. It focuses on banking problems in the United States. The second shows how restrictions on private *currency* issue in particular have historically been an especially significant cause of financial weakening; its focus is more on developments in Great Britain. Because central banking presupposes a monopoly in currency supply, the existence of central banks itself turns out to be a crucial cause of financial crises.

A "FINANCIAL WEAKENING" HYPOTHESIS

Why should banks, unlike other profit-maximizing firms, evolve in a manner that exposes them lemming-like to periodic waves of bankruptcy? I believe the answer is that they do not evolve that way at all but have been weakened by legal restrictions ultimately aimed at generating revenue for the government or at propping up special interests within the banking industry. In the United States, the adverse effects of particular restrictions are well understood. What is not appreciated is how their cumulative effects have led to the present reliance upon a lender of last resort.

Were an evil dictator to set out purposefully to weaken a fractional-reserve banking system, and to increase its dependence upon a lender of last resort, he would (1) increase the risk exposure of individual banks to enhance their prospects of insolvency; (2) create an environment conducive to "spillover" or "contagion" effects, so that individual bank failures can lead to systemwide runs; and (3) obstruct private-market mechanisms for averting crises. Banking regulations in the United States and elsewhere have unintentionally done all three things. All that can be said in these regulations' favor is that some help to mitigate the unfortunate consequences of others.

INDIVIDUAL BANK INSOLVENCY

Anti-Branching Laws. Legal restrictions subject individual banks to a higher risk of becoming insolvent by reducing their opportunities to avoid risk and by actually subsidizing bank risk taking. Of restrictions having the first effect, by far the most destructive have been laws against branch banking. Such laws account for the fact that as this is being written (1989) the United States has more than 14,000 banks and more than 3,000 "thrift" institutions, most of which are small and localized. According to Andrew Mullineaux (1987: 77), even the largest U.S. banks "are not large in relation to the size and wealth of the population," and only one of them is among the world's top 10. The smallness and lack of diversification of so many U.S. depository institutions has made them chronically failure prone: branchless or "unit" banks in the farm belt have been overexposed to farming losses, and Texas and Oklahoma banks have suffered from their involvement in oil-industry loans and in local real-estate development. In the Northwest, banks have relied excessively upon loans to the timber industry. Such overexposure of loan portfolios reflects the fact that banks' lending opportunities are, to a large extent, bound by their location. Even larger money-center banks have been adversely affected by anti-branching statutes which, by restricting their domestic business opportunities,

> have encouraged them to be outward-looking. Because of their size and their presence in the major money centers they were well placed to help in the recycling of the OPEC surpluses, especially as Latin America developed a voracious appetite for funds. Many of them consequently developed an exposure to Latin America that far exceeded their capital bases. (Mullineaux 1987: 41)

As Lawrence White (1986: 895–96) observes, restrictions against branch banking increase a bank's exposure to liability-related as well as asset-related risks. Branched banks typically rely upon a broad cushion of retail deposits gathered by local offices as their principal source of funds. Unexpected withdrawals at some branches can often be compensated for by a transfer of reserves from others. In contrast, unit banks, particularly in large money centers, have relied heavily in recent years upon "liability management," attracting wholesale deposits as an alternative means for persons far removed from the money centers to take advantage of better investment opportunities there. The danger of this approach is that, in contrast to retail deposits, wholesale deposits are much more likely to be withdrawn in response to adverse rumors, not just because their size often makes them ineligible for insurance, but also because their owners are less able to verify the truth of a rumor and are less bound by considerations of convenience than retail depositors are to remain loyal to any particular bank. The dramatic collapse of Continental Illinois was to a large extent due to its heavy reliance upon liability management—a by-product of Illinois's strict anti-branching laws—though Continental would no doubt have become insolvent anyway as a result of its unwise and excessive energy loans.

No episode illustrates more dramatically the weakening effect of anti-branching laws than the Great Depression. Between 1931 and 1933, several thousand U.S. banks—mostly small rural banks—failed. In contrast, Canada's branch-banking network did not suffer a single bank failure even though in other respects Canada was just as hard hit by the depression: it could hardly have escaped all of the adverse effects on Canadian business of a 33 percent fall in the U.S. money supply. (The Canadian money supply fell by about 13 percent.) Ironically, the United States at the time *did* have a lender of last resort, whereas Canada did not.[3]

This comparison of U.S. and Canadian experience has by now been made so often that it is in danger of becoming a cliché. Yet the comparison bears repeating because it suggests that branch banking alone would go far in rendering the U.S. banking system immune to financial crises.[4] As branching laws are liberalized, the U.S. banking system will be progressively strengthened, and its reliance upon a lender of last resort will be correspondingly reduced.

A defense of restrictions on branching is that they prevent the banking industry from becoming overly concentrated and uncompetitive. This view misconstrues both the likely effects of full interstate branching and the meaning of competition. In Gerald O'Driscoll's estimate (1988: 673), without branching restrictions the United States might still have more than 4,000 independent banking firms.[5] But even 400 banks with far-reaching branch networks would be a more-than-adequate guarantee against collusive behavior. More importantly, branch banks could really compete with one another by freely entering any locality. In contrast, the present system is one of numerous, local monopolies. Competition is not just a matter of numbers.

In addition to exposing banks to risk, anti-branching restrictions have weakened them in other, less direct ways. During the 19th century, such restrictions encouraged the growth and "tiering" or "pyramiding" of interbank deposits, with country banks remitting surplus funds to a dozen or more "reserve city" banks, and the latter sending funds to banks in New York City (Smith 1936: 138–40). By this process, the same dollar of high-powered money could be reckoned as part of several banks' reserves—a practice formally sanctioned by national banking law. This—along with legal restrictions on note issue—contributed greatly to the severity of the great money panics of 1873, 1884, 1893, and 1907, by causing illiquidity in any part of the country to have adverse repercussions everywhere else. Anti-branching laws have also stood in the way of bank mergers and acquisitions—the least disruptive way of dealing with troubled banks. Finally, anti-branching laws have indirectly weakened the financial system by providing a rationale for other legal restrictions—patchwork remedies that the supervisory authorities have embraced as a substitute for needed structural reform, many of which have ultimately served to further weaken the banking system.

Activity Restrictions. Just as anti-branching laws have subjected banks to increased risks by limiting their geographical diversification, other legal restrictions have done the same by limiting activity diversification. Laws like the Glass-Steagall Act of 1933—designed to prevent banks from holding high-risk, high-return assets—actually serve (in an otherwise deregulated setting) to *increase* the probability of bank failures.[6] As Roger Blair and Arnold Heggestad (1978: 92) explain, even the taking on of intrinsically riskier assets by a bank reduces the overall variance of returns on the bank's portfolio if fluctuations in the earnings of the riskier assets are negatively correlated to fluctuations in the earnings of the less-risky assets. Empirical evidence suggests that this has indeed been the case in recent years (Litan 1987: 84–96). It appears to have been true, moreover, between 1930 and 1933. As William Shughart (1988: 600–602) relates, despite all the rhetoric used to justify Glass-Steagall, "securities affiliates were identified as a proximate cause of failure only in the case of the Bank of the United States," which was also guilty of fraud; in general, "the presence of an affiliate appears to have reduced the probability of bank failure." The real motive behind Glass-Steagall, according to Shughart, was not to increase bank safety, but to shield both banks and investment companies from the rigors of competition.

Other legal restrictions have increased the riskiness of bank portfolios, not by restricting the investments banks can engage in, but by actually *requiring* them to make potentially risky investments. A relatively recent instance of this is the Community Reinvestment Act of 1977. Before the Civil War, so-called "free-banking" laws in numerous states forced banks to invest in state and local bonds as collateral for their note issues; in several states, the required bonds proved to be very poor investments, becoming the major cause of free-bank failures (Rolnick and Weber 1984). Nor have banks been the only financial institutions to suffer from such requirements: prior to 1981, most thrifts were restricted to mortgage lending, which overexposed them to declining real estate prices.

One especially desirable activity banks might undertake in the absence of Glass-Steagall-type restrictions would be to compete with investment companies in offering checkable mutual fund accounts. As Charles Goodhart (1987) explains, insofar as the nominal value of mutual funds is allowed to vary with the value of their underlying assets, they are (unlike bank deposit accounts) invulnerable to runs. Moreover, bank mutual fund accounts could offer distinct advantages over similar accounts offered by other firms, because bank customers could conveniently make transfers to and from their mutual fund accounts to other accounts offering different advantages (e.g., absence of minimum balance or minimum check-size requirements). Finally, were mutual fund accounts to displace deposits to any substantial degree, the burden borne by deposit-insurance schemes would be proportionately lightened, and the prospects for reforming deposit insurance—by replacing it with private insurance or by repealing it altogether—would be greatly improved.

Deposit-Rate Ceilings. Still other legal restrictions that have served to weaken banks and to create an artificial need for a lender of last resort are restrictions on deposit and loan rates of interest. Deposit-rate ceilings, also introduced by the Banking Act of 1933 (and extended by the Banking Act of 1935), were ostensibly aimed at guarding against banks bidding for customers by offering high rates on deposits, offsetting the higher cost of funds by engaging in unsafe investments with high-gross yields. But studies in recent decades, summarized by John Mingo (1981), have challenged this rationale by showing a lack of evidence of any correlation between rates paid on deposits and the quality of a bank's assets. Furthermore, if a correlation did exist, it could be because high-yielding assets lead to high deposit rates (as standard economic analysis would suggest) rather than the other way around. A more likely reason for imposing rate ceilings on banks was to preserve the market position of thrifts, which had evolved to specialize in home finance—a market position that was itself a result of prior restrictions on mortgage lending by national banks (removed in 1914 by the Federal Reserve Act). Rate ceilings also served to prop up banks with a lucrative price-fixing scheme.

Rather than reduce banks' likelihood of failure, deposit-rate ceilings have tended to have just the opposite effect by limiting their ability to bid for funds when threatened by a disintermediation or other liquidity crisis. This was dramatically evident in the 1960s, when banks and later thrifts were racked by a series of disintermediation crises. The trouble started in October 1959, when (as a result of slowly mounting inflation) Treasury bill rates rose to 5 percent—well above the 3 percent Regulation Q limits on time deposits. Banks then faced a disintermediation crisis that was a portent of further troubles to come. As inflation and short-term money rates continued to rise (in part as a result of the escalating costs of the Vietnam War), the Fed found it necessary to allow one-step increases in rate ceilings on certificates of deposit for every year from 1962 to 1965 to avoid a recurrence of the 1959 crisis. This policy left the thrifts stranded, however—their own rates being fixed at 4 percent (Wojnilower 1980: 286–87). At last, to protect the thrifts, the Fed in 1966 refused to lift bank deposit-rate ceilings again, while simultaneously putting the brakes on monetary expansion. The result was an even more severe bank "credit crunch." Finally, in August 1966, the Fed reversed its monetary policy again, this time to "rescue" the banks *from its own misguided policies*.

The banking crisis of 1966—the first "financial crisis" (to adopt the conventional, hyperbolic vernacular) in the United States since the Great Depression—was a direct consequence of Regulation Q restrictions combined with erratic Fed monetary policy. This was also true of later disintermediation crises, including the thrift crisis of 1969. If rate restrictions had been absent then as they are today, these crises would not have happened and there would not have been any need for last-resort lending by the Fed.

Deposit Insurance. The absence of crises is, however, not necessarily evidence of a strong banking system. Weak and even insolvent banks and thrifts can also be propped up by subsidies, which tend to encourage them to take on added risks that cause them, more often than not, to become even weaker and more insolvent. Deposit insurance and central bank loans have increasingly had these effects in recent years, particularly in the thrift industry where hundreds of bankrupt "zombie institutions" have been kept afloat at taxpayers' expense instead of being allowed to succumb to the Darwinian forces of the market. (Thrifts received their first direct Federal Reserve support on February 23, 1989.)

The ill effects of government deposit insurance are, as is well known, due to its lack of risk-adjusted premiums. This leads to moral hazard whereby the insured firms pursue risks that they would not pursue in an uninsured state.[7] Depositors, in turn, no longer feel any need to be concerned about the safety of particular depository institutions, and are tempted to supply funds to wherever rates are highest. According to J. Huston McCulloch (1986: 82), thanks to federal deposit insurance,

> banks and thrifts have engaged with impunity in all manner of excessive risks—foreign exchange speculation (Franklin National), speculative energy loans (Penn Square), inadequately investigated loans

(Continental Illinois), insider loans (the Butcher banks), uncollectable Third World loans (almost every top ten bank) and so forth.

According to Genie Short and Jeffery Gunther (1988), the present weakness of Texas banks and thrifts is a result not just of unit banking, but also of "policies that have removed incentives for depositors to reallocate their funds." Encouraged by the Federal Deposit Insurance Corporation's (FDIC) decision to insure even large deposits at First City Bancorp and at the First Republic Bank Corporation, depositors actually shifted funds into those troubled firms and out of stronger banks and thrifts. In the same way, insurance has been helping bad banks to drive out good banks throughout the United States. As long as such subsidies continued (together with mergers) to provide de facto full coverage, the effects of this progressive financial weakening were not apparent; but with mounting bank and thrift losses, with insurance funds themselves facing bankruptcy, and with mergers subject to increased scrutiny, the cat has been let out of the bag. The present (1989) thrift and less-developed-country–debt crises are poignant proof of this weakening. According to Edward Kane (1985: 120–21), the latter crisis is fundamentally due to "the turning on and off of deposit insurance subsidies." To the extent that the Fed is called upon to resolve these crises by acting as a lender of last resort (i.e., by forcing consumers at large to bear the cost through a weakened dollar), it will be addressing not market failure, but the failure of legal restrictions on banks and thrifts—including restrictions it has itself imposed.

The deposit-insurance crisis suggests that the argument, popularized by Milton Friedman (1960: 37–38), that deposit insurance makes a lender of last resort unnecessary may be the opposite of the truth. For as long as insurance is underpriced, it makes depository institutions more rather than less failure prone. As failures increase, the insurance funds themselves are threatened by bankruptcy. A lender of last resort is then needed to bail out the funds directly or to bail out and subsidize mergers of insolvent banks. Not to do so could lead to panic, as many depositors have no reason to trust their banks apart from the guarantees that insurance provides. The 1985 Ohio and Maryland savings and loan (S&L) crisis bears this out quite clearly.

The Lender of Last Resort Itself. By the same token, though, the Fed is also one of its own worst enemies (I am tempted to say one of its own best excuses), because it also encourages banks to take on excessive risks, leading to trouble. That lenders of last resort can also be a source of moral hazard is, of course, recognized even by their most ardent supporters (e.g., Kindleberger 1984: 280). According to Gillian Garcia and Elizabeth Plautz (1988: 112),

> Lender-of-last-resort assistance can be viewed as a form of subsidized government intervention. If potential recipients interpret such assistance to mean that the central bank would step in to bail out any institution in difficulty, the available assistance could encourage (even subsidize) additional risk-taking among institutions with lender-of-last-resort access.

This problem, which has been called "the Bagehot Problem" (after Walter Bagehot, who drew attention to it in *Lombard Street*) might be avoided if the lender of last resort followed Bagehot's advice by offering support only to solvent institutions at penalty rates. But Bagehot's advice is violated by most central banks in practice, as the rescue of Franklin National glaringly demonstrated (see Garcia and Plautz 1988: 217–28).

THE "CONTAGION EFFECT" MYTH

The preceding review suggests that legal restrictions have played a role in many, though by no means all, bank failures. Obviously failures—including failures due to outright fraud—would also occur under laissez faire. Such failures should not have to be regretted, though. On the contrary, in banking as in other industries, failures are needed to discipline and weed out bad managers; furthermore, if they lead to takeovers (or if banks are well capitalized), *isolated* failures need not cause bank customers to suffer large losses. The great fear of failure that affects regulatory authorities today reflects the widespread belief that failures, instead of being limited to poorly managed banks, will have undesirable "third-party" effects, causing panic to spread indiscriminately to other banks in the system.

Indeed, a lender of last resort is needed only when such "contagion, spillover, or domino effects" threaten "the stability of the entire monetary system" (Humphrey and Keleher 1984: 278), for otherwise runs and failures at one or several depository institutions would result in a transfer of funds to others, strengthening rather than weakening the latter. Only if panic becomes general—if depositors lose confidence in the entire banking *system*—will depositors switch to holding high-powered money, weakening all depository institutions in the process.[8] Thus, a crucial (though often implicit) assumption in the pro-lender-of-last-resort literature is, to quote Robert Solow (1982: 238), that "any bank failure diminishes confidence in the whole system," leaving no private banks in a position to stem a panic.

This is a very strong assumption, especially in view of the paucity of support one finds for it in history. In U.S. experience, Arthur Rolnick and Warren Weber (1986) found no evidence of any contagion effects from bank runs during the free-banking era (1837–60). Reviewing the national banking era (1863–1913), George Kaufman (1988: 16) found only limited evidence of contagions in the panics of 1878, 1893, and 1908; and the evidence is weak except for 1893. Even during the "Great Contraction" of 1930–33—the episode from which contemporary authorities still seem to draw all of their conclusions—contagion effects appear to have been limited regionally until late 1932; prior to 1932, moreover, runs were confined for the most part to banks suffering from prerun insolvency or to banks affiliated with insolvent firms (Wicker 1980). Even the failure of the Bank of the United States in December 1930 did not provoke any panic runs in New York City, according to Elmus Wicker (1980: 580). Finally, in their study of more recent experience, Joseph Aharony and Itzhak Swary (1983) found no evidence of any contagion effect (measured by a fall in bank stock prices) following the failures of the United States National Bank of San Diego or the Hamilton National Bank of Chattanooga; they did find evidence of a very limited contagion (involving banks known to be heavily involved in the foreign-exchange market) stemming from the failure of Franklin National. Their overall conclusion (Aharony and Swary 1983: 321) was that the "failure of a dishonestly run banking institution, even a large one, need not cause panic and loss of public confidence in the integrity of the banking system as a whole."[9]

Still more recently, the failure of Continental Illinois in 1984 also led to a slight and short-lived stock-price contagion; but it (like all previous, recent failures of large banks) did not lead to any net-withdrawal of high-powered money by noninsured depositors (Benston et al. 1986: 66). The run on Home State Savings and Loan in Ohio in 1985 did involve some withdrawals of currency and did spread to other Ohio S&Ls covered by the same insurance scheme (as well as to privately insured S&Ls there and in Maryland); however, it also did not involve any general panic but only a limited panic based upon depositors' (justified) concern over the condition of their accounts' insurers together with uncertainty as to the Fed's likely response.

In Canada also, bank runs usually do not seem to have been contagious. According to Kurt Schuler (1988: 37, 54), the only exceptions have been the panic on Prince Edward Island in 1881, which spread from the insolvent Bank of Prince Edward Island to other local banks owed money by it, and runs in 1985 on several small western banks following the failures of the Canadian Commercial and Northland banks.[10] In neither incident did runs affect any of Canada's nationwide banks. "[I]mmunity to runs," Schuler concludes, "apparently depends greatly on bank size."

All of this evidence adds up to one crucial fact: that the public generally knows more about the state of the banking system than the supervisory authorities give it credit for knowing. When certain banks or groups of banks get into trouble (or are suspected, with good reason, of being in trouble), depositors transfer funds from those banks into other, safer banks. They do not lose confidence in the banking system as a whole. This suggests that last-resort assistance by a central bank, particularly to institutions suffering from prerun insolvency, is unnecessary except on *very* rare occasions.

What about those rare occasions? Don't they supply a sufficient rationale for having a lender of last resort? The answer depends on what *causes* have given rise to contagion effects. One possible (and popular) explanation can be readily dismissed: the "random" or "bubble" theory of panics entertained by Charles Kindleberger (1978), John Bryant (1981), Douglas Diamond and Philip Dybvig (1983), Douglas Waldo (1985), and many others. According to this theory, panics need not be based upon any real shock with predictable, adverse effects on bank earnings, but may occur even in response to intrinsically irrelevant events, such as sunspots. All of the evidence reviewed above, as well as the findings of Gary Gorton (1988), disputes this view, supporting instead the alternative hypothesis that panics are based on prior, real shocks with predictable adverse repercussions on bank earnings.

Under what circumstances, then, might such shocks expose an entire banking system to contagious runs, as they seem to have done in 1932 and (perhaps) in previous crises? One possible circumstance is when banks are involved in one another's assets through correspondent relationships. As Garcia and Plautz (1988: 19) point out, the failure of a correspondent "can bring down a chain of its respondent banks." This was one justification given by the Fed for rescuing Continental Illinois. But the depth and breadth of correspondent relationships in U.S. banking is itself, as was explained earlier, a consequence of unit banking, which should become less and less important as branching restrictions are lifted. Even as matters stand, moreover, correspondent relationships are hardly extensive enough to be likely to cause a flight to currency.

Another cause of contagion effects—one that also played a crucial role in the 1932 panic—is resort to bank holidays. As George Benston and others explain (1986: 52), fears of widespread panic that inspire government officials to declare a bank holiday can easily become "a self-fulfilling prophesy": a holiday freezes up part of the money supply, reducing incomes generally and encouraging withdrawals by clients of otherwise solvent banks that fear the holiday will spread. In this way, Nevada's bank holiday in October 1932 had its own domino effect, culminating (with the help of depositors' apprehensions concerning FDR's fidelity to the gold standard) in the national bank holiday in March 1933. In the same way, Maryland depositors were inspired to run on their S&Ls in part because they feared Maryland would follow Ohio's example by declaring a holiday.

Resort to bank holidays is particularly unfortunate in that it is a substitute for a more-effective but less-dangerous alternative: this is a "restriction" or "suspension" of high-powered money payments of the kind resorted to by private banks (with the government's acquiescence) in the pre-Federal Reserve era, and that Herbert Hoover was prevented from implementing in February 1933 owing to Roosevelt's refusal to cooperate. Because a restriction allows banks to remain open to conduct lending operations and also to receive deposits and settle accounts with one another (or even, perhaps, with banks not affected by the restriction), it constitutes less of a freeze on the money supply and hence less of a reason for depositors at other banks to panic. Later I will argue that such suspensions are also consistent with maximizing banks' earnings and consumers' utility, so that they could play a role even in a fully deregulated banking system.

A third likely cause of a banking contagion is a macroeconomic shock so severe as to place all or most banks in danger of insolvency despite their best efforts to diversify. All that needs to be said about this is that the most common cause of such severe shocks has been irresponsible behavior by central banks.[11] The possibility of major macroeconomic shocks there hardly constitutes a good reason for giving central banks extra leeway (including the issue of inconvertible money) to allow them to serve as lenders of last resort.

A final and most important potential cause of contagion effects in response to real shocks is an "information externality." Such an externality may be present whenever bank depositors are unable to inform themselves of the riskiness of their own banks, and so are forced to generalize from the troubles experienced by others. To the extent that such externalities are present, the evidence reviewed above suggests that their effects are limited: depositors do seem to know *something* about their banks, so that, at worst, trouble spreads from insolvent banks to others that are, if not insolvent themselves, in some nontrivial way similar to the insolvent banks. Moreover, it will be argued below that information externalities are themselves yet another by-product of legal restrictions, which would be absent (or much less severe) under laissez faire.

MARKET SUPPORT MECHANISMS

Private Last-Resort Lending. Another implicit assumption in the lender-of-last-resort literature is that, if a central bank does not avert a financial crisis, private agents will not either: the rendering of aid to troubled banks to avoid a systemic banking collapse is regarded as a "public good" (e.g., Solow 1982: 241ff.). Here again, the assumption has little foundation in fact: although bank runs and failures may have third-party effects, these do not necessarily imply market failure. As long as some private banks are not threatened by runs (and are indeed receiving money withdrawn from other institutions), it will be in their interest to aid their solvent but illiquid rivals. Nor is there any basis for the claim, made by Jack Guttentag and Richard Herring (1983: 5) and implied elsewhere, that a government lender of last resort "may have better information than the private markets . . . and may know that [a] bank is solvent when the private market does not."

In fact, private providers of last-resort assistance are much more likely than any central bank is to conform to the "classical" recipe of lending only to solvent institutions at penalty rates, in part because doing so is entirely consistent with profit maximization. As will be seen below, by refusing last-resort assistance, central banks in the past have managed to reinforce their own privileged status—a status that rendered them peculiarly immune to confidence externalities. More recently, on the other hand, central banks have been inclined to extend aid at subsidy rates and often to insolvent institutions (Garcia and Plautz 1988: 54; Sprague 1986). In doing so, they in effect act as lenders not of last, but of first resort. Such behavior allows central banks to create an exaggerated impression of their importance. It serves, at the same time, to further weaken the banking system by creating another "moral hazard" and by discouraging the development of private arrangements for responding to crises.

Central bank aid to *insolvent* institutions is especially harmful: last-resort aid fulfills its purpose when it serves to signal the public that an institution is indeed viable. Aid to insolvent banks undermines this purpose, as the public discovers that a bank—even though it has received assistance—may still fail. Thus, an offer of last-resort aid may no longer suffice to end a run and may not suffice even if the stricken institution really is solvent, because the offer of aid no longer serves to convince a skeptical public that this is indeed the case. For this reason, the Fed alone was unable to end runs at First Pennsylvania Bank in 1980 and at Continental Illinois in 1984. As Garcia and Plautz (1988: 168) explain, private assistance had to be included in the rescue packages to those banks "to demonstrate that those with their own monies at risk were confident that the crises would be resolved without losses being incurred by uninsured depositors."

Although the rendering of emergency assistance by private banks has been quite common throughout history, legal restrictions have hampered it in numerous ways, all of which generate an artificial need for central bank assistance. The fact that central banks often underbid would-be private rescuers has already been mentioned. Branching restrictions are also to blame, for by encouraging the proliferation of small banks, such restrictions, besides making banks more failure prone to begin with, also hinder the assembly of large, wholly private rescue packages. Even an overnight loan backed by plenty of collateral, if very large (like the Fed's $23 billion loan to the Bank of New York in 1985), poses a tremendous, if not insuperable, challenge to numerous small banks that could easily be met by a group of larger banks acting in concert.

Takeovers and Mergers. Bank regulatory authorities generally agree that the best way to dispose of an insolvent bank or thrift is not to liquidate it but, if possible, to have it taken over by a solvent bank or bank holding company. Yet although they are pleased to take credit for frequently arranging such takeovers, the fact is that these authorities themselves also enforce policies that, with other legal restrictions, are the main impediments to takeovers, which could otherwise proceed in such a way as to permit greatly reduced reliance upon the central bank as a lender of last resort. John Kareken (1986: 11) sums up the situation nicely:

> If a bank is, for instance, constrained to have no branches, then neither can it acquire another bank and . . . keep the acquired bank in existence. . . . Bank acquisitions and mergers are, then, to an extent limited by state branching restrictions or, more fundamentally, by the McFadden Act. But that is not all. Under present-day federal bank regulatory policy, no bank with FDIC-insured balances can go ahead with an acquisition or merger until it has gotten the approval of the appropriate federal bank regulatory agency, whether the [Office of the Comptroller of the Currency], the FDIC, or the Federal Reserve Board (FRB), all of which are, as it were, special antitrust agencies.[12]

As if this were not enough, the Bank Merger Act of 1966 allows the Department of Justice to challenge any bank acquisition or merger approved by the above-listed agencies (Kareken 1986: 12), while Federal Reserve restrictions make bank holding company acquisitions of thrifts unattractive. All of these impediments to takeovers reflect the authorities' "bigness paranoia"—their obsession with concentration ratios in banking—which prevails despite the fact that banking in the United States is a long way from being as concentrated as banking elsewhere. Somewhat ironically, the shortage of big banks in the United States is itself a barrier to takeovers, because bigger banks can much more readily absorb the business of smaller banks than other small banks can.

Another unfortunate aspect of present policy is that, until very recently, it has permitted takeovers only of insolvent or nearly insolvent banks and thrifts. This clearly lowers the odds of finding eligible bidders for a bank or, alternatively, makes it necessary for the authorities to sweeten the pot by assuming some of the bad assets of a failed institution or by providing subsidized "leverage." Indeed, Kane (1985: 11) reports that, for large banks especially, the regulatory authorities "ordinarily make a tenacious effort through subsidizing lending to keep troubled institutions afloat well past the point of market value insolvency" using "cosmetic accounting" to hide the practice. This policy of forbearance is the equivalent of administering a "poison pill" to failing institutions in its efficacy in discouraging potential acquirers. It also encourages insolvent firms to "go for broke"—taking on risky investments in a last-ditch effort to stay alive.

The very fact that would-be takeovers or mergers must be disclosed to the authorities before they can proceed makes voluntary (i.e., hostile but non-shotgun) takeovers of poorly managed banks less likely. As Michael Jensen (1988: 44–45) explains, prior disclosure of a planned takeover of a publicly traded firm allows stockholders in the target firm to bid up the price of its stock to equal the full discounted value of any expected gain in net earnings from the takeover. Thus, nothing is left for the would-be acquirer, which (unless offered a last-minute subsidy) has every incentive to bow out.

In sum, the elimination of branch restrictions and a laissez faire policy toward mergers and takeovers would have allowed many problem banks and thrifts to be quietly absorbed by sound institutions well before their net worth became negative, and would have done so without need for last-resort subsidies made at taxpayers' expense.

THE ROLE OF CURRENCY MONOPOLY

So far I have argued that restrictions on branch banking, portfolio diversification, interest rates, and mergers, together with mispriced deposit insurance and "emergency" loans, have contributed to the fragility of the U.S. banking system, making it crisis prone and generating an artificial need for a lender of last resort. Yet this account seriously understates the case against having a central bank functioning as a lender of last resort, because it overlooks how *the very presence of even a well-behaved central bank is itself a fundamental cause of financial fragility*. This is so because central banking entails a monopoly in the supply of hand-to-hand currency, which has historically been a particularly destructive legal restriction on private banking as well as a crucial cause of monetary instability. Rather than being merely a *means* that allows central banks to act as lenders of last resort (Humphrey and Keleher 1984: 176), currency monopoly was the original raison d'être of central banks and a cause of the troubles central banks were called upon to correct only as an afterthought.

Currency monopoly directly contributes to financial fragility in three ways: (1) by preventing private banks from independently accommodating changes in the public's relative demand for currency; (2) by precluding a secondary market for bank liabilities; and (3) by creating a new and unstable form of high-powered money.

CURRENCY DEMAND

A major part of the so-called "inherent instability" of contemporary fractional-reserve banking rests upon the fact that private banks cannot issue notes. An increase in the public's demand for currency relative to its demand for deposit balances under such circumstances must lead to withdrawals of high-powered money from banks' reserves. Unless the withdrawals are somehow neutralized, they will provoke a multiplicative contraction of deposits.[13] Insofar as an increase in the relative demand for currency does not reflect a loss of confidence in banks (as is typically the case), then redeemable bank notes (which like deposits are a claim against some ultimate money of redemption) can be perfectly adequate in satisfying it. Of course, as Hugh Rockoff (1986: 629) points out, freedom of note issue cannot prevent a crisis if deposit holders do lose confidence in the banking system and therefore choose to withdraw the ultimate money of redemption (an extreme possibility to be dealt with by separate means, discussed below). But restrictions on note issue only serve to increase the likelihood of this happening by causing even non-panic-driven increases in currency demand to place a strain on the banking system, thereby helping to inspire a loss of confidence.

History is littered with instances that bear out these claims, a number of which I described in *The Theory of Free Banking* (Selgin 1988: 108–25). Perhaps the most notorious were the great "currency shortages" of 1893 and 1907 in the United States, which provided a rationale for the establishment of the Federal Reserve System. Although national banks were legally permitted to issue notes, they were hampered after 1882 by the growing scarcity of government securities, required by the National Banking Act to secure their notes. A seasonal stringency of credit emerged each year with the autumnal increase in demand for currency "to move the crops." On the aforementioned dates, this stringency degenerated into full-scale panic. Private banks, clearinghouses, and other firms issued millions of dollars worth of "currency substitutes" in partly successful efforts to stem the crises. Most of this ersatz currency was probably illegal, but its successful use helped to reveal the extent to which the crises were an avoidable consequence of legal restrictions on note issue. Here again, Canada offers an interesting counterexample, for what were "crises" in America took the form there of mere increases in the outstanding stock of private bank notes, some of which crossed the border to provide relief to Americans suffering from a shortage of exchange media.

Another example is the role of the Fed's monopoly on note issue in helping to bring on the "Great Contraction" of 1930–33. As income falls, the demand for hand-to-hand currency increases relative to the demand for deposits independently of any loss of confidence in the banking system. Thus, some of the post-1929 withdrawals of high-powered money which placed a strain on many banks might have been avoided had the banks been able to issue notes as well as create deposits.

A SECONDARY NOTE MARKET

Previously, I observed that a contagion effect could take hold in a system of unregulated deposit banks as the result of an "information externality." Because depositors lack knowledge of bank-specific risks, any real shock known to have rendered one bank insolvent may be regarded as a likely cause of serious damage to others. Thus, bad news concerning one bank spills over to apparently similar banks.

It turns out that this potential cause of a banking contagion is another consequence of legal restrictions on private, competitive note issue. As Gorton (1987) explains, prices of financial assets for which secondary markets exist will—according to the efficient markets hypothesis—tend to reflect their relative riskiness. Thus, a secondary market for bank money can, in theory, be a reliable source of information concerning bank-specific risks, which could serve to limit bank runs to truly insolvent firms. However, the secondary market for checkable deposits is too "thin" to be efficient, because checks drawn by different persons for the same amount and from the same bank are distinct assets. Therefore, freedom of note issue is necessary if market price signals are to be relied upon to stamp out a contagion.

A secondary bank-note market is typically portrayed as involving professional non-bank-note "brokers" as well as bank-note "reporters"—weekly publications with information on note discounts. If brokers do not request any risk-related discount (beyond transaction costs) to redeem a bank's notes, holders of those notes can rest assured that the bank is solvent and will not have any incentive to test its solvency by staging a run on it. On the other hand, holders of notes trading at a discount do not need to run, either, but can "walk" to a broker who charges them for assuming the risk that the notes' issuers may fail.

Though secondary note markets did indeed function this way in the United States and elsewhere in the early 19th century and before,[14] the tendency in a fully unregulated system is for brokers and bank-note reporters to give way to banks with nationwide branch networks accepting one another's notes directly or through clearinghouses at par.[15] It has been suggested (e.g., Gorton 1987: 3) that this tendency also implies the abandonment of a secondary note market and the return of an information-externality problem. The truth is rather that there is still a "virtual" secondary note market in which banks and clearinghouse associations rather than brokers become "market makers" and where notes tend to be priced either at par or altogether refused in payments to banks other than their issuer. This all-or-nothing system of note pricing suffices to avoid a contagion effect. Noteholders have reason to stage a run only on banks whose notes are not being accepted at par by other banks. Because notes—unlike checks—are fungible, a person who deposits a note with a rival bank need have no fear that the bank will refuse to credit his or her account after (unsuccessfully) trying to redeem the note. Thus, a bank's acceptance of a rival's note is, unlike its acceptance of a check, a definite token of its confidence in the rival's solvency. It is only when par acceptance of notes by rival banks is *required by statute* (as it was, for example, under the National Banking Act of 1864) instead of being voluntary that it ceases to be a reliable source of information about bank-specific risk. With freedom of note issue and exchange in *any* of its likely forms, a bank information externality would be extremely unlikely.[16]

HIGH-POWERED MONEY

It is widely believed that financial crises are most likely to occur in periods of tight money following longer periods of monetary ease (Kindleberger 1978; Minsky 1977, 1982; and many theorists of the "Austrian" school). Experience seems to confirm this view (Garcia and Plautz 1988: 7), which suggests yet another reason for viewing central banking and currency monopoly as a cause of, rather than a cure for, financial instability. The reason is that a currency monopoly makes possible much more erratic fluctuations in the money stock than can occur in banking systems where currency is issued competitively in the form of redeemable notes. When note issue is monopolized, the liabilities of the privileged bank of issue inevitably become high-powered money even though they themselves may still be redeemable in specie.[17] This high-powered money replaces specie as the principal bank reserve-medium, the consequence being that the bank of issue is relieved from suffering any adverse clearings when it overissues. Furthermore, any expansion or contraction of the privileged bank's liabilities leads to a multiple expansion or contraction of deposits at unprivileged banks, to be checked only when international specie-flows force the bank of issue to alter its course. Obviously, if a central bank suspends specie payments, or if a permanent fiat-money system is established (something relatively easy to do once notes are issued monopolistically), the privileged bank's power to inflate or deflate will, in principle at least, be unlimited.

A central bank's power to unilaterally expand or contract a nation's money stock must be compared to the relatively limited potential for similar expansion or contraction in a free-banking system. Elsewhere (Selgin 1988: 37–85), I explain in detail why free banks, unlike a central bank, cannot unilaterally or collectively affect a change in the price level or in nominal rates of interest. For this reason, and also unlike a central bank, they cannot unilaterally deplete a nation's gold stock by overissuing. This makes them incapable of creating the circumstance most frequently to blame for both American and European financial crises under the gold standard: a rising domestic price level (with or without a speculative "mania") combined with a shrinking stock of specie.[18] Needless to say, free banks would also be incapable of the hyperinflations and secular stop-and-go inflations that distinguish fiat-money regimes and are the most important cause of financial crises in more recent history.

To a remarkable extent, the literature on financial crises has turned a blind eye toward these fundamental truths. Thus, Kindleberger (1978: 52) lists the growth of private banking and financial instruments, gold discoveries, and (p. 17) the ability of competitive banks to "stretch" their reserves as causes of excessive monetary expansion,[19] while treating privileged (central) banks as sources of stability:

> Central banking arose to impose control on the instability of credit. The development of central banking from private banking, which is concerned to make money, is a remarkable achievement. By 1825, division of labor had been agreed upon: private bankers of London and the provinces financed the boom, the Bank of England financed the crisis. (Kindleberger 1978: 77)

This is a truly incredible interpretation of the history of banking in England. It would certainly have come as a surprise to the directors of the

Bank of England, both in 1825 and for many years after, to learn that they, unlike private bankers, were not "concerned to make money" or indeed that their bank's privileged status was awarded to it so that it could "impose control on the instability of credit." They would probably have been inclined to think that the whole point of the Bank's possessing the powers and privileges it possessed was precisely to enable it to make money and, more importantly, to enable it to make money more easily than other banks could in return for its sharing some of the money with the government. As regards the alleged "division of labor" in 1825, we have already seen how it is theoretically suspect. Moreover, in voicing a view made famous by the Bank directors during the Restriction, Kindleberger ought to know that he is standing on thin ice. Just as some participants in the bullionist controversy blamed the Bank of England rather than the country banks for depreciation of the pound during the Restriction (White 1984: 55–58), later writers including Henry Parnell and Robert Mushet (cited in White 1984: 63) laid blame for the 1825 crisis squarely on the shoulders of the Bank of England and its overissues of 1824–25.[20] Their view is also upheld by more recent authorities including Edward Nevin and E. W. Davis (1970: 43), who note that the country banks had been *contracting* their note issues and accumulating reserves locally and in London after 1819 in anticipation of resumption. Their policy changed after 1822, when the Bank of England—encouraged by a last-minute decision of the government to allow a continuance of country small-note circulation until 1833 (Thomas 1934: 42)—imprudently decided to employ the large reserves it had gained from the countryside by reducing its lending rate to 4 percent and extending the maturity of eligible bills from 65 to 95 days. "The country banks could hardly do other than follow these changes in the credit situation" by expanding their own issues (Nevin and Davis 1970: 43).

For some later episodes (when the "division of labor" should have been even more firmly established) the evidence against the Bank is still more conclusive. A recent case in point was the "fringe bank" crisis of 1973–74. According to Margaret Reid (1982), that crisis was based on a boom willfully engineered (with the Bank of England's help) by the Heath government in its "dash for growth." Nor has the Bank of England been the only central bank to be guilty of errors of commission (and not merely of omission) in modern times. As Garcia and Plautz (1988: 111) observe, the Fed on several occasions has set "the stage for real and financial sector insolvencies and liquidity crises." Excessive expansion of money made possible by the existence of central banks exposed financial institutions to wider and more frequent swings in nominal interest rates than could or would have occurred otherwise. An example of this cited by Kindleberger himself was the Fed's attempt to assist President Richard Nixon's 1972 reelection by expanding the money stock in the hope of lowering interest rates (Kindleberger 1988: 176). To suggest, as Kindleberger does elsewhere, that such behavior contradicts the true purpose central banks "arose" to fulfill is to ignore their historical origins entirely. It is like suggesting that lions "arose" in order to perform circus acts. The real surprise is not that central banks inflate but that many have been trained to inflate only modestly.

To conclude: monopoly in currency supply is more a cause of, than a cure for, financial fragility. This fact helps to account for the stability of past, decentralized banking systems such as those of Scotland (White 1984), Canada (Schuler 1988), Sweden (Jonung 1985), and Switzerland (Weber 1988) in the 19th century—a success that must appear paradoxical to those who regard fractional-reserve banking as inherently unstable and in need of a lender of last resort.[21]

THE POLITICAL ECONOMY OF CENTRAL BANK "HIERARCHY"

There is yet another, more subtle way in which restrictions on private currency issue have contributed to the perceived need for a lender of last resort. This is by indirectly fostering the view that private banking is *naturally* hegemonic or "hierarchical" (Gorton 1987; Gorton and Mullineaux 1987; Goodhart 1988). This view suggests that free development of a banking system would naturally lead to its being dominated by a single firm, from which other banks would borrow in times of stress, and to which they would send their reserves in normal times. What this view neglects is that the extent of hierarchy observed in contemporary banking systems is not consistent with private bankers' pursuit of their selfish interests in an unregulated setting (Selgin 1988: 16–34). Such hierarchy is another consequence of legal restrictions, including especially restrictions on note issue, that have allowed particular banks to dominate and control their rivals while also weakening the latter.

By far the most important example of this in history has been the rise to dominance of the Bank of England. The Bank's emergence as a central bank was the result of its receiving a series of legal privileges in return for large loans to the government (Smith 1936: 9, 129; Bagehot 1873: 92–100). Among the Bank's more important privileges prior to 1826 were (1) its monopoly of notes issue within a 65-mile radius of London, (2) its monopoly of limited liability and joint-stock banking, and (3) its status as exclusive holder of the government's deposits. The prohibition of limited liability and joint-stock banking outside of London was especially injurious, as it forced most of England to depend upon small, undercapitalized "country" banks as a source of currency.[22] According to Lord Liverpool (quoted in Dowd 1989: 125), this arrangement was

> one of the fullest liberty as to what is rotten and bad, but one of the most complete restrictions as to all that is good. By it a cobbler or cheesemonger [may issue notes] while, on the other hand, more than six persons, however respectable, are not permitted to become partners in a bank with whose notes the whole business of the country might be transacted.

According to Parnell (quoted in White 1984: 40), it was the presence of so many "cobblers and cheesemongers"[23] in English banking that caused hundreds of banks there to fail in 1826. In contrast, the relative freedom of Scottish banking had endowed it with several strong joint-stock banks, with nationwide branches, all of which were unharmed by the crisis in England.

The Bank of England's privileges also caused other banks to keep their specie reserves with it and to treat its liabilities as their ultimate source of liquidity.[24] This situation only served to enhance the subservience of the weaker banks to their privileged rival, causing the system to be still more top heavy and "hierarchical." The Bank had learned, furthermore, that in the event of a crisis, it could rely upon the government to protect it from bankruptcy by sanctioning its suspension of payments. Thus, while other banks were unnaturally dependent upon the Bank, it could refuse to assist them with impunity—a kind of moral hazard opposite the kind most associated with central banking today. A relatively late example of this may have been the Bank's refusal to extend aid to Overend, Gurney and Company in 1866

(De Cecco 1975: 80–82). A better example, perhaps, was the Bank of France's willful destruction of rival, provincial banks of issue in 1847–48 (Kindleberger 1984: 104–7). Such conduct by central banks only serves, of course, to further strengthen their command over remaining, underprivileged rivals.

The exalted status of the Bank of England did not just make other English banks depend on it. For London was also the financial capital of Great Britain and, indeed, the world; to dominate the London money market was, therefore, to dominate the world money market. The consequence of this was that non-English banks, including the Scottish banks during the free-banking era, occasionally looked upon the Bank of England as a potential source of emergency short-term funds.

This fact has led several writers (Cowen and Kroszner 1989; Rockoff 1986: 630; Rothbard 1988; Sechrest 1988; Goodhart 1988) to deny that banking in Scotland was ever truly free after all because it, too, depended upon access to a central bank. In arguing thus, they confuse a banking system's reliance upon access to a financial center with its reliance upon access to a privileged bank of issue. Had banking in England been free, there is no doubt that London would still have been Great Britain's (as well as the world's) financial center. In that case, Scottish banks might have relied upon any of several large, English joint-stock banks to gain access to the central money market or, better still, would simply have located their own branches (if not their headquarters) there. To really appreciate the irrelevance of this criticism of free banking, though, one should contemplate what would have happened if Scotland had set up a monopoly bank of issue while England allowed its banks to develop free of legal restrictions. Then economists might have been treated to the spectacle of a privileged central bank having to rely upon several competitive banks of issue as lenders of last resort and as conduits to the national and world money markets. What conclusions would they have drawn from this? What conclusions should be drawn from the fact that large Canadian banks have sometimes relied upon private banks in New York City both prior to and after 1913? Finally, what should one conclude from the experience of the Swedish *enskilda* banks prior to 1900—which were, as a matter of policy, refused assistance by the more privileged Riksbank but which were free of failures nonetheless—or from the similar experience of Switzerland's cantonal banks of issue in the years preceding the Franco-Prussian War? None of the latter systems can be said to have depended even indirectly upon assistance from a privileged central bank.

Thus, the hierarchy enjoyed by central banks is not a natural development but rests on "a combination of political motives and historical accident" (Smith 1936: 2), the most important motive being governments' desire to gain financial favors from particular banks. Far from being consistent with the healthy development of private banking, such hierarchy is a cause of financial weakening: the strength enjoyed by central banks is strength sapped from their would-be rivals. Moreover, the central banking "game," in which strength is transferred from several banks to one bank, has a negative sum.

Significantly, Walter Bagehot—the high priest of central banking—understood all of this. The Bank of England's special responsibilities stemmed, in his view, from its holding "the ultimate banking reserve of the country." But this fact, far from being natural, was due to the Bank's "accumulation of legal privileges . . . which no one [sic!] would now defend" (Bagehot 1873: 64, 92–100). Far from wanting to defend "the monarchical form of Lombard Street," Bagehot (1873: 66–68) called it "dangerous" and contrasted it unfavorably to the "natural" system "of many banks of equal or not altogether unequal size [that] would have sprung up if Government had let banking alone":

> In all other trades competition brings the traders to a rough approximate equality. There is no tendency to a monarchy in the cotton world; nor, where banking has been left free, is there any tendency to a monarchy in banking. . . . A monarchy in any trade is a sign of some anomalous advantage, and of some intervention from without.

Present-day defenders of central banking have neglected this part of Bagehot's teachings, twisting his "second-best" argument for central banks into a first-best argument.[25]

PANIC-PROOF FREE BANKING

I have tried to suggest above that the maximization of banking efficiency and the avoidance of fragility and crises are not conflicting goals, one of which demands competition and financial liberalization and the other of which demands regulation and control. A liberalized and hence competitive banking system is likely to be both more efficient *and* less fragile and crisis prone.

Nevertheless, even such a free-banking system would not necessarily be panic proof. As long as banks continue to have liabilities unconditionally redeemable on demand, while holding only fractional reserves, the possibility of a systemic collapse would still exist. The system could still be exposed to a sudden increase in the public's demand for the ultimate money of redemption, prompted by an invasion or revolution; or it might be threatened by a major computer malfunction (like the one that caused the Bank of New York's $23 billion default in 1985). An important question, then, is whether a lender of last resort would be necessary even in a deregulated system to guard against such rare events.

The answer, I think, is that it would not, the reason being that the widespread reliance upon bank liabilities unconditionally convertible on demand is itself an artificial consequence of legal restrictions. As Rockoff (1986: 623) points out, the Bank Notes (Scotland) Act of 1765 imposed a fine of £500 on any Scottish bank failing to redeem a note on demand; likewise, free-banking laws in the United States required state authorities to redeem *all* of a bank's notes from the proceeds of sales of deposited bonds in the event that the bank failed to redeem a single dollar on demand.[26] Such laws prevented banks from offering alternative, contingent-convertibility contracts to their customers, thereby needlessly exposing them to a higher risk of default and panic.

Contingent-convertibility contracts—contracts that make the redemption of a bank note or deposit credit contingent upon the *total value* of redemptions being requested at any moment—may take either of two forms. One allows a bank under special circumstances to "suspend" or "restrict" convertibility of deposits into high-powered money. A bank, while suspending convertibility, may still engage in other types of banking business, by issuing notes, accepting deposits, and making loans. It may also make special arrangements for continuing its settlements with other banks, thereby ensuring that notes and checks drawn from it can still be used for payments generally. The other kind of contingent-convertibility contract provides for the issuance of "option-clause" notes, which can, at the issuing bank's discretion, be redeemed either on demand or after a predetermined delay, with interest paid to the notes' holders as compensation in the latter case.

Both option-clause notes and suspension of deposit convertibility have been observed in history. The former were issued by Scottish banks prior to 1765; the latter were resorted to on several occasions by national banks in the pre-Federal Reserve era.[27] Moreover, as Kevin Dowd (1988), Gary Gorton (1985), and others have observed, their use is entirely consistent with the interests of both banks and their customers, so that legal restrictions alone have stood in the way of their more widespread use in place of unconditionally convertible liabilities. It would be only in banks' interest to exercise their option to suspend cash payments in situations where such payments become physically impossible (Postlewaite and Vives 1987: 490–91). According to Gorton (1985: 190), suspension in such circumstances prevents bank liability holders from engaging in behavior that could force their banks to suffer "fire-sale" losses: "Suspension circumvents the realization of suboptimal depositor withdrawals which are based on (rational) fears of capital losses" but which could lead to even *greater* losses than a more orderly process of liquidation. More importantly, perhaps, the mere prospect that suspension may be resorted to will, according to Dowd (1988: 327), "suffice to stabilize [a] panic and protect the banking system from collapse." Thus, contingent-convertibility contracts can provide an effective substitute for a lender of last resort or deposit insurance or other government-imposed devices for containing a banking panic.[28]

CONCLUSION

Despite frequent claims to the contrary, fractional-reserve banking systems are not inherently fragile or unstable. The fragility and instability of real-world banking systems is not a free-market phenomenon but a consequence of legal restrictions. This does not mean that deregulation is without its dangers. Dismantling bad bank regulations is like cutting wires in a time bomb: the job is risky and has to be done in carefully ordered steps, but it beats letting the thing go on ticking. Once the fuse—the legal restrictions—is dismantled, the payload—central banking and fiat money—can safely be disposed of.

PART II

BEFORE THE FED

4

THE SUPPRESSION OF STATE BANK NOTES: A RECONSIDERATION*

> Let us have a bank currency that will be recognized in the next town . . . a currency that will be recognized in New York, Philadelphia, Boston, New Orleans, Chicago, or any other part of the United States.
>
> —Rep. John F. Farnsworth (R-IL), April 28, 1864 (Cong. Globe, 38th Cong., 1st Sess.: 1934)

> [I]f the national banks, with the great advantages which they enjoy, cannot compete successfully with the State banks, it simply shows that the latter subserve better the interests of the business community, and should not be destroyed.
>
> —Rep. Francis Kernan (D-NY), February 16, 1865 (Cong. Globe, 38th Cong., 2nd Sess.: 833)

During the Civil War, a 10 percent tax was placed on any issuance of notes of state-chartered or incorporated banks, deliberately forcing state banks out of the paper currency business and making the regulation and issuance of currency a prerogative of the federal government and of federally chartered national banks.

* Originally published in *Economic Inquiry* 38, no. 4 (October 2000): 600–15. The author thanks the staff at Harvard's Baker Library in Boston and at the American Antiquarian Society for their assistance with research materials, as well as Gerald Dwyer, Lidija Polutnik, Anna Schwartz, Larry Schweikart, Warren E. Weber, Lawrence H. White, and participants at the University of Georgia Economics Department workshop for their comments and suggestions. Two anonymous referees offered helpful suggestions. This research was made possible by an Earhart Foundation grant administered by the Institute for Humane Studies.

This chapter reexamines Congress's decision to suppress state bank notes. American monetary historians have conventionally viewed the decision as reflecting (1) "the public's intolerable disgust with an unregulated currency" (Hammond 1957: 11; compare Dunbar 1922: 220), and (2) the government's desire to boost the demand for national bank charters so as to expand the market for its debt (e.g., Hughes and Cain 1998: 373–74; Dowd 1992: 230). I plan to argue that neither view accounts adequately for the 10 percent tax. The first view in particular begs important questions that have gone unaddressed: If state bank notes were clearly inferior to national bank notes, why was a prohibitive tax needed to drive them out of circulation? Just how were consumers supposed to benefit from having their choices restricted?

I explore several responses to these questions and ultimately conclude that consumers considered some state bank notes to be just as desirable as their national bank counterparts. I argue that the 10 percent tax served not to overcome any bank-note-market failure but to force the withdrawal of relatively high-quality state bank notes. I then proceed to show that the tax was not needed to secure adequate bond sales to national banks. Proponents of the tax were striving not to increase the number of applications for national bank charters but to limit growth in the aggregate money stock. I conclude by suggesting that because state banks of issue could have accommodated market demands that national banks failed to satisfy, consumers might have been better served had state bank notes been allowed to survive.

THE CHASE PLAN

When the first shots of the American Civil War were fired at Fort Sumter, the paper currency of the United States consisted of over $200 million in bank notes, issued by nearly 1,500 state-chartered banks. The quality of these bank notes varied according to their issuers' management and regulatory environment.[1] Some bank notes circulated at par only near their source and at fluctuating discounts elsewhere, so that persons carrying notes from state to state risked incurring currency exchange losses of the sort borne by international travelers today. A few were subject to especially heavy discounts or were refused altogether because their issuers' solvency was in question. Fraudulent notes were yet another source of confusion. Sen. John Sherman (R-OH), brother of Union General William T. Sherman and a leading advocate of currency reform, observed in 1863 that, of 1,500 state banks in existence two years before, all but 253 of them had had their notes counterfeited or altered at one time or another (Cong. Globe, 37th Cong., 3rd Sess.: 840ff).[2]

Five years later, the U.S. currency system had changed dramatically. Fewer than 300 state banks remained, none of which issued notes. Most of the banks present at the onset of the war had acquired national bank charters. Over $281 million in national bank notes had been issued, while less than $20 million in state bank notes remained outstanding. Unlike their state-bank counterparts, national bank notes circulated at par throughout the country. They were also fully guaranteed by the U.S. government.

These dramatic changes were the results of two pieces of Civil War legislation. The National Currency Act of February 25, 1863 (revised as the National Bank Act on June 3, 1864), provided for the establishment of federally chartered national banks. The 10 percent tax, adopted (by a narrow margin) as part of the March 3, 1865, Revenue Act and levied on any state bank notes paid out by any bank after July 1866,[3] forced state bankers either to cease issuing notes or to join the national system.[4]

Advocates of national banking, including Secretary of the Treasury Salmon P. Chase, were (in the words of New York State banking superintendent H. B. Van Dyck) unwilling "to leave [their] favorite scheme to the vindication of time and experience" (Cong. Globe, 38th Cong., 1st Sess.: 1935) and recommended a punitive tax on state bank issues in order to guarantee the wholesale conversion of state banks into nationally chartered institutions. Chase had reason to be concerned: as Table 4.1 shows, of the 584 national banks established by November 1864, only 169 were conversions of former state banks, and none of the larger state banks were among them. The tax worked as desired, so that between November 1864 and October 1865, another 731 former state banks joined the national system, the majority of them doing so after March 3.[5]

Table 4.1: Formation of National Banks, 1863–66

Dates	New Establishments	State-Bank Conversions	Cumulative Conversions	Cumulative Grand Total
Feb. 1863–Nov. 1863	133	1	1	134
Nov. 1863–Nov. 1864	282	168	169	584
Nov. 1864–Dec. 1865	283	731	922	1,601
Dec. 1865–Oct. 1866	51	11	933	1,682

SOURCE: Comptroller of the Currency, *Annual Report* (1864–1867). Figures do not sum correctly owing in part to national bank failures but perhaps also to some miscounting.

Why hadn't more state banks voluntarily joined the national system? Comptroller of the Currency Hugh McCulloch (1889: 168) listed four reasons for state banks' refusal to convert. These were (1) their fear that national banking legislation would promote "wildcat" banking; (2) their fear that a Southern victory would bankrupt the new system; (3) their fear of capricious or hostile federal interference in the future; and (4) their desire to preserve the reputational capital embodied in their brand names (which they were asked to abandon under the terms of the original National Currency Act). Interestingly, these reasons all indicate state bankers' lack of confidence in the new system—their feeling that national banking would prove *more* disreputable and *less* stable than some state banking systems had been.

Other writers, such as Fritz Redlich (1951: 107–9) and Ross Robertson and Gary Walton (1979: 379), claim that state banks were deterred by the stringent requirements of the national banking law, including its minimum capital and bond collateral requirements. Even the relatively strict New York free-banking law, for example, allowed a bank to receive and issue $100 of additional notes in exchange for $100 (face value) of additional U.S. bonds with no limit on the total value of notes issued, whereas a national bank could only receive $90 of notes in return for the same security, and then only provided that its total circulation did not exceed its paid-in capital. National bank notes were also subject to an aggregate limit until 1875, so that until that time, individual banks might be denied access to new notes despite having the requisite bonds and capital.

But the claim that national banking was resisted because it was overly burdensome is far from convincing. The constraints that national bankers labored under were offset by corresponding advantages: national banks could receive government deposits, avoid state taxes (as well the much lower but still discriminatory tax on state bank notes that preceded the 10 percent tax), and avoid the minimum reserve requirements many states imposed.[6] Thanks to these and other advantages, national banking was profitable enough to attract over 400 new entrants by the end of 1864. Many state banks also had more than enough capital to qualify for national charters, and national banking did manage to win over significant numbers of state banks. These early national banks rapidly earned a reputation for paying high dividends. In the Treasury's "Annual Report" for 1864 (48) Comptroller McCulloch observed that "the stock of State banks which have been changed into national associations has not been depreciated by the change; on the contrary, the shares of most of them have been appreciated."

Indeed, the "preference" that was, according to McCulloch (1889: 54), "everywhere given to a national currency over the notes of State banks" should have made national banking appear generally more profitable than state banking: if consumers really did prefer national bank notes to state bank notes, then, absent any currency-market failure, national banks should have captured the entire currency market, leaving state banks bereft of funds. That state banks sometimes operated under less stringent regulatory constraints would then be irrelevant, because low costs alone cannot compensate for a lack of customers.

Under the circumstances and given the aggregate $300 million ceiling on national bank notes, state banks might have been expected to apply en masse for national charters as soon as these became available. "If the Federal banks are preferable," Rep. John Ganson (D-NY) argued in 1864 (Cong. Globe, 38th Cong., 1st Sess.: 1935), "they will be organized by the capital of the country, and it will not be necessary for Congress to deprive the State institutions of their hold upon their State existence by thumb-screws."

Yet as we have seen, most state banks refused to join the national system voluntarily. The fundamental (though seldom articulated) reason for this was not that state regulations were relatively lax but that the public's demand for state-bank currency remained relatively strong: for some reason, the public did not generally refuse state bank notes in favor of supposedly superior alternatives.

DID THE BANK-NOTE MARKET FAIL?

"We would expect," writes John James (1981: 455), "that a free, self-governing, and, at times, obstreperous, people would have refused and rejected [state bank] notes with scorn, and would have made their circulation impossible, but the American people did not." Why not? Why didn't national bank notes spontaneously displace state bank notes from consumers' portfolios? One set of answers is based on the premise that in the market for currency, competition and free consumer choice alone do not maximize consumers' welfare. Although advocates of the 10 percent tax offered no explicit market-failure arguments on its behalf, the suggestion that the tax was needed to rid the U.S. economy of inferior currency carries with it the implication that the U.S. currency market had failed somehow. Therefore, I think it worthwhile to consider some market-failure arguments that may have played a tacit role in the movement to suppress state bank notes.

GRESHAM'S LAW

Three possible causes of currency-market failure that might supply a rationale for the 10 percent tax are Gresham's law, asymmetric information, and network externalities. Gresham's law asserts that "bad money drives good money out of circulation." Modern writers consider it applicable only where a single monetary unit is defined in terms of two intrinsically distinct mediums, implying an official "fixed" exchange rate between them. If this official rate differs from the two mediums' free-market exchange rate, then the officially overvalued ("bad") medium will drive the officially undervalued ("good") medium out of circulation provided that legal penalties prevent sellers from discriminating in favor of good money (e.g., by accepting bad money only at a discount).

Gresham's law takes effect, in part, because legal penalties against discrimination make it prudent for sellers to treat bad money as the de facto unit of account and for buyers to offer only bad money in exchange (Selgin 1996a). Bad money can also drive out good money in the absence of legal penalties. This occurs when prices happen (for reasons unrelated to legal sanctions) to be expressed in terms of bad money, and high transactions costs of nonpar exchange make it prohibitively costly to transact with good money. This variant of Gresham's law may be called Rolnick and Weber's law. More generally, Rolnick and Weber's law asserts that, if there are high market-based transactions costs of nonpar exchange, par monies will drive nonpar monies out of circulation (Rolnick and Weber 1986).

Was the survival of state bank notes after the passage of the national banking acts a manifestation of either Gresham's law or Rolnick and Weber's law? It clearly was not an instance of the former: gold and greenbacks (after February 1862) alone were legal tender, whereas state bank notes were not even accepted in payments to the federal government. People were therefore free to price state bank notes as they pleased or to refuse them altogether.

State bank notes were, in fact, often accepted at a discount relative to legal tender—this was, indeed, one of the chief complaints lodged against them. The complaint meant that some other medium—gold or greenbacks—was the de facto unit of account. To the extent that nonpar exchange was not costless, Rolnick and Weber's law should have favored national bank notes over state bank notes.

ASYMMETRIC INFORMATION

If some agents lack information concerning the intrinsic values of different currencies, something like Gresham's law can occur even where nonpar exchange is costless. Suppose that there are two note-issuing banks, S and N, and that bank S maintains a riskier loan portfolio and a lower reserve ratio than bank N. Bank N also redeems its notes at par in several well-placed cities, whereas bank S redeems at par only at its remote headquarters.

Because of its lower cost structure, bank S offers to pay higher rates to its depositors while lending at lower rates than bank N. If would-be borrowers and noteholders are completely unaware of the quality difference between the two banks, they will patronize bank S only, accepting, holding, and spending its notes. Bank N, in contrast, will suffer from a lack of customers. To avoid this problem, the government could supply the public with improved bank-specific information, or it could require all banks to adopt bank N's practices (see, for example, Cothren 1987; Williamson 1992).

Could consumers' ignorance account for state banks' relative lack of interest in national banking prior to March 1865? That all national bank notes were fully secured by U.S. securities and that they also were publicly receivable and (after 1864) receivable at par at any national bank was well publicized. Consumers presumably knew less about the overall quality of state bank notes; but they could refer (as merchants routinely did) to bank note reporters for information concerning note discounts. Such reporters priced both state and national bank notes, showing clearly that the former were more frequently discounted. Given the widespread availability of such information, it is highly unlikely that the persistent demand for state bank notes following the appearance of greenbacks and national bank notes was a result of consumers' inability to appreciate the differences between these distinct monies.[7]

NETWORK EXTERNALITIES

A third kind of currency-market failure occurs when "network externalities" prevent agents from switching from an inferior to a superior currency. Network externalities can be either direct or indirect. Thus, any one person's use of a particular kind of computer hardware enhances the usefulness of that same hardware to other users indirectly by creating a larger market for compatible software; whereas any one person's acquisition of a fax machine directly enhances the serviceableness of other persons' fax machines (by allowing them to trade faxes with one more person). Robert King (1983: 133) identifies a direct network externality in the market for bank notes when he observes that "an increase in the number of users of a particular note could lower the probability of meeting an individual uninformed about the value of one's note and, hence, the expected cost of trades." John P. Caskey and Simon St. Laurent (1994) appeal to indirect network externalities to explain Americans' refusal to accept the Susan B. Anthony dollar coins introduced in 1979: according to these authors, to guarantee the new coin's success, the government would have had to consider withdrawing competing paper bills from circulation.

Could a similar argument justify the 10 percent tax on state bank notes? With respect to indirect network externalities, the answer would appear to be no. Unlike the later Susan B. Anthony dollar (given then-existing cash trays and vending machines), national bank notes were fully "compatible" with the existing payments technology. Indeed, the greater uniformity of national bank notes made them more compatible with the established dollar unit of account.

What about direct network externalities? Federal authorities assured some initial network for national bank notes by making them publicly receivable. This network was further enhanced by the 1864 requirement that all national banks accept each other's notes at par. Finally, given national bank notes' guaranteed security and compatibility with the established exchange technology, it should have been strategically optimal for state banks to accept them—if not at par, then at discounts similar to ones they applied to notes of other state banks (Selgin and White 1987: 446–47).[8] In short, a newly established national bank could rely on a substantial ready-made network for its notes, at least as large as the networks enjoyed by most state banks.[9]

DID STATE BANK NOTES PASS A FAIR MARKET TEST?

If market failures weren't to blame for consumers' attachment to state bank notes, then we are compelled to wonder whether these notes were truly inferior to national bank notes.

The sweeping claims often heard concerning the poor quality of state bank notes can be highly misleading. That some banks, including the notorious "wildcats" that arose during the free-banking era, were sources of heavily discounted notes, is well known. But wildcat banks were rare, and noteholder losses from bank failures were not very large. "By 1860," Hugh Rockoff (1974: 151) observes, "note holders had probably lost less through the failure of free banks, including the wildcats, than they stood to lose in that year from a 2 percent inflation."[10]

Many banks operating during the 1850s and early 1860s enjoyed quite solid reputations, demonstrating through "a long series of years by splendid results" that the issuance of sound currency "was not beyond the reach of States' administrative powers" (White 1894: 211). The New York free banks were good enough to serve as a model for the national banking system: according to Rockoff (1975: 16), between 1850 and 1861 the average annual rate of loss on New York state bank notes was less than three-hundredths of 1 percent. The banks of the New England "Suffolk" system enjoyed an even better reputation, issuing currency that many considered to be the best in the nation, if not the world.[11] The multibranched Bank of the State of Indiana—which Bray Hammond (1957: 621) refers to as "one of the most distinguished and honored financial institutions of the country"—was among the relatively small number of Northern banks to avoid suspending during the Panic of 1857. The "uniformly successful" banks authorized under Ohio's banking laws of 1845 and 1851 (including the State Bank of Ohio and its many semi-independent branches) furnished a currency "not one dollar of which was ever lost by the holders thereof" (Knox 1900: 685). According to one-time comptroller of the currency John Jay Knox (1900: 766), many of the "excellent provisions" of the government-controlled State Bank of Iowa were followed in the national banking laws.

Several Southern banking systems also had good reputations prior to the war, including the branch-banking systems of South Carolina, whose banking laws "gave satisfaction throughout the country," and Virginia, where bank failures were unknown and bank notes "held the complete confidence of the people" (Knox 1900: 567, 529; see also Schweikart 1987: 126). The Louisiana system was another Southern banking success story. It also passed through the Panic of 1857 unscathed and went on to anger Confederate officials by continuing to remit specie to Northern creditors long after the outbreak of the war (Hammond 1957: 684; Schweikart 1987: 170).

Recognition of some of the better state bank currencies hardly suffices, of course, to establish the *overall* quality of the nation's currency in the period just prior to the enactment of the 10 percent tax. That overall quality is most readily gauged by looking at bank-note discounts. The discount placed on any bank's notes reflected both the bank's distance from the market in which the discount was quoted and the bank's perceived riskiness (Gorton 1996): if note brokers entertained any doubts concerning a bank's ability to redeem its notes at full value, they would list the notes as being of "doubtful" or "unknown" value and would refuse to accept them. A review of note prices during the Civil War reveals a state of affairs far removed from the dire image conveyed by many informal descriptions of state-bank currency. According to *Hodge's Journal of Finance and Bank Note Reporter* for October 1863 (the last date for which individual state bank circulation figures are available), discounts on bank notes in New York City tended to be quite modest: with the exception of banks in the Confederacy (the notes of which were no longer saleable in most Northern markets) and three Missouri banks (whose notes suffered discounts of 25, 30, and 50 percent), all other banks had their notes discounted by 2 percent or less, with one-fifth of 1 percent being the modal rate for all non-Confederate banks (see Table 4.2).[12] Discount rates on notes were, in other words, typically about one-fifth of the premium paid on traveler's checks today and lower by one percentage point or more than commissions paid by merchants today on charge and credit-card sales. Were the entire sum of $154,638,625 in Northern bank notes purchased at par and then sold in the New York market, the loss would have amounted to only $1,501,409, or less than 1 percent of the notes' face value, *even treating all doubtful or unknown notes as a total loss.*[13]

Although most recent discussions of bank-note prices refer to prices in Northeastern markets (New York or Philadelphia), this focus tends to overstate the extent to which bank notes depreciated away from their home markets. Because the Northeast typically enjoyed a favorable trade balance with the rest of the nation, Northeastern currency tended to command higher values in the West than Western currencies commanded in the Northeast. Thus, according to the October 1863 *Chicago Bank Note List*, of the 1,281 Northern banks that were then presumed to be either open for business, closing, or recently failed, 1,041—that is, 81.3 percent—of them issued a total of $119,813,212 in notes that traded *at par* in Chicago. Included were practically all the banks in Illinois, New England and New York, Indiana, Ohio, Delaware, and Philadelphia, as well as the State Bank of Iowa. Other banks' notes were discounted even in Chicago, but here again the discounts were generally small (see Table 4.3). In other words, by late 1863, most state-bank currency was just as acceptable in Chicago as the national bank notes that would soon supplant it.

Table 4.2: New York Bank-Note Discounts, October 1863

State	No. of Banks	Total Circulation	Modal Discount Factor	Unlisted, Doubtful, or Uknown	Discounted (difference from par)
ME	69	$5,757,072	0.002	$0	$11,514
VT	41	$5,619,603	0.002	$0	$11,239
NH	50	$4,445,112	0.002	$0	$8,890
MA	185	$26,787,703	0.002	$0	$53,575
RI	86	$6,108,828	0.002	$0	$12,218
CT	74	$11,450,126	0.002	$0	$20,500
NY	298	$27,873,087	0.00375 [a]	$0	$69,639
NJ	76	$8,826,473	0	$171,790	$11,775
DE	15	$1,265,651	0.002	$44,496	$2,920
MD	37	$6,552,720	0.00375	$66,980	$46,048
PA	87	$23,356,238	0.0075 [b]	$390,316	$144,252
OH	19 [c]	$7,043,765	0.0075	$0	$52,828
DC	3	$54,708	0.02	$0	$1,094
IL	22	$660,780	0.015	$0	$9,912
IN	15	$4,318,144	0.02	$0	$48,560
IA	2 [c]	$1,094,661	0.01	$0	$10,947
WI	64	$2,317,823	0.015	$0	$34,767
KY	9	$7,807,282	0.01	$0	$78,073
MO	9	$2,955,029	0.02	$0	$196,093
MI	4	$153,720	0.01	$0	$1,537
MN	5	$190,180	0.0075	$0	$1,426
Total U.S.	1,170	$154,638,625	0.002	$673,582	$827,827

a All New York City at par.

b All Philadelphia at 0.002.

c Branches not counted separately.

SOURCES: Note discounts from *Hodge's Journal of Finance and Bank Note Reporter* (Oct. 1863); circulation figures from Commissioner of Internal Revenue (1864).

To observe that many state bank notes had become "bankable" (or nearly so) far from home is not to deny that many states, especially ones in the West, lacked local sources of such bankable monies and therefore stood to gain something from national banking. The question is whether consumers were made better off by being limited to national bank notes alone than they would have been had they been left free to employ either national or state bank notes. Even if a locally issued state bank note was itself not bankable in some far-away market, its holder had the option by early 1862 (when the wildcats had been driven to extinction) of redeeming it at full value at its issuer's counter or perhaps offering it to a local bank in exchange for gold or greenbacks. People therefore had no more reason to refrain from employing state bank notes that were less widely accepted than greenbacks and gold than they have reason today to refrain from employing checkable deposits that are less widely negotiable than cash.[14] The presence of firmly established markets for state bank notes explains the otherwise mysterious value many state banks attached to their names—a value the original National Currency Act had not reckoned with.

To summarize: the 10 percent tax was not needed to rid the U.S. of "bad" bank notes, both because relatively few bad notes were in circulation at the onset of the Civil War and because the introduction of greenbacks and national bank notes alone should have sufficed to drive out any remaining old rags. What the tax *did* do was drive out state bank notes that had survived alongside national bank notes because the state bank notes were considered just as good for most purposes as their national counterparts. In the words of L. Carroll Root (1895: 308), the tax was found necessary "not because [state bank currency] was too bad, but because it was too good; not because people had no confidence in it, but because they preferred it to National Bank notes."[15]

Table 4.3: Chicago Bank-Note Discounts, October 1863

State	No. of Banks	Total Circulation	Modal Discount Factor	Unlisted, Doubtful, or Uknown	Discounted (difference from par)
ME	69	$5,757,072	0	$0	$0
VT	41	$5,619,603	0	$0	$0
NH	50	$4,445,112	0	$0	$0
MA	185	$26,787,703	0	$0	$0
RI	86	$6,108,828	0	$32,476	$0
CT	74	$11,450,126	0	$0	$0
NY	298	$27,873,087	0	$3,926	$0
NJ	76	$8,826,473	0	$245,422	$0
DE	15	$1,265,651	0	$79,615	$0
MD	37	$6,552,720	0.02	$380,688	$80,239
PA	87	$23,356,238	0.015	$0	$229,747
OH	19	$7,043,765	0	$0	$0
DC	3	$54,708	0.05	$0	$2,735
IL	22	$660,780	0	$0	$0
IN	15	$4,318,144	0.01	$0	$12,939
IA	2	$1,094,661	0	$0	$0
WI	64	$2,317,823	0.0025	$0	$5,795
KY	9	$7,807,282	0	$308,680	$0
MO	9	$2,955,029	0.005	$0	$32,939
MI	4	$153,720	0	$0	$0
MN	5	$190,180	0	$0	$0
Total U.S.	1,170	$154,638,625	0	$1,050,807	$364,394

SOURCES: Note discounts from *Chicago Bank Note List* (Oct. 1863); circulation figures from Commissioner of Internal Revenue (1864).

THE 10 PERCENT TAX AND WARTIME FINANCIAL POLICY

If the 10 percent tax did not serve to improve the overall quality of the U.S. currency stock, why was it enacted at all? The tax is often said to have been aimed at aiding the federal government's finances by increasing the demand for national bank charters and, hence, the demand for government bonds. The tax was part of a revenue bill, after all. But such a bare-bones fiscal explanation for the 10 percent tax is just as unsatisfactory as the claim that the tax was needed to rid the U.S. economy of inferior bank notes. It is inadequate for one simple reason: there was no shortage of applicants for national bank charters prior to March 1865. The problem that vexed Treasury officials was not a lack of applicants for national bank charters but a lack of interest on the part of state bankers. A steady stream of applications for "new" national bank charters (as opposed to applications to convert state banks) had been arriving at the comptroller's office since the passage of the National Currency Act, causing Comptroller McCulloch to decline numerous applications in an attempt to avoid a "too rapid" increase in the number of national banks (Comptroller of the Currency, *Annual Report*, 1864: 48).

Why "too rapid"? Because, the way things were progressing, the comptroller's office would have allowed the full quota of $300 million in authorized national bank notes to have been issued without seeing any corresponding retirement of state bank notes, thereby adding substantially more to the total currency stock than $100 million—the largest possible net addition if all $200 million of state bank notes outstanding on passage of the National Currency Act were retired. The 10 percent tax was supposed to persuade remaining state bankers to join other applicants for national charters. Another provision of the 1865 Revenue Act in turn officially gave former state bankers priority over other applicants.

The inflationary danger posed by the survival of state bank notes was indeed substantial: the Treasury, in having issued over $470 million in legal tender by 1867, increased enormously the nominal stock of high-powered money available to fuel bank expansion and inflation. As long as state banking legislation required banks to redeem their notes in specie, the full inflationary potential of new Treasury issues would not be unleashed. But state banks would eventually be relieved of their obligation to redeem in specie by the legal tender acts.

One way to gauge how serious inflation might have been after 1865 in the absence of the 10 percent tax is to compare the actual money stock and price level for the year 1867, when most state banks had been driven out of existence, to conjectural values for the money stock and price level assuming no tax. The money stock in 1867 amounted to $1.26 billion. Banks held reserves of $267 million. Assuming that these reserves consisted entirely of Treasury-issued high-powered money, that left another $209 million of high-powered Treasury money in circulation. Now suppose (to take the most extreme possibility) that, instead of being held by the public, the remaining $209 million of government issues were employed exclusively as reserves by state banks to support their own issues of notes and deposits. Assuming that state banks maintained a reserve ratio of 0.20 against their combined demandable liabilities (as they did in fact do just before the war), these reserves would have allowed them to support $1.045 billion in outstanding notes and deposits. The money stock would therefore have been $1.26 billion – $0.209 billion + $1.045 billion = $2.1 billion. Assuming unchanged values for real income and the velocity of money, this would imply a price-level one and two-thirds as high as that actually experienced.[16]

Salmon Chase was fully aware of the likely inflationary impact of greenbacks and national banking and was determined to soften this impact by eliminating the state banking industry. Chase was, however, inclined to oversimplify matters by disingenuously attributing the full extent of wartime inflation to "the large volume of [state] bank notes yet in circulation" and by promising that the "very considerable difference between coin and United States notes would disappear" if state bank notes were retired (U.S. Treasury, *Annual Report*, 1863: 19). Defenders of state banks could easily respond to Chase's arguments by observing that many state banks had actually reduced their issues in the years following the passage of the legal tender acts: the aggregate quantity of state bank notes, which was $202 million early in 1861, fell to $184 million by 1862, rose to $239 million in 1863, and then fell below $180 million in 1864, while the stock of Treasury currency rose continuously from a mere $16 million in 1861 to over $600 million in 1864.[17] Armed with such statistics, Rep. James Brooks (D-NY), in arguing against punitive taxation of state bank notes, took Chase to task for "attributing [the Treasury's] own expansion to the expansion of the State banks" (Cong. Globe, 38th Cong., 1st Sess.: 1731), while New York State banking superintendent H. B. Van Dyck wondered why the Treasury would "single-out the state banks for denunciation, as if they alone were responsible for the evils resulting from a redundant currency" (p. 1935).

The answer to Van Dyck's question was, of course, that the Treasury was not about to alter its wartime financial strategy, with its heavy reliance on greenbacks and bond sales to national banks, and so was unwilling to address the problem of inflation other than by treating state banks as scapegoats. Some members of Congress shared the Treasury's tendency to treat its own additions to the money stock as a fait accompli, thereby making the suppression of state bank notes the only remaining means for curtailing inflation. In defending an amendment to the Revenue Bill of 1864 which called for a prohibitive tax on state bank notes, Rep. Henry G. Stebbins (D-NY) declared, "The national financial plan" would "inflate to a still greater degree the prices of all the necessities of life" unless national banks took "the place of the local State banking system entirely" (Cong. Globe, 38th Cong., 1st Sess.: 1721). Comptroller McCulloch went a step further by holding it "indispensable for the financial success of the treasury that the currency of the country should be under the control of the government"—a goal that could not be achieved "as long as State institutions have the right to flood the country with their issues" (Comptroller of the Currency, *Annual Report*, 1864: 54). As far as Chase, Stebbins, McCulloch, and many others were concerned, the main elements—greenbacks and national banking—of the national financial plan were no longer up for debate by mid-1864. The only question left to be answered was whether to limit the inflationary consequences of these measures (and thereby enhance the Treasury's real seigniorage earnings) by forcing state banks out of the currency business.

Although defenders of state banks were able to exclude a prohibitive bank-note tax from the Revenue Act of 1864, they were unsuccessful—though only barely so—in 1865, owing in part at least to the political triumph of greenbacks and national banking. Representatives and senators who had once opposed one or both developments came reluctantly to admit the futility of such opposition, and so were prepared to support the suppression of state bank notes, not as a first-best ideal but as the sole remaining means for restricting the quantity of money.

Such was the attitude, for example, of Rep. James Wilson (R-IA), who spearheaded the fight for the 10 percent tax during the 1865 revenue revision. "I was not one of those who . . . voted for the adoption of the present national banking law," Wilson reminded his colleagues. "But it is now the established policy of the Government, and I think that it should be made the exclusive policy of the country so far as banks of issue are concerned." Reduction of the volume of currency, Wilson opined, was next in importance only to taxation in helping finance the war, "because it will make our taxes of greater value, although the same in amount, and reduce the price of everything the Government has to purchase" (Cong. Globe, 38th Cong., 2nd Sess.: 803). The question Congress had to address, therefore, was "whether, having determined to establish national banks, we will not do something to curtail the volume of the currency, instead of increasing the number of banks and thereby increasing the volume of the currency." "I know of no other way" to do this, Wilson stated, "than to prohibit the issue of notes for circulation by the local banks of the States" (p. 804).

> We have permitted an expansion of the currency beyond what we should have done. We have authorized the national banks to expand the currency to an amount equal to $300,000,000. I think that is too great an expansion. I think we have issued legal-tender notes to a greater amount than we ought to have done. But because we have done it that is no reason why we should not stop somewhere, and require at least that the local banks should not add additional volume to the currency of the country. Unless we adopt some provision of this kind, the national banks may expand their currency to the entire amount of $300,000,000, and the State banks may expand their circulation without any limitation whatever. (Cong. Globe, 38th Cong., 2nd Sess.: 834)

While references to state bank notes' contribution to inflation occur frequently during the debates over the 10 percent tax, references to the poor quality of state bank notes are relatively rare and references to any direct fiscal advantages of the tax are nonexistent. Thus, the 10 percent tax was not seen as a device for improving the quality of the currency or for extending the market for federal debt.[18] Instead, the tax was seen as a device for limiting the inflationary consequences of other revenue measures (greenbacks and national banking) by guaranteeing a fixed and controllable limit to the aggregate quantity of currency while the gold standard was suspended. As such, the tax was at best justified as a temporary expedient only—one that no longer served any beneficial purpose once resumption had been achieved.

ADVERSE CONSEQUENCES OF THE 10 PERCENT TAX

The direct losses suffered by currency holders as a result of the 10 percent tax may have been relatively small, and were perhaps offset by the tax's anti-inflationary effect. But reasons exist for thinking that the tax may have had serious indirect consequences that played out long after it had ceased to perform any anti-inflationary role. In outlawing state bank notes, legislators forced consumers to rely on a national currency that is believed by many to have suffered from two important shortcomings. First, it supposedly tended to deprive rural regions, the South especially, of access to loanable funds. Second, it is said to have lacked seasonal and cyclical "elasticity." That these supposed shortcomings of national currency were a source of substantial economic losses, and that some of those losses might have been avoided had state banks been able profitably to issue currency of their own making, are hypotheses whose detailed investigation lies beyond the scope of the present paper. Here, I merely hope to encourage such research by briefly reviewing some relevant evidence.

Numerous writings (e.g., Anderson 1933; Sylla 1972) treat the 10 percent tax, along with the unequal apportionment of national bank charters, as a major cause of the South's post–Civil War decline. The problem was not simply a regional lack of currency, as some of these writings suggest. The low homing power of national bank notes allowed them to circulate anywhere in the country, without regard to the location of the bank that had originally issued them, so that the apportionment of national bank capital had little or no influence on the ultimate apportionment of the currency stock itself (see Chapter 5 of this volume). What the South lacked after March 1865 was not currency per se but a set of institutions capable of translating local currency holdings (which formed a major part of the South's meager postwar savings) into corresponding local supplies of loanable funds (Redlich 1951: 118). State banks could not perform this task—and for many years could not operate profitably at all—owing to the 10 percent tax, which prevented them from financing their loans and investments with transactable liabilities of a form favored by their clients (p. 119; Sylla 1972: 245–46).[19] National banks could perform it only imperfectly for three reasons: first, because sparsely settled Southern communities were hard-pressed to meet the minimum capital requirement for establishing national banks (by 1869, the former Confederate states had only 65 national banks, as compared to the 205 state banks they had had at the outbreak of the war); second, because national banks were prevented until the passage of the Federal Reserve Act from lending on real estate—the South's principal collateral; and last, because national bank notes had to be fully backed by U.S. government bonds and were correspondingly less capable of financing bank loans.

Some indication of the repressive effects of Civil War banking legislation may be obtained from bank loan and circulation statistics. In 1861, the banks of what was to become the Confederacy had outstanding $7.29 in circulation, and $15.81 in loans, per capita. The corresponding figures for 1869—the year prior to an attempt at reapportionment of national bank capital—were $0.89 and $1.90. Although the decline in per capita circulation and loans was partly a reflection of an overall decline in Southern wealth, circulation and loans also declined relative to wealth: Southern currency issues represented 1.36 percent of total Southern wealth in 1861, and only 0.11 percent in 1869, while loans went from 2.95 percent of total wealth to 0.86 percent (Figure 4.1). No other part of the country suffered a similar decline in banking activity—a decline reflected in interest rates, which for decades remained systematically higher in the South than in other regions of the country (James 1981: 444).[20]

Figure 4.1: Bank Circulation and Loans as a Percentage of Wealth, by Region, 1861 and 1869

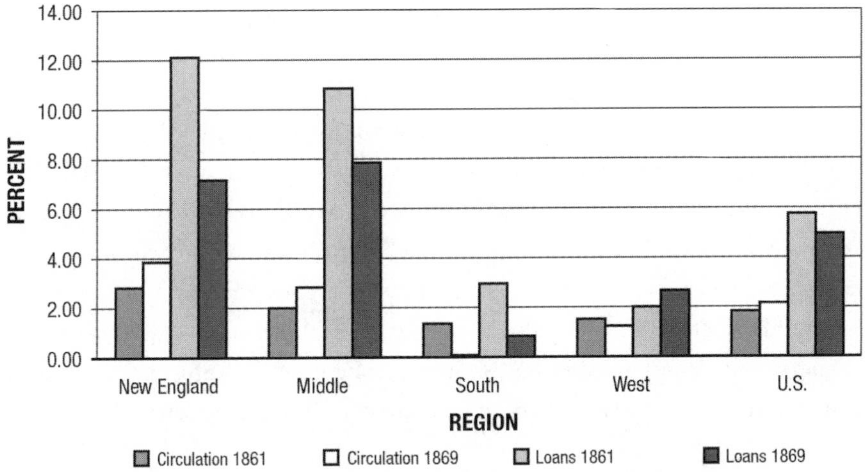

SOURCES: Population and wealth: U.S. Census Bureau (1870: 638–39); state bank loans (except Louisiana): U.S. Treasury, *Annual Statement* (1861: 306); Louisiana: U.S. Treasury, *Annual Statement* (1862: 209); national bank loans: Comptroller of the Currency, *Annual Report* (1869: 558–93); state and national bank circulation: Comptroller of the Currency, "Banking Facilities" (1870: 8).

The South gradually overcame its financial backwardness, thanks in part perhaps to a reapportionment and expansion of national bank capital in 1870, the switch to free (national) banking in 1875, and (most important) the public's growing acceptance of checks as substitutes for bank notes (which led to a revival of state banking). But while the South slowly recovered, the other shortcoming of national bank currency was becoming increasingly apparent: the low yield on required bond-security, together with administrative costs and delays involved in acquiring new notes once the requisite bonds had been purchased, discouraged most national banks from making either permanent or seasonal additions to the stock of national bank notes (Champ 1990; Cagan 1963).[21] Between 1880 and 1889, the price of 4 percent bonds of 1907—the security most commonly used to secure national bank notes during that era—soared from $103 to $129. During the same period, national bank-note circulation plummeted from a peak of approximately $360 million (or 75 percent of aggregate national bank capital) in 1882 to half that amount (or 25 percent of aggregate national bank capital) in 1891 (Root 1894: 314;

Laughlin 1898: 228 n2). Although the public could and did adapt itself to this largely supply-driven, secular decline in the currency stock through an increased reliance on checks, its only means for coping with seasonal and cyclical currency shortages (like those experienced during the panics of 1884 and 1893) was to issue millions of dollars worth of ersatz "currency substitutes." These included round-denomination certified checks and clearinghouse certificates, which (not being bank notes) managed to avoid the 10 percent tax, and leftover state bank notes, which did not (Warner 1895). The frequently voiced complaint that national bank notes lacked seasonal "elasticity" relative to "asset" currency (that is, currency that did not have to be secured by specific bond collateral) appears to be borne out by time series for national and Canadian bank notes, shown in Figure 4.2. Reformers looked on state banks as a potential source of Canadian-style asset currency.

Figure 4.2: Bank Notes in Circulation, 1880–1909, Monthly

(Millions of Dollars)

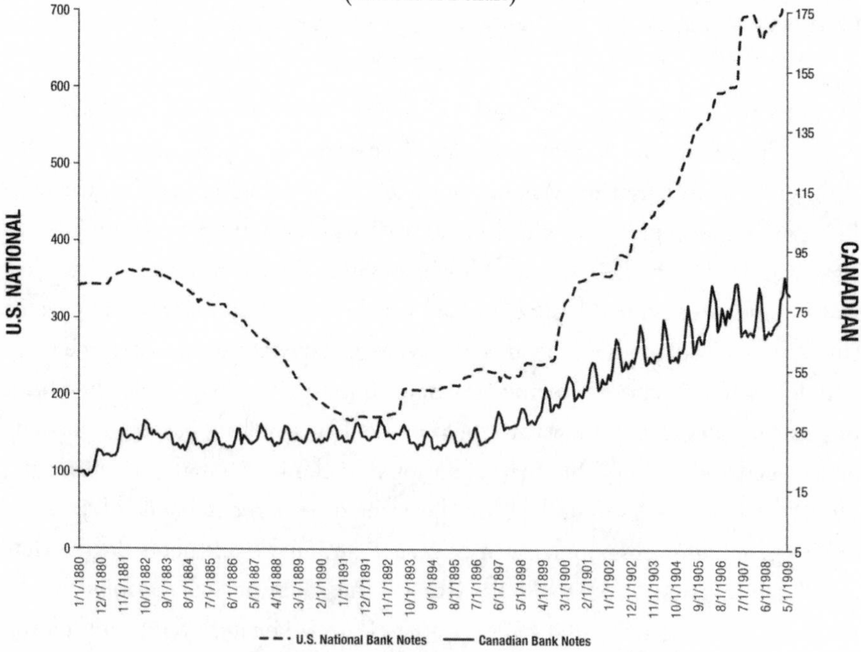

SOURCES: Data for Canadian bank notes are from Curtis (1931: 20). Data for U.S. national bank notes are from Comptroller of the Currency, *Annual Report* (various dates).

The perceived shortcomings of the national currency system spurred efforts to repeal the 10 percent tax. Such efforts had begun even before the tax went into effect and would continue until the end of the century. The Democratic platform contained a plank promising repeal as late as 1892 (Redlich 1951: 122); and between 1875 and 1892, 34 bills calling for repeal of the tax were introduced, mostly by Southern congressmen (Dunbar 1892: 55–56).[22] The Panic of 1893 brought renewed agitation for repeal, this time of a less sectional character (U.S. Congress 1895; Dodsworth 1895); even the Treasury itself, now led by John G. Carlisle, had come belatedly to see state bank notes not as a source of inflation or monetary chaos but as a desirable (if secondary) component of a reformed currency stock. But this was not the majority's view: in June 1894, a bill was introduced to remit the 10 percent tax collected on state bank notes issued during the 1893 crisis. An amendment to this bill proposed repealing the tax altogether. The amendment lost 172 to 102, and the bill as a whole was defeated (Sumner 1896: 469). The treatment of currency regulation and issuance as a federal prerogative had become firmly entrenched, and the 10 percent tax would remain on the books until 1976, when its seeming irrelevance allowed it to be quietly removed.

CONCLUSION

In the absence of a 10 percent tax, competition between note-issuing state and national banks should have sufficed to eliminate inferior state bank notes: state banks of issue could have survived the advent of national banking only by making their notes at least as desirable as national currency. The tax was implemented not to rid the nation of inferior state bank notes, or to enhance sales of government bonds, but to limit wartime inflation. Consumers may ultimately have been made worse off by the tax, which, in destroying sound state-bank currencies, prevented them from satisfying consumer wants that national banks left unfulfilled. In the market for currency, as in other markets, the presumption ought to be that more choice is better than less.

5

MONETARY REFORM AND THE REDEMPTION OF NATIONAL BANK NOTES, 1863–1913*

WITH LAWRENCE H. WHITE

THE 50 YEARS during which the national banking system operated are among the most eventful in U.S. financial and monetary history: they span the period of populist demands for free silver, the debate over returning to the gold standard, and the struggles over restrictions on bank-note issue and branch banking. During this period, the country was rocked by a series of banking panics and associated sharp depressions—particularly in 1873, 1884, 1893, and 1907—that sent policymakers and theorists alike in search of reforms that would overcome the banking system's defects.

A much-discussed shortcoming of the national banking regime was its upwardly inelastic supply of bank-note currency (see Smith 1936; Cagan 1963; Timberlake 1978; Champ 1990). The stock of national bank notes failed to expand to meet the peak demands for currency that arose seasonally with "crop moving" and cyclically with financial crises; it also failed to grow secularly with national income. That the system also suffered from

* Originally published in *Business History Review* 68, no. 2 (Summer 1994): 205–43. The authors thank the Institute for Humane Studies and the George Edward Durell Foundation for research support. Helpful comments were received from Peter Selgin, Kurt Schuler, and participants at a session of the Western Economics Association meetings. Jim Michaels provided research assistance.

downward inelasticity of the currency is nowadays seldom mentioned, though contemporaries complained forcefully that the stock of notes failed to contract in conjunction with seasonal troughs in currency demand (see, for example, Sprague 1904: 527–28). Critics attributed this problem to the lack of an effective redemption mechanism for removing excess notes from circulation. In this chapter, we examine those complaints and the associated efforts to reform the redemption system.

INTRODUCTION

Since the expiration of the charter of the Second Bank of the United States in 1836, the nation's banking functions had been carried out entirely by state-chartered banks. Incorporated state banks issued their own notes, in many cases secured by state or federal bonds and ordinarily redeemable in specie on demand. These notes moved around the country and were usually exchanged at par near home and at a discount as distance (and redemption costs) increased. There was no "national" currency save specie.

The national banking system, born during the Civil War, operated in the United States from the passage of the National Currency Act in early 1863 until the signing of the Federal Reserve Act in 1913. Shortages of reserves had caused banks to suspend specie payments in 1861. In early 1862, the Legal Tender Act authorized the federal government issue of "greenbacks"—non-interest-bearing U.S. notes not redeemable in specie but to be accepted throughout the United States as legal tender. This provided an alternative circulating currency and bank reserve medium, but it did not deal with another problem: the inability of the U.S. government to place its bonds for further war financing.

The new banking legislation, which established a series of federally chartered banks whose notes had to be backed by U.S. government bonds, was therefore most immediately motivated by the Union government's need to finance its war effort. But the movement toward national banking was given impetus by the secession of the Southern states and by the advocacy of Secretary of the Treasury Salmon P. Chase (1861–64). Secession removed the heavily Democratic (and anti–central bank) Southern members from

Congress and gave the Republicans enough votes to pass the Currency Act of February 25, 1863, soon revised by the act of June 3, 1864. These measures established the Office of the Comptroller of the Currency to administer the granting of charters to national banks and to enforce the rules under which notes could be issued and redeemed: the amount of paid-in capital required; the percentage of capital and bond valuation against which notes could be issued; the aggregate allowed volume of notes; the methods of apportioning distribution of note-issue allowances; and the methods of redeeming notes for specie or greenbacks. It is on efforts to change the workings of the redemption system that we focus here.

Although the redemption reform movement has been largely overlooked in the secondary literature, it is crucial to understanding the course of reforms aimed at securing an "elastic" currency and leading up to the Federal Reserve Act.[1] Legal restrictions were clearly responsible for the problem of upward inelasticity: note issue was restricted by a 10 percent tax on state banks and by an aggregate ceiling on national bank notes before 1875, and thereafter by the costly requirement that a national bank overcollateralize its notes with (low-yield) federal bonds. Why, then, was simple deregulation of note issue not a more popular proposal among those who complained about inelasticity? We find that the leading advocates of monetary reform, particularly those who proposed some form of deregulation to allow notes backed by ordinary banking assets ("asset currency"), understandably feared that freed-up banks might over-issue notes unless the system were equipped with an adequate redemption mechanism. Attempts to solve the redemption problem were therefore a key ingredient of the period's monetary reform proposals.

We first explain briefly why note redemption was inadequate under national banking and why that mattered. We then survey contemporary criticisms of sluggish redemption, and trace the reformers' efforts to achieve more active note redemption, both privately through banking industry cooperation and publicly through legislation. Many of these reformers correctly blamed inadequate note redemption on legal restrictions and emphasized the self-adjusting properties of a deregulated bank-note currency. Their proposals ultimately failed to be adopted because the reformers endorsed branch banking as a means toward active redemption, arousing the opposition of unit banking forces. We conclude by considering whether the Federal Reserve Act appropriately addressed the problem.

CAUSES AND CONSEQUENCES OF SLUGGISH REDEMPTION

In an unregulated banking system with plural note issue, banks naturally come to accept one another's notes. The banks promptly return collected notes to their issuers directly or through an interbank clearing system (Selgin and White 1987: 439–57). The prompt redemption of its excess notes confronts an individual bank with rising marginal liquidity costs of note issue. Issuing an additional note undesired by the public means losing an equivalent amount of reserves, and thereby increases the bank's chances of running out of reserves. The liquidity costs accompanying efficient note redemption are therefore crucial to limiting a bank's desired volume of note issues. The same costs limit a bank's desired volume of non-interest-bearing demand deposits in the standard analysis of a system lacking statutory reserve requirements (Baltensperger 1980: 1–37).

Several features of the national banking system discouraged the active redemption of notes. In particular, by requiring that national banks purchase $100 in face value of eligible government bonds for every $90 of their circulation, the regime (1) homogenized the notes of all national banks, eliminating the usual incentive for a member of the public to hold only certain preferred brands of notes while redeeming or depositing others, and (2) removed the usual profit to a bank from putting more of its own notes in circulation in place of the notes of other banks. The system thus suppressed the active interbank clearing and redemption of notes. With active redemption absent, national bank notes attained a "quasi-high-powered" status: although not a legal reserve medium, the notes circulated and were held by banks almost interchangeably with legal tender (greenbacks and gold), thus forming part of the base supporting broader monetary aggregates (Friedman and Schwartz 1963: 50, 781–82). In the aggregate, an increase in the stock of national bank notes would allow a multiple expansion of loans and deposits, much as if an equal amount of greenbacks had been issued.[2]

One especially visible symptom of the sluggish redemption of national bank notes was the notoriously poor physical condition of the notes in hand-to-hand circulation. Under ordinary conditions of plural issue, as the clearing system repeatedly sends notes home to their issuing banks, the banks can replace older notes before they become too worn. The national bank notes' lack of homing power sentenced them to remain in circulation long after becoming tattered and filthy, to the point where one observer (apparently not in jest) suggested that bank tellers faced a health risk in handling the currency (James 1938: 399–400).

An important consequence of the quasi-high-powered status of national bank notes was the absence of any reliable market-based restraint on the volume of notes. An individual bank issuing additional notes faced near-zero marginal liquidity costs. The notes could be expected to circulate indefinitely, as other banks that happened to receive them in deposits or loan payments would routinely reissue them instead of returning them to the issuer for redemption. As has been noted for the case of fiat currency, a plurality of unconstrained issuers of a homogenous high-powered money is inconsistent with monetary stability (Klein 1974: 423–53). Recognizing this problem, contemporary banking experts sharply criticized the weak homing power of national bank notes. Charles Dunbar (1904: 241), a Boston financial editor and the first chairman of Harvard's economics department, found it "singularly at variance with the principle of having a wholesome restraint upon the operations of each bank by itself, which governs our treatment of other demand liabilities." Oliver M. W. Sprague (1904: 527–28), another Harvard economist, assailed the "inelasticity on the side of contraction," which "removes from the banks individually and as a whole some of the consequences of their operations for which they should be immediately responsible."

Before 1875, the ceiling on aggregate national bank circulation ruled out any possibility of secular inflation while also creating a problem of rationing note issue among banks in different regions. Representatives of the South and West complained that their share was too small, frustrating efforts to establish new banks (Anderson 1933: 353).[3] Proposals to remove the ceiling (a policy confusingly referred to as "free banking" at the time) were met with the understandable objection that removal would lead to over-expansion and inflation unless it were accompanied by measures to ensure active redemption of notes. Fear of inflation was accompanied by concern that resumption of the gold standard (not accomplished until 1879) would be delayed. "Free banking" finally prevailed in 1875, but only following a major (though incomplete) reform of note-redemption arrangements in the previous year.

The return to the gold standard in 1879 meant that secular inflation was no longer a danger from excess note issue, but seasonal and cyclical disturbances remained a serious problem. Rather than being redeemed locally, notes unwanted in the interior during periods of slack currency demand traveled via payments or interbank deposits to the Northeast and ultimately to New York City, where they appear to have contributed to the seasonality of interest rates by spilling over into loanable funds markets. New York banks, finding an accumulation of country notes in their vaults, were hard-pressed to convert them into useful assets. Before 1874 they sometimes resorted to selling notes at a discount for greenbacks or to lending country notes at zero interest to borrowers who were expected to repay their loans in greenbacks (Friedman and Schwartz 1963: 21 n8; *Commercial and Financial Chronicle*, Jan. 22, 1870: 102–3). Much of this lending took the form of call loans for stock market speculation. In the late summer and fall, as interior banks drew cash from their correspondents to meet the peak demand for currency associated with the fall harvest, the currency movement reversed itself. The drain of cash into the interior confronted the Northeast with credit stringency, and occasionally with a currency shortage, as reserve losses forced banks to contract their balance sheets. On several occasions—including 1884, 1893, and 1907—financial stringency gave way to full-blown banking panics.

After the 1874 reform (detailed in a later section), New York banks could redeem unwanted notes and receive immediate payment from the subtreasury for them, but issuers were not called on to replenish the redemption fund immediately (Cagan and Schwartz 1991: 300–301).[4] The reform therefore did not discourage seasonal shipments of currency to the city. Redemptions at the subtreasury merely gave the New York banks excess reserves, rather than excess country notes, to lend at call and did not immediately reduce the excess reserves of country banks—thus allowing the seasonal influence on interest rates to persist. Between 1890 and 1908, increases in the excess reserves of New York banks, which largely followed interbank shipments of excess currency to New York, were associated with decreases in interest rates on call loans and on 60-day to 90-day paper in the New York money market.[5] Edwin W. Kemmerer (1910) provided evidence of such a linkage in his National Monetary Commission study of seasonal variations in money and financial markets under national banking. The seasonality of currency demand thus helps to account for the marked seasonality of interest rates between 1890 and 1919, which reinforced the effects of the seasonal credit demand emphasized by several analysts as a contributing factor in 19th-century financial crises (Allen 1986; Donaldson 1992: 277–305; Mankiw et al. 1987: 358–74).

Had there been regular active redemption of national bank notes, interior banks would not have exported local credit expansion and contraction to the Northeast. Most excess country notes would have been intercepted by rival banks, redeemed, and removed from circulation before leaving the interior. Notes that did make their way to the Northeast would have been returned to their issuers promptly for redemption instead of swelling the quantity of high-powered money in the system as a whole. The original issuing banks would not have found it profitable to issue more notes until the demand to hold their currency rose. The seasonal movements of funds to and from the Northeast would consequently have been far less pronounced, reducing the likelihood of panics. The periodic excess of high-powered money would have been halted at the source, rather than spilling over into the bond market and causing a temporary distortion in interest rates and associated distortions of savings and investment.

The contrast between variations in the currency stock and interest rates in the United States and corresponding figures from Canada serves to illustrate this point. Seasonality in the demand for currency was common to both agricultural countries. The actual circulation of bank notes showed substantial seasonal variation in Canada during 1890–1908, when there was virtually no seasonal variation in the United States (see Figure 5.1). During the same years, interest rates on Montreal call loans showed much less seasonal variation than New York or Boston rates.[6] The seasonal pattern in New York call loan rates was in fact roughly similar to the seasonal pattern in the circulation of Canadian bank notes: low in the spring and summer, high in the fall (see Figure 5.2). The greater interest-rate seasonality of the United States thus appears to have reflected in part the seasonal inelasticity of the national currency stock. Had national bank notes been actively redeemed rather than reissued, seasonality in the public's demand for currency would have led to a seasonal pattern in the quantity of notes (as it did in Canada), rather then generating spillover effects in the credit market. Such spillover effects were undesirable, because they presumably interfered with the normal function of the credit market in coordinating intertemporal allocation plans.

Figure 5.1: Bank Notes in Circulation, 1880–1909, Monthly

(Millions of Dollars)

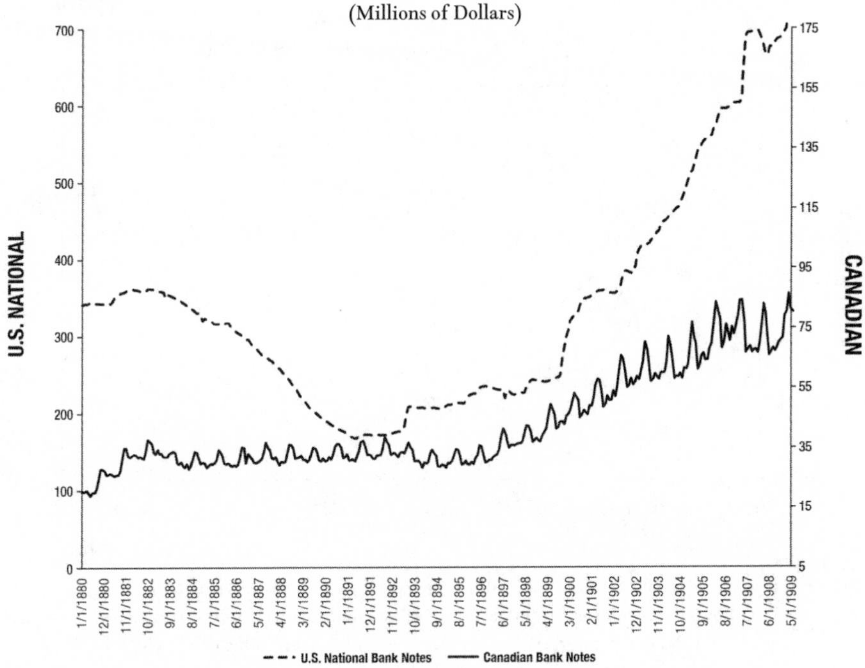

Sources: Data for Canadian bank notes are from Curtis (1931: 20). Data for U.S. national bank notes are from Comptroller of the Currency, *Annual Report* (various dates).

Figure 5.2: Bank-Note and Call Loan Rate Seasonals

Canadian Bank Notes in Circulation
Average Weekly Index Numbers, 1875–1908

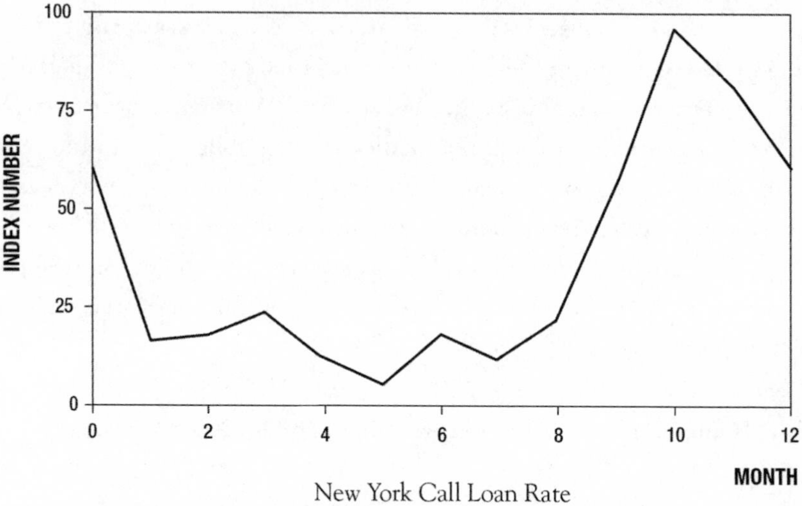

New York Call Loan Rate
Average Weekly Index Numbers, 1890–1908

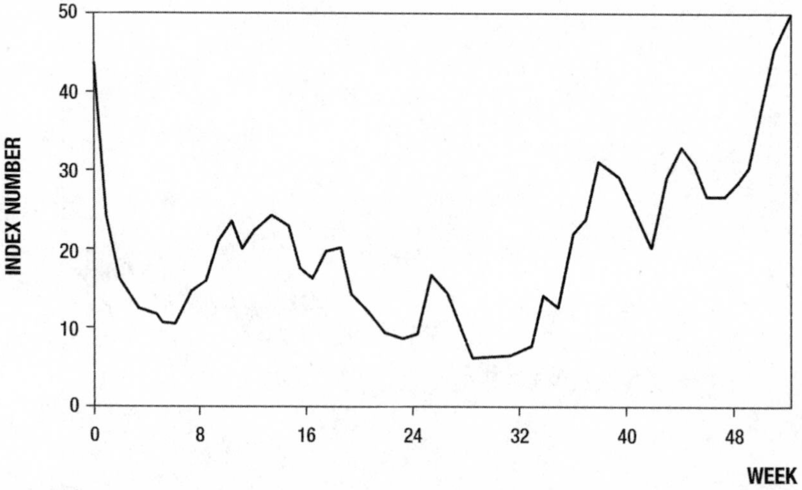

NOTES: Index numbers for the New York call loan rate and the volume of Canadian bank notes were calculated as follows. For each year in the sample, the lowest observation of the variable was assigned a value of zero, and the highest observation was assigned a value of 100. Each of the other observations for that year was then scaled correspondingly. That is, the index number for an observation of $X_i = 100 * [X_i - \min(X)] / [\max(X) - \min(X)]$, where X is the set of all observations from the same year. The average weekly (monthly) index numbers shown were constructed by taking the same week (month) from each year in the sample and averaging the corresponding index numbers.

EARLY FEARS OF OVERISSUE

The inadequate provision for active note redemption under the Currency Act was criticized even before the act became law in 1863. Rep. Stephen Baker (R-NY), in the principal speech opposing the act, warned that the lack of central redemption facilities would cause national bank notes to be discounted by banks or brokers seeking to cover high redemption costs (Bolles 1886: 215). Massachusetts representative and economist Amasa Walker (1863: 836) predicted that national bank notes would "continue to circulate as long as the material of which they are made will permit them to last." Walker argued that the act's provision making the notes receivable at par anywhere in payments to the federal government would remove any incentive for noteholders to return unneeded notes to their issuers; the notes would instead be held for government payments. Walker feared that "wildcat" national banks would spring up in remote places, issuing notes that would circulate indefinitely (pp. 833–43).

A report issued by the New York Clearing House Association also doubted that adequate redemption would occur, given that a national bank note was redeemable only at its issuer's counter:

> But how are the people to make such a presentation [at the issuing bank's counter]? Or how can even any institution, if it were disposed, afford to do it? Suppose eight or ten millions, belonging nominally in as many different states, be put afloat in New York, how can the city get rid of them? By what process procure a redemption of this uncurrent money? Whose business will it be to save a hundred dollars of this bank, and a thousand of that, and send them to Wisconsin and Dakota, only to be protested, returned to New York, then sent to Washington, and after thirty days redeemed there at par? (Williams and Everitt 1863)

The report predicted, as Walker had, that holders of bank notes would keep them for payments to the government rather than "submit to a discount of from one to five per cent" in trading the notes for local money. The report illustrated the threat of a new kind of wildcat banking through a hypothetical example of a bank "originally of $50,000 capital" that could swell its circulation and assets to $500,000 "without perhaps even having redeemed, even with legal tender, $10,000 at its remote head office" (Williams and Everitt 1863: 8–9).

Other critics envisioned that wildcat banks in the remote West would issue notes and have them "sealed up and sent to New York, where there are always debtors to the United States that could use them without trouble" (Flint 1863: 14–15). Once received by the federal government, the notes would be forced on the government's creditors, whereupon the "great centers of trade [would] be flooded with a depreciated currency" (Stearns 1864: 6). One contemporary commentator insisted that "not even the Congress of the United States [can] make a bank-bill, redeemable in New Mexico or Utah, of as much value to a merchant of Boston as one for the same amount payable in State Street" (Flint 1863: 15).

Events bore out several of these predictions. National bank notes from other parts of the country appear to have initially traded at a discount in New York City. As early as February 1864, the banks of the New York Clearing House Association resolved to accept at par only those national bank notes redeemed at par by a member bank. Other notes were to be traded as "uncurrent money," accepted only at a discount, if at all (*Hunt's Merchants Magazine*, Apr. 1864: 307).[7] Notes from all parts of the country accumulated in New York, particularly when demand to hold notes in the interior was below the spring and fall peaks. The existence of a less costly alternative to selling notes at a discount—namely, retaining them for use in payments to the government—led as predicted to few notes being sent home for redemption. The absence of a redemption constraint encouraged banks to issue all the notes for which they could get authorization. *Hunt's Merchants Magazine* (Sept. 1864: 248) reported that two national banks in New Haven, Connecticut (hardly the remote West), had $300,000 in notes outstanding for half a year or more without being asked to redeem a single dollar. According to economist Francis Bowen (1866: 773), the New Haven situation was typical. Any national bank could "pay out its bills on the morning after it receives them from the Comptroller, with a comfortable assurance of not seeing more than a stray one or two of them again for a twelve-month." Rather than returning to their sources, national bank notes, once issued, became a "part of the permanent money stock."

Congress was at first untroubled by the lack of note redemption. According to Charles Dunbar (1904: 238–39), many authorities assumed that arrangements for note redemption would be superfluous under the greenback standard then in place, because they would merely permit the exchange of one paper money for another. Johns Hopkins astronomer and economist Simon Newcomb (1865: 209–11) observed that "the law which provides for redemption provides for a mere farce. The paper in which the [national bank] bills are to be redeemed will answer no end which the bill itself will not equally answer." Sen. John Sherman (R-OH), younger brother of the Civil War general, even praised the long circulation period of national bank notes as a point of economy in the notes' favor (Dunbar 1904: 289). Both Newcomb and Sherman neglected to consider that interbank redemption of notes for reserve money would have helped to limit the volume of bank-issued money even under a greenback standard.

REFORM EFFORTS BEFORE 1874

The earliest reform effort, embodied in the 1864 revision of the National Currency Act, was motivated not by the low volume of redemptions, but in part by Congress's surprise at discovering that notes were not trading everywhere at par. Congress had expected that national bank notes would be a "uniform national currency," circulating at par throughout the country by virtue of their common collateral backing and their public receivability.

One revision proposed to the House Banking Committee in spring 1864 would have required each national bank to redeem its notes through agents in numerous specified cities as well as at its home office. Redemption agents' reserves would have been counted as part of a bank's lawful reserves. As the plan moved forward, congressmen scrambled to have cities and towns in their home districts included on the list of redemption centers (Cong. Globe, 38th Cong., 1st Sess.: 1377). In the end, 17 cities were selected, including 8 of the 9 original reserve cities from the act of 1863.[8] To soften the impact on country banks, however, the proposal was modified to allow each national bank to choose just one city from the list as a par redemption site, subject to the approval of the comptroller of the currency. National banks in reserve-redemption cities other than New York were to be required to redeem at par through a national bank in New York.

Committee members feared that allowing banks to choose a single redemption city from among the 17 would not be enough to eliminate all discounts on itinerant notes. They observed that redemption agents could be located well away from the main centers of trade where a note might be found. As New York City banker James Gallatin (1864: 15) argued, a "'uniform national currency,' issued and redeemable at different places, is a chimera. To be 'uniform' it is indispensable that it should be redeemed at some central points—say, New York, Boston, and Philadelphia." In response to this criticism, Rep. James Wilson (R-OH) recommended that all banks be required to redeem their notes at par in New York City, where most notes ended up (Cong. Globe, 38th Cong., 1st Sess.: 1378). Although the committee was convinced of the need for some further measure to keep notes from falling below par outside their limited redemption points, it nonetheless rejected Wilson's suggestion on the Populist grounds that it would make the rest of the country "pay tribute" to New York.

The committee's blunt solution, included in the revised National Currency Act of June 3, 1864 (renamed the National Bank Act in 1874), was to require all national banks to receive all national bank notes at par. This measure—which banned any national bank from discounting or refusing any national bank note—secured the uniformity of the national currency, but with unfortunate consequences for redemption. Discount charges had been instrumental in financing what little volume of note redemption there was. Once out-of-town notes could no longer be acquired at a discount, no spread remained to cover the transportation and transaction costs of redeeming them. The abolition of discounts also allowed a national bank's notes to circulate well beyond the area within which they could be returned to their issuer at relatively low cost.

The par-acceptance requirement burdened the banks of Philadelphia, Boston, and especially New York. Notes were brought to New York by the "channels of trade" and—more importantly—by shipments from correspondent banks who thereby acquired deposits in the "reserve city" banks that they could count as legal reserves.[9] The banks in all three cities had to accept large quantities of national bank notes from all over the country, without a discount to cover the costs of sorting and returning the notes to their issuers for redemption in lawful reserves. In May 1865, a committee of officers from 16 major banks in the three cities endeavored to solve this problem. The committee's preliminary plan called for all national bank notes redeemable north of Cairo, Illinois, and east of the Mississippi River, but not redeemable in Philadelphia, Boston, or New York, to be sent daily to a central "Assorting House." Notes redeemable in Philadelphia or Boston would be sent directly to assorting houses to be established in those cities, and notes redeemable in New York would be exchanged through the New York Clearing House. Banks that remitted notes would be paid immediately in negotiable interest-bearing certificates equal to 90 percent of their remittances. The certificates would be redeemable (with accumulated interest) in legal tender and canceled when the issuers or their agents redeemed the returned notes. Assorting house expenses would be assessed monthly against participating banks in proportion to their remittances.[10]

By the time a meeting was held at the New York Clearing House in September 1865 to consider the plan, the interior banks had already "conceived a not unnatural dislike" of it (*Commercial and Financial Chronicle*, Sept. 16, 1865: 354). The plan threatened to erode their profits from note issue, and several refused even to send delegates. Disagreements among the bankers present led to a "spirited and prolonged discussion" (*Bankers Magazine*, Nov. 1865: 401). Some country bankers regarded the plan as a scheme to make them keep non-interest-bearing deposits at New York, as the Suffolk Bank had required New England country banks to keep deposits at Boston earlier in the century.[11] The meeting ended without agreement on the plan.

Following that gathering, the *Commercial and Financial Chronicle* (Sept. 16, 1865: 354) pleaded with country bankers to "rise above the sordid views of private advantage" and to "promote rather than hinder" arrangements for active note redemption. The newspaper argued that the plan would ultimately work in the country banks' own interest by countering popular hostility toward national bank currency and the "double profit" (interest on collateral bonds plus interest on loans) it supposedly allowed. The committee solicited endorsements for its assorting house plan from Secretary of the Treasury Hugh McCulloch (1865–69; 1884–85) and from Comptroller of the Currency Freeman Clarke (1865–66). Clarke's statement indicated that the federal authorities were becoming concerned about the danger of monetary expansion stemming from inadequate note redemption:

> Banks have received and paid [national bank currency] out, and have had no further concern about it; consequently all have found it profitable, as they received the interest on the government bonds, pledged for its security, and lend the notes upon interest. Nearly all, therefore, are anxious to increase their circulation and, I greatly fear, will be able . . . to bring such influence to bear as will induce Congress to authorize a large increase of the national bank currency. This may be prevented if immediate action is taken to provide for the redemption and return to the place of issue the notes of existing banks. (*Commercial and Financial Chronicle*, Sept. 16, 1865: 363–64)

As noted earlier, active redemption would confront a note issuer with rising marginal liquidity costs, limiting its profit-maximizing note circulation to the quantity of its notes the public desired to hold.

The committee of city bankers reconvened in closed session on September 19, and the members voted 29 to 12 in favor of carrying its proposal forward (*Bankers Magazine*, Nov. 1865: 402). A new seven-member committee, chaired by James Gallatin, was elected to write a constitution for a National Bank Note Redemption Association. This constitution, embodying all the important features of the draft plan, was adopted on October 12, 1865.[12]

This victory for the proponents of active note redemption proved hollow, however. Many interior banks would not voluntarily cooperate with the Redemption Association or help to defray its expenses, which therefore had to be borne by the banks in the three organizing cities of New York, Boston, and Philadelphia. Although the assorting house plan promised substantial savings compared to decentralized redemption, it was costly nonetheless, and the law prohibited participating banks from discounting out-of-town notes to cover expenses. Unable to spread the costs of the assorting house scheme broadly, or to pass them on to the public, the city banks abandoned the plan. As the editors of *Bankers Magazine* (Sept. 1865: 194) had predicted, central redemption would require "more thought, more experience, more labor, and more capital" than the city banks could muster. In the next several years, two further attempts to establish a New York assorting house also failed.

After the failure of these private remedies, the movement for active note redemption focused on legislative reform. In Washington, Comptroller of the Currency Clarke advocated "compulsory redemption in the great financial and commercial centers of the country" to check monetary expansion, achieve a fairer distribution of currency across the country, and discourage the establishment of national banks purely for "the advantage arising from the issue of their own promises, without the expectation of being called upon to redeem them." Conditional on compulsory redemption "at the central and accessible points mentioned," which would eliminate the "danger of bank issues exceeding the limits prescribed by the demands of legitimate business," Clarke was willing to recommend an increase in the aggregate limit on national bank notes from $300 million to $400 million (Comptroller of the Currency, *Annual Report*, 1865: 6–8). A bill (H.R. 771) reflecting these recommendations was reported to Congress in 1866. The bill required national banks in reserve-redemption cities other than Philadelphia, Boston, or New York to maintain note-redemption agents in one of those three cities; Philadelphia and Boston banks would be required to redeem their notes at par through agents in New York. Interior banks objected to the redemption provisions of the bill, while those wishing for a rapid return to specie payments opposed the expansion of national bank notes (*Commercial and Financial Chronicle*, June 2, 1866: 674–75). The bill, minus its original provision for a raised ceiling on national bank notes, became law in 1867.

The new law had little effect on the frequency of note redemption. Clarke's successor as comptroller, Hiland R. Hulburd (1867–72), observed that, under the old law, notes of 1,320 of the 1,647 national banks had already been redeemable in Philadelphia, Boston, or New York (Comptroller of the Currency, *Annual Report*, 1866: vi).[13] The new concentration of redemption points did little to reduce the costs of sorting and transporting notes, except perhaps to allow minor economies of scale where several banks happened to share the same redemption agent. Even after 1867, redemption-agent banks in the Northeast that received notes issued by their own interior correspondents (possibly shipped by the correspondents themselves for credit to their reserve accounts) were apparently reluctant to request redemption in legal tender, for fear that they would "offend" (impose expenses on) the correspondents and drive their reserve account business elsewhere (Myers 1931: 404). The redemption-agent banks could instead dispose of the notes in hot-potato fashion by passing them back into circulation.

The summertime accumulation of unwanted country notes in the Northeast therefore continued unabated. Individual New York banks tried to dispose of the country notes by lending them free of interest for up to two weeks on the condition that the loan be repaid in greenbacks. They also sold notes to brokers, at a loss of one-tenth to one-quarter of one percent (Myers 1931; *Commercial and Financial Chronicle*, Jan. 22, 1870: 102–3). Many observers concluded that only compulsory centralized redemption of all notes in New York would prevent accumulation of the notes there. Prior to the passage of the 1867 law, Hulburd had remarked that the arguments urged in its favor "would, if carried to their logical conclusion, establish the expediency of requiring redemptions at one central point"—namely, New York (Comptroller of the Currency, *Annual Report*, 1866: vi).

Hulburd continued this theme in his subsequent annual reports. He argued that centralized redemption at New York would be "a healthy reminder to the banks that their circulation is a liability payable on demand" (Comptroller of the Currency, *Annual Report*, 1867: vii). It would also be a "first step towards specie payments," an opinion echoed by the New York Clearing House Association (*Bankers Magazine*, Jan. 1867: 496). As long as remote banks did not have to redeem their notes at New York, Hulburd warned, they would "be tempted to undue expansion by the difficulty of returning their notes for redemption." The consequence, reflecting the operation of Gresham's law under compulsory par acceptance, would be a currency dominated by "inferior" notes. Hulburd proposed that Congress establish a special nonissuing bank in New York, owned and managed by ordinary national banks, to be "the redeeming agency of the whole country, and the clearing-house of all national bank notes." He suggested, rather unconvincingly, that the bank could cover the expenses of note redemption and still return a profit to its shareholders by having a separate department devoted to "regular banking business" (Comptroller of the Currency, *Annual Report*, 1868: xxii).

The financial press in the Northeast also campaigned for compulsory note redemption in New York. *Bankers Magazine* (Jan. 1867: 496) stated that it would prove "a valuable tonic for preventing [the] succession of excitement and depression, of fever and chill" in New York financial markets. The *Commercial and Financial Chronicle* (July 10, 1869: 37–38) declared that existing redemption arrangements were "notoriously imperfect and unsatisfactory" and were responsible for the growing public outcry to replace bank notes with greenbacks. It was up to the banks themselves to protect their interests by renewing the effort to achieve redemption for all notes in New York:

> [T]he only way to make sure that the volume of bank notes shall increase when they are needed for business and shall diminish when the want has passed away, is to make it impossible for the banks to keep out their notes in excess. This is easily to be done. Banking experience has supplied an effective safe-guard. It is the safe-guard of metropolitan redemption. Let the banks be compelled to redeem their notes at the metropolis, where in time of plethora the notes are sure to accumulate, and we have the best remedy for the elasticity of the currency, which the nature of the case seems to admit.

Elsewhere, the editors of the *Chronicle* (Jan. 22, 1870: 102–3) observed that centralized note redemption would "impose a natural . . . check upon inflation" by forcing interior banks "to keep their affairs in a much more conservative condition."

Interior banks fought all proposals for centralized note redemption.[14] In doing so, they inadvertently lent credibility to the argument that active redemption would restrain their issues. The *Chronicle* (1870: 102–3) attributed the opposition to the interior banks' desire to maximize short-term profits, to their constant fear of becoming "tributary" to New York, and to the "demoralization of opinion upon banking regulations which grew out of the financial expedients of the [Civil War]."

THE REFORM OF 1874

By the early 1870s, Congress was under considerable pressure to secure active redemption of national bank notes for three reasons: to relieve New York City banks of their accumulations of excess notes; to alleviate the filthy and worn condition of the currency; and to hasten the resumption of specie payments by reining in the stock of currency. An equally powerful movement demanded that greater circulation privileges be granted to banks in the West and South. The law of June 20, 1874, enacted after a long series of conferences and amendments, reflected these pressures. It combined a plan for centralized note redemption with reapportionment of circulation privileges toward banks in the South and West in accordance with the census of 1870 (2 Cong. Rec.[1874]).[15]

The act of 1874 replaced the old system of redemption agents with a single National Bank Redemption Agency under U.S. Treasury auspices in Washington, D.C., making national bank notes redeemable through the Treasury as well as at their issuers' counters. Redemption at other locations was now prohibited.[16] The reserve requirement against notes was altered so that each bank now had to contribute legal tender equal to 5 percent of its outstanding circulation to a redemption fund held at the Treasury. When a bank's notes were redeemed, the senders would be paid immediately out of the fund, which the issuing banks would then have to replenish. Significantly, the costs of note redemption, including those for sorting and transportation, were assessed against issuing banks in proportion to the number of their notes received.

It appeared that centralized note redemption had at last been achieved, albeit with redemption centered in Washington rather than in New York. The choice of Washington, contravening the plan favored by the banks in the Northeast, was inefficient insofar as it meant additional costs of transporting notes and legal tender between the Northeast, where most notes accumulated, and Washington.[17] The choice, according to John Jay

Knox (who served as comptroller of the currency from 1872 to 1884), was designed to appease forces at the Treasury who hoped to use their new powers to encourage a greater substitution of greenbacks for national bank notes (Knox 1900: 149). The choice may also have defused the Populist suspicion that centralized redemption was a scheme to make interior banks "pay tribute" to New York.

The new law nonetheless won the approval of the northeastern banking community. The *Commercial and Financial Chronicle,* overlooking its previously expressed opinion that the Treasury's involvement in note redemption would be "bad in principle" (Jan. 22, 1870: 103), expressed the hope that the reform would finally "rid [the] banking system of one of its worst defects" (July 11, 1874: 27). *Bankers Magazine* was even more confident:

> The work of redemption seems at last to be provided for; and if carried out in good faith it will be worth more to the country than any of the other measures recently proposed to Congress. The practical difficulty of assorting the notes and presenting them for redemption is at once obviated, and the work will be greatly facilitated by the [bank charter] numbers to be hereafter stamped on all bills when issued. (*Bankers Magazine,* July 1874: 27)

The new arrangement did improve note redemption. From 1864 to 1873, the only significant redemptions had consisted of returns to the Treasury of notes unfit for further use. The annual amount of such redemptions was at most about 10 percent of the total outstanding stock of notes.[18] Following the reform, the volume of currency received rose dramatically. National banks for the first time experienced significant note returns. Shipments of worn notes surged, and the Treasury was also asked to redeem many notes still fit for circulation. During the fiscal year ending October 31, 1876, the volume of national bank notes shipped to Washington (over $209 million) exceeded 60 percent of the outstanding circulation. A year later the figure was over 75 percent.

The new law, according to *Bankers Magazine* (Aug. 1875: 82–83), "worked more efficiently than its friends had ventured to expect." Southern and western bankers who had anticipated improved opportunities for note issue were now worried that note expansion would involve marginal liquidity costs. One Arkansas banker complained that the new arrangement imposed "an unjust hardship" and "an onerous and outrageous burden" on him and his colleagues (American Bankers' Association 1875: 20).

Such worries and complaints turned out to be overblown. The Redemption Agency fell far short of achieving the ideal of comprehensive active note redemption experienced in other banking systems. Even the 75 percent redemption flow during the peak year of 1877 was a trickle compared to the estimated 1,200 percent reflow in Canada, where nationwide branch banking sponsored active note redemption. The volume of U.S. national redemptions in 1877, $214 million, was not much greater than the average annual value of New England redemptions by the Suffolk Bank during the 1840s and 1850s.[19] University of Chicago economist J. Laurence Laughlin (1898: 339) estimated that in 1890, when approximately $130 million of national bank notes were in circulation, national banks received about $4 million of one another's notes daily. Had all been redeemed, annual shipments to the Treasury would have been nearly $1 billion, about 800 percent of the stock. Allowing for notes received by state banks, which accounted for about one-third of the nation's banking-industry capital at this time, that figure represents a turnover comparable to Canada's. In contrast, the actual Redemption Agency volume in 1890 was $36 million, less than 28 percent. Even at the 1877 peak, if Laughlin's estimate roughly captures the ratio between the total circulation and the volume of notes that banks received, banks redeemed less than 10 percent of the notes received.

Most notes went unredeemed because of state banks' continued inability to issue their own notes and of some interior national banks' inability to accumulate notes rapidly enough (that is, without undue loss of interest) to meet the $1,000 minimum remittance accepted by the Redemption Agency. Most interior banks continued to reissue other banks' notes or to ship them to their city correspondents, extending the notes' circulation (Bell 1912: 45–47). The majority of notes received by the Treasury were sent by New York banks, with shipments from Philadelphia and Boston next in size.

SHERMAN'S ORDER OF 1878

Despite the relative paucity of note returns, the Treasurer's office was quickly overwhelmed by the "great amount of work suddenly thrown upon" it. The Treasurer wrote in a circular dated September 4, 1874, that "with the greatest exertions, it has been found impossible to assort enough of the redeemed national bank notes" (*Bankers Magazine*, Oct. 1874: 315). It was therefore impossible to requisition replenishment funds from issuers sufficient to avoid exhausting the 5 percent fund. Nearly $12 million of the fund's original $17.5 million was paid out before the sorting of notes even began (*Bankers Magazine*, Nov. 1874: 14). In vain, the Treasurer requested voluntary contributions to the redemption fund equal to an additional 5 percent of circulation. He finally suspended payments for several weeks, beginning September 19, so that the Redemption Agency could catch up. An act of March 3, 1875, later moved the agency from the Treasurer's office to larger quarters employing 98 full-time clerks under the secretary of the treasury's direct supervision.[20]

The Treasury regretted having taken on the burden of note redemption and soon acted to reduce it. Secretary of the Treasury John Sherman (1877–81), who as a senator in 1864 had praised the long circulation period of national bank notes for economizing on the use of paper, announced in September 1878 that, effective October 1, parties transmitting notes to Washington for redemption would have to pay their own express charges, which the Treasury had previously assessed against the issuers of redeemed notes (*Bankers Magazine*, Nov. 1878: 326–27). The new regulation, together with the standing prohibition against charging a discount for receiving other national banks' notes, meant that recipient banks would suffer losses in redeeming those notes.

The New York Clearing House Association protested to Sherman that the new rule amounted "to a penalty for forwarding National bank notes for redemption, [impeding] the practical operation of the law" of 1874 and renewing the interior banks' incentives to overissue (*Bankers Magazine*, Nov. 1878: 390). Sherman replied disingenuously that the law "did not contemplate the establishment of a grand clearing house," but aimed merely at removing worn-out notes from circulation. He declared it a "manifest injustice" to compel issuers to pay the costs of redeeming their notes, since the issuers "have no interest whatever" in having their notes returned. He regretted that some interior banks had been temporarily deprived "of the advantages of the repeal of the original act [of 1864], which required them to redeem their circulation in the large cities" (*Commercial and Financial Chronicle*, Oct. 12, 1878: 368). Sherman evidently wished to view the act of 1874 not as a remedy for the accumulation of currency in the Northeast, but solely as an expansionary measure.

Following Sherman's decision, the volume of notes sent to the Treasury fell dramatically. The volume had been $243 million in fiscal year 1877 and $213 million in FY1878; it dropped to $158 million in FY1879 and to $62 million in FY1880 (see Figure 5.3). As Sherman intended, most of the decline came in shipments of notes still fit for use, which fell from $151 million in FY1877 to $25 million in FY1880. Redemptions of worn notes also declined, from $62 million in FY1877 to $30 million in FY1880. Fearing renewed deterioration of the currency, the Treasury modified Sherman's order on December 1, 1879, to allow transportation costs for worn notes to be paid out of the 5 percent fund. This measure did not make much difference, because many banks were unwilling to undertake the costs of separating worn from fit notes and accumulating amounts sufficient for forwarding to the Treasurer (U.S. Treasury, *Annual Report*, 1880: 30). On January 13, 1881, just before Sherman left his Treasury post, his order was revoked entirely. The original arrangements of 1874 were restored, except that assorting expenses were now assessed on banks in proportion to the value rather than to the number of their returned notes (U.S. Treasury, *Annual Report*, 1882: 377).

Redemption of worn notes rebounded to over $53 million by FY1882. Returns of fit notes continued to decline, however, reaching a low mark of $3.8 million in FY1882 and not recovering their 1878 level until 1912. The principal causes of the continued low levels of fit-note redemptions were the rising price (and falling yield) of the bonds required as collateral for note issue, which made it less profitable than ever for banks to issue more notes, and the growth in the relative importance of non-note-issuing state banks.[21]

Figure 5.3: National Bank-Note Redemptions, 1875–1915, Yearly (Millions of Dollars)

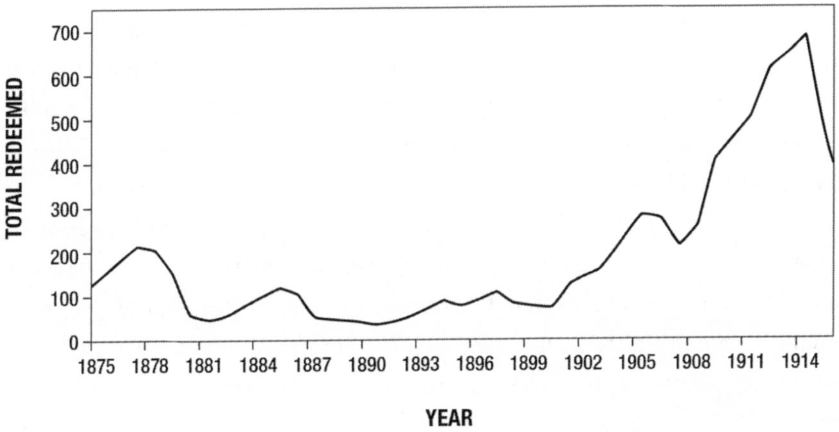

The lack of active note redemption after 1882 was both a consequence of and something of a compensation for the restrictive effects of the bond-collateral requirement. Had note redemption somehow been as active as in Canada and elsewhere despite regulatory restrictions on note issuance, high liquidity costs would have been added to the high cost of securing collateral. The secular shrinkage in the stock of national bank notes would have been even more severe. The *Commercial and Financial Chronicle* (Nov. 20, 1880: 521) pointed out the incongruity of a restriction that taxed note issue in one respect while subsidizing it in others and pleaded for reforms that would allow the stock of notes to attain a natural elasticity:

> Ought we not then to make the law so that it will be reasonably profitable for a bank to obtain and issue notes?—at the same time be sure and add to it a plan of redemption which will be prompt and effective, taking the place of the miserable make-shift, which now exists for redemption, through a Washington Bureau? In this way can be produced a perfect automatic currency machine, as obedient to the laws of trade as the circulation of blood is to the beat of the heart.

ACTIVE REDEMPTION AND THE ASSET CURRENCY MOVEMENT

The banking reform movement intensified following the panic of 1893. The House Committee on Banking and Currency considered dozens of bills, all aimed at providing a more "elastic" currency whose volume would respond appropriately to secular and especially to seasonal changes in the public's currency-holding demands.[22] The typical proposal for improving elasticity was to let banks issue an "asset" currency—that is, to allow bank notes to be matched on the balance sheet by general bank assets instead of requiring them to be overmatched by specific government bonds. This step was meant to enable banks to accommodate *increases* in currency demand. Improved redemption facilities, sometimes supplemented by a tax on circulation, were to guarantee appropriate *contraction* of the currency when demand subsided.

Freer note issue and active redemption were viewed as complementary reforms that together would give rise to an automatically adjusting currency. J. Laurence Laughlin (1898: 324), writing for the Indianapolis Commission on Monetary Reform, argued that "to secure real elasticity it is not enough that the circulation should expand when the necessities of commerce require more currency; it is just as essential that it should promptly contract when those necessities have gone by." To ensure prompt contraction, "daily and immediate redemption of notes" was a necessary counterpart to enhanced freedom of issue (p. 263). A naturally developed redemption system, which the United States lacked, would regulate the currency appropriately: "All [the] anxiety for something to force retirement of a redundant bank-currency has arisen from a failure to appreciate the important function of redemption and the way in which, when freely developed, it serves as a constant regulator of the volume of currency" (p. 325).

Banker William C. Cornwall similarly insisted that an asset currency system with active note redemption would provide automatic elasticity:

> [W]ith every bank crowding for redemption and retirement of all the notes of every other bank, and pressing out all it possibly can of its own, it is readily seen that only the actual amount needed by commerce will

> stay out. . . . This is the principle of elasticity scientifically carried out, suppressing inflation, fostering enterprise and working out its own fine end under the test of daily redemption. (American Bankers' Association 1893: 45)

It was widely believed that, in the absence of provisions for active note redemption, greater freedom of note issue might lead to "an excessive supply of circulation and an illegitimate expansion of bank credits" (Dodsworth 1895: 199).

Almost all of the reform plans considered by Congress attempted to provide for active note redemption.[23] Many plans even emphasized redemption over freer note issue, reflecting the understandable belief that getting more currency out would be easier than getting it back in again, as well as the belief that seasonal shortages of currency were largely due to maldistributions or prior overexpansions that active redemption would prevent. Proponents of reform disagreed, however, on how to implement active redemption. A minority, including the authors of the "Baltimore Plan" endorsed by the American Bankers' Association (ABA) at its 1894 Baltimore convention, argued or implied that greater freedom of note issue would itself bring about sufficiently active redemption by raising the opportunity costs to banks of reissuing rivals' notes, as experience in other nations showed. The majority, however, though recognizing "a very close connection between the ease or difficulty of issuing notes and the activity and efficiency of the redemption system" (Laughlin 1898: 326), believed that legislation redesigning the redemption system was needed to prevent overissue of asset currency.

Congress quickly abandoned the Baltimore Plan after critics pointed out that it relied on the "usual, slow process" of note redemption.[24] The majority view was bolstered by the observation that redemption under the National Banking System had been hindered not only by banks' inability to issue more of their own notes, but also by the expense of sorting and transporting the notes issued by thousands of other banks. The minority view appeared to overlook the fact that banks in the United States were much more numerous and dispersed than banks in other nations.

LEGISLATIVE PROPOSALS FOR ACTIVE REDEMPTION

An obvious but unpopular route to active note redemption was to repeal the requirement that national banks receive one another's notes at par. This idea, proposed by Comptroller Knox in 1873, was revived in the late 1890s by Virginia banker William L. Royall. In testimony before the House Banking Committee (U.S. Congress 1897: 199), Royall blamed par acceptance for the seasonal glut of notes in New York: "[I]f you put out notes in a backwoods community that are good at par in New York, those notes will leave the backwoods community and go to New York."[25] Nonpar acceptance would make sorting and returning notes profitable and would prevent notes from circulating far from their places of issue and redemption. Royall cited the case of antebellum Virginia notes, which traded at a discount in New York and consequently were seldom taken there.

The same sort of localness characterized Canadian bank notes before 1890.[26] Nonpar valuation eventually disappeared, as discounts paved the way for improved redemption facilities. A nonpar currency was nevertheless viewed in the United States as decidedly retrograde. Thomas G. Bush of the Indianapolis Monetary Commission told the House Banking Committee that proponents of such a solution "in coming to Washington ought to have taken the stagecoach instead of the railroad train," as outdated means were "more in keeping with their views" (U.S. Congress 1898: 277).

A second proposal for encouraging active note redemption was to make it illegal for national banks to pay out one another's notes, as Massachusetts had done for state banks in 1843. This proposal, recommended by Charles Dunbar (1904: 243), was considered but ultimately abandoned by the authors of the bill (H.R. 3333) submitted to the 55th Congress by Rep. Joseph Walker (R-MA), chair of the House Banking and Currency Committee (U.S. Congress 1898: 260). The proposal failed to reckon with country banks' option of sending unwanted notes to their reserve-city correspondents. Instead of helping to spread the redemption process more widely, it would have increased the burden on city banks struggling to dispose of excess notes.

A third and more popular proposal was to increase the number of common locations at which banks were obliged to redeem their notes. Various subtreasuries could officially be required to serve as redemption bureaus along with the Redemption Agency in Washington, as some already were doing unofficially (Cagan and Schwartz 1991). Alternatively, national banks could be officially required to redeem their notes at par at private clearinghouses approved by the comptroller of the currency. The bill supported by New York banker Richard B. Ferris (H.R. 2699) and read before the 54th Congress, as well as the ones submitted by Secretary of the Treasury Lyman Gage (H.R. 5181) and the Indianapolis Monetary Commission (H.R. 5855) to the 55th Congress, embodied the subtreasury approach. The Treasury Department proved unwilling, however, to take on any additional burden. The clearinghouse approach found its way into a large number of proposals, including an early Walker bill and at least four others.[27] The banking community opposed these bills because they would have imposed high costs on banks.

A fourth and still more popular approach, following the Canadian and Scottish models, was to allow interstate branch banking by national banks while requiring each branch to redeem at par the notes issued by its head office. Branching would permit banks to expand profitably into new areas where their notes might circulate. The branch-redemption requirement would make them devote some share of the resulting earnings to maintaining more widespread redemption facilities. The inclusion of branching privileges in asset currency plans was seen by some as essential for getting any part of the banking industry to support legislated redemption provisions. Others, particularly Rep. Charles N. Fowler (R-NJ)—a member (and later chairman) of the House Banking and Currency Committee, a member of the Indianapolis Monetary Commission, and an uncompromising promoter of asset currency—viewed branch banking as a means to active note redemption and thereby as a key to the success of an asset currency (Laughlin 1898).

Branch banking, however, had politically influential opponents. The smaller interior banks feared the consolidation of the banking industry that interstate branching would bring. The unit banking lobby was able to prevent the passage of any measure that even hinted at banking across state lines throughout the 1890s and beyond.[28] The path of least resistance, evident in the Gold Standard Act of 1900, was therefore to relax bond-collateral requirements without making any improvements in note redemption to provide an offsetting restraint. As one commentator observed, "[T]he plans of the theorists contemplated that the bank issues should be at the same time expansible and contractible. But legislation has adopted only one-half of the project, for it has seized upon the idea of expanding the bank issues but made no provision for their contraction" (Falkner 1900: 47).[29]

THE ULTIMATE FAILURE OF THE ASSET CURRENCY MOVEMENT

By obstructing potential improvements in note redemption, the defenders of unit banking helped to undermine the asset currency movement. They did so knowingly. Andrew J. Frame, a Wisconsin banker who was one of branch banking's more outspoken opponents, made his position clear in a 1907 address: "Enforced quick redemption . . . will work under a branch banking system, but it is impracticable under ours. For one, I do not propose to be accessory to my own hanging by aiding in bringing about any branch banking system, which I confidently believe is the ultimate end in view of many of the asset currency advocates" (American Bankers' Association 1907: 138).

By 1907 the asset currency movement had abandoned "its moorings in branch banking" (Livingston 1986: 155). It instead attempted to devise second-best means for achieving an elastic currency with active note redemption. The clearest example of a second-best proposal, and the last important effort to establish an actively redeemed asset currency, was a joint product of the ABA's Currency Commission and the Committee on Finance and Currency of the New York State Chamber of Commerce. Their proposal, put before Congress in 1907 as H.R. 23017, recommended that national banks be allowed to issue unsecured "credit" notes to supplement their bond-secured notes. The comptroller of the currency would "designate certain cities conveniently located in the various sections of the United States for the current daily redemption" of the credit notes.

Both the New York committee and the ABA Currency Commission stressed the importance of note redemption. Economists Charles Conant and Joseph French Johnson, writing for the New York committee, held that active redemption was a matter "of the first importance," and that multiple redemption points were necessary to secure it: "If the volume of bank notes is to vary sensitively with the need for them, there must be incessant daily redemption, and this can be had only when the redemption points are so numerous that no bank will be more than 24 hours distant from one" (Claflin et al. 1906: 13–14). James B. Forgan, president of the First National Bank of Chicago and a member of the ABA Currency Commission, argued that creating an asset currency "without providing means for its contraction . . . would only enhance the evils of our present system." He elaborated,

> It is, therefore, no expansion of the currency that we are advocating, but the adjustment of it to fluctuating demands of commerce with an adequate power to contract as these demands are reduced. . . . *There is only one possible way by which this attribute of elasticity can be given to it; that is, by active redemption and practical cancellation of bank notes which are not kept in circulation by the requirements of commerce.* (American Bankers' Association 1907: 167–68; emphasis in original)

Drawing on his experience as a former employee of both Scottish and Canadian banks, Forgan claimed that, with adequate redemption facilities, national bank notes would circulate "on exactly the same basis as checks, bank drafts, and other similar obligations," being "presented along with these through the Clearing House for redemption" instead of being treated like gold or greenbacks.

Others were skeptical that multiple redemption points alone, unaccompanied by branch banking, could achieve active note redemption. Frame dismissed the proposal as "an expensive luxury" that would make "a picnic for the express companies" at great expense to the national banks (American Bankers' Association 1907: 138). But skepticism was not confined to the unit banking interests. Frank Vanderlip, a former assistant secretary of the treasury and a member of the New York currency committee, also came to doubt "whether the creation of numerous redemption points would be sufficient to drive in the redundant circulation."[30] The New York committee and the ABA commission responded by proposing a tax on credit notes in circulation. Taxing circulation, however, penalizes notes generally, not only excess notes, and does nothing by itself to drive redundant notes to their issuers.[31] Forgan admitted that once a note has been issued, it may, tax or no tax, remain "entirely beyond the reach of the bank that wants to redeem it" if no mechanism exists for returning it promptly (American Bankers' Association 1907: 164–65).

By endorsing a circulation tax, the sponsors of H. R. 23017 played into the hands of the opponents of asset currency, led by Sen. Nelson Aldrich (R-RI). Aldrich favored allowing a supplemental currency, to be issued only during "emergencies" and subject to a heavy tax aimed at achieving its prompt withdrawal. The Aldrich-Vreeland Act of May 30, 1908, embodied a compromise between Aldrich and the supporters of H. R. 23017, authorizing an emergency asset currency under a heavy tax but denying an ordinary asset currency with active redemption. The act was, moreover, adopted only as a temporary expedient (expiring June 30, 1914) while the National Monetary Commission, which it authorized, looked into permanent reform solutions. Ultimately it gave way, not to any asset currency, but to the Federal Reserve Act of 1913.

The Federal Reserve System provided even less adequately than the National Banking System had for active note redemption. Each of the 12 regional Federal Reserve Banks was required to receive and prohibited from reissuing (except at a 10 percent penalty) the notes of any other reserve bank, but the banks seldom had the opportunity to redeem one another's notes. The public, as before, did not seek to redeem unwanted notes directly, but found it easier to deposit them in their accounts at commercial banks. State and national banks preferred to hold and reissue Federal Reserve notes rather than to redeem them for gold, even though the banks could not yet count the notes as part of their legal reserves. The Federal Reserve notes were the favored currency medium of the public, and the national banks' own profits from note issue were dwindling. The holding and reissue of Federal Reserve notes was also encouraged by a rule preventing a bank from directly receiving reserve-balance credit from its district reserve bank for a deposit of notes issued in other districts. Member banks were thus encouraged to return their own reserve bank's notes, but not to send in the notes issued by other district reserve banks (Taylor 1914: 456–58).

Federal Reserve notes were therefore as lacking in "homing power" as national bank notes had been before. Economist Fred M. Taylor (1914: 460) concluded that "the new law does not promise to give to the note issue the degree of contractibility which has hitherto been considered desirable." The *Commercial and Financial Chronicle* (Aug. 17, 1915: 398) noted the irony of this outcome in light of the original aim of providing a downwardly elastic currency:

> What is now being done . . . is just the reverse of what was intended. . . . Instead of notes being retired, when their mission as a medium for carrying mercantile paper has been fulfilled, they are being forced into circulation and a determination exists to keep them afloat indefinitely. Mr. [Benjamin] Strong [Governor of the Federal Reserve Bank of New York] argues that this does no harm and that if the notes become redundant they will quickly come in and be presented for redemption. As a matter of fact unless some crisis intervenes they will stay out just as long as the banks and the trust companies continue to pay them out.

The Federal Reserve Act had introduced a currency whose volume was "elastic" only in the sense that it could be increased or reduced at the Federal Reserve's discretion. Although this sort of discretionary elasticity did succeed in smoothing interest rates and (for a time) in avoiding financial crises by eliminating seasonal accumulations of currency in New York City, it was far from providing the automatic elasticity that reformers throughout the national banking era had tried to achieve (Miron 1986: 125–40).

CONCLUSION

The inadequacy of note redemption under the National Banking System in the late 19th and early 20th centuries was appreciated by many reformers, who sought improved opportunities for redemption as a complement to greater freedom of issue. According to their diagnosis of the banking system's problems, the interventions of the federal government prevented the stock of bank notes from adjusting, in an automatic and desirable way, in response to changes in the demand to hold notes. The reformers' goal of an elastic currency was co-opted, and their deregulatory program ultimately discarded, in the fashioning of the Aldrich-Vreeland and Federal Reserve acts. Recent work on the self-adjusting properties of the note supply under deregulated conditions suggests, however, that the reformers' diagnosis was essentially correct.[32] Their program deserved a better hearing.

6

NEW YORK'S BANK: THE NATIONAL MONETARY COMMISSION AND THE FOUNDING OF THE FED*

LEGISLATION CALLING FOR the establishment of a Centennial Monetary Commission "to examine the United States monetary policy, evaluate alternative monetary regimes, and recommend a course for monetary policy going forward," was introduced in both the House and the Senate in July 2015, with the essential provisions of the bill passing the House in November.[1] The commission is to consist of 12 voting members (8 Republicans and 4 Democrats, given the existing majority and minority composition of Congress), together with two nonvoting members: one chosen by the secretary of the treasury and the other, consisting of a Federal Reserve Bank president, chosen by the Fed chair.

According to Rep. Kevin Brady (R-TX), the measure's original sponsor, the commission is to consider "all points of view . . . with respect to the proper role envisioned for our central bank" (Brady 2014: 393). Brady's proposal was subsequently incorporated into the 2016 Financial CHOICE Act.

Prompted by the subprime financial crisis, and particularly by a belief that the crisis revealed significant shortcomings of the Federal Reserve System, the Centennial Monetary Commission plan draws inspiration from the National Monetary Commission convened over a century ago, in response to the Panic of 1907.[2] It was, perhaps somewhat ironically, mainly owing to the efforts of that earlier commission, which was also charged with studying

* Originally published as Cato Institute Policy Analysis no. 794 (June 21, 2016).

alternatives to, and proposing a plan for reforming, the then-existing U.S. monetary system, that the Federal Reserve Act itself was passed.

In this chapter, I review the National Monetary Commission's origins, organization, and achievements. I mainly wish to identify that Commission's shortcomings, with the aim of offering some advice concerning how a new commission might do better. But I also wish to respond to conventional, celebratory accounts of the Fed's establishment by drawing attention to the way in which special interests, and representatives of the major New York City banks in particular, seized control of the pre-Fed currency reform movement, taking it in a direction better suited to preserving and enhancing Wall Street's profits than to ending financial crises.

I begin by reviewing the financial crises that first gave rise to a movement for monetary reform, and the progress of that movement up to the passage of the Aldrich-Vreeland Act in 1908, by which the National Monetary Commission was established. I then show how the Commission became a façade behind which its chair, Sen. Nelson Aldrich (R-RI), pursued a personal monetary reform agenda heavily influenced by major New York bankers. I show how the Commission's successful public relations campaign overcame resistance to the measures Aldrich and his advisers favored, including a "National Reserve Association," to the point of compelling the Democrats to include similar provisions in their alternative to the Aldrich plan, which became the Federal Reserve Act. I show that the Fed was, in fact, more effective in preserving New York's financial hegemony than in securing financial stability. Finally, I draw from this review of history some lessons concerning how a new monetary commission might replicate the earlier Commission's achievements, while avoiding its flaws.

FINANCIAL CRISES UNDER THE NATIONAL CURRENCY SYSTEM

The National Monetary Commission was an outgrowth of crises that beset the pre–Federal Reserve monetary system. A review of those crises and the circumstances that gave rise to them is therefore essential to a proper understanding of that Commission's origins and purpose.

During the last decades of the 19th century, and the first decade of the 20th, the cost of credit in the United States tended to vary with the seasons, especially by rising every autumn as farmers drew on banks for funds with which to "move the crops." The seasonal tightening was largely a reflection of the fact that moving the crops meant paying migrant workers, who had to be paid in cash. When farmers asked their banks for cash, national banks, despite being authorized to issue their own in the form of circulating bank notes, tended to draw instead on their reserves, sometimes by withdrawing funds from their city correspondents. Unless they were located in New York, the correspondent banks in turn withdrew funds from their own correspondents in that city. To avoid having their reserves fall below legal requirements, correspondent banks everywhere, but New York banks especially, cut back on lending until the harvest season ended and withdrawn cash gradually found its way back into the banking system.

In most years, tightening of credit was the whole story. But in others, mere tightening gave way to panic. Between the end of the Civil War and 1913, the United States endured five major financial crises: in 1873, 1884, 1890, 1893, and 1907. With the exception of the 1884 panic, which broke out in May, the crises all took place during the fall harvest; and all, with the exception of the 1893 panic, were triggered by the failure of some important firm or firms, often (though not always) located in New York. The failures led to further tightening of the New York money market, including the market for "call" money used to finance stock purchases, and thence to falling stock prices. Falling stock prices in turn aggravated New York banks' usual seasonal liquidity problems by making it impossible for them to recall many of their loans, and by triggering suspensions of payment, sometimes in New York only, and sometimes nationwide. On several occasions, suspensions were avoided only because Leslie Shaw, secretary of the treasury from 1902 to 1907, averted them by shifting cash from the Treasury's coffers to various national banks in anticipation of the harvest-time drain, and took it back again afterwards (Timberlake 1963).

That the crises tended to get worse over time was particularly disturbing. The Panic of 1893 was more serious than that of 1884; while the Panic of 1907 was the most severe of all. Senator Aldrich, who was to play the central part in organizing and leading the National Monetary Commission, described that last crisis as follows:

> Suddenly the banks of the country suspended payment, and acknowledged their inability to meet their current obligations on demand. The results of this suspension were felt at once; it became impossible in many cases to secure funds or credit to move the crops or to carry on ordinary business operations; a complete disruption of domestic exchange took place; disorganization and financial embarrassment affected seriously every industry; thousands of men were thrown out of employment, and wages of the employed were reduced. The men engaged in legitimate business and the management of industrial enterprises and the wage-earners throughout the country, who were in no sense responsible for the crisis, were the greatest sufferers. (Aldrich 1910: 4)

THE ROLE OF REGULATION

Frequent financial crises were, by the last decades of the 19th century, mainly a U.S. phenomenon. No other relatively developed nation suffered from them. What set the United States apart?

During the late 1880s, the United States, like most advanced industrial nations, operated on a gold standard, which meant that its money consisted either of actual gold coins or of paper currency and deposits redeemable in such coins.[3] Until the Civil War, U.S. paper currency consisted solely of the circulating notes of numerous state-authorized banks. The outbreak of the war led to legislation authorizing the Treasury to issue its own paper money, known officially as United States Notes and, unofficially, as "greenbacks." A subsequent suspension of gold payments placed the nation on a greenback standard.

Wartime legislation also provided for the establishment, by the federal government, of national currency-issuing banks, while subjecting state banks to a prohibitive 10 percent tax on their outstanding notes so as to compel them to switch to national charters.[4] Consequently, when gold payments were resumed in 1879, the stock of U.S. paper currency consisted entirely of greenbacks, the quantity of which was absolutely fixed, and of national bank notes.

Although several foreign nations—including England, France, and Germany—had by this time established paper currency monopolies, the United States was hardly unique in allowing numerous banks to issue paper money. On the contrary: until well into the 20th century, competitive or "plural" note-issue systems were the rule rather than the exception.[5] What set the United States apart were destabilizing financial regulations peculiar to it. Two sorts of regulations were especially at fault. The first allowed national bank notes to be issued only to the extent that they were fully backed by government securities. Indeed, until 1900, the requirement was that for every $90 of their notes outstanding, the banks had to have surrendered to the comptroller of the currency authorized bonds having a face value of at least $100.

The bond-deposit requirement caused the supply of national bank notes to vary, not with the public's changing currency needs, but with the availability and price of the requisite bonds. The requirement's presence within the National Currency and National Bank acts of 1863 and 1864 reflected those measures' original purpose of helping the Union government to finance its part in the Civil War.

During the last decades of the 19th century, the government, instead of being desperate for funds, ran frequent budget surpluses, which it chose to apply toward reducing the federal debt. As it did so, bonds bearing the banknote circulation privilege became increasingly scarce, and national banks, instead of trying to put more notes into circulation as the economy grew, did just the opposite, retiring their notes so as to be able to sell and realize gains on the bonds that had been backing them. Between 1881 and 1890, a period of general business expansion and rapid population growth, the outstanding stock of national bank notes shrank from over $320 million to just under $123 million! Because the quantity of greenbacks, the nation's only other paper currency, was fixed by statute, the total money stock was no more elastic than national bank notes were. National banks were especially unwilling to acquire and hold costly bonds just for the sake of meeting temporary currency needs, such as those of the harvest season, because doing that meant having stacks of notes resting idle in their vaults for much of the year, and incurring correspondingly high opportunity costs.

The other important source of U.S. financial instability consisted of laws and other provisions that prevented many U.S. banks, including all national banks, from establishing branches away from their home office. Besides improving banks' ability to geographically diversify their assets and liabilities, branching would have allowed them to shift funds to and from different markets, in response to shifting patterns of demand, while still retaining full control of those funds.

An early source of opposition to branching—state authorities' narrow construal of rights conferred by banks' charters—was subsequently reinforced, according to Oliver M. W. Sprague (1903: 242), by "[p]rejudices aroused in the course of Jackson's war against the Second Bank of the United States; a somewhat absurd fear of an impossible monopoly in banking; and the self-regarding interests of [established] local bankers." Even despite such prejudices, branch banking flourished prior to the Civil War in some parts of the South and Midwest. It was only after the passage of the national banking acts and the 10 percent tax on state bank notes (the last of which came close to wiping out all state banks) that "unit" banking "became a distinguishing feature of the United States economy" (McCulley 1992: 13–14).

National banks were themselves unable to branch, not owing to any specific provisions of the national banking laws, but to the way in which those laws were interpreted. This fact must be kept in mind in light of frequent claims that unit banking was either an inevitable or an unalterable feature of the pre-Fed U.S. economy:

> [N]o evidence exists that the framers of the 1863 and 1864 legislation meant to preclude branch banking. Nevertheless Hugh McCulloch, the first comptroller of the currency, and succeeding comptrollers, interpreted two clauses in the National Banking Act to prohibit branch banking. The act required persons forming an association to specify "the place" where they would conduct banking and required that the transaction of usual business be "an office or banking house" located in the city specified in the charter. Thus the administration of the

> National Banking Act further directed American banking toward a unit structure and prevented the development of large banks with branches, a system more typical of modern economies. (McCulley 1992: 14)

More than any other factor, unit banking made the U.S. economy vulnerable to panics. It limited banks' opportunities for diversifying their assets and liabilities. It made coordinated responses to panics more difficult. Finally, it forced banks to rely heavily on "correspondent" banks for out-of-town collections, and to maintain balances with them for that purpose. Correspondent banking, in turn, contributed to the "pyramiding" of bank reserves: country banks kept interest-bearing accounts with Midwestern city correspondents, sending their surplus funds there during the off-season. Midwestern city correspondents, in turn, kept funds with New York correspondents, and especially with the handful of banks that dominated New York's money market. Those banks, finally, lent the money they received from interior banks to stockbrokers at call (White 1983: 66ff; Calomiris and Haber 2014: 184).

The pyramiding of reserves was further encouraged by the National Bank Act, which allowed national banks to use correspondent balances to meet a portion of their legal reserve requirements. Until 1887, the law allowed "country" national banks—those located in rural areas and in smaller towns and cities—to keep three-fifths of their 15 percent reserve requirement in the form of balances with correspondents or "agents" in any of 15 designated "reserve cities," while allowing banks in those cities to keep half of their 25 percent requirement in banks at the "central reserve city" of New York. In 1887, St. Louis and Chicago were also classified as central reserve cities. Thanks to this arrangement, a single dollar of legal tender held by a New York bank might be reckoned as legal reserves, not just by that bank, but by several. Thus, a spike in the rural demand for currency might find all banks scrambling at once, like players in a game of musical chairs, for legal tender that wasn't there to be had, playing havoc in the process with the New York stock market, as banks serving that market attempted to call in their loans (Graves 1903: 88–89; McCulley 1992: 18; White 1983: 69–71).

The financial condition of half a dozen New York banks thus became "the most important single factor to be considered in estimating the strength of the system as a whole" (Sprague 1910: 13). "In a dramatic way," Benjamin Beckhart and James Smith observe in their 1932 volume on the New York money market, "the panic of 1907 demonstrated the evils inherent in the concentration of reserve funds in New York City." They continue,

> The social peril of a dominating financial center and the alleged withdrawal of funds from the farming West for speculation in the East furnished fuel for constantly burning issues. It would probably be no exaggeration to say that this problem in itself was sufficient to give impetus to the banking reform movement which eventually resulted in the establishment of the Federal Reserve system. (Beckhart and Smith 1932: 155)

Nationwide branch banking, by permitting one and the same bank to operate both in the countryside and in New York, would have avoided this dependence of the entire system on a handful of New York banks, as well as the periodic scramble for legal tender and ensuing market turmoil. As Sprague (1903: 243–44) explains,

> The bank with many branches can concentrate its reserves wherever the demand arises. In a measure this is true in the United States at present, under the system of bankers' deposits in reserve cities; but the transfer of cash would be more immediate and automatic under a branch system. Moreover, the existing system is exceedingly unsatisfactory during periods of acute distress. . . . [E]xperience shows that at such times country banks withdraw deposits to protect themselves, even when they are in no immediate danger. The credit structure as a whole is weakened, reserves become unavailable at points of greatest danger, and banks fail which might have survived with a little timely assistance.

Although it exposed them to occasional crises, the correspondent business was both very lucrative to the most powerful New York banks and crucial to their success, having come to surpass in importance the business they did with individual depositors. By October 1913, the eight largest New York banks collectively managed $462.2 million in bankers' balances, as opposed to just $361 million in individual deposits (see Table 6.1). It was owing to those banks' concern to preserve their correspondent banking business that they came to play a prominent part in shaping the course of subsequent banking and currency reform efforts.

Table 6.1: Deposits of the Eight Largest New York City Banks, October 21, 1913 (Millions Of Dollars)

Bank	Bankers' Deposits	Individual Deposits
National Bank of Commerce	66.6	58.7
Chase National	76.0	38.7
First National	54.9	47.6
Hanover National	66.3	25.5
Liberty National	14.2	12.7
Mechanics and Metals National	30.0	29.7
National City	92.5	108.6
National Park	61.7	39.7
Total	462.2	361.2
Total all NYC national banks	641.3	715.6
Eight largest as percentage of all NYC banks	72.1%	50.5%

Source: Watkins (1929: 21, Table 4).

THE ASSET CURRENCY MOVEMENT

In light of existing regulations' contribution to U.S. monetary instability, it was only natural for those seeking to improve the U.S. banking and currency system to recommend getting rid of, or at least substantially relaxing, the troublesome regulations. In particular, they favored letting national banks issue notes backed by their general assets—that is, by the same general assets those banks held against their deposits. Some also favored doing away with the prohibitive tax on state bank notes.

Although some early calls for "asset currency" predate the Panic of 1893, the movement first achieved prominence in the wake of that crisis, when "the business and financial community was nearly unanimous in its desire to abolish bond-secured currency and issue a new national bank note secured by the [general] assets of the issuing banks" (West 1977: 43). "The appeal of an asset-based currency," Elmus Wicker (2005: 2) notes, "resided in its simplicity. It did not require further intrusion by government into the banking industry. No major institutional changes were necessary."

The asset currency movement drew inspiration from several nations that had long relied on asset-backed currency, and especially from Canada, where several dozen banks supplied such currency while managing more than 1,000 branch offices scattered across the country. Although it involved practically no government regulation save certain minimum capital requirements, Canada's system managed to accommodate fluctuating currency needs without difficulty and without any losses to the public. "As surely and regularly as the autumn months come around and the inevitable accompanying demand for additional currency begins to manifest itself," wrote L. Carroll Root (1894: 322), so "does the currency of the banks automatically respond." Credit crunches and panics were unknown. As one prominent Canadian banker put it, "The Canadians never know what it is to go through an American money squeeze in the autumn" (Root 1894: 322).[6] The stark contrast between the behavior of the currency stock in the United States and its behavior in Canada is shown in Figure 6.1.

Proposals to eliminate or relax regulatory restrictions on banks' ability to issue notes had as their counterpart provisions that would allow banks to branch freely. The Canadian system supplied inspiration here as well. Canadian banks enjoyed, and generally took full advantage of, nationwide branching privileges. What's more, by an ironic twist, many also had branches in New York City, and so had direct access to a valuable market that was denied to most of their U.S. counterparts.

Many asset currency proposals called upon the comptroller of the currency to allow national banks to branch, while also requiring banks to redeem their notes—that is, to exchange them, on demand, for gold or greenbacks—at their branches as well as at their head offices, both as an alternative to correspondent banking (and the consequent pyramiding of reserves) and as the most straightforward means for absorbing redundant bank notes: unlike unit banks, banks with nationwide branch networks could resort to local exchanges or "clearings" of notes and checks as a less costly and more expeditious alternative to shipping them to one or more central clearinghouses or redemption agencies. Besides aiding the prompt mopping-up of excess currency, and reducing interior banks' reliance upon city correspondents, branch banking would also enhance banks' safety through greater diversification of bank assets and liabilities. For these reasons, pleas for branch banking quickly became "an integral part" of the asset currency movement (Livingston 1986: 80).

Figure 6.1: Bank Notes in Circulation, 1880–1909, Monthly

(Millions of Dollars)

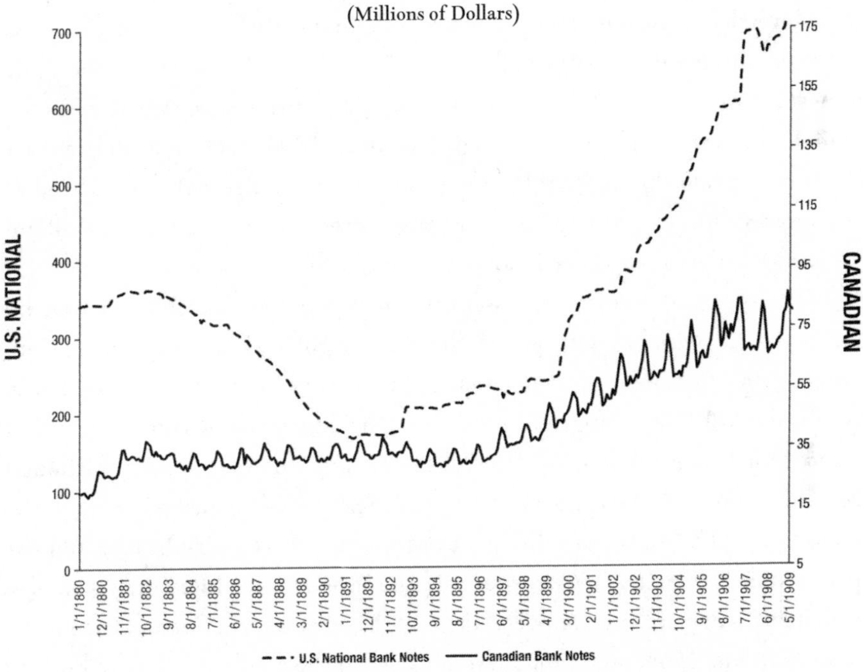

SOURCES: Data for Canadian bank notes are from Clifford Curtis (1931: 20). Data for U.S. national bank notes are from Comptroller of the Currency, *Annual Report* (various dates).

Despite the emphasis they placed on deregulation, asset currency plans often called upon either banks or the government to take various positive steps, many of which were aimed at assuaging critics' fears that asset currency might be less secure than bond-backed notes, or that banks might overissue it. To protect noteholders from losses due to bank failures, most plans provided for a bank-note "safety" or "guarantee" fund, typically to be kept equal to 5 percent of the total value of asset-backed notes. To guarantee that excess notes would be redeemed promptly, even in the absence of widespread bank branches, many also called for the establishment of bank-note redemption facilities in major commercial centers across the country. Like other asset currency measures, such proposals looked to Canada for inspiration, for Canadian banks also took part in a bank-note guarantee fund, while being required to provide for the redemption of their notes in each of Canada's seven provinces.

More than a dozen asset currency bills found their way into Congress between the Panic of 1893 and the Panic of 1907. Until 1897, the most important of these, and the basis for many later proposals, was the "Baltimore Plan," so called because it originated in an 1894 meeting of Baltimore's bankers. During the mid-1890s the movement was sidelined when its more active participants went to battle against "Free Silver."[7] But with William McKinley's election victory it sprang back to life.

Of various McKinley-era asset currency plans, the most important by far was that which grew out of the Indianapolis Monetary Convention, where 300 businessmen-delegates, representing more than 100 cities, resolved to convince Congress to appoint a monetary commission and, if that effort failed, to establish an 11-member commission of their own. Although McKinley himself favored a government-sponsored commission, and the House passed a bill to establish it, the Senate, led by Aldrich, rejected the plan (Kolko 1963: 148). Consequently the Indianapolis Monetary Commission itself, a private and nonpartisan body that was a sort of prototype for the later National Monetary Commission, took up the challenge of developing a reform proposal. The Commission's impressive 600-page report, including its proposed currency and banking reform, was published and offered to Congress in January 1898 (Laughlin 1898). The report would remain the most comprehensive of all arguments in favor of asset currency.

J. Laurence Laughlin, a University of Chicago economics professor, was the most important of the Indianapolis Monetary Commission's 11 members, and the uncredited author of its report. He had criticized some earlier asset currency plans, and the Baltimore Plan in particular, for failing to provide adequately for the active redemption of national bank notes, by means of branch banking or otherwise (Laughlin 1894). Laughlin would remain a key figure in the currency reform movement until the passage of the Federal Reserve Act, to which he also contributed. However, in 1898 Laughlin stood so squarely in the asset currency camp that his report contained only one passing reference to a "central bank." As Roger Lowenstein (2015: 24) notes, the Indianapolis delegates whose views Laughlin represented "were headed in the other direction—they wanted the government *out* of banking."

Despite the Indianapolis Commission's impressive report, Congress rejected its asset currency plan and various bills inspired by it.[8] Instead, with the Gold Standard Act of March 14, 1900, Congress put into effect those parts of the Indianapolis proposal addressing the question of the standard, while making it somewhat easier for national banks to issue bond-backed notes. It allowed national banks to issue notes up to deposited bonds' par value, rather than 90 percent of that value; and it cut the tax on outstanding notes in half. Most importantly, it provided for conversion of expensive bonds that were about to mature into others running 30 years and paying a lower rate.[9]

Although the Gold Standard Act reversed the downward movement in the stock of national bank notes, the relief this brought didn't last long: in the fall of 1901, credit tightened again, as New York "experienced the greatest difficulty meeting the autumnal call from the interior" (McCulley 1992: 99), reminding everyone that another crisis would come sooner or later.

By then, asset currency had gained a new and influential advocate in Charles N. Fowler—a Republican congressman from New Jersey, and Congress's "most persistent and articulate champion of financial reform." (McCulley 1992: 43). Fowler had been made chair of the House Committee on Banking and Currency when Teddy Roosevelt took office the previous March. Between 1902 and 1907, Fowler introduced several asset currency bills, all of which were endorsed by the American Bankers' Association (ABA) and various chambers of commerce (McCulley 1992: 43). But despite this support, and his considerable status, Fowler's attempts fared no better than other asset currency proposals had. Although several were reported favorably in the House, they died when the Senate Banking Committee refused to take them up.

OPPONENTS OF ASSET CURRENCY

Despite its popularity among experts, and the persuasive evidence that Canadian experience supplied, the asset currency movement faced stiff opposition both within the government and from representatives of the banking industry.

The banking industry's attitude toward asset currency is best grasped by referring to Richard T. McCulley's (1992) treatment of the late-19th-century politics of banking reform as a struggle among three banking industry interest groups: Wall Street, Main Street, and LaSalle Street. The last, meaning the bankers of Chicago but also those of other relatively large Midwestern cities, spearheaded the asset currency movement, hoping by means of it "to improve their competitive position vis-à-vis the East, and to expand at the expense of smaller rural bankers" (Wiebe 1962: 62). Country or "Main Street" bankers were, on the other hand, generally opposed to branch banking, fearing, as one of them put it in assessing Fowler's 1902 plan, that the major banks of the great money centers "would be able to plant their branches in every city or town where they pleased, and . . . would soon drive the local institutions out of business" (Pugsley 1907: 305). A 1903 resolution of bankers of Kansas and Nebraska went still further, condemning branch banking, not only as "tending to establish a monopoly . . . in the hands of a few millionaires," but also as "unpatriotic, un-American, unbusinesslike" (Fowler 1902: 56).

Because plans calling for it were often joined by calls for letting banks branch, in the eyes of country bankers asset currency became "blackened by the company it kept" (Wiebe 1962: 65). According to H. Parker Willis, writing at the end of 1903,

> [W]hen the question of bond security has come up in Congress, the influence of small banks has been thrown forcibly against any change,

> and the general apathy of members, coupled perhaps with a feeling that the matter was a good one for use as the basis in political huckstering, has tended to keep things *in status quo*. (Willis 1903: 137–38)

Small bankers' tendency to assume that "complicated reforms . . . always originated with the 'sinners' and 'plutocratic combinations' in Wall Street," was only part of the problem (Wiebe 1962: 62). "Strangely enough," Louis Ehrich (a prominent Colorado businessmen and asset currency proponent) remarked at a 1903 dinner at New York's Reform Club, "the primal hindrance to a reform of the currency has been the indifference, and even opposition, of this very banking class, this so-called Money Power" (Ehrich 1903: 13).

In fact there was nothing at all surprising about the Money Power's unwillingness to join the movement for asset currency. Far from being uninterested in the course of reform, the major New York banks, which by 1900 had come to specialize in investment rather than commercial banking (McCulley 1992: 90), were determined to oppose any proposal that threatened to undermine their lucrative correspondence-banking business. By the time of the 1907 panic, New York banks collectively held about 35 percent of all correspondent balances, amounting to about $500 million. Eighty percent of this amount was held by the city's "big six" national banks, including the National City Bank, the National Bank of Commerce, and the First National Bank (Tallman and Moen 2012: Table 1).[10] Thus, it happened that Main Street unwittingly joined forces with Wall Street, whose machinations it most feared, with both battling against the LaSalle Street–led asset currency campaign.[11]

Banking-industry opposition to asset currency had as its counterpart the opposition of two powerful politicians, politically as far removed from one another as Main Street and Wall Street. The first of these was William Jennings Bryan.

Though better known for having campaigned for free silver and against a gold standard, Bryan was no less opposed to commercial bank-note currency, his belief being that government alone should issue paper money. As a Democratic congressman (1891–95), Bryan consistently opposed measures calling for asset currency, as well as attempts to repeal the 10 percent tax on state bank notes. When President Grover Cleveland urged that the prohibitive tax be removed in the wake of the Panic of 1893, Bryan "delivered an impassioned speech" in which he not only opposed that step but expressed his desire to see all national bank notes retired in favor of government money (Coletta 1964: 33).

Although he lost his presidential bids both in 1896 and in 1900, Bryan maintained control of the powerful, progressive minority within the Democratic Party. "If you said anything against Bryan," a Democratic representative of long standing recalled many years later, "you got knocked over, that is all" (Dunne 1964: 9). Using this influence, Bryan waged "incessant war against asset currency," treating it, without warrant, as part of a conspiracy of major financiers to assert control over the nation's money supply (Dunne 1964: 9).

During the Panic of 1907, Bryan, far from moderating his blanket opposition to any relaxation of existing currency laws, insisted on it all the more vehemently. In response to the many "editorials in the city dailies, demanding an asset currency," Bryan (1907) claimed that the panic was itself "a part of the plutocracy's plan to increase its hold upon the government." "The big financiers," he wrote, "have either brought on the present stringency to compel the government to authorize an asset currency or they have promptly taken advantage of the panic to urge the scheme which they have had in mind for years." It followed, Bryan argued, that Democrats were "duty bound to . . . oppose asset currency in whatever form it may appear." Democrats, he said,

> should be on their guard and resist this concerted demand for an asset currency. It would simply increase Wall Street's control over the nation's finances, and that control is tyrannical enough now. Such elasticity as is necessary should be controlled by the government and not by the banks. (Bryan 1907)

The other major political opponent of asset currency could not have been less like Bryan in every other respect. Nelson Aldrich was a wealthy, blue-blooded Republican, who served on the Senate Finance Committee for

30 years, and chaired it from 1881 to 1911. He was for that reason alone by far the most powerful shaper of monetary policy and reform during that time. According to McCulley (1992: 224), "Aldrich was at the same time the most logical and the least promising figure to lead the reform of American banking." The very "embodiment of the Republican congressional 'Old Guard,'" he was notorious for his role in "shielding eastern banking and corporate interests from greater public accountability and government control" (pp. 224–25). Until the 1907 panic, Aldrich employed his power not to encourage monetary reform, but to stand in its way, especially by foiling every plan for asset currency (Lowenstein 2015: 33).

Fowler's asset currency bills became particular targets of Aldrich-led opposition. According to Willis, who assisted in drafting the Indianapolis Commission Plan, and who would later assist Carter Glass in drafting the Federal Reserve Act, Fowler's first, 1902 asset currency bill was scuttled by a June 1902 Republican caucus:

> The whole tone of the caucus . . . was one of contempt for the movement to gain a currency not based on bonds. . . . The outcome was a crushing defeat for the original Fowler measure and therewith for credit currency—a defeat which was only deepened by the slightly less contemptuous but still very hostile attitude of the Republicans toward the revised and simplified Fowler bill which appeared . . . at the next session of Congress. (Willis 1903: 141)[12]

Although President Roosevelt had been prepared to support Fowler's 1903 attempt, Aldrich refused to cooperate. "Our currency," he told A. Barton Hepburn, one of the plan's proponents, "is as good as gold. Why not let it alone?" (Lowenstein 2015: 38). To more effectively counter Fowler's attempt, the big New York bankers first denounced it as one that would give rise to "second-class currency." They then arranged to have Aldrich introduce an alternative "proposing a limited expansion of the currency with notes issued against selected state, municipal, and railroad bonds"—that is, with bonds of the very sort that had been the basis of the notoriously "second-class" currencies and "wildcat" banking of the antebellum era.[13]

Aldrich was, however, more concerned with making his bill attractive to his fellow Republican senators and the special interests they represented than with keeping the nation's currency safe. As Paul Warburg, who played a major part in shaping subsequent reforms, put it, Aldrich "believed in bond-secured currency and, at a pinch, in still more bond-secured currency" (Warburg 1930: 19). Wrote Willis:

> It was natural that the conservative banking interests should be attracted by the Aldrich bill and repelled by the Fowler bill, partly because the Aldrich bill proposed no radical changes, partly because it promised to enhance the price of certain existing securities. The Fowler bill took a step in the direction of greater freedom of competition in banking . . . while it possibly squinted toward the ultimate introduction of a branch banking measure, though this, of course, would be entirely a matter for the future. (Willis 1903: 125)

Democratic filibustering ultimately prevented a Senate vote on the Aldrich bill. In the meantime, the measure's Republican supporters attempted to bypass Fowler's committee, which also would have put paid to it, by having a similar bill introduced in the House as a *revenue* measure, with the intent of having it reported to the Ways and Means Committee (McCulley 1992: 106–7). Fowler protested, and the House Speaker sustained him, so Aldrich's bill would have died anyway. Still, the episode illustrates the lengths to which Aldrich and the rest of the Republican Old Guard were prepared to go to counter any threat to the monetary status quo.

In December 1906, Fowler tried again, introducing legislation embodying a new asset currency plan developed during the preceding months by the ABA's Currency Commission. The plan would have allowed national banks to issue asset-backed notes up to 25 percent of their capital, or 40 percent of their outstanding bond-secured notes (depending on which limit was lower) subject to a low (2.5 percent) tax. This attempt died on the House floor.

By the summer of 1907, a few prominent proponents of asset currency, having become discouraged by the movement's lack of political success, began to desert it and to instead join those who were prepared to limit the privilege of issuing notes not backed by bonds either to a central bank or to a handful of regional banks or bank associations (Livingston 1986: 171–72). One of the defectors was Frank Vanderlip, who was to play a prominent behind-the-scenes part in the National Monetary Commission.

Vanderlip had been the assistant of Lyman Gage, McKinley's secretary of the treasury who, like his chief, "attributed the inept U.S. currency system to serious legal constraints" (Wicker 2005: 39). But his views changed after he was employed by National City Bank, which he quickly turned into "the nation's largest holder of interior bank deposits" (McCulley 1992: 91). In his 1906 Chamber of Commerce Committee report, Vanderlip, instead of insisting as he once had on the need for asset currency and financial deregulation, proposed a central bank of issue, authorized to deal, but not to compete with, other banks, controlled by a board consisting partly of presidential appointees.

Despite desertions from its supporters' ranks and powerful opponents in Congress, until the Panic of 1907, asset currency remained a relatively popular reform alternative. It continued to command the almost universal support of leading monetary economists. And although it faced stiff resistance, resistance to the alternative of a central bank was even stiffer. Warburg's partner, Jacob Schiff, who himself favored a central bank, summed the matter up well in addressing the New York Chamber of Commerce in anticipation of the release of its 1906 report:

> The American people at the time of Andrew Jackson, and more so today, do not want to centralize power. They do not want to increase the power of Government. They know that every increase in the power of government, beyond the legitimate functions of government, means the suppression of private energy, and they also know that a central bank would, more or less, just as the Sub-Treasuries are today, be a government institution. . . . They do not want to have this mass of deposits, these large deposits, which the government would have to keep in this bank, controlled by a few people. They are afraid of the political power it would give and the consequences. That is the feeling of the people of this country. (New York Chamber of Commerce 1907: 50)

According to Wicker (2005: x), even as late as the first half of 1908 "no one . . . thought a central bank would be at the top of the banking system reform agenda." Although it is too strong to say, as Wicker does, that asset currency plans still "monopolized the banking reform debate," such plans remained prominent.[14] While the central bank plan "appealed to a handful of journalists and professors," it had no friends in Congress, where preferences were divided between those who favored an asset currency reform and others, including Aldrich, who still remained "enamored of the system of National Bank Notes secured by government bonds" (Lowenstein 2015: 75).

The currency reform movement had thus reached an impasse that only Aldrich himself could break. By electing to convene and direct a National Monetary Commission, Aldrich did at last break it. But he did so in a manner that was to decisively sway the balance of the movement in favor of a central bank.

THE ALDRICH-VREELAND ACT

Although an interval of economic expansion between August 1904 and May 1907 reduced the pressure for monetary reform, the Panic of 1907 led to calls for immediate legislation (Laughlin 1908: 490). "Reform," Lowenstein (2015: 73) writes, "was suddenly the rage. Proposals poured into Congress."

The more authoritative proposals once again called for asset currency, including yet another Fowler bill essentially repeating his 1906 attempt. But because of the Aldrich-led Senate Finance Committee's "stern opposition . . . against any form of 'asset-currency'" (Laughlin 1908: 493), the measure that ultimately won approval—the Aldrich-Vreeland Act of May 30, 1908—amounted not to a permanent and coherent plan for currency reform, based on asset currency or otherwise, but, in the words of Indianapolis Plan author J. Laurence Laughlin, to "a curious compound of conflicting views, compromise, haste, and politics" (p. 490).

The compromise to which Laughlin refers began as one between Fowler's asset-currency bill and another reply by Aldrich. Aldrich's plan, renewing his 1903 call for allowing national banks to secure their notes with the same sorts of bonds that had secured the notes of antebellum wildcat banks, was for that and other reasons "riddled in the House by the representatives of industry and banking" (Laughlin 1908: 494). "One can scarcely avoid the conclusion," Laughlin observed in his own scathing assessment of Aldrich's plan, that it "represented only the stolid personal prejudices of a very few mistaken politicians, who held the reins of power" (p. 494).

Fowler's proposal was, on the other hand, exceedingly ambitious: unlike some previous asset currency plans, it called for national banks to retire all of their bond-secured notes at once, rather than gradually, while allowing them to issue asset-backed notes up to 100 percent of their capital, rather than up to 40 or 50 percent of that capital. Realizing that neither the Fowler bill nor the Aldrich alternative could succeed, Rep. Edward Vreeland (R-NY) offered a compromise measure resembling Aldrich's but allowing commercial paper as well as bonds to serve as backing for emergency note issues. Fowler, however, refused to report Vreeland's bill from his committee. Fowler's refusal to compromise cost him the support of a House that "was not ready to throw over all bond security" (McCulley 1992: 153), as well as that of the ABA, which instead of endorsing his plan, developed its own less aggressive asset currency proposal.

The Republican leadership answered Fowler's intransigence by calling a party caucus to bring Vreeland's bill before the House. The House, in turn, resolved to discharge the bill from Fowler's committee, guaranteeing the bill's passage there. Fowler in the meantime reintroduced a more moderate version of his bill, only to have what was now Vreeland's committee set it aside unceremoniously in favor of one of Vreeland's measures. When the Senate rejected the Vreeland bill, the matter was referred to a conference committee, which came up with the Aldrich-Vreeland compromise by incorporating large chunks of the Aldrich bill into the House proposal.

The Aldrich-Vreeland Act was passed on May 30, 1908. Although "there was little enthusiasm for the bill among bankers, and none among the public" (Lowenstein 2015: 79), the measure was approved owing to the keen sense of urgency engendered by the recent panic, and the fact that the actual reforms it provided for, instead of being permanent, were originally scheduled to expire on June 30, 1914. (The Federal Reserve Act would later extend them for an extra year.) Those reforms "authorized banks to form local currency associations and, with the approval of the Treasury secretary, to issue additional National Bank Notes in an emergency" (Lowenstein 2015: 79). The emergency notes were to be backed first by government securities and second by commercial paper.

The temporary emergency currency provisions of the Aldrich-Vreeland Act were as close as the United States would ever come to establishing a decentralized asset currency. Although the act did not allow national banks to directly issue asset-backed notes, it at least allowed some of them to do so indirectly, albeit subject to a stiff tax, by organizing themselves into currency associations.[15]

Although it didn't last long, the Aldrich-Vreeland asset currency experiment was to prove both beneficial and enlightening. When World War I broke out some months before the Federal Reserve Banks opened for business, the ensuing panic confronted the U.S. monetary system with its "biggest gold outflow in a generation" (Silber 2007: 285). Put to its only test, the Aldrich-Vreeland emergency currency passed with flying colors.[16]

Of far greater bearing upon the ultimate course of monetary reform than the Aldrich-Vreeland Act's emergency currency provisions was the act's single paragraph establishing a National Monetary Commission, the mission of which was "to inquire into and report to Congress, at the earliest date practicable, what changes are necessary or desirable in the monetary system of the United States or in the laws relating to banking and currency." According to Vreeland's April 20, 1908, testimony before the House Committee on Banking and Currency (U.S. Congress 1908: 9), although Aldrich promised that the Senate would draft a bill providing for such a commission, no such legislation was introduced there. "The main thing," Vreeland continued, "is that we shall have a commission . . . which shall study the need of such revisions in our banking laws as may be necessary, and who shall take time to do it intelligently, and report at a future session of Congress upon the whole matter." Vreeland therefore allowed his own bill to be amended to provide for the proposed Monetary Commission.[17] In short, had the matter been left to Aldrich's own committee, the commission that would determine the future course of U.S. monetary reform, over which Aldrich was to preside like Suleiman, might never have been launched.

THE COMMISSION

Officially, the National Monetary Commission had 18 members, including Aldrich and Vreeland, who served as its chair and vice chair, respectively. The rest consisted of 8 senators appointed by the vice president, Charles Fairbanks, and 7 representatives chosen by the speaker of the house, Joseph Cannon. Of the senators, 4 were Republicans and 4 were Democrats, while of the representatives, 4 were Republicans and 3 were Democrats. Arthur Shelton, who served on Aldrich's staff, was the Commission's 18th member, as well as its secretary. A. Piatt Andrew, finally, served as the Commission's special assistant.

To accomplish its task, the Commission was expected "to examine witnesses and to make such investigations and examinations, in this or other countries, of the subjects committed to their charge as they shall deem necessary."[18] These interviews, examinations, and investigations were supposed, in Andrew's words, to serve as the "foundation" for the Commission's report to Congress, which was to include its proposed legislation.

The Commission's first gathering took place at Rhode Island's Narragansett Pier in July 1908. There the Commission "voted to send representatives . . . to the leading countries of Europe to collect information with regard to the organization of banking in these countries" (Andrew 1909: 378). The European tour began on August 12 and ended on October 13, 1908, although most Commission members returned in late August, leaving Aldrich and Andrew to complete the mission.

The investigations of both foreign and domestic monetary arrangements undertaken or otherwise sponsored by the Commission were complemented by an equally impressive U.S. "education" campaign. "Reform," wrote *Wall Street Journal* editorial assistant Sereno S. Pratt to Aldrich in February 1908, "can only be brought about by educating the people up to it" (Livingston 1986: 182). In fact, Aldrich had understood all along that "the public had to be educated before he could propose legislation." Consequently, as soon as the Commission had formulated its proposals, he and his associates proceeded "to blanket the country with educational literature" (Lowenstein 2015: 99). The *Wall Street Journal* itself took part in this campaign, by publishing a 14-part series of opinion pieces authored by Charles Conant, a journalist and member of the New York Chamber of Commerce Commission on Currency Reform, which had earlier reported in favor of establishing a U.S. central bank.

The first fruits of the Commission's efforts, consisting of 23 volumes of studies commissioned and interviews undertaken by it, began to appear in the autumn of 1910. Although they were completed around the same time, the Commission's report and actual reform plan were not made public until January 17, 1911. The midterm election had, in the meantime, handed control of the House to the Democrats. Consequently Aldrich, who had originally intended to present his plan to Congress immediately following its completion, chose to withhold it for another year with the aim of gaining broader support for it, including the ABA's much-coveted endorsement. With that strategy in mind the draft bill was sent to leading bankers and economists, who were asked to suggest revisions. According to Andrew (cited by Gray 1971: 73), "as many as twenty modified drafts were printed during the course of that year as a result of continuous consultation with hundreds of important people." Having at last gained the ABA's approval, Aldrich introduced his bill to the Senate in January 1912. That step having at last been taken, the business of the National Monetary Commission was formally over.

The centerpiece of the Aldrich plan was a National Reserve Association, located in Washington and operated as a cooperative of subscribing state and national banks, with 15 branches assigned to districts throughout the country. The districts would in turn be divided into portions assigned to local associations, each made up of at least 10 banks. The local associations of each district would select both their own boards and, collectively, that of the Reserve Association's district branch. Subscribing banks would also directly or indirectly select 40 of the National Reserve Association's 46 directors. The rest would consist of government appointees, including the secretary of the treasury, the secretary of commerce and labor, the secretary of agriculture, and the comptroller of the currency.

The National Reserve Association would have the power, through its branches, of issuing notes against its members' prime commercial paper, and so would serve as an indirect means by which those members could place currency into circulation that was not backed by government bonds. But although it provided in this way for a kind of asset currency, Aldrich's proposal was a far cry from genuine asset currency plans such as those devised at Baltimore and Indianapolis, or those offered later by Congressman Fowler. While "asset currency" in its original sense meant currency backed by ordinary bank assets, rather than by government bonds, the Aldrich plan allowed banks to acquire currency only in exchange for short-run commercial paper. Regardless of the soundness of their other assets, banks that lacked such paper would have no more access to currency than they would have had without the reform.

Instead of having them apply for currency to a semicentralized agency, on terms established by that agency, genuine asset currency plans also allowed national banks themselves, if not all banks, to issue their own asset-backed notes. The idea was to let national banks stand on their own two feet, instead of having them lean on other institutions, whether private or public. Far from seeking the same end, the Aldrich plan went in precisely the opposite direction, by calling for the eventual *substitution* of National Reserve Association notes for those of national banks themselves. In other words, the plan called for removing banks altogether from the currency business, and turning that business over to a semipublic monopoly.

A TROJAN HORSE FOR WALL STREET

Although it pretended to be an objective and bipartisan body of 18 senators and representatives, all working together to determine the best means for ridding the U.S. economy of financial crises, in truth the National Monetary Commission served from the very beginning as a sort of Trojan horse, the purpose of which was to convey Aldrich's—which is to say Wall Street's—preferred scheme for currency and banking reform through Congress.

According to no less an authority than A. Piatt Andrew, the Commission's special assistant who was responsible for composing its report and editing its other publications, the Commission "was a one-man show" (Gray 1971: 73). Aldrich, Andrew says, "expected little help from the members of the commission, most of whom had little to offer in the way of scholarship and experience in financial matters and all of whom he knew he could control. . . . So far as the Commission itself was concerned, the Senator's principal idea was to keep its members happy until he had a bill ready and then get their approval." Aldrich held bimonthly meetings with Commission members in New York so as to assure them that "they were not being left out of the picture." But those meetings were otherwise of no real significance. "Occasionally some member would have an idea to which the Senator would listen patiently, but following some general discussion one of his friends on the Commission would usually move that 'the matter be left to the Chairman with the power to act,'" and that would be the end of that (Gray 1971: 73).

If one man's dominance of a commission of inquiry wasn't necessarily a bad thing, it certainly was so in this instance, for Aldrich was notorious for being "fiercely partisan" (Gray 1971: 63). "[T]he old leopard," said Gray of Aldrich, "could not change his spots, and his identification with the crusade did not enhance its political prospects." Despite Piatt Andrew's having "made every effort to enlist bipartisan support," the Commission's proposal "was universally dubbed the 'Aldrich Plan'" (p. 64). The fortunes of that plan thus remained inextricably intertwined with those of the Republican Party itself.

Handicapped as it was by Aldrich's partisanship, the Commission was rendered still more so by its chairman's notoriously cozy relationship with Wall Street. "In the marriage of business and government," Lowenstein (2015: 41–42) observes, "Aldrich felt no discomfort." His close ties to Wall Street were especially conspicuous. In "The Treason of the Senate," his muckraking *Cosmopolitan* series, David Graham Phillips (1906) described Aldrich as "the intimate of Wall Street's great robber barons" and "the chief agent of the predatory band which was rapidly forming to take care of the prosperity of the American people."

The popular perception of Aldrich—or at least that of Democrats and many western Republicans—was no different. It is well captured by a 1905 cartoon depicting him as the crowned king of the Senate, a tiny Teddy Roosevelt prostrate before him. Other Republican senators around him are busy welcoming "The Trusts" into the Senate Chamber, reading a ticker tape, or otherwise enjoying the fruits of crony capitalism. At the cartoon's upper right corner the senator's office door appears, with "VESTED INTERESTS" painted below his name on its etched-glass window.

Aldrich's close ties to Wall Street were evident in his choice of advisers. Although he treated his fellow commissioners as mere ciphers, he did not hesitate to take the advice of powerful financiers to heart, particularly ones closely associated with J. P. Morgan and John D. Rockefeller. It is now common knowledge that the Aldrich plan, despite having been presented as the fruits of the Commission's labor, was entirely the work of Aldrich and his small circle of advisers—Henry P. Davison, Frank Vanderlip, Paul Warburg, Piatt Andrew, and (according to Vanderlip) Benjamin Strong—who cobbled it together during their November 1910 "duck hunt" at Jekyll Island.[19]

The Jekyll Island meeting is now notorious, but it remained a well-kept secret until Aldrich's biographer, Nathaniel Stephenson, spilled the beans in 1930. No word of it had ever been breathed to the other Commission members. The need for secrecy was perfectly obvious. By 1910, a lack of "Wall Street influence" had become, in Lowenstein's words, "the litmus test of monetary reform," and one that President William Taft himself had promised the National Monetary Commission would pass (2015: 97). Yet the Jekyll Island gathering had Wall Street written all over it. The island itself was a Morgan retreat, while the participants, apart from Andrew, were all Wall Street luminaries. Davison, who arranged the retreat, besides being a senior Morgan partner, was vice president of the First National Bank of New York, a founder of Banker's Trust, and a director of four other major New York City banks or trusts.[20] Vanderlip was then president of the Morgan-controlled National City Bank, and would soon help the Morgan interests to gain control of the National Bank of Commerce. Warburg had been a partner in Kuhn, Loeb & Co. since 1902. Strong, finally, was vice president of Bankers Trust.[21]

Gaudy conspiracy theories have portrayed the Jekyll Island gathering as a plot aimed, as Lowenstein (2015: 117) puts it, at "confiscating the people's wealth." But to portray the participants as "patriotic conspirators" who merely wished "to achieve a worthy public reform," as Lowenstein himself does (p. 118), is no less misleading. The truth, as McCulley (1992: 231–32) observes, is that the Jekyll Island bankers were concerned, above all, about "the viability of the banks that they represented," and particularly about how those banks' "interior correspondents continued to subject them to sudden calls for cash" that often "placed an almost unbearable strain on the financial center." Vanderlip, in particular, had reason to be concerned:

> While National City Bank officials increasingly bound their assets to a declining securities market, the bank's interior balances doubled between 1900 and 1910. . . . Heightened financial instability at New York rendered problematic Vanderlip's numerous projects for expanding the National City Bank's activities both domestically and internationally and severely impaired his bank's ability to smoothly channel financial resources to its corporate clients. (McCulley 1992: 231–32)

Aldrich's advisers wanted stability. But they only wanted as much of it as they could have while preserving the pyramiding of bank reserves in New York. They therefore rejected reforms that would have made other banks less dependent upon them, by granting those banks direct access to the New York money market and enhancing their freedom to issue bank notes. Although the dismissal of such popular and sensible alternatives would have been surprising had the Aldrich team merely "wanted a more resilient banking system" (Lowenstein 2015: 118), allowing for those authors' vested interests, it wasn't surprising at all. Nor was it surprising that, instead of referring to the adverse effects of unit banking and other structural sources of U.S. financial instability, as asset currency proposals had done, the National Monetary Commission's official report ignored them (Dewald 1972: 942).

Instead of allowing banks to branch, so that they might maintain control of their own reserves while still employing those reserves efficiently, the Aldrich plan asked them to maintain deposits at 15 district "reserve associations," each of which acted as a branch of a National Reserve Association in Washington. The plan also prohibited reserve associations from paying interest on reserves, while making no change in the National Banking Act's provisions allowing banks to count correspondent balances in reserve city and central reserve city banks as part of their legal reserves. These arrangements were designed to assure city correspondent banks, and the big New

York banks especially, that the new reserve associations would not compete with them for bankers' deposits (McCulley 1992: 238). As Alfred Crozier observes in *U.S. Money vs. Corporation Currency*, an excoriating, 400-page assessment of the Aldrich plan,

> The chief curse and evil of the present banking system is the law that years ago was instigated by Wall Street, under which a large portion of the entire cash of the country held by the banks, nearly one-third of it, by means of the reserve system is concentrated in a few big Wall Street banks. . . . And this Aldrich bill practically makes no change in this reserve system. The banks of the entire country can go on depositing their "cash reserve" in Wall Street, and will do so, because Wall Street banks pay interest on such deposits and the National Reserve Association is prohibited from doing so. (Crozier 1912: 90)

Piatt Andrew, who composed the Commission's report, had no qualms about catering to Wall Street's needs. Almost uniquely among economists at the time, he was himself a champion of unit banking who, instead of seeing it as a source of weakness and instability, waxed poetic over its supposedly egalitarian tendencies. "Nowhere else," he observed, on the eve of the 1907 panic, "will one find such equality of importance among the banks . . . or such mutual independence of action" (White 1983: 86).[22] That the New York banks, whose agenda he helped to carry out, were more "equal" than all the others, doesn't appear to have weakened Andrew's determination to preserve the correspondent system status quo.

To allow Wall Street to steer the Commission to an outcome it considered favorable was one thing; to publicly justify the course taken was another. Aldrich tried to accomplish the last goal by claiming that branch banking was insufficiently popular to have merited the Commission's attention:

> Of course, I realize that there are in this country a great many intelligent men who think we ought to have a system of branch banking like the Canadian [sic]; but unless I greatly mistake the character of the American people that will not be possible. In my judgement any system

> which is to be adopted in this country must recognize the rights and independence of the 25,000 separate banks in the United States. . . .
>
> The men who deposit in or borrow from small country banks, or banks in the large towns, who have been accustomed to dealing with men who are their neighbors and friends who have a sympathetic appreciation of their wants, will not be willing to consent that legislation shall authorize the displacing of such banks by agents sent from the banks of New York or Chicago to conduct business in these smaller communities. (Aldrich 1910: 24)

The palpable weakness of Aldrich's argument betrays its insincerity. If clients of "small" banks really did prefer them to potential interlopers from New York or Chicago, that was a reason for other banks to refrain from entering the smaller banks' markets, rather than one for legally prohibiting such entry. In truth, Aldrich cared not about the well-being of small banks' country clients, but about that of New York bankers who stood to lose their correspondent business if branch banking was permitted.

The Commission's out-of-hand rejection of branch banking was but one component of its general rejection of the asset currency approach to monetary reform in favor of a central bank–based alternative. Instead of drawing attention to the part bond-deposit requirements had played in making the currency supply inelastic, as all previous discussions of the topic had done, the Commission made hardly any mention of it; and far from recommending that those requirements be repealed or at least relaxed, its plan looked forward to the complete replacement of commercially supplied bank notes with those issued by the National Reserve Association.

Aldrich understood perfectly well, of course, that a call for any sort of central bank would face resistance as stiff, if not stiffer, than one for unlimited branch banking. He also understood that his planned National Reserve Association was but a thinly disguised central bank, and that it would be widely recognized as such. Addressing the Economic Club of New York in November 1909, he admitted that the Commission's plan was likely to meet with the objection "that no organization which we may suggest can be adopted on account of political prejudices of the past or of the present"

(Aldrich 1910: 27). But this time, rather than regarding public resistance as fatal, he expected to prevail against it:

> I have the utmost confidence in the intelligence and ultimate good judgement of the American people, and I believe if it should be thought wise by the commission, supported by the consensus of intelligent opinion of the people of the United States, to adopt any system, that neither the political prejudice of the past nor the ghost of Andrew Jackson . . . will stand in the way. (Aldrich 1910: 27)

In the event, the ghost of Andrew Jackson was indeed laid to rest. But if the Commission was able to manage that, surely it might also have managed to overcome objections to branch banking, and therefore to asset currency, had it only been willing to pursue this alternative agenda.

In truth, the Aldrich plan, rather than reflecting the state of public opinion, reflected Aldrich's personal preferences, as informed by his intimate circle of advisers. Of those preferences, the most significant consisted of Aldrich's "conclusion that a central bank was the solution to the United States banking problem," which, according to McCulley (1992: 225), he appears to have arrived at "with unseemly haste" after a long career as Congress's "leading defender of the financial status quo." Here again, Aldrich's preferences aligned with Wall Street's, for the Wall Street bankers, and Vanderlip in particular, had come to see a central bank as the best means for preserving their correspondent business whilst protecting them from the shocks to which that business exposed them.

The first evidence of Aldrich's own conversion to central banking occurs in the National Monetary Commission's fall 1908 European itinerary, which concentrated on the central bank–based arrangements of England, Germany, and France (Dewald 1972: 940).[23] A similar bias is evident in the Commission's publications—nine, five, and three volumes of which are respectively devoted to studies of the German, French, and English banking systems. When these studies were being commissioned, only 21 countries—a third of the world total—had central banks. Yet of the remaining countries, Canada alone is represented, in volumes (both excellent) by Joseph French Johnson

(1910) and Roeliff M. Breckenridge (1910). In short, rather than supplying an objective foundation for the Commission's conclusions, the Commission's studies instead constituted, in Livingston's (1986: 198) words, "a formidable brief on behalf of a central bank."[24]

Nor was there any compelling a priori reason for the central bank–oriented nature of the Commission's investigations. Although Aldrich's claim that the central bank systems that received the lion's share of the Commission's attention had witnessed fewer financial panics than the United States, it was also true, as Calomiris and Haber (2014: 184) note in their survey of banking crises, that "the U.S. was the *only* country in the world still suffering from these kinds of panics at the end of the nineteenth century" (emphasis added).

What is less clear is whether Aldrich intended all along to "prosecute the ideological struggle for central banking," as Livingston (1986: 189) claims, or whether he only "became a convert" to the central banking alternative after visiting the Reichsbank, as Wicker (2005: x) maintains. There is perhaps some truth to both positions. While the Commission's European itinerary itself suggests that some central bank bias was present from the start, according to Warburg, who had long been a lone champion of the central bank alternative, it was only after the European trip that Aldrich, who had previously shown little interest in Warburg's plan, not only expressed his approval of it, but chided Warburg for having been "too timid about it" (Warburg 1930: 56).

WARBURG'S INFLUENCE

That Paul Warburg himself played a major role in shaping the Aldrich plan is beyond doubt. Warburg had favored central banking along German lines ever since his arrival in the United States in 1902, and had been tirelessly campaigning for a U.S. central bank since the beginning of 1907. He first met Aldrich on the day after Christmas 1907. According to Piatt Andrew, although Aldrich "disliked the tenacity with which Warburg would press his points," he also realized that Warburg knew more about central banking than other bankers whose advice he sought. Aldrich had been particularly impressed by

Warburg's speech on "A United Reserve Bank for the United States" (Warburg 1911), which was originally delivered at the New York YMCA on March 23, 1910, with thousands of copies distributed by the New York Merchant's Association. And although, at Jekyll Island, the too-frequently needled senator often cut Warburg off in mid-sentence, he did so "only to reintroduce later the point Warburg had been making as his own" (Gray 1971: 74).

Warburg had no patience for proposals calling for a decentralized asset currency and related, deregulatory reforms. Rather than ever delving into the root causes of U.S. financial instability, as other reformers had done, he took as his starting point the assumption that the German system, with which he was most familiar, was ideal.[25] Noting that that system avoided the "inelasticity" that plagued the U.S. arrangement, he, like many commentators since, concluded that the U.S. currency system was inelastic *because it lacked a central bank*—a diagnosis that allowed for only one cure. In a January 1908 address at Columbia University, for example, Warburg dismissed as "bad" any reform measure "which accentuates decentralization of note issue and of reserves" or "which gives to commercial banks power to issue additional notes against their general assets without restricting them in turn in the scope of their general business, and without creating some additional independent control, endorsement, or guarantee" (Warburg 1930: 25).

A comparison of Warburg's opinion—that the best way to have plenty of cash available for an emergency was to keep it all in a "central reservoir"—with Walter Bagehot's (1873) very different perspective, as set forth in *Lombard Street*, is highly instructive. England had long had what Bagehot termed a "one reserve" banking system. "All London banks," he observed, "keep their principal reserve on deposit in the Banking Department of the Bank of England. This is by far the easiest and safest place for them to use. The Bank of England thus has the responsibility of taking care of it" (p. 27). But far from viewing this concentration of reserves as a blessing, Bagehot saw in it the ultimate cause of British financial instability. "I shall have failed in my purpose," he wrote,

> if I have not proved that the system of entrusting all our reserve to a single board, like that of the Bank directors, is very anomalous; that it is

> very dangerous; that its bad consequences, though much felt, have not been fully seen; that they have been obscured by traditional arguments and hidden in the dust of ancient controversies. (Bagehot 1873: 66)

A far safer alternative, in Bagehot's opinion, was the "natural" one "of many banks of equal or not altogether unequal size," each keeping its own reserves, "which would have sprung up if Government had let banking alone" (Bagehot 1873: 67). It was only because he believed that "[n]othing could persuade the English people to abolish the Bank of England" that Bagehot, instead of proposing that England "return to a natural or many-reserve system of banking" (p. 69), instead offered the now-famous advice that there ought to be

> a clear understanding between the Bank and the public that, since the Bank holds our ultimate banking reserve, they will recognize and act on the obligations which this implies; that they will replenish it in times of foreign demand as fully, and lend in times of internal panic as freely and readily, as plain principles of banking require. (Bagehot 1873: 71)

As if to settle any doubt as to his first-best ideal, Bagehot ended *Lombard Street* with a final apology for having proposed something else:

> I know it will be said that in this work I have pointed out a deep malady, and only suggested a superficial remedy. I have tediously insisted that the natural system of banking is that of many banks keeping their own cash reserves, with the penalty of failure before them if they neglect it. I have shown that our system is that of a single bank keeping the whole reserve under no effectual penalty of failure. And yet I propose to retain that system, and only to mend and palliate it.
>
> I can only reply that I propose to retain this system because I am quite sure it is of no manner of use proposing to alter it. . . . You might as well, or better, try to alter the English monarchy and substitute a republic, as to alter the present constitution of the English money market, founded on the Bank of England, and substitute for it a system

> in which each bank shall keep its own reserve. There is no force to be found adequate to so vast a reconstruction, and so vast a destruction, and therefore it is useless proposing them.
>
> No one who has not long considered the subject can have a notion of how much this dependence on the Bank of England is fixed in our national habits. (Bagehot 1873: 330)

Thus, Warburg, like many central banking apologists since, took as his scientific ideal an arrangement that Bagehot had considered fundamentally unsound. He did this, moreover, despite the fact that the idea of a central reserve bank, far from having been fixed in *American* habits, was one Americans had long opposed.

THE FATE OF THE ALDRICH PLAN

The long interval between the National Monetary Commission's launch and the completion of its report was due to Aldrich's involvement in the tariff debate of 1909, and to his consequent preoccupation with attacks upon him by insurgent Republicans that would ultimately lead to his decision to retire from the Senate. The delay meant that the Aldrich plan could not be completed until after the 1910 election, which gave Democrats a majority in the House for the first time in 16 years. The lame-duck senator's other critics were thus joined by New York bankers, who "publically chastised Aldrich for procrastination that endangered the movement for a central bank" (McCulley 1992: 227).

The plan's hopes now rested on the success of the National Citizens' League—an organization launched in April 1911, at Warburg's urging, to "carry on an active campaign of education and propaganda for monetary reform, on the principles . . . outlined in Senator Aldrich's plan" (Warburg 1930: 569). The league's purpose was to win support for the plan from progressives who tended—with good reason—to regard any scheme with which Aldrich was associated as one hatched by Wall Street. Consequently, Warburg arranged to have its executive committee consist entirely of Chicago businessmen and politicians, with Laurence Laughlin (who, like Vanderlip, had by then abandoned the cause of a fully decentralized asset currency) serving as its chairman. To gain progressives' support for the Aldrich plan, the league argued in favor of its essential elements, while studiously avoiding any reference to it by name, in lectures it sponsored and in *Banking Reform*, its monthly magazine. The league also took pains to insist that the measures it favored, far from catering to Wall Street, or amounting to a call for a central bank, were the best means for avoiding these outcomes.

The National Citizens League was to do more than any other body to overcome Americans' longstanding aversion to the idea of a U.S. central bank. Yet despite the league's efforts, Aldrich's hopes for the success of his own bill were dashed. The bill found no supporters in the Senate. "Republicans were embarrassed by the Aldrich Plan and Democrats were beholden to oppose it" (Lowenstein 2015: 150). The plan's bipartisan trappings fooled no one. Nor did it help that Aldrich chose to submit the plan in his own name. "Certainly," Warburg (1930: 76) later wrote, "it was not to be expected that [Democratic representatives] would endorse a bill which carried the name of the outstanding Republican leader." On the contrary: they considered Aldrich anathema (Lowenstein 2015: 90). Within Aldrich's own party, on the other hand, his plan was opposed by progressives, and especially by Sen. Robert La Follette (R-WI), who detected excessive Wall Street influence. As the November election approached, even Taft himself gave the plan the cold shoulder.

Nor did the Jekyll Island gathering's cloak of secrecy prevent many from concluding that Aldrich's plan was, in fact, a Wall Street concoction. A month before it was finally submitted to Congress, Charles Lindbergh Sr. assailed the plan as a scheme to preserve, and even enhance, the "Money Trust's" share of the nation's bank reserves, by requiring state as well as national banks subscribing to the proposed National Reserve Association to conform to the National Bank Act's reserve requirements (U.S. Congress 1911: 46–47).

Rather than take up the Aldrich bill, the House Banking Committee resolved itself into two subcommittees. The first, assigned to Arsène Pujo (D-LA), who had served on the National Monetary Commission, took on the task of investigating the Money Trust—which is to say, the very same banking interests that had played so prominent a part in shaping the Aldrich plan. The other, headed by Carter Glass (D-VA), a conservative Democrat, was assigned the task of developing an alternative plan for currency reform. Although this division prevented Pujo himself from being made responsible for currency reform, the Money Trust investigations put any plan even vaguely associated with Wall Street on the defensive. This more than countered the National Citizens' League's efforts, while causing its leaders to put as much distance as possible between their own proposals and the one put forward in the name of Aldrich's Commission. Had the true authorship of the Aldrich plan been known at the time, it is doubtful that any measure resembling it would have been passed even by a Republican Congress.

As the November elections loomed, Aldrich's last hope was that Woodrow Wilson, who was looking increasingly strong in his bid for the White House, might favor his plan; as an academic (and a lecturer on economics), Wilson had spoken favorably of European-style central banking. In the course of his campaign, however, Wilson had publicly declared—with noteworthy accuracy—that any plan bearing Aldrich's name "must have been drawn in the offices of the few men who, in the present system of concentrated capital, control the banking and industrial activities of this country" (Lowenstein 2015: 145). Despite every effort, Aldrich's accomplices were unable to prevent Wilson from categorically rejecting the plan for the sake of gaining Bryan's support. It was, in fact, Bryan himself who had drafted most of the Democratic Party's platform, including the plank stating, "We oppose the so-called Aldrich Bill or the establishment of a central bank" (Lowenstein 2015: 164).

But whether Bryan, Wilson, and other Democrats realized it or not, Aldrich's efforts had set the parameters of their own proposal. As Wicker (2005: 6) remarks in his history of the pre-Fed currency reform movement, "The debate no longer centered on whether or not to have a central bank but on what kind of central bank." At least in this one important respect, despite all the opposition they encountered, the National Monetary Commission's efforts—or, more precisely, Aldrich's efforts—were to prove strikingly successful.

THE FEDERAL RESERVE ACT

Despite the defeat of the Aldrich plan, and Democrats' particular determination to have nothing to do with it, many of that plan's essential features ended up being replicated in the Democrats' own reform alternative. That alternative—the Federal Reserve Act—was, as William Dewald (1972: 931) has observed with only slight exaggeration, "fundamentally the same" as the defeated Aldrich bill. Wicker (2005: ix) likewise concludes that "Senator Nelson Aldrich of Rhode Island deserves equal billing with Carter Glass as a cofounder of the Fed." In the first of two massive volumes making up his *History of the Federal Reserve Act*, Paul Warburg himself (1930: 178–406) documents the many similarities between the two measures.[26]

How did the Democratic plan end up being so similar to Aldrich's? First of all, the Democrats, despite their determination to quash the Aldrich bill, had developed no plan of their own as of early 1912. Also, thanks to the efforts of the National Citizens' League and other Aldrich-inspired propaganda, representatives of the banking industry had been won over to the general idea of having some kind of central agency, rather than existing banks themselves, take responsibility for supplying an "elastic" currency. To attempt to redirect bankers' support to any substantially different plan was to risk losing that support altogether.

Most importantly, H. Parker Willis—whom Carter Glass hired to assist him in coming up with a Democratic plan for currency and banking reform, and who would dominate the Glass Committee much as Aldrich had dominated the National Monetary Commission—was a former student and long-time aide of Laurence Laughlin. Laughlin was the University of Chicago economist who, after campaigning for asset currency on behalf of the Indianapolis Monetary Commission, took charge of the Aldrich-inspired National Citizens' League. Whether despite Willis's close connection to Laughlin, or because he was unaware of that connection, Glass hired him on the recommendation of his two sons, who had learned economics from Willis at Washington and Lee University. Consequently, it happened that the economist put in charge of formulating a Democratic plan for currency and banking reform was a protégé of the man who had been among the chief advocates of that plan's Republican rival.

For the Democrats to have openly imitated the Aldrich plan was, of course, out of the question. But this didn't prevent them from allowing many of that plan's main features to be incorporated in new and otherwise more palatable legislation. By taking this approach, they managed to gain for the new plan the support of many who had previously favored the Republican measure, but who realized that the prospects for that measure's passage had melted away. Indeed, despite the fulminations of the National Citizens' League's New York branch, Laughlin eventually offered to throw his own support behind a Democratic plan so long as it retained what he regarded as the essential features of Aldrich's proposal (Kolko 1963: 218–22).[27]

A major obstacle to be overcome was, of course, William Jennings Bryan, who had been "exceedingly disturbed at those provisions of the Glass bill contemplating currency in the form of bank notes rather than greenbacks" (Dunne 1964: 9). Bryan's resistance was, however, ultimately overcome by means of a stipulation—most likely the work of William McAdoo, Woodrow Wilson's secretary of the treasury—making Federal Reserve notes obligations, not only of the Federal Reserve banks themselves, but of the U.S. government (p. 10). A second obstacle was Sen. Robert Owen (D-OK), chairman of the Senate Banking Committee, who favored greater centralization and government representation, and whose sentiments Wilson himself shared. But although both favored an all-government Federal Reserve Board, they also proved willing to settle for one that was merely dominated by government appointees.

Oddly enough, Aldrich himself, in condemning the Federal Reserve Act as "revolutionary, socialistic, and unconstitutional" in an October 1913 speech at the Academy of Political Science at Columbia University, unwittingly contributed to its success: although Aldrich's aim had been that of preventing his own bill's former supporters from supporting Glass's bill instead, he managed, according to Gray (1971: 74), to "convince a number of hitherto wavering members of the Bryan wing of the Democratic party to vote for the Federal Reserve Act" on the grounds that "any bill criticized so vehemently by Aldrich was, ipso facto, a good thing."

Of the differences between the Federal Reserve Act and the Aldrich plan, the least trivial—and the main bone of contention between their respective advocates—had been that, while the 46-member board of the Aldrich plan's National Reserve Association was to consist mainly of bankers chosen by other bankers, the Federal Reserve Board was to consist of seven members only, five of whom, including the secretary of the treasury and the comptroller of the currency (who were members ex officio), were to be appointed by the president. Even this difference was to prove more apparent than real: when the actual board members were chosen, they included Frederic Delano, a former director of the National Citizens' League, and, most hearteningly so far as the Aldrich bill's former proponents were concerned, Paul Warburg. Important posts at the various Federal Reserve banks were also secured by former Aldrich plan proponents, with Benjamin Strong landing what would quickly become the most powerful position of all: governorship of the Federal Reserve Bank of New York. Notwithstanding the appearance of decentralization and government control, control of the Fed had, in fact, been "captured" by Wall Street, which thereby secured for itself a position of dominance over the rest of the U.S. financial system far greater even than that which it had commanded under the previous national bank-note regime.

A DEFECTIVE SOLUTION

Of the more immediate outcomes of the Federal Reserve Act, perhaps none was to prove more disappointing to sincere proponents of reform, including many of that act's champions, than its utter failure to address the pyramiding of bank reserves in New York City, and the consequent employment of such reserves to finance stock purchases. As Lawrence Clark (1935: 346) observed two decades after the Fed's establishment, the tendency of reserves to become concentrated in New York had been one of the most "persistently and vehemently denounced" shortcomings of the national banking system, and one that the Federal Reserve Act was supposed to correct. As Senator

Owen told President Wilson a month before the act gained his signature, one of the measure's "most far-reaching results" would be "to gradually withdraw these reserves, which have heretofore been pyramided in the three great central reserve cities" (p. 348).

Yet instead of countering either Wall Street's influence, or the tendency of reserves to pile up there, the Federal Reserve Act had just the opposite effect. Instead of declining, balances in the three reserve cities grew rapidly, with those in New York growing most rapidly of all. By 1926, banker's balances in New York City national banks were almost $200 million greater than they had been just prior to the Fed's establishment, while the share of such balances belonging to the six-largest banks had risen from 65 percent to almost 78 percent (see Table 6.2). New York City's position also improved relative to that of Chicago and St. Louis, the other central reserve cities (see Figure 6.2). In short, despite what many of the Federal Reserve Act's proponents had anticipated, "the Federal Reserve system . . . made the New York call money market more attractive than it ever was before the establishment of the central banking system" (Clark 1935: 358).

Table 6.2: Bankers' Balances in Six Largest New York National Banks, 1913 and 1926 (Millions of Dollars)

Bank	Bankers' Balances (October 21, 1913)	Bankers' Balances (December 31, 1913)
National Bank of Commerce	66.6	149.9
Chase National	76.0	176.1
First National	54.9	77.3
Hanover National	66.3	82.4
National City	92.5	102.9
National Park	61.7	62.3
Total	418.0	650.9
Total all NYC national banks	641.3	837.2
Six largest as percentage of all NYC banks	65.2%	77.7%

SOURCE: Watkins (1929: 21, Table 4; 60, Table 15).

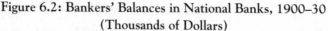

Figure 6.2: Bankers' Balances in National Banks, 1900–30 (Thousands of Dollars)

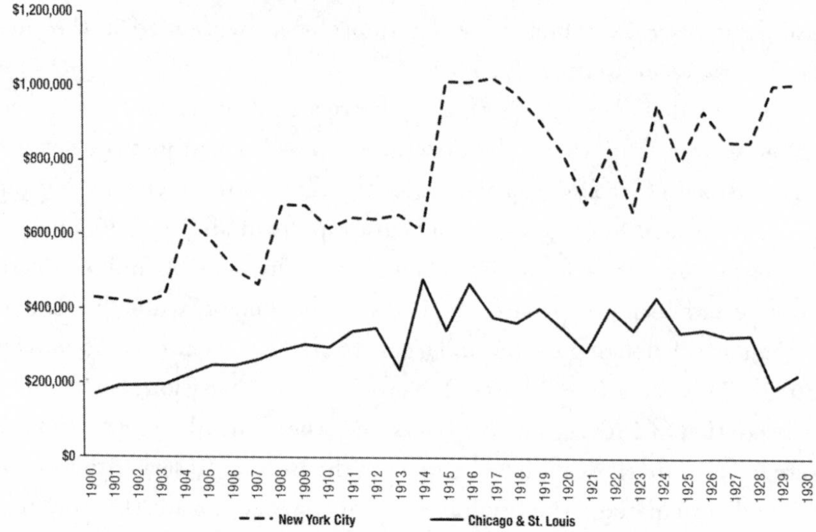

SOURCES: Beckhart and Smith (1932: 203, Chart 19) and Comptroller of the Currency, *Annual Report* (various dates).

Thanks to the new system's reserve requirements, the degree of credit pyramiding—that is, of leveraging of available gold reserves—grew even more dramatically than the concentration of reserves:

> Whereas under the national banking system, the New York City banks had to keep a 25 per cent gold reserve against their deposits, under the Federal Reserve system, they have had to keep only [a] 13 per cent reserve against such deposits, and that not of gold, but of deposit credit in the Federal Reserve Bank. Upon the basis of this 13 per cent reserve, which itself was capable of a huge increase until the ratio of the Reserve Bank's gold to its deposits amounted to 35 per cent, it has been possible to effect the tremendous expansion in the superstructure of credit which has taken place by means of the central banking system. (Clark 1935: 353)

How is it that the Fed, instead of reducing the extent of reserve pyramiding, as intended, ended up doing just the opposite? First of all, the Fed's discount facilities made it appear less likely that New York banks would ever have to suspend payments, and therefore less risky for other banks to send funds to them. In addition, the new arrangement, while reducing overall reserve requirements, still allowed non–New York City banks to keep up to one-third of their required reserves in the form of reserve city bankers' balances, at the discretion of the comptroller of the currency. The Fed was also prevented, just as the Aldrich plan's reserve associations would have been, from competing with reserve city banks by paying interest on its members' reserve balances. Finally, many state banks found that, by refraining from joining the new system while keeping surplus funds in New York, they could gain indirect access to the Fed's discount facilities, whilst still earning interest on their reserves (Calomiris et al. 2015).

As for the Fed's own decentralized arrangement, McCulley (1992: 301) observes that, rather than having served, as was intended, to "dilute Wall Street power," it "enabled the New York Reserve Bank to overshadow the others and to exercise disproportionate influence on the system." And although Democrats assumed that having the president appoint the Federal Reserve Board would guarantee that monetary policy "conformed with the public good rather than banker interest," that assumption also proved to be mistaken. "Some of Wilson's appointees to the board, not to mention those of his less progressive successors, shattered any notion that this procedure necessarily yielded a board not unduly sympathetic to the financial community" (McCulley 1992: 301).

A more important question is, how could the designers of the new system have come up with an arrangement that failed so conspicuously to achieve their avowed objectives? The answer, of course, is that in incorporating large chunks of the Aldrich bill into their own measure, they unwittingly included features calculated by their original authors to enhance, rather than undermine, Wall Street's dominant position.

If the Federal Reserve Act catered to Wall Street almost as effectively as Aldrich's plan might have, it also shared—if it didn't compound—the Republican measure's chief shortcomings. In particular, both measures provided a form of elasticity that Chicago First National Bank President James Forgan (1903: 66) once characterized as being of the (chewing) "gum" rather than "rubber band" sort: they made it possible for the supply of currency to expand when more was needed, but *without* assuring that it would contract as demand subsided.

In his testimony on the Federal Reserve bill before the House Committee on Banking and Currency, Fowler (U.S. Congress 1913: 1876)—by then a private citizen—elaborated upon the "chewing gum" problem by observing, quite correctly, that once a Federal Reserve note was put into circulation, "there will be no natural impulse to send it home, as in the case of a bank credit [i.e., asset] currency." In modern parlance, Federal Reserve notes differed from ordinary, competitively supplied bank notes in being "high-powered" money—that is, money that other banks would treat, not like so many checks in need of collection, but as part of their cash reserves. Fowler also worried that, owing to the proposed structure of the Federal Reserve Board, monetary policy would, in practice, fall under the control of the secretary of the treasury and therefore, indirectly, under that of the president (p. 1901).

That the Federal Reserve Act should have provided so inadequately against the risk of a redundant currency and consequent inflation was ironic, as one fear often raised against asset currency was that *it* could prove redundant, even though, being competitively supplied, it was more likely to be routinely presented for collection. What was said by the Fed's supporters to have been *inadequately* provided for in some asset currency plans wasn't *at all* provided for by the Federal Reserve Act! The Democratic plan, Elihu Root observed in a trenchant critique delivered days before its passage, "provides an expansive currency, but not an elastic one." Furthermore,

> It provides a currency which may be increased, always increased, but not . . . any provision compelling reduction. . . . I am not speaking of what the reserve board may do. . . . The universal experience, sir, is that the tendency of mankind is to keep on increasing the issue of currency. Unless there is some very positive and distinct influence tending toward the process of reduction, that tendency always has . . . produced its natural results, and we may expect it to produce its natural results here. (Root 1913: 12)

Those natural results, Root went on to explain, consisted of "a period of inflation, of false prosperity, and of inevitable catastrophe" (1913: 14).

In reply to Root's remarks, Owen (1913) insisted that such worries were unfounded. "Our currency bill," he said, "does not forecast a period of inflation, to be followed by a hideous panic that will shake the world to its foundations." Instead, Owen argued, Federal Reserve notes

> could not expand or remain expanded beyond the requirements of our commerce, because, unless a bank needed currency, it would not call for these notes, and as soon as the need for currency was past the bank would return the currency to the Reserve Bank and the Reserve Bank would return such currency to the Federal Reserve agents. (Owen 1913)

Owen didn't explain why other banks would bother exchanging Federal Reserve notes for gold or greenbacks when, thanks to their status as government obligations, those notes were themselves practically the same as greenbacks—and more convenient than gold. As for commercial banks exchanging the notes for Federal Reserve credits, that in itself would not threaten the Fed with any loss of reserves and, therefore, could not be counted on to result in any reduction in its balance sheet. The only reserve drain the Fed had to fear, apart from one caused by a run on the dollar itself (as happened in 1933), was an external or foreign one.

Owen's arguments betray his belief in the "real-bills doctrine." That doctrine, to which Willis also subscribed wholeheartedly, held that a bank could never issue too much currency so long as it did so only in exchange for short-term "real" bills (that is, bills of exchange representing inventories or deliveries of actual goods). Although superficially appealing, the doctrine overlooks the fact that the nominal value of real bills presented to a bank, rather than being strictly related to the real value of goods in the process of being finished or sold, depends both on the general level of prices, and on the central bank's discount rate—that is, the rate at which it agrees to supply cash in exchange for immature commercial IOUs. The lower the discount rate, the greater the volume of bills that banks will be tempted to discount, and the greater the increase in the money stock. If the rate is sufficiently low, the money stock will increase to the point where prices begin to rise, increasing the nominal quantity of real bills. Consequently, a vicious cycle of expansion can occur, with prices rising without limit, despite strict adherence to the real-bills rule. If paper currency is redeemable in gold, requests for redemption will ultimately put a stop to the inflation by forcing issuers to either raise their discount rates or default—but perhaps not without triggering a crisis.[28]

While the convertibility of paper notes into gold also limits monetary expansion in a decentralized asset currency system like the ones Fowler proposed, and does so regardless of the assets backing the notes, the check involved in that case is much more immediate. In a decentralized system, the different banks of issue pursue independent discount policies, and those that discount too liberally face immediate gold (or legal tender) losses as a result of regular interbank settlements. A systematic overissuance of notes is therefore unlikely to continue to the point of causing inflation.[29]

It would not be long before events proved Owen's confidence misplaced, while vindicating Root's pessimism. Although Federal Reserve currency did indeed prove more elastic than national bank notes had been, its elasticity was far from being the sort needed to achieve financial stability.

Although the Federal Reserve avoided inflation at first, it proved far less successful than its proponents promised it would be in accommodating seasonal peaks in the demand for currency and credit, and in thereby reducing the tendency for interest rates to rise every autumn. Although, as Jeff Miron (1986) and others have shown, interest rates exhibited less seasonal variation in the years immediately following the Fed's establishment, until 1917 the improvement appears to have been due not to Federal Reserve actions, but to wartime gold inflows (Fishe 1991). It was only following the June 1917 amendments to the Federal Reserve Act, relaxing the backing requirements for Federal Reserve notes, that the Fed found itself able to fully accommodate seasonal peaks in currency demand (Fishe 1991).

But the 1917 amendments were implemented, not so the Fed might meet the public's seasonal currency needs, but so it could serve the government as an instrument of inflationary war finance (Fishe 1991: 314–16). Just as Fowler had predicted, once the United States entered the war, the Fed proceeded to operate as if it were a branch of the Treasury. Although, as Jim Grant (2014: 53; see also Timberlake 1993: 258) explains, the Fed did not simply "shovel funds directly into the Treasury," it did the next-best thing, "lending against the collateral of Treasury securities at artificially low rates," so that member banks might in turn finance, at equally favorable rates, both their own and their customers' purchases of Liberty Bonds. According to Friedman and Schwartz (1963: 221), virtually all of the 75 percent increase in the U.S. money stock between 1916 and 1920 went, directly or indirectly, toward financing the war effort. During the same period, general prices nearly doubled.

Nor did it take long for Root's "inevitable catastrophe" to materialize. Freed by the Armistice from its role in war finance, the Fed first allowed interest rates to rise and then, starting in November 1919, began tightening in earnest in an effort to curtail inflation. Although the Dow Jones Industrial Average rallied one last time between early 1918 and the autumn of 1919, more than making up for the decline it suffered during the half-year following the U.S. decision to enter the war, in October 1919 another decline commenced which, by August 1921, had wiped out those post-1918 gains. The decline in stocks heralded an even more rapid decline in general prices—the severest on record. Wholesale prices fell by almost 37 percent between January 1920 and July 1921, while consumer prices declined by roughly half that amount. Even so, the declines weren't rapid enough to prevent a sharp increase in unemployment and an accompanying sharp decline in real output—proportionately larger, according to Victor Zarnowitz (1996), than any witnessed between the Civil War and the Fed's establishment.

The 1930s would, of course, witness still more severe crises, including a series of banking panics. To say, as Michael Bordo and David Wheelock (2013: 59) do, that during that episode "the Fed's performance as lender of last resort . . . failed to live up to the promises of those who designed the System," is to indulge in understatement.[30] Those authors neither understate nor exaggerate, however, in blaming the recurrence of banking crises on the Federal Reserve Act's failure "to replace the crisis-prone unit banking system with a more stable, concentrated branch banking system" (p. 61).

By most measures the post-1914 economy was, in fact, less stable than the pre-Fed economy had been. According to Miron, comparing the 25-year period commencing with Fed's establishment with the preceding 25-year period, one finds that

> the variance of both the rate of growth of output and of the inflation rate increased significantly, while the average rate of growth of output fell, and real stock prices became substantially more volatile.

Miron reports, furthermore, that "all of these conclusions hold even when one excludes the Great Depression from the post-Fed sample period," and that the deterioration in stability, far from having been a result of developments that were beyond the Fed's control, can be attributed directly to its actions (1988: 2).

In Chapter 8 of this volume, my coauthors and I survey the entire post–Federal Reserve macroeconomic record. We find that

> (1) the full Fed period has been characterized by more rather than fewer symptoms of monetary and macroeconomic instability than the decades leading to the Fed's establishment; (2) while the Fed's performance has undoubtedly improved since World War II, even its postwar performance has not clearly surpassed that of its (undoubtedly flawed) predecessor; and (3) alternative arrangements exist that might do better than the presently constituted Fed has done. (p. 212)

LESSONS FROM THE NATIONAL MONETARY COMMISSION

The National Monetary Commission did make positive contributions to the cause of monetary reform. In particular, as William Dewald (1972: 932) has observed, it "played a constructive role in establishing interest and understanding in monetary reform both in Congress and nationwide." It did so most obviously through its many publications. "Whatever may be the legislative outcome of the Commission's labors," Wesley Mitchell (1911: 593) quite justly observed after most of these had appeared, "it has already performed a notable service by gaining fresh and diffusing old knowledge of the objects with which it deals."

Just as impressive, and considerably more influential, than the Commission's lengthy list of publications was the nationwide education campaign launched by Aldrich and his associates, which, as Wicker (2005: 6) notes, "did more than perhaps anything else to increase public support for a central bank." The campaign's success, despite Americans' almost universal opposition to a central bank at the time of the Aldrich-Vreeland Act's passage, was certainly the Commission's most impressive and enduring achievement. That even the Democratic Party, whose opposition to a central bank had been especially fierce, was compelled to embrace the idea, made the campaign's success especially remarkable.

But remarkable as the National Monetary Commission's achievements were, they were matched by no less remarkable shortcomings that did lasting damage to the cause of monetary reform. These consisted most obviously of the fact that, appearances notwithstanding, the Commission was in truth a mere façade behind which Aldrich led his own one-man monetary reform campaign. Aldrich's domination of the Commission's proceedings had many unfortunate consequences. It turned what was supposed to be a bipartisan effort into a blatantly partisan one and, by doing so, linked the fate of the Commission's recommendations to that of the Republican Party, as well as to Aldrich's own popularity within that party. Finally, and most unfortunately, it introduced a strong pro–central bank bias into the Commission's proceedings, including its publications and educational efforts, while altogether dismissing the initially more popular and arguably superior asset currency alternative. That the United States established a central bank when it did was, to a surprising degree, the accidental result of one man's having been led to embrace that solution, while dismissing alternatives, after a long career in which he showed no interest at all in monetary reform, except to the extent needed to stand firmly in its way.

Aldrich's preference for a central bank solution reflected another of the National Monetary Commission's serious shortcomings, to wit: its having catered to Wall Street, even to the point of allowing powerful representatives of the New York City banking interests to determine its plan for reform. It was only to be expected that Wall Street would favor a plan protective of its interests—and of New York's correspondent banking business in particular—while opposing any alternative that might harm those interests. For that reason, the public was right to be suspicious of Wall Street's involvement, and had to be kept in the dark concerning its extent—something that would not have been possible had control of the Monetary Commission been more widely shared.

Might a new monetary commission avoid the National Monetary Commission's shortcomings? I believe it could, if properly designed. Such a commission would first of all have to meet the requirements set forth by the Indianapolis Board of Trade, in its 1896 memorial laying the groundwork for the Indianapolis Monetary Commission. "No [currency reform] movement could or should succeed," wrote the memorialists, "that is not based upon the broadest possible justice and intelligence, and the entire interest of the whole people" (Laughlin 1898: 3). Consequently, they continued, responsibility for conducting needed investigations and framing legislation based on them

> should only be entrusted to those who are great enough to rise above all party relation and prejudice, to discard all former ideas when confronted with better methods, and fairly and honestly deal with the great question for the general good and for defense against instability of values, which has caused such immeasurable losses to the people of this country within the few years just past. (Laughlin 1898: 3)

For their part, the Board of Trade's governors, in resolving to heed these principles in forming the Indianapolis Commission, observed that

> The commission to be ultimately selected must be of such attainments and character as not only to allay all suspicion of any influence of class or sectional interest, but it must be of such fitness as to inspire the confidence in the mind of the fair-minded citizen of the republic that its work will be done for the permanent welfare of the whole nation. (Laughlin 1898: 6)

That Representative Brady's statement of the principles informing his Centennial Monetary Commission proposal resembles the Indianapolis declarations from 110 years ago is encouraging. Brady writes,

> In thinking about a national monetary commission, one must start with the question, What are the characteristics, and what is the design of a commission that produces a solid result? First it has to be open-process, which I would call brutally bipartisan. It has to be equally balanced between parties, equally balanced between policymakers within Congress, and include bright minds and thinkers outside of Congress as well. It needs to allow for a fair fight, in which the best and brightest ideas on monetary policy going forward can prevail. (Brady 2014: 393)

The experience of the National Monetary Commission points to the particular importance of having as chair of any new commission someone—whether a politician or a "thinker outside Congress"—with a reputation for independence and open-mindedness.

It is also encouraging, in light of past experience, to note that Brady seems determined to have the new commission avoid the Wall Street influence that tainted its predecessor's proceedings. "Among our problems right now," he writes, "is that our current monetary policy has tilted the playing field in favor of Wall Street and away from average working families in America" (2014: 390). Awareness of the Fed's origins suggests that the tilt, far from being a recent development, is a defect built into the Fed's very foundation.

Calling for avoidance of undue Wall Street influence is one thing. Achieving it is another. What practical steps must a Centennial Monetary Commission take if it is to avoid becoming a plaything of powerful vested interests within the financial industry? Most obviously, a new commission must avoid letting representatives of major financial firms from Wall Street and elsewhere, and especially ones whose firms have benefited from the Federal Reserve's largesse, sit on the commission or otherwise play any direct part in shaping its report or proposal. Instead, the commission's members, whether congressmen or outside experts, should be free of any close ties to Wall Street or of any affiliation with financial industry special interests.

But that's not all. The overseers of the new commission must also recognize in the Federal Reserve itself an extremely powerful financial institution that has a stake greater than all others in the monetary status quo, and that is likely to oppose any reform that might reduce its current discretionary and regulatory powers and privileges. The alacrity with which Fed officials recently opposed legislation that would merely have allowed for unrestricted U.S. Government Accountability Office "audits" (that is, investigations) of the Fed's activities, supplies ample proof of this.[31]

Yet forming a new monetary commission that avoids undue Federal Reserve influence will be anything but easy. In its current form, the proposed Centennial Monetary Commission provides for two nonvoting members, one of whom is to be appointed by the secretary of the treasury, and the other of whom is to be "the president of a district Federal Reserve bank appointed by the Chair of the Board of Governors of the Federal Reserve System."[32] This provision alone must introduce some status quo bias into the commission's proceedings. But even if it didn't, and even if no other Federal Reserve officials took part, the danger of such a bias would not necessarily be avoided. As Lawrence H. White (2005) has shown, the Fed employs more monetary economists full time than all the major academic research departments combined, while employing many others either part time or as occasional visitors. Fed-associated economists also dominate the editorial boards of the leading scholarly monetary economics journals, thereby indirectly influencing the research agendas of monetary economists not otherwise connected to the Fed, especially (according to Boston College professor Ed Kane) by encouraging them to take for granted the existing, Fed-dominated monetary control system, while ignoring "the broader principal-agent conflicts comprised in the information and incentives subsystems of monetary policy-making" (Kane 1990: 290). Of all the hurdles the proposed Centennial Monetary Commission must overcome, none is likely to prove more challenging than that of locating qualified participants who, though well informed about the monetary status quo, are also prepared to objectively assess reforms that do more than tinker with it.

PART III

THE FEDERAL RESERVE ERA

7

THE RISE AND FALL OF THE GOLD STANDARD IN THE UNITED STATES*

THERE IS, IN informal discussions and even in some academic writings, a tendency to treat U.S. monetary history as divided between a gold standard past and a fiat dollar present. For some, the dividing line marks the baleful abandonment of a venerable pillar of sound money; for others, it marks the long-overdue deconsecration of an antediluvian relic.

In truth, the "money question"—which is to say, the question concerning the proper meaning of a "standard" U.S. dollar—was hotly contested throughout most of U.S. history. Partly for this reason, a functioning (if not formally acknowledged) gold standard was in effect only for a period comprising less than a quarter of the full span of U.S. history, surrounded by longer periods during which the dollar was either a bimetallic (gold *or* silver) or a fiat unit. A review of the history of the gold standard in the United States must therefore consist of an account both of how the standard came into being, despite not having been present at the country's inception, and of how it eventually came to an end.

THE GOLD STANDARD DEFINED

Any history of the gold standard must begin with a clear description of what such a standard is and, no less importantly, what it isn't. In a genuine gold standard, the basic monetary unit is a specific weight of gold alloy of some

* Originally published as Cato Institute Policy Analysis no. 729 (June 2013). An earlier version was prepared for the Hillsdale College Free Market Forum on "Markets, Governments, and the Common Good," Houston, Texas (October 4–5, 2012).

specific purity, or its equivalent in fine gold, and prices are expressed in the unit or in some fractional units based upon it. Assuming that coinage is a government monopoly, the government offers to convert gold bullion into "full-bodied" gold coins, representing either the standard unit itself or multiples or fractions thereof, in unlimited amounts. This policy of providing for the unlimited minting of gold bullion is known as "free" coinage. Money is created through public demand to convert bullion to coin.

That coinage is "free" doesn't necessarily mean that persons bringing bullion to the mint don't pay a fee to have it coined. Coinage might be "gratuitous," with minting costs paid out of public funds; but the mint might instead deduct the costs of coin manufacture, or "brassage," and even some profit or "seigniorage," from the amount of coin it supplies in exchange for bullion. In that case, coins will command a premium above their bullion value representing the total coinage fee, and the monetary unit can be understood to stand either for the weight of fine gold that must be surrendered in order to obtain the nominal equivalent in gold coin, or for its coined representative.

The other requirement of a genuine gold standard is that actual exchange media other than full-bodied coins themselves must consist either of paper money that is readily convertible, by either domestic or foreign holders, into full-bodied coin, or of "token" or "subsidiary" coins, generally representing small fractions of the standard money unit, that may consist of other metals but that are rated well above their metallic worth. The value of such coins, which are necessarily coined not freely but on the government's own initiative, derives either from direct limitation of their quantity or from their also being made freely redeemable in full-bodied coin.

As for what a gold standard is *not*, it is not, first of all, a standard or "measure" of *value*. Under a gold standard, prices—not "values"—are expressed in gold units, and those prices indicate nothing more concerning values than that sellers of goods value the gold in question more than the goods they are prepared to exchange for it. The treatment of the gold standard as a "standard of value" invites the mistaken conclusion that, insofar as it does not rule out variations in the general level of prices, such a standard must be "inaccurate" and therefore faulty. The conclusion is mistaken both because it rests upon a faulty analogy and because inflation and deflation, whether under a gold standard or under any other sort of monetary standard, are not necessarily symptoms of either a superabundance or a shortage of money.[1]

Nor is the existence of a gold standard a matter of gold coins having "legal tender" status. Such a status, though it may play a role in establishing or propping up a gold standard, is neither necessary nor sufficient to sustain such a standard. In fact, although some U.S. states employed their constitutional right to make either gold or silver legal tender, the federal government, which was ultimately responsible for the establishment of the gold standard in the United States, never made any sort of money legal tender until 1862, when it conferred that status, not upon gold, but upon greenbacks.

Substantial "backing" of paper money by gold is also both unnecessary and insufficient to make such paper "as good as gold." For that, what's usually required is unrestricted convertibility of paper money into gold coin, for which fractional gold reserves not only may suffice, but in practice usually have sufficed. Thus, "silver certificates" issued by the U.S. Treasury between 1878 and 1933, though "backed" by silver, were worth their nominal value—not in the silver for which they were exchanged (the market value of which was well below its then-inoperative mint value), but in gold, thanks to the limited number of certificates issued and (after 1890) to their being redeemable for gold.

To say that a genuine gold standard doesn't call for any particular degree of "backing" of paper money by gold is to insist, contra both Milton Friedman (1961a) and Murray Rothbard (1962), that a gold standard can be genuine without being "pure." That is, the standard is genuine despite the presence of paper money (or spendable bank deposits) backed by assets apart from gold itself. The emergence of redeemable substitutes for gold coin, backed only by fractional gold reserves and consisting either of circulating notes or transferable deposit credits, appears to have been both an inevitable occurrence as well as one that, despite setting the stage for occasional crises, has also contributed greatly to economic prosperity.

A genuine gold standard must, nevertheless, provide for *some* actual gold coins if paper currency is to be readily converted into metal even by persons possessing relatively small quantities of the former. A genuine gold standard is therefore distinct from a gold "bullion" standard of the sort that several nations, including the United States, adopted between the two world wars. The Bank of England, for example, was then obliged to convert its notes into 400 fine ounce gold bars only, making the minimum conversion amount, in circa 1929 units, £1,699, or $8,269.

Equally mistaken is the claim that a gold standard is an instance of government price fixing. Although the claim has some merit in the case of certain degenerate forms of the gold standard, in which responsibility for converting paper claims into gold has been placed entirely in the hands of public or semipublic authorities that might repudiate that responsibility with impunity, a genuine gold standard arrangement is one in which the convertibility of paper money into gold rests upon a binding contractual obligation that is no more an instance of price-fixing than, say, the obligation of a cloakroom to redeem claim tickets in the coats or hats originally handed over in exchange for them. In a genuine gold standard, in other words, it makes no sense to speak of exchanges of paper claims for gold as so many "purchases" or "sales" at fixed "prices."

Finally, a gold standard needn't be either established or administered by government. In principle, it might be a purely market-based arrangement, with private mints supplying gold coins and private banks supplying both notes and deposits redeemable in privately minted gold.[2] In practice, however, the universal tendency of governments to monopolize the minting of coins of all sorts made those same governments responsible for establishing and administering metallic monetary standards, with free (if not gratuitous) coinage serving as the approximate, monopolistic equivalent of competitive coinage.

THE BIMETALLIC DOLLAR

The first steps toward establishing an official U.S. monetary standard were taken prior to the Constitutional Convention. In 1785, Congress made the Spanish (silver) dollar the United States' official unit of account; and in 1786, the Board of Treasury fixed the weight of that dollar at 375 and 64/100s grains of fine silver. (A troy ounce of gold, in comparison, is equivalent to 480 grains of fine gold.) These steps pointed toward a (monometallic) silver standard, but as yet no actual coining had been provided for.

The Constitution itself granted Congress "the power to coin money" as well as to "regulate the value thereof." In exercising this power, Congress passed the Coinage Act of April 2, 1792. The act established the U.S. dollar—a somewhat lightened version of its former Spanish counterpart—as the United States' basic monetary unit, providing for the free coinage of silver into dollar coins containing 371.25 grains of pure silver. But as the act also provided for the free coinage of gold into 10-dollar "eagles" containing 247.5 grains of pure gold, it made the new dollar not a silver unit but a bimetallic one, standing either for a definite amount of silver or for a different but no less definite amount of gold.

Why bimetallism? Because, apart from being the arrangement most familiar to the founders, owing to its long employment in the British Isles, bimetallism had the advantage of being capable of providing the nation with exchange media covering a wide range of desirable denominations with a minimum need for either bank-issued paper or token coins. Full-bodied gold coins would be too valuable to serve conveniently as anything other than money of fairly large denominations, while full-bodied silver coins would be suitable for smaller denominations, but not for larger ones. Though paper money and token coins might in contrast serve for all denominations, the former was anathema to at least some of the Founders, while the latter was at best a necessary evil, to be adopted only for those tiny denominations for which even silver wasn't suitable, and even then with trepidation, owing to the risk (all too familiar from both British and colonial experience) of rampant counterfeiting.[3]

The first Coinage Act established a ratio of mint "prices" for gold and silver that made an ounce of gold worth 15 times as many dollars as an ounce of silver. When the act was passed, this mint ratio was more or less the same as the ratio of the two metals' world market prices. Under the circumstances, either gold or silver bullion might be brought to the mint for coining, to satisfy a perceived need for coins of either metal, allowing bimetallism to be fully operative. But if for any reason the market ratio came to differ substantially from the mint ratio, the metal that was relatively undervalued at the mint would cease to flow there. For this reason, and because the relative market prices of gold and silver tend to change—sometimes substantially—official bimetallism might in practice degenerate into de facto "alternating" monometallism, with a de facto silver standard in one period giving way to a de facto gold standard in the next.

Even before the new U.S. Mint was completed in Philadelphia, a few years after the Coinage Act had passed, the world gold-to-silver market price ratio rose substantially above 15:1. It then became profitable for the mint's clients to exchange gold for silver in the open market, since the silver could in turn be rendered into more dollars than the gold itself would have yielded. Consequently, the flow of gold to the new mint, feeble from the start, eventually stopped altogether, and although the United States remained officially committed to bimetallism, for much of the period from 1792 until 1834, it was really on a silver standard, with extant gold coins being sold for their commodity value instead of circulating by tale (that is, at face value).

The Appalachian gold discoveries of the early decades of the 19th century caused the price of gold to decline, but not enough to stop it from being legally undervalued. The new gold mining interests, however, pressured Congress to raise gold's mint price so as to revive gold coinage. In fact, Congress did more than that: while the world market gold-to-silver price ratio in 1834 was about 15.625:1, Congress made the new gold dollar consist of just 23.2 grains of gold, implying a mint price for gold of just under $20.672 dollars per ounce, and a corresponding mint ratio just above 16:1.[4] The new ratio was, therefore, almost as far *above* the market ratio as the old mint ratio had been below it. The predictable result was, not an operational bimetallic standard, but a switch from de facto silver monometallism to de facto gold monometallism.[5] From 1834 onward, silver coinage would be limited, either by necessity or by design, to fractional "token" coins which, being rated well above their metal content, were minted only by government order.

The California and Australian gold finds of 1848 and 1851, by quadrupling world gold output, placed further downward pressure on the value of gold, reinforcing the effect of the 1834 legislation and assuring that the U.S. mint equivalents would continue indefinitely to sponsor a de facto gold standard. By 1859, the market ratio was again close to where it had been in 1792, which meant that, at a mint equivalent of 16:1, there was little likelihood of a revival of silver coinage, or of silver being employed to pay off debts contracted on a gold basis.

THE GREENBACK ERA

The rapidly mounting expenses of the Civil War caused both sides in the conflict to resort to inconvertible paper money. With the exception of the banks of New Orleans, which continued to remit specie until ordered to cease doing so by the Confederate government in Richmond in September 1861, banks throughout what was to become the Confederacy suspended specie payments shortly after South Carolina seceded. Their suspensions were eventually sanctioned, subject to varying conditions, by state authorities, allowing the banks in question to advance a substantial part of their still-considerable specie reserves to the Confederate Treasury, which arranged to pay for it with paper notes. Although the first such notes were for large denominations not intended to serve as currency, the Confederacy soon issued large amounts of smaller denomination paper that would serve as the region's standard money until the North's victory rendered it worthless.

In the Union, Salmon P. Chase, Lincoln's first secretary of the treasury, discovered upon taking office that the government had available "less than $2,000,000, all of which was appropriated ten times over" (Hammond 1957: 720). Between his appointment and June 1861, the Treasury had expenditures of $23.5 million against receipts of only $5.8 million; on July 1, 1861, when the national debt had risen to $90 million, Chase informed Congress that the government needed another $320 million.

The immediate cause of suspension in the Union was a decision by Chase that warrants the adjective "Jacksonian." Having convinced the bankers of New York, Boston, and Philadelphia to collectively purchase $50 million in Treasury securities, with the option of buying two further installments of the same size, Chase surprised them by insisting that they actually deliver $50 million in gold to the subtreasury, instead of allowing the loan to take the form of deposit balances credited to the government that it might in turn draw upon by check. Chase thus ignored an August 5, 1861, reform allowing commercial banks to serve as government depositories and, by so doing, made it impossible for banks to go on meeting the Treasury's needs without suspending specie payments. Finally, on December 30, 1861, the banks, finding their specie holdings cut in half, with many on the verge of violating their minimum reserve requirements, suspended. The Treasury, in turn, had to suspend payment on the $5, $10, and $20 "Demand Notes" it had been using to pay the Union's military expenses since August 1861.

The change in Demand Notes' status from redeemable to unredeemable currency paved the way for the passage of the first Legal Tender Act on February 25, 1862, authorizing the issuance of $150 million in "United States Notes"—better known as "greenbacks"—which were to be legal tender except for the payment of custom duties and interest on government bonds.[6] Two subsequent Legal Tender acts expanded the ceiling to $450 million. The scale of the new issues would eventually cause prices to rise substantially, while causing gold to command a substantial premium relative to its (currently inoperative) mint price. That premium meant that greenbacks had supplanted gold as the North's medium of account.

In California and Oregon, however, the greenbacks were themselves treated as a commodity rather than as money, thanks to merchants' refusal to either accept them or pay them out to their customers—a refusal informed by the prior prohibition of banks of issue in both states (Lester 1939: 161–71). The West Coast thus remained on a gold standard, keeping some $25 million in metallic money in open circulation after such money had all but vanished from the rest of the country, avoiding almost all of the inflation that afflicted the rest of the country, and proving that a gold standard can prevail despite legal tender legislation favoring an altogether different standard.

After the South's defeat, the general consensus was that specie (meaning, given the relative world values of gold and silver at the time, gold) payments ought to be resumed, with most favoring a return to the prewar gold parity. But as the price level had approximately doubled in the course of the war, and the market price of gold was as yet 50 percent above its former mint price, restoring the old parity would require considerable deflation, which could only be achieved by either contracting the nominal stock of government currency or by allowing real output growth to bring prices down gradually.

Congress at first let Hugh McCulloch, Lincoln's third secretary of the treasury, pursue his preferred policy of "immediate and persistent contraction of the currency." But once faced with the painful side effects, including increased unemployment, arising from McCulloch's harsh prescription, Congress was compelled, first, to reduce the rate of greenback contraction and then, in February 1868, to end the contraction altogether in favor of letting the economy "grow up" to its still-enlarged money stock (Timberlake 1993: 88–91).

Unfortunately, the economy grew only very slowly in the years immediately following this change, and then contracted after the Panic of 1873, which dealt resumption a further setback by provoking the issuance of another $26 million in greenbacks. Progress toward resumption was finally renewed thanks to the Resumption Act of January 1875, which provided for further contraction of the stock of U.S. notes from the $382 million then outstanding to $300 million. To overcome opposition to monetary contraction from "greenbackists"—a mainly agrarian movement that favored currency expansion to combat deflation—that act also removed a previous ceiling on the overall quantity of national bank notes, while providing that only $80 in greenbacks could be retired for every $100 addition to the quantity of such notes. The measure thus allayed greenbackists' fears. The catch, whether intended as such or not, was that greenback retirements were based on *gross* rather than net increases in national bank-note circulation—that is, on the extent of new national bank-note issues not adjusting for the fact that some of these issues merely compensated for the redemption of previously outstanding notes. So, notwithstanding appearances to the contrary, the new policy led to a reduction in the quantity of both forms of currency (Timberlake 1993: 112).

BIMETALLISM ABANDONED

At last, on January 1, 1879, specie payments were officially resumed. As had been anticipated at the war's end, "specie," in practice, meant gold. But while the revival of a de facto gold standard would have been the natural outcome of official bimetallism in 1865, in 1879 that outcome was something else altogether: it was—at least as far as champions of silver or genuine bimetallism were concerned—nothing less than a "crime."

The so-called "Crime of '73" refers to the failure of the Coinage Act signed by President Ulysses S. Grant in February of that year to provide for the coinage of full-bodied or standard silver dollars. This failure meant that, once resumption of metallic payments was achieved, the mint's undertaking to coin silver freely would remain a dead letter, with silver employed only in making subsidiary coins, despite a substantial decline in silver's relative world price. Although the measure and its potential consequences were scarcely noticed at first, after 1875, when the world gold-to-silver price ratio began to rise well above 16:1, and especially after 1879 when specie payments were at last resumed, the reality that silver had been quietly demonetized became increasingly evident. Indeed, after two subsequent decades of persistent deflation, this development came to occupy center stage in American politics. The occasion was the presidential election of 1896, in which the Democrats chose William Jennings Bryan, a prominent free silver advocate, to run against William McKinley.

Earlier administrations had quieted the movement to revive free silver coinage by passing the Bland-Allison Act of 1878 and the Sherman Silver Purchase Act of 1890. Although neither measure restored the free coinage of silver, the first called upon the Treasury to purchase and coin into dollars on its own account up to $4 million of silver per month. The second increased the monthly purchases to $6 million while allowing those extra purchases to be paid for using new Treasury notes. The last step, however, almost caused the gold standard to come to grief when, during the Panic of 1893, the Treasury was only able to meet large-scale Treasury note redemptions thanks to last-minute support from a bankers' syndicate. The perception that it had contributed to the panic caused the Silver Purchase Act to be repealed on November 1, 1893. It was against this background that Bryan gave his famous "cross of gold" speech and otherwise made free silver a central plank in the Democratic Party platform. But while Bryan managed thereby to become the nominee of both the Democratic and Populist parties, he failed to win over urban wage earners, who feared the prospect of a free-silver-based inflation as much as farmers and silver miners welcomed it.

McKinley's victory put an end to any immediate prospect of a revival of bimetallism. The Gold Standard Act, passed on March 14, 1900, proved something of an anticlimax, but it was more than a mere formality. It was intended to end, once and for all, speculation that the United States might once again "do something for silver" by reinstating the free coinage of that metal.

Why had the U.S. financial community favored the demonetization of silver? Had bimetallism proved to be inherently flawed? Not according to Milton Friedman (1992: 155): "Far from being a thoroughly discredited fallacy," he writes, "bimetallism has much to recommend it, on theoretical, practical, and historical grounds, as superior to monometallism." Until the post-1848 increase in world gold production, the French market was big enough to make France's bimetallic ratio of 15.5:1 the dog that wagged the world market price ratio tail. That outcome was attributable in part to John Law's infamous paper money scheme, which instilled in the French a lasting aversion to paper money.

Silver's relatively low value was also no reason for abandoning it. Gold monometallists sometimes argued that a progression from less to more precious metal was a "natural" if not inevitable consequence of progress, with its accompanying increase in the average size of economic transactions. Therefore, just as Rome eventually gave up bronze for silver, the United States and other industrializing nations were bound, they insisted, eventually to give up silver for gold. But the tendency in question, much as it may have operated in ancient times, ceased to do so after the development of reliable bank money and token coins, which made the bulkiness of full-bodied coins irrelevant, and did so even to the point of allowing such coins to be largely dispensed with.

Neither was the variability of silver's relative price a reason for demonetizing the metal. On the contrary, as Friedman (1992: 154) observes, silver's real price was actually less variable than gold's during the century that followed Britain's official abandonment of bimetallism in 1819. Moreover, had Britain abandoned gold rather than silver, its decision, by encouraging other nations to make the same choice, might eventually have caused gold rather than silver to become known as "the restless metal."

In short, there is no good reason for supposing that commercial considerations alone made a prosperous nation's unilateral transition from either a silver standard or bimetallism to a gold standard especially desirable, much less inevitable. Instead, the most important factor favoring the U.S. switch was simply that so many other nations had already switched to gold, or were in the process of doing so. That the advantages of any sort of money depend positively on how widely it is employed makes money a quintessential "network" good; and this in turn means that, as the international popularity of any particular monetary standard increases, it becomes a more attractive bandwagon for other nations to jump on.

Great Britain's own decision to officially abandon silver was, again according to Friedman (1992: 156), "the pebble that started an avalanche" favoring gold. Britain's example was especially influential because Britain's financial preeminence made stable exchange rates between sterling and other currencies particularly desirable (Gallarotti 1995: 141–80). That preeminence itself came more and more to be understood, rightly or wrongly, as having been aided by Britain's decision to embrace gold (Feavearyear 1963: 212–13).

The response to Britain's decision was nevertheless slow in coming. At first, network effects favored bimetallism at the French ratio, if they favored any particular metallic system. The gold finds of 1848 and 1850 fortuitously reaffirmed Britain's decision to abandon its "ancient standard." But a genuine golden "avalanche" didn't begin until Germany joined Britain in the aftermath of the Franco-Prussian war, tipping the scales decisively in gold's favor. Between 1870 and American resumption in 1879, numerous countries embraced gold monometallism. France itself ended free coinage of silver on September 6, 1873, while the rest of the Latin Monetary Union followed in 1876. But it was above all Germany's decision to switch to gold that prompted the United States to demonetize silver, both by making the gold network larger than its main rivals and by boosting the world gold-to-silver price ratio to an extent that threatened to prevent the United States from ever joining that network unless it took steps to close its mints to silver.[7]

THE "CLASSICAL" GOLD STANDARD

Great Britain's own switch to gold was far from deliberate. The pound "sterling" originally referred to a pound weight (troy), or 5,560 grains, of silver, or its equivalent in silver coin. But subsequent debasements reduced the pound's silver content. In early Tudor times, one troy pound of sterling silver was divided into 20 silver shillings, each containing a mere 144 grains of metal. The Great Debasement of the reigns of Henry VIII and Edward VI took the reduction of the pound's silver content much further, giving rise to the "60-shilling" standard (that is, a standard by which 60 silver shillings, or the equivalent of three nominal pounds sterling, were cut from one troy pound of silver) which prevailed until 1601, when it in turn gave way to the 62-shilling standard, which was to prevail, officially, until the early 19th century.

Although several attempts were made between 1489 and 1662 to introduce a gold "pound" or 20 shilling coin, the gold coins in question all ended up commanding more than their intended values, thanks either to the debasement of the silver coinage or to the relative appreciation of gold bullion. The pound thus remained a silver unit, still equivalent to 20 shillings, though those 20 shillings collectively contained far less than a pound-weight of silver.

And though Great Britain did not officially abandon bimetallism until 1819 (when silver was formally demonetized), and did not have a gold standard that was both official and operating until 1821 (when specie payments were resumed), an unofficial and generally unacknowledged switch to gold had already taken place there more than a century before. The first step toward that switch consisted of Great Britain's prior switch from a simple silver standard to official bimetallism, which occurred when it provided for free and gratuitous coinage of both silver and gold in 1666.

Because the gold coinage at the time consisted only of guineas, which (after an initial attempt to rate them at 20 shillings in 1662) were allowed to float against silver, there was as yet strictly speaking no "mint price" of gold, or implied mint gold-silver equivalent. But the transition to bimetallism was completed with Isaac Newton's decision, in 1717, to officially rate the guinea at 21 shillings, which established a mint price for gold of £3 17s 10½d per troy ounce. Although Newton hadn't intended it, his rating of the guinea undervalued silver, and so cut off the flow of that metal to the mint. England thus found itself on a de facto gold standard, which (despite great inconvenience caused by the lack of silver coin) prevailed until it gave way to the paper pound in 1797. In 1798, free coinage of silver, then long in desuetude, was formally ended, just as it would be ended under similar circumstances in the United States three-quarters of a century later. Finally, the Coinage Act of 1816 introduced the 20-shilling gold sovereign, reaffirming gold's former mint price. The 1816 act thus served, like its U.S. counterpart of 1900, both to codify and to entrench the status quo ante.

Claims to the contrary notwithstanding, that Great Britain played a crucial part in the establishment of the international gold standard does not mean that the Bank of England, alone or in conjunction with other central banks, played an essential part in "managing" that standard. "Not only can we say," Giulio Gallarotti (1995: 140) concludes, "that the Bank did not manage the international monetary system, but it is questionable whether it even managed the British monetary system." And although central banks involved in the system did occasionally assist one another with loans, they drew just as often upon private lenders for similar assistance.

In truth, the world's most successful international monetary arrangement appears to have worked automatically, with deliberate planning playing an even more minor part in its operation than it had played in its emergence. The institutional setup consisted, first of all, of nothing other than the sum of national gold standard arrangements: there was nothing in it akin to the International Monetary Fund or Special Drawing Rights or other such centralized and bureaucratic facilities. Indeed, as T. E. Gregory (1935: 7–8) observes, "The only intelligible meaning to be assigned to the phrase 'the international gold standard' is the simultaneous presence, in a group of countries, of arrangements by which, in each of them, gold is convertible at a fixed rate into the local currency and the local currency into gold, and by which gold movements from any one of these areas to any of the others are freely permitted by all of them." The most notable achievements of the classical gold standard—including its tendency to keep international exchange rates from fluctuating beyond very narrow bounds and, thereby, encourage the growth of international trade and investment—appear to have required nothing more, in other words, than a resolve on the part of the involved countries to keep their own gold standards in good working order.

The mechanism by which the international gold standard automatically regulated national money stocks and price levels was long assumed to be the so-called "price-specie-flow" first explained by David Hume. According to Hume, excessive expansion of the stock of paper money in any one gold-standard country will raise prices there, but not in other gold standard countries. At some point, it becomes worthwhile to import from abroad goods previously purchased at home. An adverse trade balance thus develops, causing gold to flow from the country where prices are relatively high to those where they are not, encouraging monetary expansion in those countries and monetary contraction in the one suffering a gold drain. Equilibrium is reestablished when a given quantity of gold once again has approximately the same purchasing power everywhere, at least with regard to internationally tradable goods.

Hume's price-specie-flow mechanism will operate only if nations' price levels differ enough to move exchange rates beyond so-called gold (or gold-export) "points," reflecting transport and other costs associated with importing goods from abroad. In practice, though, the mechanism was seldom triggered under the classical gold standard. Instead, so long as gold convertibility commitments remained credible, speculators tended to buy currencies that depreciated in the foreign exchange market, and to sell those that appreciated. Capital movements thus served to keep exchange rates from varying beyond the gold points, thereby avoiding any need for current-account gold transfers to preserve international equilibrium.

There was, in any event, no need for deliberate central bank regulation of national money stocks, much less for deliberately coordinated policies, to achieve and preserve international monetary equilibrium. That is, there was no need for central bank "cooperation." Indeed, many of the countries that were part of the classical gold standard did not even have central banks at the time. These included the United States, which was the largest participant, and Canada, Australia, and Switzerland, all of which were among those most successful in adhering to the standard. Central banks were, on the other hand, behind some of the least robust gold standards of Latin America and Asia.[8]

When central banks did seek to exert some influence, they generally sought, not to expedite, but to forestall the gold standard's normal operation, avoiding adjustments needed to preserve or restore international equilibrium (Gregory 1935: 37–38). In particular, instead of managing their discount rates as if to mimic the response of decentralized arrangements, central banks attempted to take advantage of the ability their monopoly privileges gave them to defy the gold standard "rules" by sterilizing gold transfers. But while such attempts might succeed for a time in deferring needed adjustments, more often they proved entirely futile. Under the classical gold standard, Trevor Dick and John Floyd (1992: 5) conclude, "central banks face[d] constraints, not rules," and could not sterilize the effects of gold flows or control their domestic money stocks even if they wanted to.

For some, of course, the impotence of central banks operating under the classical gold standard's constraints is a reason for condemning that arrangement as a barbarous relic. For others, though, it was a key to the classical gold standard's success in stabilizing both money's long-run purchasing power and international exchange rates—a success that, as we shall see, twice inspired government attempts to replicate the former system's success. That those initiatives *did* depend, and depend heavily, on central bank cooperation, and that neither succeeded in replicating the older arrangement's achievements, suggests that those achievements were realized despite, rather than because of, central bankers' involvement.

The long-term stability, under the gold standard, of world prices, and of the U.S. price level in particular, reflected the connection under that standard of price level changes to changes in gold's average cost of production. For any given state of gold supply, a growing demand for money would place downward pressure on the money prices of all goods apart from gold itself (the dollar value of which was, of course, fixed), including the prices of labor and other inputs in gold mining. The decline thus enhanced the profitability of gold mining and gold prospecting, ultimately promoting greater output of gold, which would end if not reverse the tendency of prices to fall. When, on the other hand, gold mining became less costly—owing to new discoveries or to more economical extraction techniques—the mines' increased output resulted in both increased coinage of gold and greater deposits of gold into the banking system. The consequent monetary expansion would then raise the general demand for goods and, ultimately, world prices. In the long run, inflation following gold discoveries and gold-mining innovations tended to just offset the deflation that took place during intervals between gold supply improvements, leaving the price level unchanged in the long-run.

Still, the deflationary intervals could be long; and one such interval—the one that began in the early 1870s and ended in 1896—was notoriously so. That interval's persistent deflation caused some 20th-century authorities to refer to it (in the British case) as a (first) "Great" depression and (in the U.S. case) as the "Long" depression. Yet in neither instance was there any persistent decline in aggregate real income or employment. Instead, those who characterized them as depressions appear to have simply assumed, mainly on the basis of the experience of the 1930s, that deflation and depression inevitably go hand in hand. Instead actual statistics for the interval in question reveal healthy average growth rates for both total and per capita real income in both nations, with declining prices reflecting, not flagging demand (as they did in the 1930s), but robust productivity growth.[9]

This isn't to deny, of course, that the United States and other countries experienced occasional, and sometimes sharp, contractions during the gold standard era. In the United States there was indeed a relatively long depression of real activity beginning in 1873—but "relatively long" here means two or perhaps three years, not more than two decades! There were also major U.S. financial crises in 1884, 1893, and 1907. But it is by no means clear that the gold standard was to blame for these episodes. That it wasn't to blame for the 1873 downturn should be obvious enough, as the United States was then still on a greenback standard, and had as yet not even taken its first steps toward resumption. As for the other crises, the fact that Canada largely avoided them, and much other evidence besides, strongly suggests that they were due not to the gold standard but to monetary and banking regulations peculiar to the United States (see Chapter 3 of this volume).

Despite their regulatory origins, U.S. financial crises of the gold standard period were to supply a rationale, not for financial deregulation (as some reformers had recommended), but for the passage of the Federal Reserve Act in 1913. As the original act itself makes clear, the Fed was not supposed to override the gold standard, but to secure and preserve it by preventing it from being undermined by further financial panics. In fact, by placing responsibility for gold convertibility entirely with a semipublic authority instead of with numerous private firms, the legislation represented a step—albeit an unintended and largely unrecognized one—toward the gold standard's eventual downfall.

WORLD WAR I AND THE RECONSTRUCTED GOLD STANDARD

On the eve of the outbreak of World War I, and before the Federal Reserve System was operating, the U.S. monetary system faced still another crisis. The closing of London's acceptance and discount houses caused foreigners to start liquidating their holdings of U.S. securities, causing heavy gold exports. A suspension of American gold payments and bank credit contraction were both avoided thanks to the closing of the New York Stock Exchange and to the issuance of emergency currency authorized by the Aldrich-Vreeland Act, a temporary measure set up in the wake of the Panic of 1907 that was set to expire once the Fed was up and running.[10]

The actual outbreak of the war brought an immediate suspension of gold payments by all of the Continental belligerents. Great Britain did not formally suspend, but the British government allowed the Bank of England to place obstacles in the way of persons attempting to withdraw gold from it. The Bank also began a publicity campaign against "unpatriotic" gold hoarding.

The United States also avoided outright suspension after it declared war on Germany in April 1917. Five months after it did so, however, President Wilson issued a proclamation requiring all persons seeking to export gold from the country to secure permission to do so from the secretary of the treasury. Because that permission was almost always denied, the proclamation, which remained in effect until June 1919, amounted to an embargo on gold exports, and hence a partial suspension of gold payments.

The combination of reduced European production and a monetary policy aimed at boosting the demand for Liberty Bonds (and no longer constrained by the risk of an external gold drain) resulted, during the war, in a 70 percent increase in the U.S. narrow (M1) money stock. That increase, in turn, produced an increase in prices of more or less the same magnitude as that which had taken place during the Civil War (Crabbe 1989: 427). But when the Fed continued to pursue the same policy after the gold embargo was lifted in 1919, the result was a net gold drain which, having already reached $300 million by March 1920, threatened to drive the Fed's gold reserve ratio below its legal minimum. In response, the Fed banks slammed the brakes on credit growth, sharply raising their discount rates and keeping them raised for the better part of a year. The policy U-turn succeeded in bringing the Fed's gold reserve ratio well above its minimum level, thereby avoiding a suspension or renewed restriction of gold payments, but not without plunging the United States into a deep (though short-lived) depression.

Other belligerent nations also hoped to reestablish their prewar gold standards, and to do so despite far more substantial wartime increases in their national money stocks and price levels. Not all of them succeeded. Germany, Austria, and Hungary experienced hyperinflations that led to the establishment of new currencies. France abandoned its former gold coin standard in favor of a gold bullion standard, while also electing—with several other nations—to permanently reduce the gold content of its currency. But largely haphazard, seat-of-the-pants settings of new gold parities led to precisely the sort of substantial (gold) price-level disparities that Hume's price-specie-flow theory takes as its starting point, but which were for the most part avoided under the classical gold standard. The parities chosen by Denmark, Italy, and Norway appear in retrospect to have overvalued their currencies—that is, to have made those countries' price levels, expressed in terms of a common gold unit, high relative to other nations'. In contrast, the parities chosen by France, Germany, and Belgium caused their currencies to become relatively cheap.

Great Britain's strategy for restoring gold payments was to prove particularly ill advised. Despite the substantial increase in the British money stock and price level since the outbreak of the war, it was determined to restore the pound's prewar gold parity, and to do so not gradually (as the United States had done after the Civil War and as Great Britain itself did after the French wars), but quickly. Churchill's now much-maligned decision to resume gold payments on April 28, 1925, is supposed by most authorities to have overvalued the pound by about 10 percent, severely depressing British exports, provoking a general strike, and giving rise to what were euphemistically termed balance-of-payments "difficulties."

The obvious alternatives for bringing the pound back into purchasing-power parity with the (undiminished) U.S. dollar were further deflation (and corresponding depression) or devaluation. British authorities, however, opted for "none of the above." Drawing inspiration from the 1922 Genoa Conference, they responded to the general strike by means of a further expansion of bank credit, while attempting to address the "gold shortage" (that is, the now further enhanced "overhang" of sterling monetary liabilities), first, by abandoning (as France had already done) the prewar gold coin standard in favor of a gold bullion standard, and second and more importantly, by convincing other central banks to treat sterling balances rather than gold itself as their principal reserve asset.

These steps by Great Britain created the "gold exchange" standard, under which Bank of England promises became, together with those of the Federal Reserve, the principal reserve and settlement medium of many gold standard nations. England's "one reserve system," condemned long before by Walter Bagehot (1873) as an "unnatural" and destabilizing byproduct of the Bank of England's monopoly privileges (see also Chapter 2 of this volume), was thus transformed into an *international* one-reserve system that was correspondingly more dangerous because it tended to delay still further "the moment when the braking effect that would otherwise have been the result of the gold standard's coming into play would have been felt" (Rueff 1972: 19). Thanks to the gold exchange, Great Britain was able, for a while, to go on being a debtor to other nations without running short of bullion.

Unlike the classical gold standard, the interwar gold exchange standard depended crucially upon central bank cooperation. Moreover, it required such cooperation, not just to run smoothly, but to run at all. A decision on the part of any major participating central bank to defect might easily have sufficed, given the Bank of England's modest gold reserve holdings, to cause the whole arrangement—and the gold economization it was designed to achieve—to come tumbling down. The result would have been worldwide deflation, or widespread devaluations, or some combination of the two. The arrangement was, in short, exceedingly fragile. On the other hand, as we shall see, when national central banks did cooperate in an attempt to keep it from collapsing, they sometimes found that they could do so only by sacrificing internal stability.

The United States for the most part cooperated with Great Britain after 1924. It had switched from easy to tight money in 1920, sterilizing gold inflows and thereby putting pressure for some years on sterling (Crabbe 1989: 428ff.). But beginning in 1924, the United States leaned the other way, largely in order to assist Great Britain with its own effort to restore gold payments. U.S. gold holdings, having reached a peak of $4,234 million in August 1924, started declining thereafter in response to the resumption of gold payments, first by Germany (in accordance with the Dawes Plan), then by Holland, and finally by Great Britain itself (Anderson 1949: 153). Nevertheless, the Federal Reserve Banks for the most part kept their discount rates low and, when that proved insufficient to stem British gold losses, resorted for the first time to a large-scale open market purchase of government securities as a means for fueling bank expansion and combating deflation (pp. 155–56).

Ultimately, it was France's efforts to restore the gold franc that would prove the gold exchange standard's undoing. France's de facto stabilization of 1926 undervalued the franc approximately as much as Great Britain's 1925 decision had overvalued sterling. In the spring of 1927, in an attempt to stem the sterling inflow by compelling the Bank of England to raise its discount rate, France began converting its sterling balances, putting the Bank of England under a severe strain. The conversion of sterling balances into gold was further accelerated by the French Monetary Law of June 25, 1928, which called for 100 percent gold backing of the Bank of France's note circulation. Between the passage of that law and the onset of 1932, France's share of world gold reserves shot up from just 7 percent to a whopping 27 percent.

Under the classical gold standard, France's accumulation of gold would have prompted monetary expansion there, while necessitating contraction elsewhere, and so would have been self-limiting. France, however, chose to sterilize its gold inflows. Still, it does not follow—as some authorities[11] have claimed—that had France not chosen to hoard gold, the outcome would have been similar to what would have happened under a true gold standard. Instead, increased lending by the Bank of France might ultimately have served only to inspire still more lending by the Bank of England, perhaps forestalling but not avoiding the gold exchange standard's eventual demise. In this respect, the interwar standard resembled, not a genuine gold standard, but, as Jacques Rueff (1972: 21) put it, a "child's game in which one party had agreed to return the loser's stake" after every contest. The fundamental problem was not that France was a "gold sink," but that neither France nor any other country could be expected to accumulate foreign currency reserves indefinitely, instead of taking advantage of the right to cash them in.

Having failed in his efforts to convince the Bank of France to remain content to hold sterling instead of gold, Montagu Norman, governor of the Bank of England, turned again for help to the United States. At a secret conference arranged by Benjamin Strong at the New York Fed, to which representatives of the Reichsbank and Bank of France were also invited, Norman succeeded in convincing Strong, but not the others, to cheapen credit still further. Strong arranged to do his part by having the Fed undertake more large security purchases and by calling for the further lowering of regional Fed bank discount rates.[12]

According to several economists, most notably F. A. Hayek and Lionel Robbins, the Great Depression began, not as a response to post-1929 deflation, but as the collapse of a prior "malinvestment" boom fueled by the Fed's easy money policy of the latter 1920s. According to Benjamin Anderson (1949: 146–47), the Fed "was created to finance a crisis and to finance seasonal needs for pocket cash. It was not created for the purpose of financing a boom, least of all for financing a stock market boom. But from early 1924 to the spring of 1928 it was used to finance a boom and to finance a stock market boom."

The Fed's efforts nevertheless proved inadequate to save the pound. That currency's convertibility, already jeopardized by France's actions, was dealt a further, fatal blow by the Austrian banking crisis, which in turn triggered a general abandonment of sterling and, hence, of the exchange standard. As Gregory (1935: 57) explains, the attacks on sterling were understandable, if not justified, for under the gold exchange set-up, "any failure of London to meet demands in gold meant that the security behind, e.g., the Dutch currency, was in effect reduced in value. The anxiety of certain Central Banks to draw out gold at a time when gold withdrawals appeared highly embarrassing to the Bank of England must not be put down to blind panic or selfishness on the part of those Banks." Great Britain withstood the attacks until September 1931, when it elected at last to devalue the pound.

Ideally, Britain's abandonment of the parity dating back to Newton's 1717 rating of the guinea might have done "nothing more than restore Great Britain's competitive position to what it would have been if the gold standard had been restored at a lower gold content, or if it had not been restored at all, in 1925" (Gregory 1935: 71). But happening when it did, after so many nations had made the convertibility of their own currencies dependent upon the inviolability of sterling, it led to the general abandonment of gold parities that had been so laboriously established or reestablished since the war. Thus, just as one "domino effect" led from Great Britain's adoption of the gold standard to that standard's general adoption, another, more cataclysmic domino effect now led from Great Britain's abandonment of gold to its almost universal abandonment. As Gregory (p. 145) explained at the time:

> The ability to maintain a local currency at par with gold carried with it economic consequences of the most far-reaching kind. But every breach in the system of gold standard countries diminishes the advantages of the system. If only a single country remained upon gold, its price structure and its foreign exchange rates with the rest of the world might be more unstable than those of the remaining areas *inter se*. (Gregory 1935: 145)

The mechanics of gold's downfall were, however, different from those that assisted its rise. There were at work not merely the usual advantages of remaining in a fixed, sterling-based exchange network, but the tendency of gold to flow from those nations that clung to the gold standard to Great

Britain and others that had abandoned it. This tendency only served to further encourage other countries, and important suppliers of crops and raw materials especially, to follow Great Britain's example. Great Britain's move was therefore, in Gregory's words, "highly infectious" (1935: 74). Following it, chunk after chunk of the remaining gold block broke off and floated away. By the close of 1932, Canada, Denmark, Egypt, Finland, Japan, Norway, Rhodesia (Northern and Southern), Siam, South Africa, and Sweden had all gone off gold. At the same time, the gold standard's allure gave way to the perception that it was to blame for the worldwide economic catastrophe.

But was it? The commonly heard claim is that "the gold standard" was what fell apart in the 1930s, after having brought about the world's worst depression. That claim betrays a failure to appreciate the crucial difference between the genuine gold standard that prevailed until the outbreak of World War I and the far more fragile gold exchange standard that was cobbled together after the war. It was the latter standard that failed, with cataclysmic consequences, in the early 1930s.

It remains true, nevertheless, that the collapse of the interwar gold exchange standard ultimately had the effect of discrediting not only that particular sort of gold standard, but the gold standard broadly understood. Some years before Great Britain's suspension, when France first began to cash in its pounds, a Bank of England official had anticipated this very outcome. "If one country decides to revert to the [classical] Gold Standard," he observed, "it may lay claim to more gold than there is any reason to expect the gold centre to have held in reserve against legitimate Gold Exchange Standard demands. What is then endangered is not merely the working of the Gold Exchange Standard, but the Gold Standard itself" (Johnson 1997: 133).

GOLD AND THE U.S. DEPRESSION

Despite the gathering momentum favoring abandonment of gold, reinforced by international runs on the dollar in both 1931 and 1932, the United States clung to its gold standard until March 6, 1933, when a run on the New York Fed's gold reserves led to President Roosevelt's declaration of a national bank holiday. That holiday would ultimately keep all U.S. banks closed until March 13. In the course of it, Roosevelt ordered commercial banks to exchange their remaining gold reserves for Federal Reserve notes and credits and to submit lists of persons who had withdrawn gold or gold certificates since February. He also prohibited gold exports except by special arrangement with the secretary of the treasury. Finally, in his executive order (no. 6073) concerning banks' reopening, he stipulated that "no permission to any banking institution to perform any banking functions shall authorize such institution to pay out any gold coin, gold bullion or gold certificates except as authorized by the secretary of the treasury, nor to allow withdrawal of any currency, for hoarding, nor to engage in any transaction in foreign exchange except such as may be undertaken for legitimate and normal business requirements, for reasonable traveling and other personal requirements, and for the fulfillment of contracts entered into prior to March 6, 1933."

These emergency measures already amounted to an indefinite suspension of the gold standard. Then, on April 5, 1933, yet another executive order required all U.S. residents to exchange, on or before May 1, most of their holdings of gold coin, bullion, and gold certificates for Federal Reserve notes and token coins valued at the then still-official rate of $20.67 per troy ounce; the order made subsequent possession of monetary gold a criminal act. For the remainder of 1933, the dollar remained inconvertible, while its foreign exchange value was allowed to float. Finally, the Gold Reserve Act of January 30, 1934, established a new, official price of gold of $35 per troy ounce, while requiring that all gold and gold certificates held by the Federal Reserve be surrendered to the U.S. Treasury.

The United States' decision to cling to its pre–World War I gold standard until the spring of 1933 has since been blamed for both the severity and persistence of the U.S. Great Depression. But the facts do not support such a simple interpretation. Although there can be little doubt that the post-1929 "Great Contraction" of the U.S. money stock, and the consequent collapse in nominal spending, played a major part in the Depression, the gold standard as such cannot be said to have been responsible for this contraction. The Fed could have combated the collapse without sacrificing its ability to convert gold into dollars. As Leland Crabbe (1989: 417), a Board of Governors staff member, succinctly puts it, "Because the [Fed's] gold reserve requirement rarely restrained policy between 1914 and 1933, the Federal Reserve had broad discretionary powers to manage the nation's money supply in the advancement of domestic objectives."

The Federal Reserve Act required that the Fed maintain a gold reserve equal to not less than 35 percent of its deposits and not less than 40 percent of its outstanding notes. Although the Fed came close to being constrained by those requirements during the 1920–21 crisis, it subsequently accumulated substantial excess reserves by sterilizing gold inflows from Europe. The accumulation continued not only throughout the remainder of the 1920s but also after the onset of the Depression. "At the same time that Fed policymakers refused to provide relief to member banks," Richard Timberlake (1993: 270–71) observes, "gold in Fed Banks was piling up. By August 1931, Fed gold had reached $3.5 billion (from $3.1 billion in 1929), an amount equal to 81 percent of outstanding Fed monetary obligations and more than double the reserves required by the Federal Reserve Act." Although it lost gold during both the autumn of 1931 and the summer of 1932, the Fed enjoyed a net increase in gold in both years. Mounting fears of devaluation during the early months of 1933 led to both extensive earmarking of gold for foreign accounts and an internal run on gold.[13] But even at its nadir, at the end of the bank holiday, the Fed's gold stock stood at $4,282 million, leaving the Fed with more than $1 billion in excess reserves. What's more, the Fed's gold constraint, however tight it became, could always be loosened, since the Federal Reserve Board had the authority to suspend the Fed's gold reserve requirements altogether, and for an indefinite period, in an emergency.[14]

Nor, despite suggestions to the contrary (Elwell 2011: 9), is it certain that more aggressive Fed expansion to combat the Great Contraction would have posed a threat to the dollar's convertibility. Michael Bordo and colleagues (2002) find that, even had there been perfect capital mobility (which was far from the case), open market purchases on a scale capable of preventing the monetary collapse would not have sponsored gold outflows large enough to pose a threat to the dollar's convertibility. Chang-Tai Hsieh and Christina D. Romer (2006), drawing on both statistical and narrative evidence, reject the more specific hypothesis that, prior to 1933, the Fed had been compelled to refrain from expansionary policies out of fear that expansion would provoke a speculative attack on the dollar. The U.S. monetary contraction, Hsieh and Romer (2006: 142) conclude, took place, not because the Fed was encumbered by "Golden Fetters," but because its administration was inept. Finally, although it is true that the bank holiday of March 1933 was itself triggered by fears of an impending devaluation, those fears arose, not owing to the perception that the Fed was in danger of running out of gold reserves, but owing to the newly elected president's unwillingness to unequivocally commit to maintaining the gold standard (Wigmore 1987).

In brief, the decision to suspend the dollar's convertibility into gold was as unnecessary as it was contrary to the proclaimed purpose of the Federal Reserve System. That system, Gregory (1935: 102) reminds us,

> was expressly created in 1913 for the purpose of avoiding any suspension of cash payments in the future, for the received tradition of central banking contains no place for a suspension of cash payments as a remedy for banking panic. On the contrary, the received tradition is that, so long as the foreign exchanges continue favourable, the way to avoid suspension of cash payments is to lend freely against adequate security, but at a rate of interest sufficiently high to deter irresponsible borrowing and at the same time to attract back to the country a portion of its outstanding short-term assets.

The U.S. decision to abandon gold, Gregory (1935: 103) concludes, was "an arbitrary act of statesmanship, which may indeed be justified on political or psychological grounds, but which was certainly not inevitable on technical economic grounds."

Although both the Great Contraction and the banking crises that accompanied it might have been prevented without abandoning the gold standard, that does not mean that devaluation of the dollar played no part in the post-contraction economic recovery. By reducing the dollar's official gold content to 59 percent of its former content, the Roosevelt administration increased the nominal monetary gold stock from $4,033 million to $7,438 million overnight, thereby compensating somewhat, though belatedly, for the Federal Reserve's past failure to take advantage of its unused capacity to expand credit.[15] By cheapening U.S. exports, devaluation may also have contributed to subsequent, substantial net U.S. gold receipts, though those appear to have been mainly due to the growing likelihood, following Hitler's assumption of power, that Europe would once again find itself engulfed by war.

BRETTON WOODS AND THE FIAT DOLLAR

Although, according to our understanding of the meaning of a gold standard, the United States abandoned that standard during the national bank holiday in 1933, officially the abandonment of gold was a gradual process completed only in the 1970s.

The collapse of the interwar gold standard left the world monetary system in a state of disarray. It would remain in that state throughout World War II, as the prewar problem of unstable exchange rates gave way to one of extensive exchange controls. The war completed the process, begun during World War I, by which sterling hegemony gave way to dollar hegemony in world monetary affairs. Whereas substantial U.S. gold receipts during World War I had given way to substantial gold losses afterward, the close of World War II only served to revive net gold flows to the United States that had begun before the war's outbreak. Those inflows ultimately left the United States in possession of roughly three-quarters of the world's monetary gold. By then, the U.S. dollar was the only major world currency still meaningfully linked to gold.

Various proposals for restoring other currencies' convertibility eventually gave rise to the Bretton Woods plan, calling for the establishment of a new exchange standard that was to have been based upon both sterling and the U.S. dollar. Ultimately, convertibility came to be based upon the dollar alone.[16] That meant participating nations' currencies were to be "pegged" not to gold directly but to U.S. dollars, which would remain uniquely convertible into gold. The pegged exchange rates were subject to adjustment with the approval of the newly established International Monetary Fund (IMF), so named because it also administered a dollar endowment to which participants held specific "drawing rights" for use in maintaining their currencies' par values.

Under Bretton Woods, although it remained impossible for U.S. citizens to convert U.S. dollars into gold, foreign central banks had the right to convert dollars into gold at the new official rate of $35 per ounce. Furthermore, U.S. dollars could be freely sold in the London gold market, where in 1961 a gold "pool" was established for the purpose of aiding such conversions. The Fed contributed half of the pool, and a consortium of European central banks contributed the other half. It was thus possible, in practice, for any foreigner to acquire gold in exchange for U.S. dollars at the official rate, and to do so anonymously. Because most system currencies did not become fully convertible at the new par values established for them in 1946 until the close of 1958, the system only became fully operative at the latter date.

The Bretton Woods system was supposed to reproduce the most desirable features of the classical gold standard while nevertheless allowing participating central banks some freedom to pursue independent monetary policies. For a time, it seemed to achieve its purpose, by reestablishing a system of stable exchange rates accompanied by low inflation. However, the system's apparent stability masked serious inherent flaws that became especially serious once the dollar emerged as its only "key" currency. That status ultimately led U.S. authorities to take advantage of the system to engage in inflationary finance, ultimately exposing the dollar to speculative attacks like those to which the interwar sterling-based exchange standard had succumbed. "As outstanding dollar liabilities held by the rest of the world monetary authorities increased relative to the U.S. monetary gold stock," Michael Bordo (1993: 51) explains, "the likelihood of a run on the 'bank' increased. The probability of all dollar holders being able to convert their dollars into gold at the fixed price declined."

In two respects at least, the Bretton Woods arrangement was even more vulnerable to speculative attacks than its interwar predecessor had been. The Bretton Woods exchange rate commitments were, first of all, known to be subject to change. Secondly, interwar devaluations, and the devaluation of the U.S. dollar itself especially, gave speculators more reason than ever before to distrust the new regime's commitments—to view them, not as so many binding contractual obligations, but as a mere exercise in government price fixing that might be abandoned with relative impunity. For these reasons, the Bretton Woods system was especially likely to come under attack in the event of a perceived shortage of gold cover.

Still, U.S. authorities were unconcerned with the system's strength, despite the restoration of the (dollar) convertibility of system currencies. In 1960, U.S. gold holdings stood at $17.8 billion, while the U.S. gold tranche ("ordinary drawing rights") at the IMF stood at $1.6 billion, giving the United States total reserves of $19.4 billion against foreign private and official U.S. dollar holdings of $18.7 billion (Rueff 1972: 208). But beginning around that time, persistent and mounting U.S. balance of payment deficits caused the ratio of U.S. gold stock to foreign dollar holdings to decline almost continuously to such levels as no longer supplied grounds for sanguinity.[17] In June 1967, France became the first country to act upon growing doubts about the dollar's future convertibility by quitting the gold pool and starting to shift gold from New York and London to Paris. France's move put sterling under severe pressure that led, in November 1967, to its devaluation, which, in turn, dealt a mortal blow to confidence in the dollar's convertibility into gold. The United States' creditors, having long since become, according to Jacques Rueff (1972: 208), "tired of having to accept indefinitely growing amounts of U.S. currency which were totally useless to them," at last began to convert substantial portions of their dollar balances into gold. Mounting gold withdrawals during late 1967 and early 1968 gave way in mid-March of the latter year to a massive run.

U.S. authorities responded to the run by terminating the gold pool on March 17. This step stanched the gold outflow by forcing requests to convert dollars into gold at their official par value "through the narrow channel of some U.S. monetary authority," limiting requests to foreign monetary authorities and making them "obvious and conspicuous" (Rueff 1972: 184–85). The change, besides ruling out private conversions, discouraged those countries that depended on the United States either for military protection or for economic aid, or that simply wished to maintain friendly diplomatic relations with it, from cashing in dollars.

Although it came close to converting the Bretton Woods gold-exchange standard into a de facto dollar standard, the new arrangement also succeeded for a time, with the help of special drawing rights created to supplement the previously available IMF gold tranches, at preserving the appearance of some sort of gold standard. But as the supply of foreign-held dollars continued to increase, their holders overcame their politically motivated reluctance to cash them in: "Piling up dollars," Rueff (1972: 190) observed, will eventually "make people allergic to them." By the end of 1970, U.S. gold holdings had fallen to just $11,100 million, with total reserves (including IMF drawing rights) at $14,500 million (p. 210), while total external dollar balances amounted to over $45,700 million, or more than three times available reserves. The Fed managed to accommodate requests for gold for another eight months, but on August 15, 1971, its "gold window" was closed for good. Even so, appearances were to some extent kept up: in March 1972 the dollar was officially devalued to $38 per ounce, though no U.S. agency was actually prepared to exchange gold for dollars at that price. A further, official devaluation in December 1973 was still more meaningless, for gold was then already trading for more than its new, official price of $42.22, to which it was never to return. Official acknowledgment that the dollar was no longer based on gold did not come until October 1976; and to this day, U.S. gold holdings continue to be carried on the Fed's books at $42.22 per ounce, although general inflation and a recent bull market in gold have raised gold's market price to about $1,600 per ounce.

A REVIVED GOLD STANDARD?

Although a genuine and official gold standard prevailed in the United States only for about half a century, that experience was successful enough to give rise to a widespread (though by no means universal) perception that, notwithstanding the *theoretical* advantages of an ideally managed fiat money, the gold standard was uniquely capable of keeping both exchange rates and the general price level relatively stable and predictable. Nor has this perception been a popular one only, unsupported by expert opinion. Jürg Niehans (1978), for example, observed that while "a non-commodity system, since it gives monetary policy more freedom, can if it is ideally managed, always do at least as well as any commodity money system and probably better. . . . from a practical point of view, commodity money is the only type of money that, at the present time, can be said to have passed the test of history in market economies."[18]

Indeed, the double-digit inflation that had taken hold in the United States when Niehans wrote led not long afterward to the establishment of a Gold Commission, charged with conducting "a study to assess and make recommendations with regard to the policy of the U.S. government concerning the role of gold in domestic and international monetary systems." The measure's sponsors, Sen. Jesse Helms (R-NC) and Rep. Ron Paul (R-TX), had each attempted to introduce legislation aimed at reestablishing a gold standard of some sort, but had been unsuccessful. They hoped the Gold Commission would produce new support for a gold revival, and so were disappointed when the newly elected Reagan administration, instead of showing enthusiasm for such a revival, allowed its own appointees to the commission to join what became a substantial anti-gold majority. That majority's final report recommended, unsurprisingly, against reestablishing a gold-based dollar, prompting two of the dissenting commissioners, Ron Paul and Lew Lehrman, to prepare and publish a minority report (Paul and Lehrman 1982).[19]

Since the convening of the Gold Commission, several other (usually Republican) politicians have ventured to defend the gold standard and in some instances to urge its revival. The general consensus, however, has remained that reached by the commission: that despite the infirmities of the present fiat dollar standard, a transition back to gold convertibility would likely prove difficult.

Some popular arguments against proposals for a new gold standard are not very compelling. The claim that the real price of gold has become too volatile to allow that metal to be relied upon as a standard, for example, overlooks the extent to which gold's price depends on the demand for private gold hoards, which has become both very great and very volatile precisely because of the uncertainty that fiat money regimes have inspired. The claim also overlooks the tendency, discussed earlier, for a metal's price to become more stable as it becomes more widely adopted as a monetary standard.

Nor is it the case that there is not enough gold in the United States to support a new gold standard. Saying so doesn't mean, of course, that it would be possible to make dollars redeemable in gold at gold's official bookkeeping price of $42.22 per ounce, much less at any of the still lower prices that pertained before the gold standard was abandoned. Any such parity would confront the United States with a monetary "overhang," and a corresponding need for monetary contraction and deflation, such as would make the overhang Great Britain faced in 1925 seem trivial in comparison. But there need be no monetary overhang or gold shortage, provided that the dollar is given a new gold parity closer to its current market price. According to Lawrence White (2012: 416), the Treasury's gold stock—assuming that it is indeed what the Treasury claims and given an official gold price of $1,600 per troy ounce—would be worth almost 20 percent of 2012 M1, making for "a more than healthy reserve ratio by historical standards." Indeed, even at a gold price of only $800 per ounce, the gold reserve ratio would under normal circumstances be quite adequate, and especially so if, as White assumes, the restoration of gold convertibility reduced the demand for gold itself as an inflation hedge.[20]

There are, however, some more compelling reasons for doubting that a return to gold would prove worthwhile, even allowing that a system that could perform as the classical gold standard did would be well worth having. One is the prospect that any restoration of the convertibility of dollars into gold might be so disruptive that the short-run costs of the reform would outweigh any long-run gains it might bring. The problem here is not that there is no new gold parity such as would allow for a smooth transition, but that the correct parity cannot be determined with any precision and must instead be discovered by trial and error. Consequently, the transition could involve either costly inflation or its opposite—a deflationary crisis such as the one Great Britain confronted when it resumed gold payments in 1925 (White 2012: 416).

A second compelling reason has to do with the specific disadvantage of a unilateral return to gold. Here, once again, it must be recalled that the historical gold standard that is remembered as having performed so well was an *international* gold standard, and that the advantages in question were, to a large extent, advantages due to belonging to a very large monetary network. Consequently, a gold standard that is limited to a single country—even a very large country—cannot be expected to offer the same advantages as a multicountry gold standard or set of gold standards. The problem here was already evident to T. E. Gregory in 1934, when the prospect of a general gold revival was far less remote than it is today. "One may take it as axiomatic," he wrote, "that none of the countries at present off gold is likely to want to go back without others going back simultaneously" (Gregory 1935: 168). To arrange for a coordinated revival, an international conference would have to be convened; but then, Gregory observed, "the danger is that the proposed Conference will degenerate into a mere wrangle over new [gold] parities."[21]

Finally and perhaps most importantly, it is more doubtful than ever before that any government-sponsored and -administered gold standard would be sufficiently credible to either be spared from or to withstand redemption runs. "If a government can go on a gold standard," James Hamilton (2005) has remarked, "it can go off, and historically countries have done exactly that all the time. The fact that speculators know this means that any currency adhering to a gold standard will . . . be subject to a speculative attack." The breakdown in the credibility of central bank exchange rate commitments since World War I cannot be easily repaired, if it can be repaired at all. Consequently, nothing short of the removal of responsibility for enforcing such commitments from public or semipublic authorities to the private sector—that is, a return to private and competitive currency issuance—is likely to be capable of establishing a robust and sustainable gold standard (see Selgin and White 2005).

In brief, if they are to recreate a gold standard capable of being both stable and credible, governments must be both able and willing to engineer a concerted return to gold, and yet must also be prepared to renounce their currency monopolies or otherwise deny themselves the ability to revise their countries' convertibility commitments with impunity. To say that the prospects for both requirements being met are remote is to understate matters considerably. The truth is rather that the brief institutional efflorescence we call the classical gold standard is unlikely ever to be realized again.

8

HAS THE FED BEEN A FAILURE?*

WITH WILLIAM D. LASTRAPES
AND LAWRENCE H. WHITE

> No major institution in the U.S. has so poor a record of performance over so long a period, yet so high a public reputation.
>
> —Milton Friedman (1988)

In the aftermath of the Panic of 1907, the U.S. Congress appointed a National Monetary Commission. In 1910, the Commission published a shelf-full of studies evaluating the problems of the postbellum national banking system and exploring alternative regimes. A few years later Congress passed the Federal Reserve Act.

Today, in the aftermath of the Panic of 2007, and as the 100th birthday of the Federal Reserve System approaches, it seems appropriate to once again take stock of our monetary system. Has our experiment with the Federal Reserve been a success or a failure? Does the Fed's track record during its history merit celebration, or should Congress consider replacing it with something else? Is it time for a new National Monetary Commission?

* Originally published in the *Journal of Macroeconomics* 34, no. 3 (September 2012): 569–96. The authors thank David Boaz, Don Boudreaux, Tyler Cowen, Christopher Hanes, Jeff Hummel, Arnold Kling, Jerry O'Driscoll, Scott Sumner, Alex Tabarrok, Dick Timberlake, Randy Wright, and numerous blog commentators for their helpful suggestions, while absolving them of all responsibility for the paper's arguments and conclusions. William D. Lastrapes is a professor in the department of economics at the University of Georgia's Terry College of Business.

The Federal Reserve has, by all accounts, been one of the world's more responsible and successful central banks. But this tells us nothing about its absolute performance. To what extent has the Fed succeeded or failed in accomplishing its official mission? Has it ameliorated to a substantial degree those symptoms of monetary and financial instability that caused it to be established in the first place? Has it at least outperformed the system that it replaced? Has it learned to do better over time?

We address these questions by surveying available research bearing upon them. The broad conclusions we reach based upon that research are that (1) the full Fed period has been characterized by more rather than fewer symptoms of monetary and macroeconomic instability than the decades leading to the Fed's establishment; (2) while the Fed's performance has undoubtedly improved since World War II, even its postwar performance has not clearly surpassed that of its (undoubtedly flawed) predecessor; and (3) alternative arrangements exist that might do better than the presently constituted Fed has done. These findings do not prove that any particular alternative to the Fed would, in fact, have delivered superior outcomes: to reach such a conclusion would require a counterfactual exercise too ambitious to fall within the scope of what is intended as a preliminary survey. The findings do, however, suggest that the need for a systematic exploration of alternatives to the established monetary system, involving the necessary counterfactual exercises, is no less pressing today than it was a century ago.

As far as we know, the present study is the first attempt at an overall assessment of the Fed's record informed by academic research.[1] Our conclusions draw importantly on recent research findings, which have dramatically revised economists' indicators of macroeconomic performance, especially for the pre–Federal Reserve period. We do not, of course, expect the conclusions we draw from this research to be uncontroversial, much less definitive. On the contrary: we merely hope to supply prima facie grounds for a more systematic stock-taking.

In evaluating the Federal Reserve System's record in monetary policy, we leave aside its role as a regulator of commercial banks. Adding an evaluation of the latter would double an already large task. It would confront us with the problem of distinguishing areas where the Fed has been responsible for policymaking from those in which it has simply been the policy-enforcing agent of Congress. It would also raise the thorny problem of disentangling the Fed's influence from that of other regulators, because every bank the Fed regulates also answers to the Federal Deposit Insurance Corporation (FDIC) and a chartering agency. Monetary policy, by contrast, is the Fed's responsibility alone.[2]

THE FED'S MISSION

According to the preamble to the original Federal Reserve Act of 1913, the Federal Reserve System was created "to furnish an elastic currency, to afford means of rediscounting commercial paper, to establish a more effective supervision of banking in the United States, and for other purposes." In 1977, the original act was amended to reflect the abandonment of the gold standard some years before, and the corresponding increase in the Fed's responsibility for achieving macroeconomic stability. The amended act makes it the Fed's duty to "maintain long-run growth of the monetary and credit aggregates commensurate with the economy's long-run potential to increase production, so as to promote effectively the goals of maximum employment, stable prices, and moderate long-term interest rates." On its website, the Board of Governors adds that the Fed also contributes to "better economic performance by acting to contain financial disruptions and preventing their spread outside the financial sector."

These stated objectives suggest criteria by which to assess the Fed's performance, namely, the relative extent of pre– and post–Federal Reserve Act price level changes, pre– and post–Federal Reserve Act output fluctuations and business recessions, and pre– and post–Federal Reserve Act financial crises. For reasons already given, we do not attempt to address the Fed's success at bank supervision.

INFLATION

The Fed has failed conspicuously in one respect: far from achieving long-run price stability, it has allowed the purchasing power of the U.S. dollar, which was hardly different on the eve of the Fed's creation from what it had been at the time of the dollar's establishment as the official U.S. monetary unit, to fall dramatically. A consumer basket selling for $100 in 1790 cost only slightly more, at $108, than its (admittedly very rough) equivalent in 1913. But thereafter the price soared, reaching $2,422 in 2008 (Officer and Williamson 2009). As the first panel of Figure 8.1 shows, most of the decline in the dollar's purchasing power has taken place since 1970, when the gold standard no longer placed any limits on the Fed's powers of monetary control.

Figure 8.1: Quarterly U.S. Price Level and Inflation Rate, 1875–2010

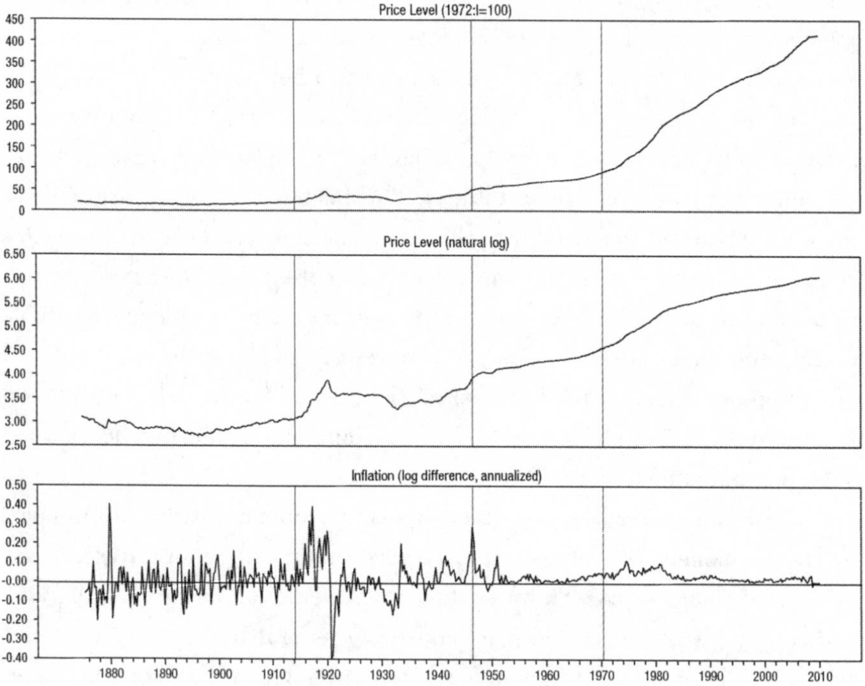

NOTES: Gross national product (GNP) deflator (Balke and Gordon [1986] series spliced to Department of Commerce series in the fourth quarter of 1946). Vertical lines indicate the founding of the Fed, the end of World War II, and the effective end of the gold standard in the United States.

The highest annual rates of inflation since the Civil War also occurred under the Fed's watch. The high rates of 1973–75 and 1978–80 are the most notorious, though authorities disagree concerning the extent to which Fed policy was to blame for them.[3] Yet those inflation rates, in the low "teens," were modest compared to annual rates recorded between 1917 and 1920, which varied from just below 15 percent to 18 percent, with annualized rates for some quarters occasionally approaching 40 percent (see Figure 8.1, third panel). Significantly, both of the major post–Federal Reserve Act episodes of inflation coincided with relaxations of gold standard–based constraints on the Fed's money-creating abilities, consisting of a temporary gold export embargo from September 1917 through June 1919 and of the permanent closing of the Fed's gold window in 1971.[4]

Although the costs of price level instability are hard to assess, the reduced stability of prices under the Fed's tenure has certainly not been costless. As the Board of Governors itself has observed,

> Stable prices in the long run are a precondition for maximum sustainable output growth and employment as well as moderate long-term interest rates. When prices are stable and believed to remain so, the prices of goods, services, materials, and labor are undistorted by inflation and serve as clearer signals and guides to the efficient allocation of resources. . . . Moreover, stable prices foster saving and capital formation, because when the risk of erosion of asset values resulting from inflation—and the need to guard against such losses—are minimized, households are encouraged to save more and businesses are encouraged to invest more. (Board of Governors of the Federal Reserve System 2009)

More specifically, as Ben Bernanke (2006: 2) observed in a lecture several years ago, besides reducing the costs of holding money, stable prices

> allow people to rely on the dollar as a measure of value when making long-term contracts, engaging in long-term planning, or borrowing or lending for long periods. As economist Martin Feldstein has frequently pointed out, price stability also permits tax laws, accounting rules, and the like to be expressed in dollar terms without being subject to distortions arising from fluctuations in the value of money.

Feldstein (1997) had, in fact, reckoned the recurring welfare cost of a *steady* inflation rate of just 2 percent—a cost stemming solely from the adverse effect of inflation on the real net return to saving—at about 1 percent of gross national product (GNP).[5]

As Bernanke's remarks suggest, *unpredictable* changes in the price level have greater costs than predictable changes. Benjamin Klein (1975) observed that, although the standard deviation of the rate of inflation was only a third as large between 1956 and 1972 as it had been from 1880 to 1915, inflation had also become much more persistent. The price *level* had consequently become less rather than more predictable since the Fed's establishment. Robert Barsky (1987) reported in the same vein that, while quarterly U.S. inflation could be described as a white-noise process from 1870 to 1913, it was positively serially correlated from 1919 to 1938 and from 1947 to 1959 (when the Fed was constrained by some form of gold standard), and has since become a random walk. These findings suggest that, as the Fed gained greater control over long-run price level movements, those movements became increasingly difficult to forecast.

Our own estimates from an autoregressive–moving-average (ARMA) (1, 1) model yield conclusions similar to Klein's. Although the standard deviation of inflation was greater before the Fed's establishment than it has been since World War II, the postwar inflation process includes a large (that is, above 0.9) autoregressive component, whereas that component was small and negative before 1915 (see Table 8.1).[6] Relatively small postwar inflation-rate innovations have consequently been associated with relatively large steady-state changes in the price level (see Figure 8.2). A GARCH (1, 1) model of the errors from the ARMA model accordingly reveals a stark difference between the conditional variance of the inflation process before and since the Fed's establishment, with almost no persistence in the variance of inflation prior to the Fed's establishment, and a very high degree of persistence afterwards, especially since the closing of the Fed's gold window (Table 8.1, second panel).[7] Lastly, by treating six-year rolling standard deviations for quarterly inflation and price level series as proxies for the uncertainty associated with each, we confirm Klein's finding that, while the rate of inflation has tended to become more predictable as inflation has become more persistent, forecasting future price levels has generally become more difficult, with the degree of difficulty increasing with the forecast horizon (Figure 8.3). The conditional variances implied by the GARCH model are shown in Figure 8.4.[8]

Table 8.1: Characteristics of Quarterly Inflation

	1875–1914	1947–2010	1915–2010	1971–2010
Sample Statistics				
Mean	-0.05%	3.39%	3.16%	3.84%
Standard deviation	8.33%	2.54%	6.78%	2.51%
Autocorrelation, 1 lag	0.18	0.80	0.70	0.89
Autocorrelation, 2 lags	-0.16	0.72	0.43	0.84
Autocorrelation, 3 lags	0.01	0.65	0.29	0.81
Autocorrelation, 4 lags	-0.03	0.54	0.26	0.78
Autocorrelation, 5 lags	-0.04	0.49	0.19	0.71
Autocorrelation, 6 lags	-0.01	0.42	0.11	0.69
Autocorrelation, 7 lags	0.06	0.38	0.05	0.62
Autocorrelation, 8 lags	0.10	0.41	0.02	0.60
Autocorrelation, 9 lags	0.06	0.39	0.01	0.57
Autocorrelation, 10 lags	0.01	0.45	0.09	0.56
Autocorrelation, 11 lags	0.10	0.43	0.16	0.54
Autocorrelation, 12 lags	0.13	0.43	0.16	0.52
Coefficients from ARMA(1,1)–GARCH(1,1)				
Constant	0.008	0.0015	0.0002	0.0009
AR(1)	-0.467	0.9372	0.9078	0.9567
MA(1)	0.689	-0.4530	-0.3705	-0.4616
Constant in variance	0.00026	0.000006	0.000005	0.000002
ARCH(1)	0.049	0.260	0.351	0.1128
GARCH(1)	—	0.714	0.695	0.8531
Conditional variance (5yr)	0.350	0.230	—	—
Conditional variance (30yr)	0.843	1.135	—	—
Conditional variance (100yr)	1.530	2.263	—	—

NOTE: Inflation is quarterly log difference of the price level, adjusted to an annual rate, using the data described in Figure 8.1.

Figure 8.2: Price Level Response to Standard Deviation Inflation Shock, Various Subperiods

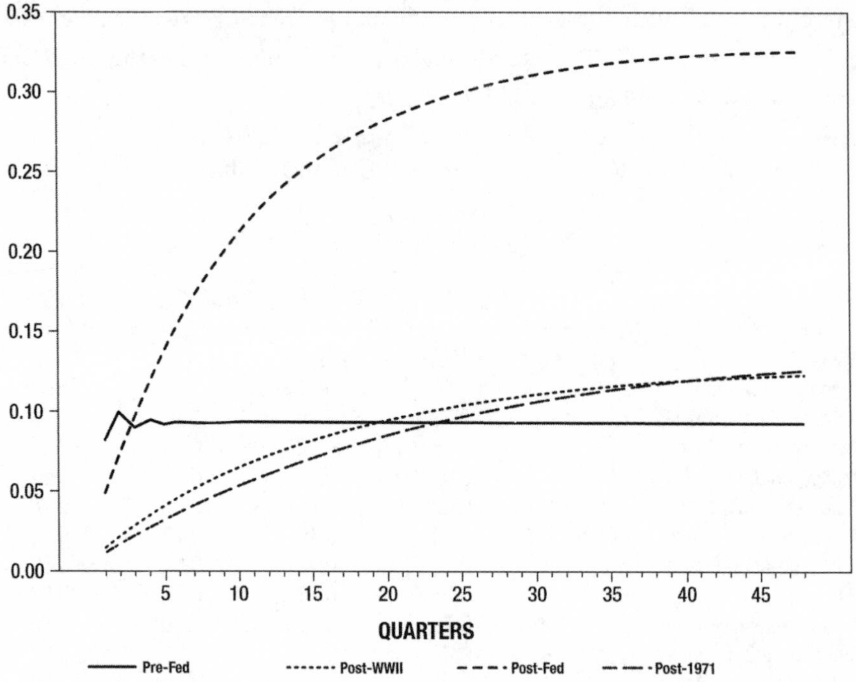

NOTE: Impulse responses as a function of forecast horizon, implied by the ARMA coefficient estimates in Table 8.1.

Figure 8.3: Price Level and Inflation Uncertainty

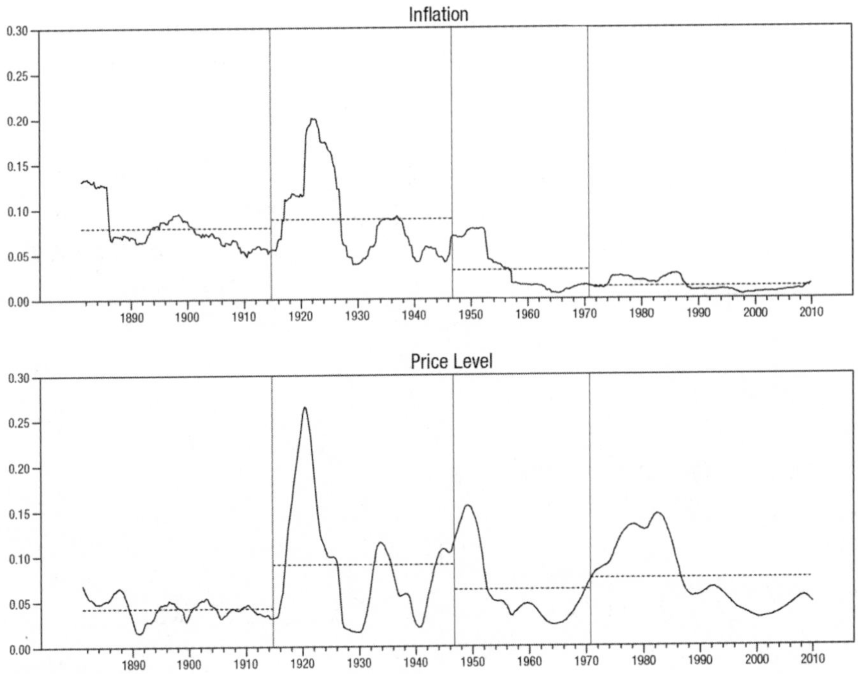

NOTES: Six-year rolling standard deviations of the quarterly inflation rate and the price level, using data shown in Figure 8.1.

Figure 8.4: Conditional Variances of the Price Level Forecast Errors, Various Horizons

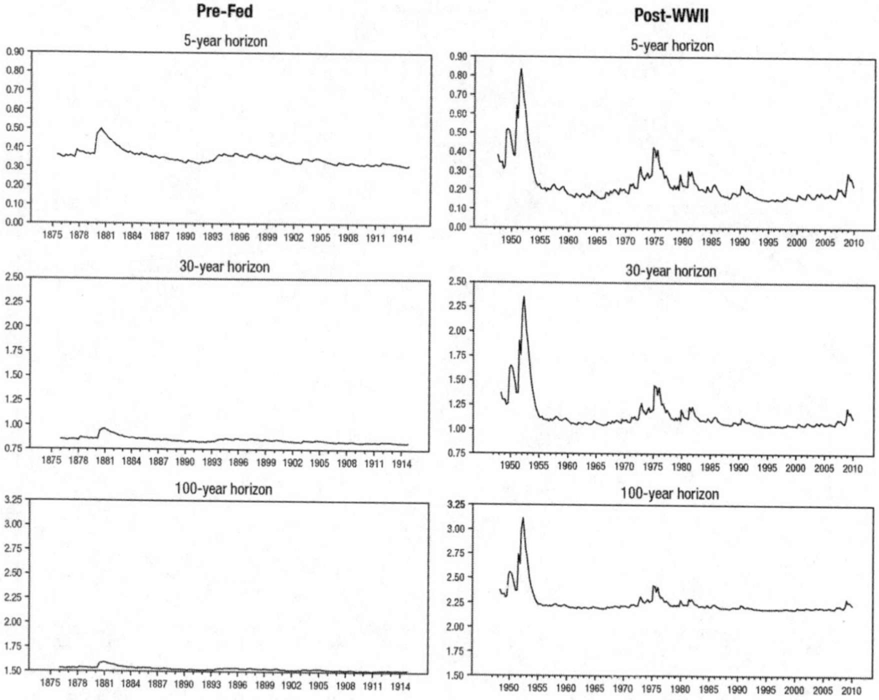

NOTE: Fitted values at various horizons of conditional variance of the price level as implied by coefficient estimates in Table 8.1.

The last panel of Figure 8.4 makes it especially easy to appreciate why corporate securities of very long (e.g., 100-year) maturities, which were common in the decades just prior to the passage of the Federal Reserve Act, have become much less common since. To the extent that its policies discouraged the issuance of longer-term corporate debt, the Fed can hardly be credited with achieving "moderate long-term interest rates."[9]

DEFLATION

While it has failed to prevent inflation, the Fed has also largely succeeded, since the Great Depression, in eliminating deflation, which was a common occurrence under the pre-Fed, post–Civil War U.S. monetary system.

Between 1870 and 1896, for example, U.S. prices fell 37 percent, or at an average annual rate of 1.2 percent (Bordo and Redish 2004; Figure 8.1, panel 2).

The postwar eradication of deflation would count among the Fed's achievements were deflation always a bad thing. But is it? Many economists appear to assume so. But a contrasting view, supported by a number of recent studies, holds that deflation may be either harmful or benign depending on its underlying cause. Harmful deflation—the sort that goes hand in hand with depression—results from a contraction in overall spending or aggregate demand for goods in a world of sticky prices. As people try to rebuild their money balances they spend less of their income on goods. Slack demand gives rise to unsold inventories, discouraging production as it depresses equilibrium prices. Benign deflation, by contrast, is driven by improvements in aggregate supply—that is, by general reductions in unit production costs—which allow more goods to be produced from any given quantity of factors and which are therefore much more likely to be quickly and fully reflected in corresponding adjustments to actual (and not just equilibrium) prices.[10]

Historically, benign deflation has been the far more common type. Surveying the 20th-century experience of 17 countries, including the United States, Andrew Atkeson and Patrick Kehoe (2004: 99) find "many more periods of deflation with reasonable growth than with depression, and many more periods of depression with inflation than with deflation." Indeed, they conclude "that the *only* episode in which there is evidence of a link between deflation and depression is the Great Depression (1929–1934)." This finding stands in stark contrast with the more common view exemplified by Bernanke's (2002a) assertion, in a speech aimed at justifying the Fed's low post-2001 funds target, that "Deflation is in almost all cases a side effect of a collapse in aggregate demand—a drop in spending so severe that producers must cut prices on an ongoing basis in order to find buyers."

Atkeson and Kehoe's arresting conclusion depends on their having looked at inflation and output growth statistics averaged across five-year time intervals and over a sample of 17 countries. There have, in fact, been other 20th-century instances in which deflation coincided with recession or depression in individual countries over shorter time intervals. In the

United States, this was certainly the case, for example, during the intervals 1919–21, 1937–38, 1948–49 (Bordo and Filardo 2005a: 814–19) and, most recently, 2008–09. It remains true, nonetheless, that taking both 19th- and 20th-century experience into account, it is, as Michael Bordo and Andrew Filardo (p. 834) observe, "abundantly clear that deflation need not be associated with recessions, depressions, and other unpleasant conditions."

Although the classical gold standard made deflation far more common before the Fed's establishment than afterwards, episodes of "bad" deflation were actually less common under that regime than they were during the Fed's first decades (Bordo and Filardo 2005a: 823). Benign deflation was the rule: downward price level trends, like that of 1873–96, mainly reflected strong growth in aggregate supply. Occasional financial panics did, however, give rise to brief episodes of bad deflation. We take up below the question of whether the Fed has succeeded in mitigating such panics.[11]

Taking these findings into account, the Fed's record with respect to deflation does not appear to compensate for its failure to contain inflation. It has, on the one hand, practically extinguished the benign sort of deflation, replacing it with persistent inflation that masks the true progress of productivity. On the other hand, it bears at least some responsibility for several of the most severe episodes of harmful deflation in U.S. history.

VOLATILITY OF OUTPUT AND UNEMPLOYMENT

If the Fed has not used its powers of monetary control to avoid undesirable changes in the price level, has it at least succeeded in stabilizing real output? Few claim that it did so during the interwar period, which was by all accounts the most turbulent in U.S. economic experience.[12] In fact, according to the standard (Kuznets-Kendrick) historical GNP series, thanks to that turbulent interval, the cyclical volatility of real output (as measured by the standard deviation of GNP from its Hodrick-Prescott filter trend) has been somewhat greater throughout the full Fed sample period than it was during the pre-Fed (1869–1914) period.

The same data also support the common claim (see, for example, Burns 1960; Baily 1978; DeLong and Summers 1986; Taylor 1986) that the

Fed has made output considerably more stable since World War II than it was before 1914 (Table 8.2, row 1, and Figure 8.5, first panel). Christina Romer's (1986a, 1989, 2009) influential work has, however, cast doubt even on this more attenuated claim. According to her, the Kuznets-Kendrick pre-1929 real GNP estimates overstate the volatility of pre-Fed output relative to that of later periods, in part because they are based on fewer component series than later estimates and because they conflate nominal and real values, but mainly because the real component series are almost exclusively for commodities, the output of which is generally much more volatile than that of other kinds of output. From 1947 to 1985, for example, commodity output as a whole was about two and a third times more volatile than real GNP.

Table 8.2: Output Volatility, Alternative GNP Estimates (Percentage Standard Deviation from Trend)

Series	1869–1914	1915–2009	1915–1946	1947–2009	1984–2009	ratio	ratio	ratio	ratio
	(1)	(2)	(3)	(4)	(5)	(2)/(1)	(3)/(1)	(4)/(1)	(5)/(1)
Standard	5.064	5.764	9.323	2.554	1.706	1.138	1.841	0.504	0.337
Romer	2.664	5.716	9.224	2.554	1.706	2.145	3.463	0.959	0.640
Balke-Gordon	4.270	6.291	10.195	2.773	1.696	1.473	2.388	0.649	0.397

NOTES: Trend is measured using the Hodrick-Prescott filter. "Standard" series, 1869–1929: original Kuznets series, with adjustments by Gallman and Kendrick (see Rhode and Sutch 2006: 3–12). "Romer" series, 1869–1929: real GNP from Christina Romer (1989: Table 2). "Standard" and "Romer" series, 1929–2009: spliced to real GNP (Bureau of Economic Analysis of the Department of Commerce, retrieved from FRED, Federal Reserve Bank of St. Louis, https://fred.stlouisfed.org). "Balke-Gordon" series, 1869–1983: real GNP from Nathan Balke and Robert Gordon (1986: App. B, Table 1); 1984–2009: spliced to Bureau of Economic Analysis real GNP.

SOURCE: All data are from Carter et al. (2006).

According to Romer's own pre-1929 GNP series, which relies on statistical estimates of the relationship between total and commodity output movements (instead of Kuznets' naïve one-to-one assumption), the cyclical volatility of output prior to the Fed's establishment was actually lower than it has been throughout the full (1915–2009) Fed era (Table 8.2, row 2, and Figure 8.5, second panel). More surprisingly, pre-Fed (1869–1914) volatility (as measured by the standard deviations of output from its Hodrick-Prescott trend) was also lower than post–World War II volatility, though the difference is slight.[13]

Figure 8.5: Percentage Deviations of Real GNP from Trend

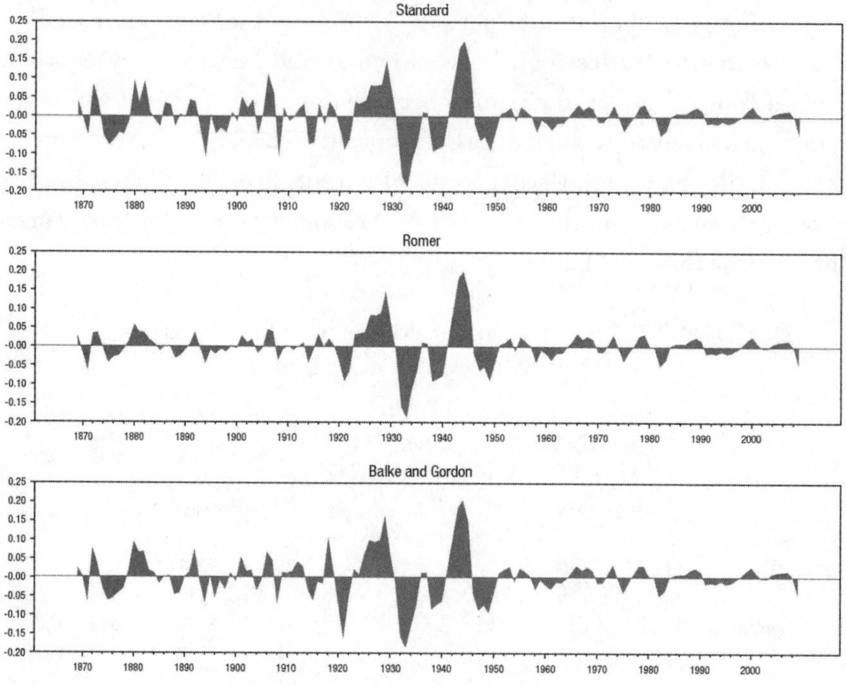

NOTES: See Table 8.2 for series definitions and sources. Shaded area is deviation from trend, where trend is measured using Hodrick-Prescott filter.

Complementary revisions of historical unemployment data by Romer (1986b) and J. R. Vernon (1994), displayed in Figure 8.6, likewise suggest that the post-1948 stabilization of unemployment apparent in Stanley Lebergott's (1964) standard series is an artifact of the data. Because Vernon's revised unemployment series is based on the Balke-Gordon (1986) real GNP series, which is more volatile than Romer's GNP series, and because his series includes the relatively volatile 1870s, Vernon finds a somewhat larger difference between 19th-century and postwar unemployment volatility than that reported by Romer. Nevertheless, he finds that his estimates "indicate depressions for the 1870s and 1890s which are appreciably less severe than the depressions perceived for these periods by economists such as Schumpeter and Lebergott" (Balke and Gordon 1986: 707).

Figure 8.6: U.S. Unemployment Rate, 1869–2009

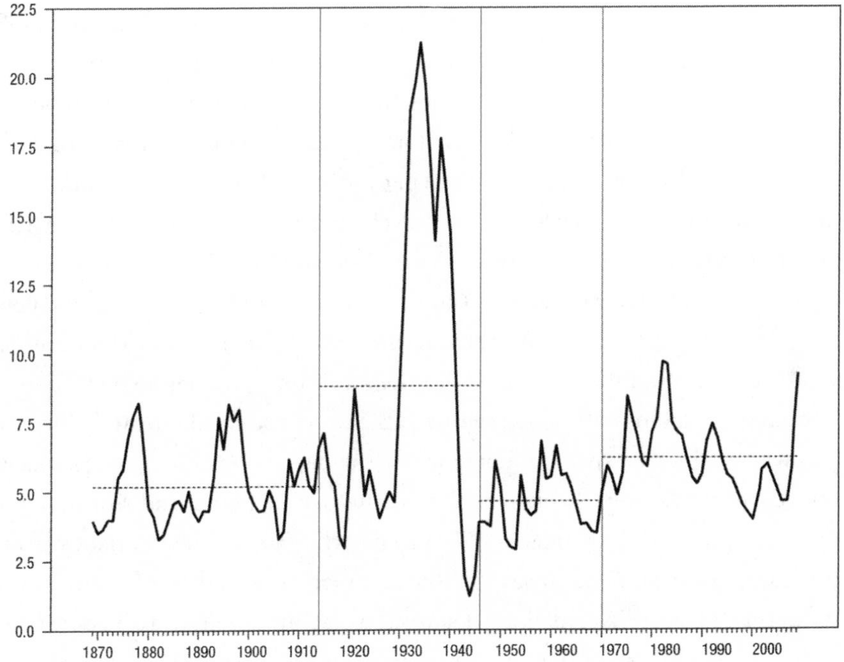

NOTE: Dashed lines indicate subperiod sample means.

SOURCES: 1869–99 (Vernon 1994); 1899–1930 (Romer 1986b, adjusted series); 1931–40 (Coen 1973, adjusted series); 1941–2009 (Bureau of Labor Statistics).

Romer's revisions have themselves been challenged by others, however, including Victor Zarnowitz (1992: 77–79) and Balke and Gordon (1989).[14] The last-named authors used direct measures of construction-, transportation-, and communication-sector output during the pre-Fed era, along with improved consumer price estimates, to construct their own historic GNP series. According to this series, the standard deviation of real GNP from its Hodrick-Prescott trend for 1869 to 1914 is 4.27 percent, which differs little from the standard-series value of 5.10 percent. Balke and Gordon's findings thus appear to vindicate the traditional (pre-Romer) view (Table 8.2, row 3, and Figure 8.5, third panel).

More recent work helps to resolve the contradictory findings of Romer, on one hand, and Balke and Gordon, on the other. Rather than rely on conventional aggregation procedures to construct historic (pre-1929) real gross domestic product (GDP) estimates, Albrecht Ritschl and colleagues (2008) employ "dynamic factor analysis" to uncover a latent common factor capturing the comovements in 53 time series that have been consistently reported since 1867. According to their benchmark model, which assumes that the coefficients ("factor loadings") relating individual series to the latent factor are constant, there was, in fact, "no change in postwar volatility relative to the prewar [that is, pre–World War I] period" (p. 7). Allowing instead for time-varying factor loadings (and hence for gradual structural change), they find that post–World War II volatility was a third *greater* than pre-Fed volatility (p. 29, Table 1). These findings reinforce Romer's conclusions.[15] But Ritschl and his colleagues are also able to reproduce Balke and Gordon's postwar moderation using a common factor based on their nonagricultural real time series only, which resemble the series Balke and Gordon rely upon for their GNP estimates. Here again, the moderation vanishes if factor loadings are allowed to vary. Balke and Gordon's finding of a substantial reduction in post–World War II output volatility relative to pre-Fed volatility thus appears to depend on their focus on industrial output and the implicit assumption that the relative importance of different components of that output had not changed.

Even if one accepts the Balke-Gordon GNP estimates, it does not follow that the Fed deserves credit for (belatedly) stabilizing real output. It may be that aggregate supply shocks, the real effects of which monetary policy is unable to neutralize, were relatively more important before 1914 than they have been since World War II. The effects of this reduced role for supply shocks might then be misinterpreted as evidence of the Fed's success in limiting output variations by stabilizing aggregate demand.

Using the Balke-Gordon output series, John Keating and John Nye (1998) estimate a bivariate vector autoregression (VAR) model of inflation and output growth for the United States over the periods 1869–1913 and 1950–94.

They then identify aggregate demand and supply shocks by assuming, in the manner of Olivier Blanchard and Danny Quah (1989), that supply shocks alone have permanent real effects, which allows them to decompose the variance of output into separate supply- and demand-shock components. Doing so, they find that aggregate supply shocks were of overwhelming importance in the earlier period, accounting for 95 percent of real output's conditional forecast error variance at all horizons (Keating and Nye 1998: 246, Table 3). During the post–World War II period, in contrast, the fraction of output's forecast error variance attributable to supply shocks has been just 5 percent at a one-year horizon, rising to only 68 percent after a full decade (Keating and Nye 1998: 240, Table 2).

Keating and Nye (1998) themselves, however, question the validity of these findings because, according to their identification scheme, a positive pre-Fed "supply" shock causes the price level to increase rather than to decline. But this seemingly "perverse" comovement may simply reflect the tendency, under the international gold standard regime, for supply shocks involving exportable commodities, such as cotton, to translate into enhanced exports and thus into increased gold inflows (see Davis et al. 2009). A more recent study by Michael Bordo and Angela Redish (2004) allows for this possibility by extending the Keating-Nye model to include a measure of the pre-Fed money stock and by assuming that the price level is uninfluenced in the long run by either aggregate supply or aggregate demand shocks at the national level—an assumption consistent with the workings of the international gold standard. According to their estimates, which again rely upon Balke and Gordon's quarterly output data, aggregate supply shocks accounted for 89 percent of pre-Fed output variance at a 1-year horizon and for almost 80 percent of such variance after 10 years. These findings differ little from Keating and Nye's for the pre-Fed period.

Bordo and Redish examine the pre-Fed era only, and so do not offer a consistent comparison of it with the post–World War II era. To arrive at such a comparison, while shedding further light on the Fed's contribution to postwar stability, we constructed a VAR model allowing for four distinct macroeconomic shocks—to aggregate supply, the investment-saving (IS) schedule, money demand, and the money supply—which are identified using different and plausible identifying restrictions for the pre-Fed and post–World War II sample periods. Using this model (and relying once again on the Balke-Gordon GNP estimates), we find that aggregate supply shocks account for between 81 percent and 86 percent of the forecast error variance of pre-Fed output up to a three-year horizon, as opposed to less than 42 percent of the variance after World War II (Table 8.3).[16] In terms familiar from recent discussions of the causes of the post-1983 "Great Moderation" in output volatility (discussed below), our findings suggest that the post–World War II period taken as a whole enjoyed better "luck" than the pre-Fed period.

Table 8.3: Contribution of Aggregate Supply Shocks to Output Forecast Error Variance

Horizon (quarters)	Pre-Fed	Post-WWII
1	81.1373	36.2475
2	83.0815	35.2230
3	85.7569	41.2518
4	86.5508	46.4824
5	86.3244	51.7597
6	86.3275	56.7460
7	86.5984	60.9029
8	86.8482	64.2719
12	88.9045	72.8033
16	90.7820	77.4053
20	91.8888	80.4573
24	92.7255	82.7308

SOURCE: Lastrapes and Selgin (2010).

Our model also shows no clear improvement after World War II in the dynamic response of output to aggregate demand shocks. Whereas one might expect the Fed, in its role as output stabilizer, to tighten the money supply in the face of positive IS (spending) shocks and to expand it in response to positive shocks to money demand, the response functions we estimate indicate instead that the Fed has tended to *expand* the money stock in response to IS shocks, causing larger and more persistent deviations of output from its "natural" level than would have occurred in response to similar shocks during the pre-Fed period (Figure 8.7, left-hand-side panels). At the same time, the Fed was *less* effective than the classical gold standard had been in expanding the money supply in response to unpredictable reductions in money's velocity.

Figure 8.7: Dynamic Responses of Output and Money to Aggregate Demand Shocks, Pre-Fed and Post–World War II

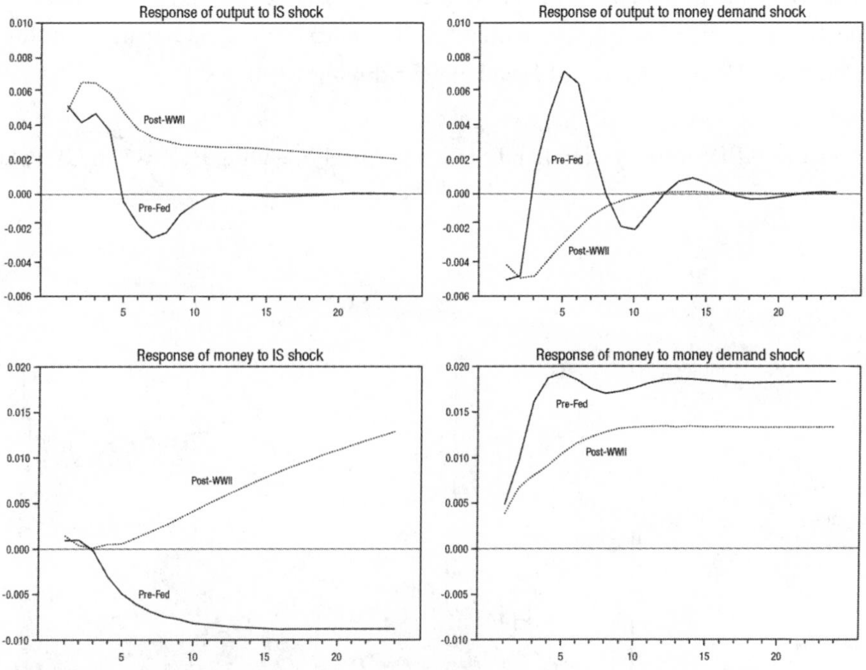

NOTES: Responses to an unanticipated increase in the IS curve (aggregate spending) and to an unanticipated increase in the demand for real money balances, as a function of forecast horizon in quarter. See Lastrapes and Selgin (2010).

Fiscal stabilizers, whether "automatic" or deliberately aimed at combating downturns, are also likely to have contributed to reduced output volatility since the Fed's establishment, when state and federal government expenditures combined constituted but a fifth as large a share of GDP as they did just before the recent burst of stimulus spending (Figure 8.8). Thus Bradford DeLong and Lawrence Summers (1986) claim that the decline in U.S.

output volatility between World War II and the early 1980s was due, not to improved monetary policy, but to the stabilizing influence of progressive taxation and countercyclical entitlements. Subsequent research documents a pronounced (though not necessarily linear) relationship between government size and the volatility of real output (e.g., Gali 1994; Fatás and Mihov 2001; Andres et al. 2008; Mohanty and Zampolli 2009). According to Madhusudan Mohanty and Fabrizio Zampolli (2009), a 10 percent increase in the government's share of GDP was associated with a 21 percent overall decline in cyclical output volatility for 20 countries in the Organisation for Economic Co-operation and Development during 1970–84.[17]

Figure 8.8: Annual Federal and State and Local Spending Relative to GDP, 1902–2009

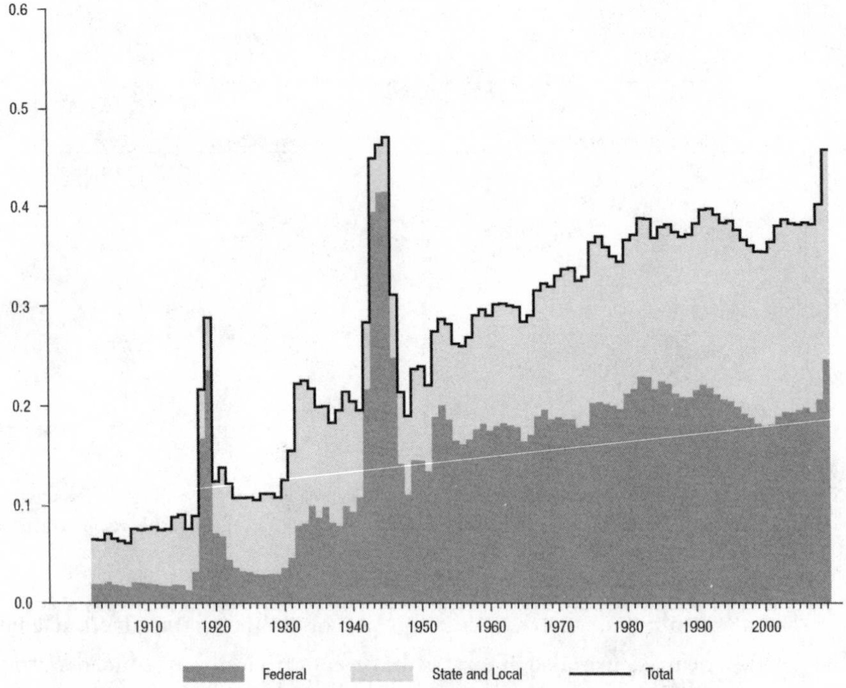

NOTES: Federal spending is federal net outlays from the Office of Management and Budget (retrieved from FRED, Federal Reserve Bank of St. Louis, https://fred.stlouisfed.org). State and local expenditures are from http://usgovernmentspending.com.

Fiscal stabilizers appear, on the other hand, to have played no significant part in the post-1984 decline in output volatility (as well as in both the average rate and the volatility of inflation) known as the "Great Moderation." Consequently, that episode seems especially likely to reflect a genuine if belated improvement in the conduct of monetary policy. We next turn to research concerning this possibility.

THE "GREAT MODERATION"

The beginning of Paul Volcker's second term as Fed chairman coincided with a dramatic decline in the volatility of real output that lasted through the Alan Greenspan era. Annual real GDP growth, for example, was less than half as volatile from 1984 to 2007 as it was from 1959 to 1983. The inflation rate, having been reduced to lower single digits, also became considerably less volatile. Many, including Alan Blinder (1998), Romer (1999), Thomas Sargent (1999), and Bernanke (2004), have regarded this "Great Moderation" of inflation and real output as evidence of a substantial improvement in the Fed's conduct of monetary policy—a turn to what Blinder (1998: 49) terms "enlightened discretion."[18] Bernanke (2004), conceding that the high inflation in the 1970s and early 1980s was largely due to excessive monetary expansion aimed at trying to maintain a below-natural rate of unemployment, argues similarly that Fed authorities learned over the course of that episode that they could not exploit a stable Phillips curve; Romer (1999: 43) claims that, after the early 1980s, the Fed "had a steadier hand on the macroeconomic tiller."[19]

The "enlightened discretion" view has, however, been challenged by statistical studies pointing to moderating forces other than improved monetary policy. A study by James Stock and Mark Watson (2002: 200; see also 2005) attributes between 75 percent and 90 percent of the Great Moderation in U.S. output volatility to "good luck in the form of smaller economic disturbances" rather than improved monetary policy. Subsequent research has likewise tended to downplay the contribution of improved monetary policy, either by lending support to the "good luck" hypothesis or by attributing the Great Moderation to financial innovations, an enhanced "buffer stock" role for manufacturing inventories, an increase in the importance of the service sector relative to that of manufacturing, a change in the age composition of the U.S. population, and other sorts of structural change.[20] As usual, there are exceptions, prominent among which is the study of Jordi Gali and Luca Gambetti (2009), which finds that improved monetary policy, consisting of an increased emphasis on inflation targeting in setting the federal funds target, did play an important part in the Great Moderation.

Most authorities do attribute the substantial decline in both the mean rate of inflation and in inflation volatility since the early 1980s to improved monetary policy. Yet, even here, the contribution of enlightened monetary policy may be less than it appears to be: according to Robert Barro and David Gordon's (1983) theory of monetary policy in the presence of a time-inconsistent temptation to improve current-period real outcomes using surprise inflation, the higher the natural rate of unemployment, the greater the inflationary bias in the conduct of monetary policy, other things equal. According to Peter Ireland (1999) and to Henry Chappell and Rob Roy McGregor (2004), both the actual course of inflation in the 1970s and afterwards and the arguments on which the Federal Open Market Committee based its decisions conform to the predictions of the theory of time-inconsistent monetary policy.[21]

In the presence of supply shocks, moreover, the time-inconsistency framework implies that higher inflation will be accompanied by a more marked "stabilization bias" and, hence, by greater inflation volatility. Richard Dennis (2003; see also Dennis and Söderström 2006) explains:

> [T]o damp the inflationary effect of the adverse supply shock, central bankers have to raise interest rates more today, generating more unemployment than they would if they could commit themselves to implement the tight policy that they promised. In this scenario, the effect of the time-inconsistency is called stabilization bias because the time-inconsistency affects the central banker's ability to stabilize inflation expectations and hence stabilize inflation itself. The stabilization bias adds to inflation's variability, making inflation more difficult for households, firms, *and* the central bank, to predict.

As Chappell and McGregor (2004: 249–50) observe, to the extent that the Great Moderation conforms with the predictions of the theory of time inconsistency, that moderation supplies no grounds for complacency about the Fed:

> Policy-makers may have greater appreciation for the importance of maintaining price stability, but the fundamental institutions by which monetary policy decisions are made have not changed, nor has the broader political environment. Shocks similar to those that emerged in the 1970s could do so again. While Blinder (1997) would comfort us with the argument that the time inconsistency problem is no longer relevant, a more troublesome interpretation is possible. The current time-consistent equilibrium is more pleasant than the one prevailing in the 1970s, not just because the Fed is more enlightened, but also because of a fortunate confluence of exogenous and political forces.

Recent experience has, of course, made it all too evident that prior reports of the passing of macroeconomic instability were premature. According to Todd Clark (2009: 7), statistics gathered since the outbreak of the subprime crisis reveal "a partial or complete reversal of the Great Moderation in many sections of the U.S. economy." Clark himself, in what amounts to the flip side of the Stock-Watson view, characterizes the reversal as a "period of very bad luck" (p. 25), asserting that "once the crisis subsides . . . improved monetary policy that occurred in years past should ensure that low volatility is the norm" (Clark 2009: 27; compare Canarella et al. 2010). Those who believe, in contrast, that "luck" was no less important a factor in the moderation than it has been in the recent reversal, or who—like Taylor (2009a)—see the subprime crisis itself as a byproduct of irresponsible Fed policy, are unlikely to share Clark's optimism.

FREQUENCY AND DURATION OF RECESSIONS

Some of the hazards involved in attempting to compare pre– and post–Federal Reserve Act measures of real volatility can be avoided by instead looking at the frequency and duration of business cycles. Doing so, Francis Diebold and Glenn Rudebusch (1992: 993–34) observe, "largely requires only a qualitative sense of the direction of general business activity," while also allowing one to draw on indicators apart from those used to construct measures of aggregate output.

The National Bureau of Economic Research's (NBER) conventional business cycle chronology suggests that contractions have been both substantially less frequent and substantially shorter on average, while expansions have been substantially longer on average, since World War II than they were prior to the Fed's establishment. Because it is based on aggregate series that avoid the excessive volatility of conventional pre-Fed output measures (Romer 1994: 582 n28), and because it only classifies contractions of some minimum duration and amplitude as business cycles, the chronology does in fact avoid some of the dangers involved in comparing pre-Fed and post–World War II output volatility.

The NBER's chronology has nonetheless been faulted for seriously exaggerating both the frequency and the duration of pre-Fed cycles and, thereby, exaggerating the Fed's contribution to economic stability. According to Romer (1994: 575), whereas the NBER's post-1927 cycle reference dates are derived using data in levels, those for before 1927 are based on detrended data. This difference alone, Romer notes, results in a systematic overstatement of both the frequency and the duration of early contractions compared to modern ones.[22] The NBER's pre-1927 indexes of economic activity, upon which its pre-Fed chronology depends, are also based in part on various nominal time series—which (for reasons considered above) are a further source of bias (Romer 1994: 582; see also Watson 1994).

Using both the Fed's and an adjusted version of her own indexes of industrial production (see Miron and Romer 1990), Romer arrives at a new set of reference dates that "radically alter one's view of changes in the duration of contractions and expansions over time" (Romer 1994: 601). According to this new chronology, although contractions were indeed somewhat more frequent before the Fed's establishment than after World War II (though not, it bears noting, more frequent than in the full Federal Reserve sample period), they were also almost three months *shorter* on average, and no more severe.

Recoveries were also faster, with an average time from trough to previous peak of 7.7 months, as compared to 10.6 months. Allowing for the recent, 18-month-long contraction further strengthens these conclusions. And while the new dates still suggest that expansions have lasted longer since World War II than before 1914, that difference, besides depending mainly on one exceptionally long expansion during the 1960s (p. 603), is also much less substantial than is suggested by the NBER's dates.

Because the Miron and Romer (1990) industrial production series begins in 1884, Romer does not attempt to revise earlier business cycle dates. That project has, however, been undertaken more recently by Joseph Davis (2006) who, using his own annual series for U.S. industrial production for 1796–1915 (Davis 2004), finds no discernible difference at all between the frequency and average duration of recessions after World War II and their frequency and average duration throughout the full national banking era. Besides suggesting that the NBER's recessions of 1869–70, 1887–88, 1890–91, and 1899–1900 should be reclassified as growth cycles (that is, periods of modest growth interrupting more pronounced expansions) Davis's chronology goes further than Romer's in revising the record concerning the length of genuine pre-Fed contractions, in part because it goes further in distinguishing negative output growth from falling prices. The change is most glaringly illustrated by the case of the recession of 1873. According to NBER's chronology, that recession lasted from October 1873 to May 1879, making it by far the longest recession in U.S. history and, therefore, an important contributor to the conclusion that recessions have become shorter since the Fed's establishment. According to Davis's chronology, in contrast, the 1873 recession lasted only two years, or just six months longer than the subprime contraction.[23]

In comparing pre– and post–Federal Reserve Act business cycles, we have again tended to set aside the interwar period, as if allowing for a long interval during which the Fed had yet to discover its sea legs. Nevertheless, the Fed's interwar record, and especially its record during the Great Depression, cannot be overlooked altogether in a study purporting to assess its overall performance. And that record was, by most modern accounts, abysmal. The truth of Milton Friedman and Anna Schwartz's (1963: 299ff.)

thesis that overly restrictive Fed policies were responsible for the "Great Contraction" of the early 1930s is now widely accepted (e.g., Bernanke 2002b; Christiano et al. 2003), as is their claim that the Fed interfered with recovery by doubling minimum bank reserve requirements between August 1936 and May 1937. Romer (1992) has shown, furthermore, that although monetary growth was, despite the Fed's errors, the factor most responsible for such recovery as did take place between 1933 and 1942, that growth was based, not on any expansionary moves on the part of the Fed, but on gold inflows from abroad prompted first by the devaluation of the dollar and then by increasing European political instability.[24]

Some economic historians, most notably Barry Eichengreen (1992), have blamed the Great Depression in the United States on the gold standard rather than on the Fed's misuse of its discretion, claiming that the Fed had to refrain from further monetary expansion in order to maintain the gold standard. But Elmus Wicker (1996: 161–62) finds that gold outflows played only a minor role in the banking panics that were the proximate cause of the monetary collapse of 1930–33, while Michael Bordo and colleagues (2002) show that, even had there been perfect capital mobility (which was far from being the case), open market purchases on a scale capable of having prevented that collapse would not have led to gold outflows large enough to pose a threat to convertibility. Chang-Tai Hsieh and Romer (2006), finally, draw on both statistical and narrative evidence to examine and ultimately reject the specific hypothesis that the Fed was compelled to refrain from expansionary policies out of fear that expansion would provoke a speculative attack on the dollar. Instead, they conclude (p. 142), "the American Great Depression was largely the result of inept policy, not the inevitable consequence of a flawed international monetary system."[25]

BANKING PANICS

If the Fed has not reduced the overall frequency or average duration of recessions, can it nonetheless be credited with reducing the frequency of banking panics and, hence, of the more severe recessions that tend to go along with such panics? A conventional view holds that the Fed did indeed make panics less common by eliminating the currency shortages and associated credit crunches that were notorious features of previous panics; and Jeff Miron's (1986) research appears to support this view by showing how, in its early years at least, the Fed did away with the seasonal tightening of the money market, and consequent spiking interest rates, that characterized the pre-Fed era.

However, more recent and consistent accounts of the incidence of banking panics suggest that the Fed did not actually reduce their frequency. Andrew Jalil concludes, on the basis of one such new reckoning, "that contrary to the conventional wisdom, there is no evidence of a decline in the frequency of panics during the first 15 years of the existence of the Federal Reserve" (Jalil 2009: 3). That is, there was no reduction between 1914 and 1930 and, hence, none until the conclusion of the national bank holiday toward mid-March of 1933. Jalil's findings agree with Wicker's conclusion, based on his comprehensive analyses of financial crises between the Civil War and World War II (Wicker 1996, 2000), that previous assessments had exaggerated the frequency of pre-Fed banking panics by counting among them episodes in "money market stringency coupled with a sharp break in stock prices" or collective action by the New York Clearinghouse but no "widespread bank runs or failures" (Wicker 2000: xii). In fact, Wicker states,

> there were no more than three major banking panics between 1873 and 1907 [inclusive], and two incipient banking panics in 1884 and 1890. Twelve years elapsed between the panic of 1861 and the panic of 1873, twenty years between the panics of 1873 and 1893, and fourteen years between 1893 and 1907: three banking panics in half a century! And in only one of the three, 1893, did the number of bank suspensions match those of the Great Depression. (Wicker 2000: xii)

In contrast, Wicker (1996) elsewhere reports, the first three years of the Great Depression alone witnessed five major banking panics. No genuine post-1913 reduction in banking panics, or in total bank suspensions, took place until after the national bank holiday of March 1933; and credit for that reduction belongs, not to the Fed, but to the Reconstruction Finance Corporation (RFC), which purchased $1.1 billion in preferred stock from some 6,500 banks between March 1933 and May 1934, and, starting on January 1, 1934, deposit insurance (see Figure 8.9). "As the RFC and FDIC became more important to stabilizing the banking system," financial historian Robert Lynn Fuller (2009: 535) observes, "the Federal Reserve Bank became less so . . . because its primary purpose—to provide liquidity to the system—had become irrelevant in a system awash in liquidity."[26]

Figure 8.9: U.S. Bank Failures as Percentage of All Banks, 1896–1955

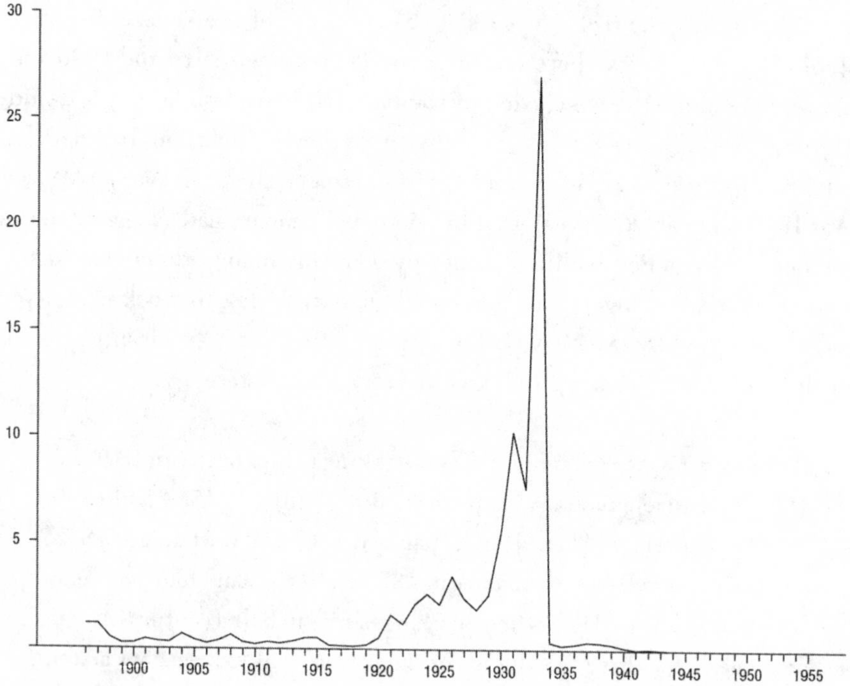

SOURCES: Board of Governors of the Federal Reserve System (1943, 1959); Comptroller of the Currency, *Annual Report* (1917).

Besides supplying a more accurate account of the frequency of banking panics before and after the Fed, Jalil's chronology of panics allows him to revise the record concerning the bearing of panics on the severity and duration of recessions. Whereas DeLong and Summers (1986), employing their own series for the incidence of panics between 1890 and 1910, conclude that banking panics played only a small part in the pre-Fed business cycle, Jalil (2009: 34) finds that they were a "significant source of economic instability." Nearly half of all business cycle downturns before World War II involved panics, and those that did tended to be both substantially more severe and longer lasting than those that did not: between 1866 and 1914, recessions involving major banking panics were on average almost three times as deep, with recoveries on average taking almost three times as long, as those without major panics (p. 35).[27] This evidence suggests that, by serving to eliminate banking panics, deposit insurance also served, for a time at least, to reduce the frequency of severe recessions. This fact, in turn, points to the need for a further, downward reassessment of the Fed's post-1933 contribution to economic stabilization.

Finally, those banking panics and accompanying, severe recessions that did occur before 1914 were not inescapable consequences of the absence of a central bank. Instead, according to Wicker (2000: xiii) and White (1983), among others, banking panics both then and afterwards were fundamentally due to misguided regulations, including laws prohibiting both statewide and interstate branch banking. Besides limiting opportunities for diversification, legal barriers to branch banking, together with the reserve requirement stipulations of the National Banking Act, encouraged interior banks to count balances with city correspondents as cash reserves. The consequent "pyramiding" of reserves in New York, combined with inflexible minimum reserve requirements and the "inelasticity" of the stock of national bank notes (which had to be more than fully backed by increasingly expensive government bonds, and which could not be expanded or retired quickly even once the necessary bonds had been purchased, owing to delays in working through the Office of the Comptroller of the Currency) all contributed to frequent episodes of money market stringency, some of which resulted in numerous bank suspensions, if not in full-blown panics.

Other nations' experience illuminates the role that misguided regulations, including those responsible for the highly fragmented structure of the U.S. banking industry, played in making the U.S. system uniquely vulnerable to panics. Bordo (1986) reports that, among half a dozen western countries he surveyed (the others being the United Kingdom, Sweden, Germany,

France, and Canada), the United States alone experienced banking crises. Charles Calomiris (2000: Chapter 1), also drawing on international evidence, attributes the different incidence of panics to differences in banking industry organization.

Given its proximity to and economic integration with the United States, Canada's experience is especially revealing. Unlike the United States, which had almost 2,000 (mainly unit) banks in 1870, and almost 25,000 banks on the eve of the Great Depression, Canada never had more than several dozen banks, almost all with extensive branch networks. Between 1830 and 1914 (when Canada's entry into World War I led to a run on gold anticipating suspension of the gold standard), Canada experienced few bank failures and no bank runs. It also had no bank failures at all during the Great Depression, and for that reason experienced a much less severe contraction of money and credit than the United States did. Although the latter outcome may have depended on government forbearance and implicit guarantees which, according to Lawrence Kryzanowski and Gordon Roberts (1993), made it possible for many Canadian banks to stay open despite being technically insolvent for at least part of the Great Depression period,[28] the fact remains that Canada was able to avoid banking panics without resort to either a central bank or explicit insurance.[29]

LAST-RESORT LENDING

That the Federal Reserve System was not the only solution to pre-Fed banking panics—that it may, in fact, have been inferior to deregulatory reforms aimed at allowing the U.S. banking and currency system to develop along stronger, Canadian lines—and that credit for the absence of panics after 1933 mainly belongs not to the Fed but to deposit insurance, does not rule out the possibility that the Fed has occasionally contributed to financial stability by serving as a lender of last resort (LOLR).

The traditional view of the lender-of-last-resort role derives from Walter Bagehot (1873). In Bagehot's view, a LOLR is a second-best remedy for a banking system weakened by legal restrictions, including those awarding monopoly privileges to favored banks (first best to Bagehot was a minimally restricted and, hence, stronger system like Scotland's).[30] The LOLR can help prevent financial panics, without creating serious moral hazard, by supporting illiquid but not insolvent banks. Bagehot's classical rules for last-resort lending instructed the Bank of England to extend credit "freely and vigorously," but only to borrowers that passed a solvency test (Bagehot's was posting "good banking securities" as collateral), and only at a higher-than-normal rate of interest. As Brian Madigan, director of the Federal Reserve's division of monetary affairs, has noted, "Bagehot's dictum can be viewed as having a sound foundation in microeconomics":

> Specifically, lending only to sound institutions and lending only against good collateral sharpen firms' incentives to invest prudently in order to remain solvent. And lending only at a penalty rate preserves the incentive for borrowers to obtain market funding when it is available rather than seeking recourse to the central bank. (Madigan 2009: 1)

In Bagehot's day, the solvency requirement was intended to protect the then-private Bank of England's shareholders from losing money on last-resort loans. Today it serves to protect taxpayers from exposure to public central bank losses.

Judged from a Bagehotian perspective, how well has the Fed performed its LOLR duties? According to Thomas Humphrey, a former Federal Reserve economist and an authority on classical LOLR doctrine, it has performed them very badly indeed, honoring the classical doctrine "more in the breach than in the observance" (Humphrey 2010: 22). While Humphrey does identify episodes—including the October 1987 stock market crash, the approach of Y2K, and (in some respects) the aftermath of 9/11—in which the Fed seems to have followed Bagehot's advice, he notes that this has not been its usual practice.[31]

During the Great Depression, for example, the Fed departed from Bagehot's doctrine first by failing to lend to many solvent but illiquid banks, and later (in 1936–37) by deliberately reducing solvent banks' supply of liquid free reserves (Humphrey 2010.: 23). Since then, it has tended to err in the opposite direction, by extending credit to insolvent institutions. The Fed made large discount window loans to both Franklin National and Continental Illinois before their spectacular failures in 1974 and 1984, respectively; and between January 1985 and May 1991, it routinely offered extended credit to banks that supervisory agencies considered in imminent danger of failing. Ninety percent of these borrowing banks failed soon afterwards (U.S. Congress 1991; Schwartz 1992).

During the subprime crisis, Humphrey (2010: 333) observes, the Fed "deviated from the classical model in so many ways as to make a mockery of the notion that it is a L[O]LR." It did so by knowingly accepting "toxic" assets, most notably mortgage-backed securities, as loan collateral, or by purchasing them outright without subjecting them to "haircuts" proportionate to the risk involved, and by supplying funds directly to firms understood to be insolvent (Humphrey 2010: 24–28; see also Feldstein 2010: 136–37).[32] As the two panels of Figure 8.10 show, until September 2008, the Fed also sterilized its direct lending operations through offsetting Fed sales of Treasury securities, in effect transferring some $250 billion in liquid funds from presumably solvent firms to potentially insolvent ones—a strategy precisely opposite Bagehot's, and one that tended to spread rather than to contain financial distress (Thornton 2009a, 2009b; Hetzel 2009a; Wheelock 2010: 96). This strategy may ultimately have harmed even the struggling enterprises it was supposed to favor, for according to Daniel Thornton (2009b: 2), if instead of attempting to reallocate credit, the Fed had responded to the financial crisis by significantly increasing the total amount of credit available to the market, then "the failures of Bear Stearns, Lehman Brothers, and AIG may have been avoided and, so too, the need for TARP." Moreover, according to several authorities, it was thanks to the Troubled Asset Relief Program (TARP) itself, or rather to the gloom-and-doom warnings Ben Bernanke issued in his effort to secure the passage of TARP, that a "relatively modest contraction of economic activity due to . . . the deflation of house prices became the Great Recession" (Goodfriend 2010: 18; see also Taylor 2009a: 25–30).

Figure 8.10: Federal Reserve Credit and Components, Monetary Base, and Excess Reserves, 2007–10

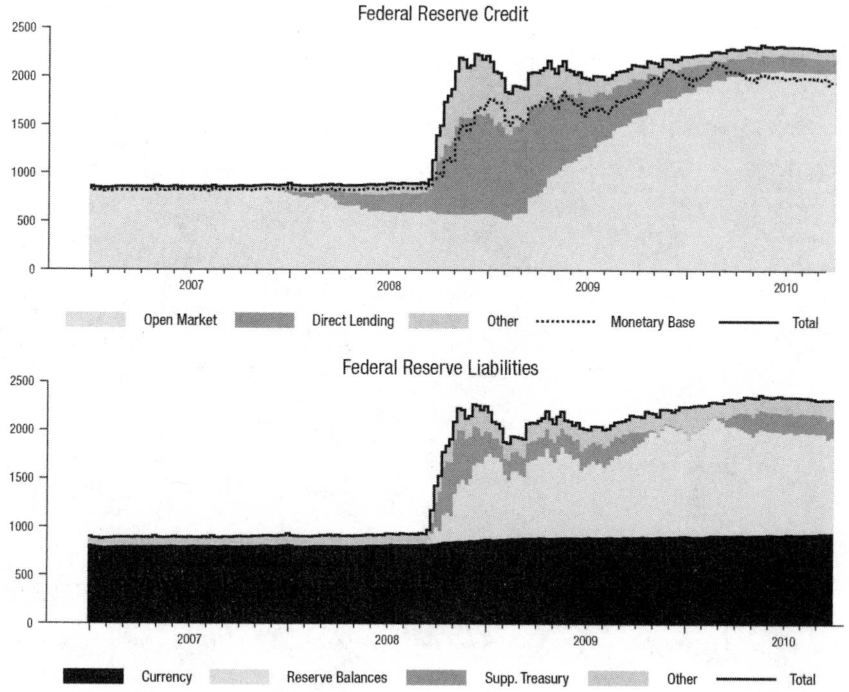

NOTES: Weekly data. "Open market" includes all securities held outright, including mortgage-backed securities, plus repurchase agreements. "Direct lending" includes term auction credit, all other loans, and all net portfolio holdings of the Fed's special investment vehicles.

SOURCE: FRED, Federal Reserve Bank of St. Louis, https://fred.stlouisfed.org.

In September 2008, the Fed at last turned from sterilized to unsterilized lending, and on such a scale as resulted in a doubling of the monetary base over the course of the ensuing year. At the same time, however, it began paying interest on excess reserves, thereby increasing the demand for such reserves, while also arranging to have the Treasury sell supplemental bills and deposit the proceeds in a special account. Thanks in part to these special measures, bank lending, nominal GDP, and the Consumer Price Index (CPI), instead of responding positively to the doubling of the monetary base, plummeted (see Figure 8.11).[33]

Figure 8.11: Nominal GDP Growth and Inflation, 2000–10

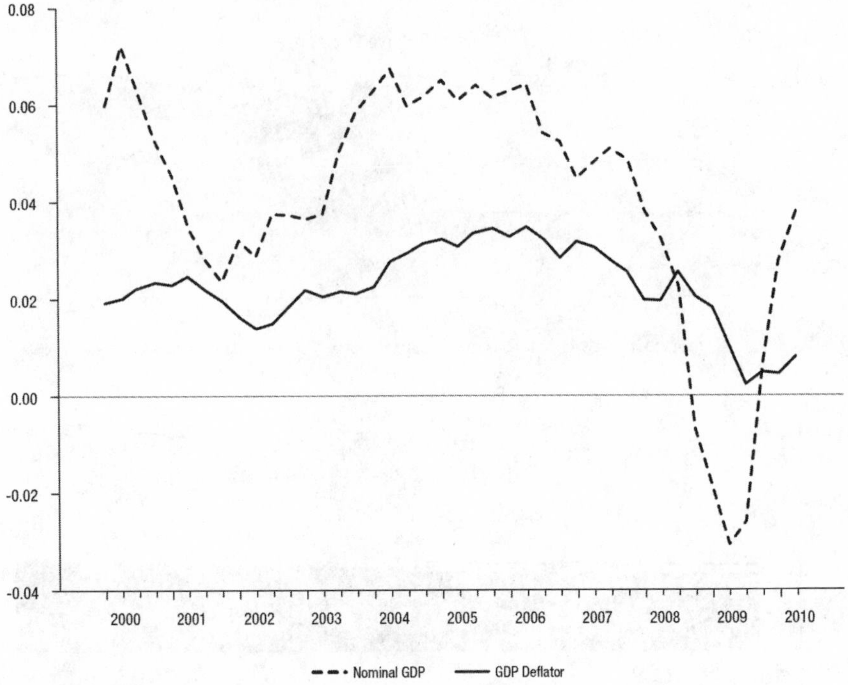

NOTES: Quarterly data, year-to-year growth rates.

Finally, rather than pursue a consistent policy—a less emphasized but not less important component of Bagehot's advice—the Fed unsettled markets by protecting the creditors of some insolvent firms (Bear Stearns) while allowing others (Lehman Brothers) to suffer default. Former Fed Chairman Paul Volcker (2008: 2) remarked, in the aftermath of the Fed's support (via its wholly owned subsidiary Maiden Lane) of JPMorgan Chase's purchase of Bear Stearns, that the Fed had stretched "the time honored central bank mantra in time of crisis—'lend freely at high rates against good collateral'—to the point of no return."

The Fed has been increasingly inclined to lend to insolvent banks in part because creditworthy ones have been increasingly able to secure funding in private wholesale markets. As Stephen Cecchetti and Piti Disyatat (2010) observe, under modern circumstances "a bank that is unable to raise funds in the market must, almost by definition, lack access to good security for collateralized loans." Prior to the recent crisis, the development of a well-organized interbank market ready to lend to solvent banks led many economists (Friedman 1960: 50–51; Goodfriend and King 1988; Kaufman 1991; Schwartz 1992; Lacker 2004: 956ff.) to declare the Fed's discount window obsolete and to recommend that it be shut for good, leaving the Fed with no lender-of-last-resort responsibility save that of maintaining systemwide liquidity by means of open market operations, while relying upon private intermediaries to distribute liquid funds in accordance with Bagehot's precepts. Notwithstanding Cecchetti and Disyatat's (2010: 12) claim that "a systemic event almost surely requires lending at an effectively subsidized rate . . . while taking collateral of suspect quality," open market operations have in fact proven capable of preserving market liquidity even following such major financial shocks as the failure of the Penn Central Railroad, the stock market crash of October 1987, the Russian default of 1998, Y2K, and the 9/11 terrorist attacks.[34]

The subprime crisis has, however, led many experts to conclude that it is Bagehot's precepts, rather than direct central bank lending to troubled firms, that have become obsolete. Some justify recent departures from Bagehot's rules, or at least from strict reliance on open market operations, on the grounds that the crisis was one in which the wholesale lending market itself was crippled, so that even solvent intermediaries could not count on staying liquid had the Fed supplied liquidity through open market operations alone. "With financial institutions unwilling to lend to one another," argues Kenneth Kuttner (2008: 2; compare Kroszner and Melick 2011: 151–52), "the Fed had no choice but to step in and lend to institutions in need of cash." Years before the crisis, Mark Flannery and George Kaufman (1996: 821) made the case in greater detail:

> The discount window's unique value arises when disarray strikes private financial markets. If lenders cannot confidently assess other firms' conditions, they may rationally withdraw from the interbank loan market, leaving solvent but illiquid firms unable to fund themselves. . . . In response to this sort of financial crisis, government may need to do more than assure adequate liquidity through open market operations. Broad,

> short-term [N.B.] discount window lending, unsecured and at (perhaps) subsidized rates, may constitute the least-cost means of resolving some types of widespread financial uncertainties.

But even when ordinary open market operations appear insufficient, it doesn't follow that direct Fed lending, let alone lending at subsidized rates to presumably insolvent firms, is necessary. Instead, the scope of Fed liquidity provision can be broadened by relaxing its traditional "Treasuries only" policy for open market operations to allow for occasional purchases of some or all of the private securities it deems acceptable as collateral for discount window loans.[35] Willem Buiter and Anne Sibert (2008) argue that such a modification of the Fed's open market policy—what they term a "market maker of last resort" policy—would have sufficed to reliquify nonbank capital markets, and primary dealers especially, while heeding both Bagehot's principles and the stipulations of the Federal Reserve Act. It would also have avoided any need for the Term Auction Facility (TAF), the Term Securities Lending Facility (TSLF), special purpose vehicles, and other such "complicated method[s] of providing liquidity" that unnecessarily exposed the Fed "to the temptation to politicize its selection of recipients of its credit" (Bordo 2009: 118) while compromising its independence (Thornton et al. 2009; Bordo 2010; Goodfriend 2010).[36]

Even the potential failure of financial institutions deemed "systematically important" does not necessarily warrant departures from classical LOLR precepts. Consider the case of Continental Illinois, the first rescue to be defended on the grounds that certain financial enterprises are "too big to fail." Although the FDIC claimed, in the course of congressional hearings following the rescue, that the holding company's failure would have exposed 179 small banks to a high risk of failure, subsequent assessments by the House Banking Committee and the Government Accountability Office placed the number of exposed banks at just 28. A still later study by Kaufman (1990: 8) found that only *two* banks would have lost more than half of their capital. The 1990 failure of Drexel Burnham Lambert had no systemic consequences, and there is no evidence, also according to Kaufman (2000: 236), that the failure of Long-Term Capital Management eight years later "would have brought down any large bank if the Fed had provided liquidity during the unwinding period through open market operations" while also backing the counterparties' unwinding plan.

During the subprime crisis, financial enterprises far larger than either Continental or Drexel Lambert either failed or were threatened with failure. Yet there are doubts concerning whether even these cases posed systemic risks that could only be contained by direct support of the firms in question. When it was placed into FDIC receivership in September 2008, Washington Mutual was five times larger, on an inflation-adjusted basis, than Continental Illinois at the time of its failure. Still, the FDIC was able, after wiping out its shareholders and most of its secured bondholders, to sell it to JPMorgan Chase without either inconveniencing its customers or disrupting financial markets (Tarr 2010).[37]

Or consider Lehman Brothers. It was one of the largest dealers in credit default swaps (CDSs). Peter Wallison (2009: 6; see also Tarr 2010) nevertheless found "no indication that any financial institution became troubled or failed" because of its failure.[38] Wallison (2009: 6) explains:

> Lehman's inability to meet its obligations did not result in the "contagion" that is the hallmark of systemic risk. No bank or any other Lehman counterparty seems to have been injured in any major respect by Lehman's failure, although of course losses occurred. . . . Although there were media reports that AIG had to be rescued shortly after Lehman's failure because it had been exposed excessively to Lehman through credit default swaps (CDSs), these were inaccurate. When all the CDSs on Lehman were settled about a month later, AIG's exposure turned out to be only $6.2 million. Moreover, although Lehman was one of the largest players in the CDS market, all its CDS obligations were settled without incident.

Wallison's statement should be amended to allow for the fact that, on the Tuesday following Lehman's Monday bankruptcy filing, the Reserve Primary money market mutual fund, having written off its large holdings of unsecured Lehman paper (and having lacked sponsors capable of making up for the loss), had to reduce its share price below the pledged $1 level to 97 cents. Reserve Primary's "breaking the buck" led to several days of large redemptions from other (especially institutional) prime money market funds and, thereby, to a sharp drop in the demand for commercial paper. Significantly, government money market funds, including Treasury-only funds, experienced inflows; and it is possible that the redemptions would have subsided on their own as it became clear that most funds would remain able to meet all redemption requests at $1 per share. The Treasury nevertheless intervened on Friday to guarantee all money-market share prices at $1.[39]

In deciding not to rescue Lehman Brothers, the Fed abided by the classical rules of last-resort lending. It earlier chose, on the other hand, to rescue the creditors of Bear Stearns by paying about $30 billion for the firm's worst assets so that JPMorgan Chase would purchase the firm and assume its debts. Later, it also chose to rescue AIG. On what grounds did it determine that Bear Stearns and AIG were "too big to fail," while Lehman Brothers was not?[40] Bear Stearns, like Lehman Brothers, was an investment bank, and AIG was an insurance company and CDS issuer. Both Bear Stearns and AIG had played highly risky strategies and were caught out. Neither was a commercial bank involved in retail payments, and neither performed functions that couldn't have been performed just as well by other private firms. Creditors and counterparties stood to lose, but it isn't clear that many of the numerous broker-dealers and hedge funds that did business with Bear Stearns would not have survived its default or that the failure of some of them would have had extensive knock-on effects. In fact, the Fed has never explained the precise nature of the "systemic risk" justifying its intervention in these instances. Nor has it ever made public its criteria for determining which failures posed a systemic threat that could not be handled in classical fashion.

The Fed's departures from classical doctrine also do not seem to have been very effective in achieving its short-run objective. The rescue of Bear Stearns did not keep Lehman or AIG from toppling. Instead, it appears to have encouraged those firms to leverage up further by persuading reassured creditors to lend to them even more cheaply. In any event, the Fed's actions did not suffice to substantially improve conditions in the money market. The root of the problem was not a lack of liquidity but of solvency. As Kuttner

(2008: 7) and many others have observed, "no amount of liquidity will revive lending so long as financial institutions lack sufficient capital."

The Fed's unprecedented violations of classical LOLR doctrine during the recent crisis threaten ultimately to further undermine financial stability both by impeding its ability to conduct ordinary monetary policy and by contributing to the moral hazard problem. Regarding the former problem, Kuttner (2008: 12) writes:

> Saddling the Fed with bailout duties obscures its core objectives, unnecessarily linking monetary policy to the rescue of failing institutions. Moreover . . . loan losses could compromise the Fed's independence and thus weaken its commitment to price stability in the future.

In light of such considerations, it would be better, according to Kuttner (2008: 12), "to return to Bagehot's narrower conception of the LOLR function, and turn over to the Treasury the responsibility for the rescue of troubled institutions, as this inevitably involves a significant contingent commitment of public funds."

But the most important costs that must be set against any possible short-run gains from Fed departures from classical LOLR doctrine consist of the moral hazard problems caused by such departures, including the problem of zombie institutions gambling for recovery. As Kaufman (2000: 237) puts it, "there is little more costly and disruptive to the economy than liquid insolvent banks that are permitted to continue to operate." It is a common misconception to think that imposing losses on management and shareholders, while shielding counterparties and creditors, is enough to contain moral hazard. So long as bank creditors can expect high returns on the upside, with implicit government guarantees against losses on the downside, they will lend too cheaply to risky, poorly diversified banks, making overly high leverage (thin capital) an attractive strategy. Normal market discipline against risk-taking is thus significantly undermined (see Roberts 2010). Already by 2002, according to one estimate (Walter and Weinberg 2002), more than 60 percent of all U.S. financial institution liabilities, including all those of the 21 largest bank holding companies, were either explicitly or implicitly guaranteed. Overly risky financial practices were a predictable consequence. As Charles Calomiris (2009a) observes, the extraordinary risks taken by managers of large financial firms between 2003 and 2007 were the result, not of "random mass insanity," but of moral hazard resulting in large part from the Fed's willingness—implicit in previous practice—to depart from classical last-resort lending rules to rescue creditors of failed firms.

Likewise, according to Buiter (2008a: 103), although unorthodox Fed programs may have succeeded in enhancing market liquidity during 2007 and 2008, some—including the TAF, the TSLF, the Primary Dealer Credit Facility (PDCF), the opening of the discount window to Fannie and Freddie, and the rescue of Bear Stearns—appear "to have been designed to maximize bad incentives for future reckless lending and borrowing by the institutions affected by them."[41] Far from being an unquestionably worthwhile departure from classical last-resort lending rules, the unprecedented granting of support to insolvent firms during the subprime crisis may well prove the most serious of all failures of the Federal Reserve System.[42]

ALTERNATIVES TO THE FED, PAST AND PRESENT

Our review of the Fed's performance raises two very distinct questions: (1) might the United States have done better than to have established the Fed in 1914, and (2) might it do better than to retain it today? While the first question is of interest to economic historians, the second should be of interest to policymakers.

The questions are distinct because the choice context has changed. One major change is that the gold standard is no longer in effect. Under the gold standard, the scarcity of the ultimate redemption medium was a natural rather than a contrived scarcity. The responsibilities originally assigned to the Fed did not need to include, and in fact did not include, that of managing the stock of money or the price level. The gold standard "automatically" managed those variables under a regime of unrestricted convertibility of bank notes and deposits into gold. The Fed's principal assignments were to maintain the unrestricted convertibility of its own liabilities and to avoid panics that threatened the convertibility of commercial bank liabilities.

Consequently, it is relatively easy to identify viable alternatives to the adoption of the Federal Reserve Act in 1913. At a minimum, the continuation of the status quo was an option. In light of the severe Great Contraction of the early 1930s under the Fed's watch, worse than any of the pre-Fed panics, Friedman and Schwartz (1963: 168–72, 693–94) argued that continuing the pre-Fed status quo would have had better results. Under the pre-1908 status quo, panic management was handled by commercial bank clearinghouse associations. The clearinghouses lent additional bank reserves into existence, met public demand for currency by issuing more, and, when necessary, coordinated suspensions of convertibility to prevent systemic contraction (Timberlake 1993: 198–213). According to Wicker (2000: 128–29), a "purely voluntary association of New York banks that recognized its responsibility for the maintenance of banking stability was a feasible solution to the bank panic problem." In particular, Wicker maintains, the Gilded Age might have been rendered entirely panic-free had the 1873 recommendations of the New York Clearing House Association, as contained in the so-called Coe Report (recommending that Congress formally grant the association authority to oversee the efficient allocation of member banks' reserves during crises), been adopted.

Congress did, in fact, implement a reform along the lines suggested by the Coe Report in the shape of the 1908 Aldrich-Vreeland Act, which assigned the issue of emergency currency, which was illegal for clearinghouses but clearly helpful, to official National Currency Associations that could lawfully do what the clearinghouses had been doing without legal authority. The system of emergency currency issue by National Currency Associations had one test, when the onset of World War I triggered a sharp demand for currency in 1914 (before the Fed was up and running), and it passed the test well (Silber 2007).

An alternative, deregulatory alternative to a central bank also received serious attention in the decades prior to the passage of the Federal Reserve Act. This was a plan endorsed by the American Bankers' Association at its 1894 convention in Baltimore, and thereafter known as "the Baltimore plan." The Baltimore plan treated the panic-free and less-regulated Canadian banking system as a model (White 1983: 83–90; Bordo et al. 1996; Calomiris 2000: Chapter 1). Under a system devised to sell government bonds during the Civil

War, federally chartered ("national") banks were required to hold backing for their notes in the form of federal bonds. The backing requirement increasingly constrained the issue of notes as the eligible bonds became increasingly scarce. (State-chartered banks were prevented from issuing notes by a prohibitive federal tax.) Reformers for good reason viewed this requirement as the source of the notorious secular and seasonal "inelasticity" of the National Bank currency (Noyes 1910; Smith 1936). Under the Baltimore plan, federally chartered banks would have been allowed to back their note liabilities with ordinary bank assets, a reform that some proponents called "asset currency."

The Baltimore plan was blocked in the political arena by the power of a vested interest, the small bank lobby. Asset currency reformers worried that a surfeit of currency might arise if the existing restrictions on note issue were lifted without any accompanying system for drawing excess currency out of circulation. They observed that Canada's nationwide branched banks were an efficient note-collection system, and so favored not only Canadian-style deregulation of note issue but also deregulation of branching. They failed to overcome the political clout of the small bankers who were determined to block branch banking (White 1983: 85–89; Selgin and White 1994).

Coming up with alternatives to the Fed today takes more imagination. Assuming that there is no political prospect of replacing the fiat dollar with a return to the gold standard or other commodity money system, for the dollar to retain its value, some public institution or law must keep fiat-base money sufficiently scarce. In this respect at least, our finding that the Fed has failed does not by itself indicate that it would be practical to entirely dispense with some sort of public monetary authority. But neither does it indicate that the only avenues for improvement are marginal revisions to Fed operating procedures or additions to its powers. On the contrary, the Fed's poor record calls for seriously contemplating a genuine change of regime. In particular, it strengthens the case for precommitment to a policy rule that would constrain the discretionary powers that the Fed appears to have used so ineffectively. Whether implementing such a new regime should be called "ending the Fed" is an unimportant question about labels.

A detailed blueprint or assessment of any particular policy rule would be out of place here, but it is useful to sketch some alternatives that merit consideration, to underscore the point that the Fed as presently constituted may carry an opportunity cost.[43]

CONTEMPORARY ALTERNATIVES TO DISCRETIONARY MONETARY POLICY

The general case for a monetary rule is well known. Milton Friedman (1961b) and Robert Lucas (1976) argue empirically and theoretically that the Fed lacks the informational advantage over private agents that it would have to have in order to out-forecast them and improve their welfare through activist policy. Finn Kydland and colleagues (1977) make the point that even a well-informed and benevolent central bank is weakened by lack of precommitment when the public, in forming its inflation expectations, takes into account the central bank's temptation to use surprise inflation to improve the economy's unemployment or real output. At the most philosophical or jurisprudential level, the case for a constitutional constraint on monetary policymakers derives from the general case for "the rule of law rather than rule by authorities." The rule of law means constraints against arbitrary governance so that citizens can know what to expect from their government (White 2010). Taylor (2009b: 6) writes: "More generally, government should set clear rules of the game, stop changing them during the game, and enforce them. The rules do not have to be perfect, but the rule of law is essential."

COMMODITY STANDARDS

Based on its long history, the gold standard warrants consideration as an alternative to discretionary central banking.[44] Dismissals of the gold standard as a viable option have often been based on flawed assessments of its past performance (see Kydland and Wynne 2002: 7–9). The instability in the U.S. financial system during the pre-Fed period was due to serious flaws in the U.S. bank regulatory system rather than to the gold standard. Indeed, the Federal Reserve Act, which retained the gold standard, was predicated on this view. Canada adhered to a gold standard during the same period but, with a differently regulated banking system, experienced no such instability.

Perhaps the leading indictment of the gold standard today is Barry Eichengreen and Peter Temin's (2000) charge that it was "a key element—if not the key element—in the collapse of the world economy" at the outset of the Great Depression. Here, it is important to distinguish a classical gold standard from the structurally flawed interwar gold exchange standard. The latter was created by European governments to assist their misguided (and ultimately futile) attempts to restore prewar gold parities despite having pushed up prices dramatically by use of printing-press finance during wartime suspensions of gold redeemability. The massive deflation that became unavoidable when France ceased to play along with the precarious postwar arrangement (Johnson 1997; Irwin 2010) was not a failing of the classical gold standard. Neither were postwar exchange controls or "beggar thy neighbor" trade policies.[45]

It is an automatic system like the classical gold standard that is worth reconsidering, certainly not the interwar system. The classical gold standard did not depend on central bank cooperation—indeed many leading participants did not even have central banks—so it was less vulnerable to defection by any particular central bank, and therefore more credible, than the interwar arrangement (Obstfeld and Taylor 2003). Although Eichengreen and Temin (2000) acknowledge the benefits of the prewar gold standard, they never explain why it was necessary to abandon the gold standard altogether rather than to simply allow for one-time devaluations by the countries that had suspended and inflated.

A second indictment of the gold standard derives from fear of secular deflation. We noted above the importance of distinguishing benign from harmful deflation, while also observing that the secular deflation that characterized much of the classical gold standard period was benign, accompanying vigorous real growth. It is true that spokesmen for the interests of farmers complained about secular deflation. They appear to have believed, mistakenly, that overall deflation was lowering their real or relative incomes, as though nominal rather than the real factors were lowering the prices of what they sold relative to the prices of what they bought. Or they were seeking a bit of unexpected inflation to reduce, ex post, the real value of the debts they had incurred in farm mechanization. Their complaints reflected misperception or special-interest pleading rather than any genuine harm being done by a benign deflation (Beckworth 2007).

A third and long-standing objection to a gold standard by economists—the main reason why John Maynard Keynes famously called it a "barbarous relic"—is that it needlessly incurs resource costs in extracting and storing valuable metal for monetary use. A fiat standard can, in principle, replicate (if not improve upon) a gold standard's price-level stability without any such resource costs (Friedman 1953). In practice, however, fiat standards have *not* replicated gold's price-level stability (Kydland and Wynne 2002: 1). Nor, ironically, have they even lowered resource costs. The inflation rates of postwar fiat standards have by themselves imposed estimated deadweight costs greater than the reasonably estimated resource costs of a gold standard (White 1999: 48–49). Meanwhile, the public has accumulated gold coins and bullion as inflation hedges, adding more gold to private reserves than central banks have sold from official reserves. The real price of gold is much higher today than it was under the classical gold standard, encouraging the expansion of gold mining (see Figure 8.12). Thus, the resource costs of gold extraction and storage for asset-holding purposes have *risen* since the world's departure from the gold standard.

Figure 8.12: Real Price of Gold, 1861–2009

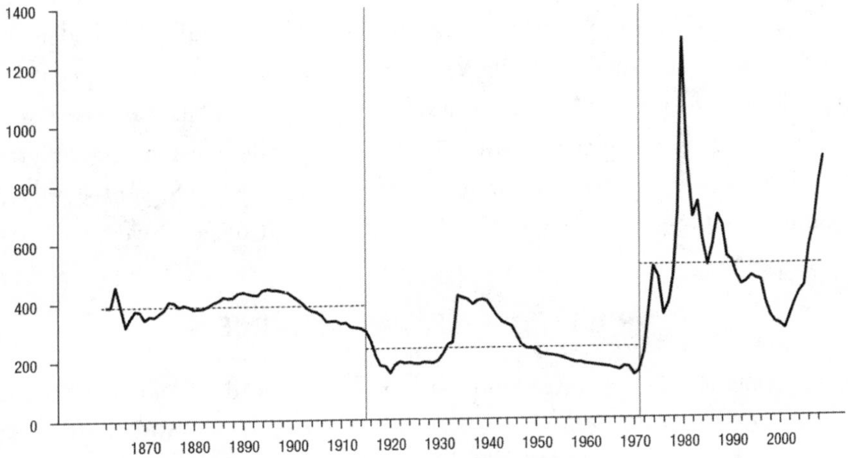

NOTES: Annual average gold price based on London P.M. fix relative to the GNP deflator.

SOURCES: For gold prices: data from 1861 to 1899 are from Global Financial Data, average of high and low; data from 1900 to 2009 are from Global Insight (http://www.ihs.com).

At least three serious problems do confront any proposal to return to a gold standard. The first is choosing a gold definition of the dollar that avoids transitional inflation or deflation (see White 2004). The second is securing a credible commitment to gold. As James Hamilton (2005) has remarked: "If a government can go on a gold standard, it can go off, and historically countries have done exactly that all the time. The fact that speculators know this means that any currency adhering to a gold standard (or, in more modern times, a fixed exchange rate) may be subject to a speculative attack." Hamilton (1988) argues that a drop in the credibility of governments' commitment to fixed parities, leading to a speculative rise in the demand for gold, contributed to the international deflation of the early 1930s. To remove the threat of speculative attack may require the further reform of moving currency redemption commitments out of monopolistic and legally immune (hence, noncredible) central banks and returning them, as in the pre-Fed era, to competing private issuers constrained by enforceable contracts and reputational pressures (Selgin and White 2005).

The third problem, which argues against any nation's unilateral return to gold, is that a principal virtue of the classical gold standard was its status as an *international* standard. A single nation's return to gold would not reestablish a global currency area and would achieve only a relatively limited reduction in the speculative demand for gold as an inflation hedge. As it would also fail to substantially increase the transactions demand for gold, it could not be expected to make the relative price of gold as stable as it was under the classical system (White 2008). To provide considerably greater stability than the present fiat-dollar regime, a revived U.S. gold standard would probably need to be part of a broader international revival.[46]

RULE-BOUND FIAT STANDARDS

Given that the postwar fiat standards managed by discretionary central banks have generally failed to deliver the long-run price stability that was delivered by the gold standard, Finn Kydland and Mark Wynne (2002: 1) ask whether a better fiat regime is possible. They note that the "hard pegs" of dollarization or currency boards have proven successful at delivering more stable nominal environments in countries that have adopted them. But, they naturally ask, "What about the large country, the 'peggee'? What rule or regime can a large country such as the United States . . . adopt to guarantee long-term price stability?"

A well-known and very simple type of monetary rule is a fixed growth path for M2, as advocated by Milton Friedman in the 1960s. It is arguably no longer appropriate in the current environment where the velocity of M2 (or any other monetary aggregate) is no longer stable. A number of more sophisticated rules that accommodate unstable velocity have been more widely discussed in recent years.

(1) A *Taylor rule*, which continuously updates the federal funds target according to a fixed formula based on measured departures of inflation and real output from specified norms, can be viewed as a description of Fed policy over the recent past, with notable exceptions. The exceptions—that is, the departures from the fitted Taylor rule—appear to have been harmful (Taylor 2009a). A federal funds rate well below the Taylor rule–path for an extended period fosters an asset bubble; a rate too high precipitates a recession. A firm commitment to a fully specified Taylor-type rule could helpfully constrain monetary policy.

(2) A *McCallum rule* is similar to a Taylor rule, except that the monetary base (rather than the federal funds rate) is the instrument, and feedback comes from base velocity growth and nominal income growth. A McCallum rule amounts to a type of nominal-income rule, with the corrective policy response to nominal income above or below its target level fully specified in terms of adjustment to monetary base growth. Bennett McCallum's (2000) simulation study claims that adhering to the rule would have improved the economy's macroeconomic performance over the actual performance under the Fed's discretionary policymaking.

(3) Scott Sumner (1989, 2006; Jackson and Sumner 2006) and Kevin Dowd (1995) have each proposed constraining monetary policy to a *nominal income target*. In contrast to McCallum's backward-looking feedback from observations on realized nominal income, they propose forward-looking feedback from the expected level of nominal income implied by futures markets indicators.

(4) Toward the end of his career, Friedman (1984) proposed simply *freezing the monetary base* and—reminiscent of the Canadian alternative in 1913—allowing seasonal and cyclical variations in the demand for currency relative to income (variations in velocity's inverse) to be met by private note-issue.

CONTEMPORARY ALTERNATIVES TO A PUBLIC LENDER OF LAST RESORT

An important argument for retaining a discretionary central bank is that, as a lender of last resort, the central bank can helpfully forestall panics or liquidity crises in the commercial banking system. In the usual understanding, a lender of last resort injects new bank reserves whenever a critical insufficiency of reserves would otherwise arise. To evaluate the argument, we need to ask why the banking system might face insufficient reserves. Harry G. Johnson (1973: 97) points out that commercial bankers should be presumed capable of optimizing their reserve holdings:

> At least in the presence of a well-developed capital market, and on the assumption of intelligent and responsible monetary management by the central bank, the commercial banks should be able to manage their reserve positions without the need for the central bank to function as "lender of last resort."

Johnson's "well-developed capital market" refers to the fact that a U.S. commercial bank with low reserves due to random outflows can quickly replenish its reserves by borrowing overnight in the federal funds market. His "assumption of intelligent and responsible monetary management by the central bank" means assuming that the central bank has not sharply reduced the monetary base and, thereby, the total of available bank reserves. (The possibility of a crisis due to contractionary central bank policy itself hardly justifies having a central bank.) Under those conditions, a critical shortage of reserves in the banking system as a whole implies an unexpected spike in the demand for reserve money, presumably due either to banks raising their desired reserve ratios or to the public draining reserves from the banking system.

A spike in demand for reserve money, left untreated, implies the shrinkage of the money multiplier and, thus, of the broader monetary aggregates. What is called the "lender of last resort" function can thus be viewed as an aspect of a central bank's duty, under a fiat standard, to prevent the flow of spending from unexpectedly shrinking. However, last-resort lending is also aimed at preserving the flow of bank *credit* by preventing solvent financial firms from failing for want of adequate liquidity. A central bank with a target for M1 or M2 automatically injects base money as the money multiplier shrinks. A central bank precommitted to a Taylor rule or a nominal income target does likewise.

A central bank in a modern financial system can readily make the necessary reserve injections through open market purchases of securities. For reasons considered above, it need not and generally should not make loans to particular institutions, for the sake of avoiding moral hazard and favoritism. A central bank's readiness to lend to troubled or otherwise favored banks, providing explicit or implicit central bank bailout guarantees, promotes bad banking.

Jeffrey Lacker (2007: 7) reminds us that 19th-century writers, like Walter Bagehot who famously urged the Bank of England to *lend* to other banks in times of credit stringency, "wrote at a time when lending really was the only way the central bank provided liquidity." He continues:

> Indeed, when the Fed was founded in 1913, discount window lending was envisioned as the primary means of providing reserves to the banking system. Today, the Fed's primary means of supplying reserves is through open-market operations, which is how the federal funds rate is kept at the target rate. In fact the effect of discount window loans on the overall supply of liquidity is automatically offset, or "sterilized," to avoid pushing the federal funds rate below the target. So it is important to distinguish carefully a central bank's monetary policy function of regulating the total supply of reserves from central bank credit policy, which reallocates reserves among banks.

Given a monetary policy rule that automatically injects reserves to counteract an incipient monetary contraction, and especially allowing for occasional (but presumably rare) departures from a Treasuries-only open market policy, there is no need for a *lender* (as opposed to a "market maker") of last resort. That is, the Fed's discount window can be closed without impeding its role of maintaining financial system liquidity. A case for keeping the discount window open would have to be made on the (unpromising) grounds that the Fed should intervene in the allocation of reserves among banks, or should use the window to lend cheaply (or purchase assets at above-market prices) to inject capital into banks on the brink of insolvency.

Historical evidence indicates that official discount window lending is not necessary to avoid banking panics—scrambles for liquidity characterized by contagious runs on solvent institutions. Panics have been a problem almost exclusively in countries where avoidable legal restrictions have weakened banks (Benston and Kaufman 1995; see also Chapter 3 of this volume). The United States in the late 19th to early 20th century is the prime example of a legislatively weakened and relatively panic-prone system. Even in that system, clearinghouse associations limited the damage done by panics by organizing liquidity-sharing and liquidity-creation arrangements, including temporary resort to clearinghouse "loan" certificates, and, if necessary, by arranging for a suspension or "restriction" of payments (Timberlake 1993: 207–9; Dwyer and Gilbert 1989).[47] Bagehot himself, as we noted previously, did not see any need for a lender of last resort in a structurally sound banking and currency system—though for him this meant a system in which currency was not fiat money and was not supplied monopolistically.

Central bank lending that, contra Bagehot, puts insolvent institutions on life support can be replaced by policies for promptly resolving financial institution insolvencies. In recent years, such proposals as expedited bankruptcy and "living wills," possibly requiring that losses be borne by holders of subordinated debt or "contingent capital certificates," have been widely discussed (Board of Governors of the Federal Reserve System 1999; Calomiris 2009b; Flannery 2009). Outright bailouts, on "too big to fail" grounds, can be left to the Treasury. As Kuttner (2008: 12) has suggested, it would be best "to return to Bagehot's narrower conception of the LOLR function, and turn over to the Treasury the responsibility for the rescue of troubled institutions, as this inevitably involves a significant contingent commitment of public funds." Such a reform, Kuttner (2008: 13) adds, would simplify the implementation of monetary policy by avoiding bailout-based changes to the supply of bank reserves, while reducing the risk of higher inflation or reduced Fed independence.[48]

CONCLUSION

Available research does not support the view that the Federal Reserve System has lived up to its original promise. Early in its career, it presided over both the most severe inflation and the most severe (demand-induced) deflations in post–Civil War U.S. history. Since then, it has tended to err on the side of inflation, allowing the purchasing power of the U.S. dollar to deteriorate considerably. That deterioration has not been compensated for, to any substantial degree, by enhanced stability of real output. Although some early studies suggested otherwise, recent work suggests that there has been no substantial overall improvement in the volatility of real output since the end of World War II compared to before World War I. Although a genuine improvement did occur during the subperiod known as the Great Moderation, that improvement, besides having been temporary, appears to have been due mainly to factors other than improved monetary policy. Finally, the Fed cannot be credited with having reduced the frequency of banking panics or with having wielded its last-resort lending powers responsibly. In short, the Federal Reserve System, as presently constituted, is no more worthy of being regarded as the last word in monetary management than the National Currency System it replaced almost a century ago.

The Fed's record suggests that its problems go well beyond those of having lacked good administrators, and that the only real hope for a better monetary system lies in regime change. What sort of change is a question beyond the scope of this paper, which has only indicated some possibilities. We hope that it will also encourage further research exploring those alternatives' capacity to contribute to a genuinely improved monetary system.

9

OPERATION TWIST-THE-TRUTH: HOW THE FEDERAL RESERVE MISREPRESENTS ITS HISTORY AND PERFORMANCE*

FOR A PRIVATE-SECTOR FIRM, success can mean only one thing: that the firm has turned a profit. No such firm can hope to succeed, or even to survive, merely by *declaring* that it has been profitable. A government agency, on the other hand, can succeed in either of two ways. It can actually accomplish its mission. Or it can simply *declare* that it has done so, and get the public to believe it.

That the Federal Reserve System has succeeded, in the sense of having prospered, is indisputable. At the time of its 100th anniversary, its powers are both greater and less subject to effective scrutiny than ever, while its assets, now exceeding $3 trillion, make it bigger than any of the world's profit-oriented financial firms.[1] And, criticism from some quarters notwithstanding, the Fed enjoys a solid reputation. "The Federal Reserve," Paul Volcker observed recently, "is respected. And it's respected at a time when respect and trust in all our government institutions is all too rare. It's that respect and trust that, at the end of the day, is vital to the acceptance of its independence and to support for its policies" (Bordo and Roberds 2013: 400). Besides securing support for it at home, a Dallas Fed brochure (FRBDI)[2] proudly declares, the Fed's status has caused "emerging democracies around the globe" to treat it as a model for their own monetary arrangements.

* Originally published in the *Cato Journal* 34, no. 2 (Spring/Summer 2014): 229–63.

But what has the Fed's reputation to do with its actual performance? Not much, according to Milton Friedman. "No major institution in the U.S.," Friedman (1988) observed some years ago, "has so poor a record of performance over so long a period, yet so high a public reputation."[3] The Fed has succeeded, not by actually accomplishing its mission but by convincing the public that it has done so, through publicity that misrepresents both the Fed's history and its record.

What follows is a survey of such propaganda as it occurs in official Federal Reserve statements aimed at the general public, which are properly regarded as reflecting the views of "the Fed," rather than those of particular Fed employees.[4] In showing how Fed authorities misrepresent the Fed's record, I do not mean to suggest that they always do so intentionally. Groupthink, conditioned by employees' natural desire to defend the institution they work for—or to at least avoid biting the hand that feeds them—undoubtedly plays a part. But whatever the motives behind it, the misrepresentation in question harms the public, by causing it to overrate the status quo when considering possible reforms.

ORIGINS

No Fed propaganda has contributed more to its stature than that devoted to convincing the public that any other arrangement would have resulted in a less stable U.S. monetary system. To support this belief, the Fed has had to overcome the American public's long-standing resistance to the idea of having a central bank in the United States. The Fed's architects were able to do this easily enough, by denying that the Federal Reserve System was a central bank at all, and official Fed publications still vaunt its "decentralized" structure.[5] But the Banking Act of 1935, in making the newly constituted Board of Governors the acknowledged seat of Federal Reserve power, put paid to that conceit, forcing Fed apologists to instead insist that a central bank was, after all, the only arrangement capable of providing the nation with a stable currency system.

To take such a stand is to claim that the infirmities of the pre-Fed U.S. monetary system were the inevitable consequences of a lack of Fed oversight. "In the early years of our country," says the Philadelphia Fed's video "The Federal Reserve and You" (FRBPI), "there was very little supervision or regulation of banks at all." Consequently, the video continues, "financial crises and panics took their toll." Ben Bernanke, responding to a question raised by Rep. Ron Paul (R-TX) at a congressional hearing, likewise observed that the Fed was created because "there were big financial panics and there was no regulation there and people thought that was a big problem" (Bernanke 2009).

In an article on "The Founding of the Fed," the Federal Reserve Bank of New York (FRBNYI) refers specifically to the shortcomings of the U.S. monetary system between the demise of the Second Bank of the United States and the outbreak of the Civil War. "For the next quarter century," the article observes,

> America's central banking was carried on by a myriad of state-chartered banks with no federal regulation.[6] The difficulties brought about by this lack of a central banking authority hurt the stability of the American economy. There were often violent fluctuations in the volume of bank notes issued by banks and in the amount of demand deposits that the banks held. Bank notes, issued by the individual banks, varied widely in reliability.

According to the San Francisco Fed (FRBSFI), some of the banks in question "were known as 'wildcat banks' supposedly because they maintained offices in remote areas ('where the wildcats are') in order to make it difficult for customers to redeem their notes for precious metals."

The suggestion such remarks convey of pre-Fed American banking as a free-for-all is, to put it mildly, extremely misleading. "The early years of the republic," Bray Hammond (1957: 185–86) observes in his Pulitzer-prize-winning study of banking in antebellum America,

> are often spoken of as if . . . government authority refrained from interference in business and benevolently left it a free field. Nothing of the sort was true of banking. Legislators hesitated about the kind of

conditions under which banking should be permitted but never about the propriety and need of [sic] imposing regulations.

So far as the Federalists and Jeffersonians who dominated American politics at the time were concerned, "the issue was between prohibition and state control, with no thought of free enterprise."[7]

Although the federal government withdrew from the banking business between 1836 and 1863, banking continued to be regulated by state authorities. That remained the case, moreover, despite "free-banking" laws passed, first by Michigan (in 1837), and subsequently by 17 other states. Despite their name, which some Fed officials appear to take literally, and despite providing something akin to a general incorporation procedure for banks, these laws did not open the floodgates to unregulated banking. On the contrary, banks established under them were often subjected to more burdensome regulations than those common to charter-based arrangements (Ng 1988). Among other things, American "free" banks were universally prohibited from branching. They were also required to "secure" their notes with assets chosen by state regulators.

Thanks to research by Hugh Rockoff (1975) and Arthur Rolnick and Warren Weber (1983, 1984), among others, we now know that the "free-for-all" account of antebellum banking is about as faithful to reality as a 1950s Hollywood western. Fly-by-night banks were few and far between, and while many banks failed, the most common cause of failure, besides under-diversified loan portfolios that went hand in hand with unit banking, was heavy depreciation of the securities that some "free" bankers were forced to purchase in order to "secure" their notes.

Official Fed sources also fail to point out how antebellum banking regulations stood in the way of the establishment of a "uniform" U.S. currency. In a brief, sepia-toned segment of the Philadelphia Fed's video, "The Federal Reserve and You" (FRBPI), a pair of farmers, complete with dungarees and open-crown hats, ponder a stack of state bank notes as they try to settle a sale, while a voice-over relates that there were 30,000 different kinds of notes in circulation back then (a much inflated figure, actually, unless one includes every sort of forged note), with certain notes commanding far less than their face value. What the video *doesn't* say is that both the great variety of state bank notes and the discounts to which they were subject were further fruits of unit banking laws. In Scotland and elsewhere, during that same era, note-issuing banks were allowed to establish nationwide branch networks, and no special government intervention was needed to achieve a uniform currency.

The Philadelphia Fed video also fails to mention how, despite unit banking, discounts on state bank notes had fallen to *very* modest levels by the early 1860s—so modest that, had someone in the autumn of 1863 been foolish enough to purchase every (non-Confederate) bank note in the country for its declared value, in order to sell the notes to a broker in New York or Chicago, that person's loss would have amounted to less than 1 percent of the notes' face value, even reckoning "doubtful" notes as worthless (see pp. 76–77 of this volume).[8]

That improvement didn't stop the northern government from passing legislation authorizing U.S. Treasury notes ("greenbacks"), establishing national banks, and subjecting outstanding state bank notes to a prohibitive 10 percent tax. As Fed sources point out, these measures did away with remaining bank-note discounts, and so gave the United States an entirely uniform currency at last. But those sources (as well as many non-Fed writings) misstate both the motivation behind the steps taken—which was actually that of replenishing the Union's empty coffers—and the precise means by which discounts were eliminated. Despite what is often suggested, discounts didn't vanish simply because the notes of all national banks were subject to the same regulations and backed by government bonds. Those similarities alone couldn't have prevented national banks from applying discounts to rival banks' notes sufficient to cover the cost of returning them for payment. Instead, a provision of the 1864 National Bank Act, a revised version of the 1863 National Currency Act, simply compelled every national bank to accept other national banks' notes at par.[9]

That "bank runs and financial panics continued to plague the economy" after the Civil War is of course readily acknowledged by official Fed publications (FRBP2). The main reason for this, according to one of those sources (FRBNY1), was "[t]he inability of the banking system to expand or contract currency in circulation or provide a mechanism to move reserves throughout the system." Here again, Fed officials treat what was really a consequence of misguided regulation as having been due to a *lack* of regulation. In particular, instead of explaining how regulations kept national banks from issuing more currency when it was needed, engendering the notorious "inelasticity" of the U.S. currency stock, they blame that inelasticity on "the absence of a central banking structure" (FRBNYI). Put it that way and—presto!—a central bank becomes the only conceivable remedy.

In fact, the U.S. currency stock might have been made perfectly elastic simply by doing away with barriers to branch banking and repealing Civil War–era laws regulating banks' ability to issue notes, including the requirement that national bank notes be backed 110 percent by U.S. government bonds. (Those laws, it bears recalling, were part of the Union's strategy for funding the war, and as such were obsolete.) That such deregulation could have worked, and worked better than the Fed did, is strongly suggested by Canada's experience. Canada didn't have a central bank until 1935, yet it avoided the crises that rattled the U.S. economy in 1873, 1884, 1893, and 1907. Canada's relatively stable system consisted of several dozen nationally branched banks-of-issue, all of which were able to issue notes backed by their general assets, and subject to no further restriction save one (itself relaxed in 1907) based on their paid-in capital. Canadian banks' relative freedom allowed them to meet both secular growth and seasonal peaks in currency demand, while nationwide branching, by facilitating note redemption, saw to the mopping-up of excess currency (Selgin and White 1994: 237–40).

Canada's example didn't go unnoticed by those seeking to fix the U.S. currency system, and quite a few legislative attempts were made—the Indianapolis, Carlisle, and Fowler plans among them—to replicate it. Alas, all were doomed, thanks in part to their call for branch banking, which was vigorously opposed by bankers in smaller towns as well as those in New York City. "Main Street" feared the competition to which branching would expose it, while "Wall Street" was anxious to hold on to the large correspondent balances that were a by-product of the status quo.[10]

It was only when Canadian-style currency reform proved a dead end that reformers generally abandoned it in favor of a central bank–based alternative. Instead of calling for deregulation of the existing banking and currency system, this alternative involved having a new bank (or, as it were, set of banks) vested with the exclusive right to both branch and issue notes backed by assets other than government bonds. Because the new banks, which were to do business only with established banks and the U.S. government, posed no direct threat to established banks, and because it left the structure of the commercial banking industry more or less unchanged, the new plan steered clear of concerted bankers' opposition. A central bank was, in short, no more than a second-best solution—if that—to the ills of the pre-1914 U.S. currency and banking system.

Yet one would never guess such from the Fed's own accounts of its history, which for the most part don't even mention Canada's successful arrangement, the various asset currency plans inspired by it, or how banking industry insiders were instrumental in seeing to it that those plans were set aside in favor of a central bank alternative. According to one of Ben Bernanke's recent George Washington University lectures (Bernanke 2012a), for example, it was only after the 1907 crisis "that Congress began to say, 'Well, wait a minute, maybe we need to do something about this, maybe we need a central bank, a government agency that can address the problem of financial panics.'"

INDEPENDENCE

"Most studies of central bank independence," a San Francisco Fed publication informs us, "rank the Fed among the most independent in the world" (FRBSF 1999a). The Fed's independence is supposed to allow it to "conduct monetary policy with relative autonomy from the federal government," especially by insulating its decisions "from short-term political influence" (FRBA3; see also Board of Governors 2013b). Particular arrangements that supposedly rule out such "short-term political influence" include the fact that members of the Board of Governors serve staggered 14-year terms, and the fact that the Fed, instead of relying on Congress for funding, uses its seigniorage revenue to cover its costs and pay shareholder dividends (Board of Governors 2013a, 2013b; FRBD2).

But despite these arrangements, and no matter how independent the Fed may be compared to other central banks, the truth is that it has always conducted monetary policy with an eye toward satisfying the desires of the general government. That the Fed was a mere handmaiden to the Treasury before 1951 is sufficiently obvious that at least one official Fed educational document concedes the point. "From its founding in 1913," a Philadelphia Fed publication (FRBP2) recognizes, "to the years up to and following World War II, the Fed largely supported the Treasury's fiscal policy goals."

Until 1935, the secretary of the treasury and his second-in-command, the comptroller of the currency, served as the chairman and vice chairman, respectively, of the Federal Reserve Board. Although the Banking Act of 1935 removed Treasury representatives from what then became the Board of Governors, while establishing the present terms of appointment, it did not end the Treasury's influence. On the contrary, that influence actually increased. "From 1935 to 1951," Richard Timberlake (n.d.) observes, "the secretary of the treasury, with the compliance of Fed Board Chairman Marriner Eccles, continued to dominate Fed policies." During World War II especially, and for some years afterwards, monetary policy again became entirely subordinated to the Treasury's wants, with the Fed holding down interest rates on government securities by serving, in effect, as the Treasury's bond buyer of last resort, which meant having monetary policy play second fiddle to government funding.

Fed outreach materials all agree, on the other hand, in proclaiming 1951 as the year in which the Fed achieved complete independence. "When the Korean War broke out," the aforementioned Philadelphia Fed publication observes,

> Fed chairman William McChesney Martin again faced pressure from the Treasury to maintain low interest rates to help provide funds for the war effort. Martin, however, worked closely with the Treasury to break the long-standing practice of supporting government bond interest rates. Since then, the Fed has remained staunchly independent in its use of open market operations to support its monetary policy goals. (FRBP2)

Actually, the Fed's chairman at the time of the so-called Treasury Accord was not Martin but Thomas B. McCabe. Martin took part in the accord, not as the Fed's representative, but as the Treasury's, having at the time been its assistant secretary for monetary affairs. But let us not quibble. The big question is, did the accord really free the Fed from politics? According to Robert Weintraub (1978: 354), the claim is "at best a half truth." The accord allowed the Fed to reduce its Treasury purchases to the extent allowed by its agreement to swap unmarketable 2 3/4 bonds for 2 1/2 ones already outstanding. In turn, the Fed promised to raise its discount rate only with the Treasury's permission, which was unlikely to be given except under "very compelling circumstances" (pp. 353–54).

As if to make clear who held the upper hand, days after the accord was reached President Harry Truman had chairman McCabe tender his resignation, appointing McChesney Martin in his place. Far from daring to flex the Fed's muscles, Martin proved a pushover when it came to resisting government influence (Meltzer 2003: 712). Although the Fed avoided inflation during most of the 1950s, that was so only because the decade was one of small government deficits (with occasional surpluses) and because Dwight Eisenhower, who succeeded Truman in 1953, was a resolute inflation hawk. When John F. Kennedy and then Lyndon Johnson took command, Martin had no trouble switching to the more activist and inflationary stance they favored, and although he did offer some resistance to Johnson's demand for further help in financing the Great Society programs and the Vietnam War, that resistance proved too feeble to keep the inflation rate from rising (Cargill and O'Driscoll 2013).[11]

When Martin retired at last, his replacement, Arthur Burns, upheld Martin's doctrine of "independence within government." As if to render that meaning of that doctrine crystal clear, during the 1971 election campaign Nixon and his staff pressured Burns to pursue an expansionary monetary policy, even though doing so might mean losing control of inflation, in part by leaking to the press that "the Federal Reserve would lose its independence if interest rates were not kept low" (Day 2013; see also Abrams 2006). Burns complied, with consequences that are all too well known. He then went on to conduct monetary policy during the remaining Nixon, Ford, and Carter years "with the same political sensitivity" (Cargill and O'Driscoll 2013: 422).

Although Paul Volcker managed to rein in inflation and, thereby, restore the Fed's reputation as an independent agency devoted to keeping prices stable, he was able to do so only because he was backed by presidents who were themselves convinced that inflation had become the nation's top economic problem (Cargill and O'Driscoll 2013: 423). "Political pressure," Thomas Cargill and Gerald O'Driscoll (2013: 423) observe, "is political pressure even if it happens to lead to correct policy."

More recently still, political pressure appears to have played a part in the Fed's ill-fated decision to keep interest rates low despite evidence of an overheating housing market. On the occasion of his testifying before the Financial Crisis Inquiry Commission, Alan Greenspan pointed out "that if the Federal Reserve had tried to slow the housing market amid a 'fairly broad consensus' about encouraging homeownership, 'the Congress would have clamped down on us'" (Cargill and O'Driscoll 2013: 424–25).[12]

In short, while the Treasury Accord may ultimately have relieved the Fed of its former duty to serve as the Treasury's "bond buyer of last resort," it did not otherwise free monetary policy from political influence. Instead, as Weintraub (1978: 353) observes, Fed chairmen ever since McCabe have understood perfectly well that "a Chairman of the Federal Reserve Board who ignores the wishes of the President does so at his peril."

INFLATION AND DEFLATION

Of the many challenges the Fed faces in trying to put a favorable spin on its record, none is more daunting than that of pretending that it has kept prices stable. The U.S. consumer price level was approximately the same when the Fed was founded as it was at the time of the dollar's establishment as the official U.S. monetary unit. It is now about 24 times higher. The dollar has thus lost over 96 percent of its pre-Fed value, with most of the loss occurring since 1971. Before then, the Fed was still somewhat constrained by an obligation to redeem its notes in gold.

Since the Fed can hardly deny outright that, by any reasonable measure, it has failed to keep prices stable, it must settle for suggesting that it has done so while carefully avoiding any reference to the actual course of prices since its establishment. A particularly flagrant instance of this approach occurs in the Atlanta Fed video "The Fed Explains Good versus Bad Standards" (FRBA2). That video starts by comparing the need for a reliable standard of value to that for reliable standards of weight and measurement. "Over the years," the narrator observes, "we have come to appreciate the importance of maintaining consistent standards in our measurements, and the measurement of value is no different. Keeping that standard stable is vital to keeping our economy operating at its maximum efficiency." Did the gold standard do the trick? "Not really," the narrator explains:

> Fluctuations to [sic] the purchasing power of gold made gold a poor standard on which to base our measure of value, and that made trade difficult since no one knew what a dollar would buy from day to day. Eventually, the United States separated from the gold standard and Congress tasked the Federal Reserve to set its policies in order to maintain price stability. Now, the Fed is in charge of keeping the purchasing power of a dollar stable so that when people want to buy or sell something everyone has a clear understanding of the measure of value.

The video implies—though it never *says*—that the dollar has been a more reliable "measure of value" since the Fed's establishment, and particularly since 1971 (when the U.S. "separated" from the gold standard), than it was before. In a like manner, another Atlanta Fed video (FRBA1) shows a cartoon car (the real economy) heading along a road strewn with obstacles (the macroeconomic environment, presumably). "Because the Federal Reserve is keeping an eye on inflation," a voice tells listeners, "you can keep an eye on the road." In truth, of course, it has become both more necessary and more difficult for businessmen and consumers to keep track of inflation since 1914 than it was during most of the preceding century.[13]

When it isn't claiming, implicitly or otherwise, to have prevented it, the Fed portrays inflation, not as evidence of its own lack of monetary restraint, but as a kind of menace-from-without, while portraying itself as a heroic, if not invincible, inflation fighter. "If the price level begins to rise too quickly," the Atlanta Fed video tells listeners, "central banks, like the Federal Reserve, will *try* to adjust monetary policy in order to slow this advance of prices" (emphasis added). A still more blatant example of this tactic occurs in the New York Fed's educational comic book, "The Story of Monetary Policy" (FRBNY 1999), with its panel showing the Fed, depicted as a superhero—complete with blue bodysuit and yellow cape—thrusting an elbow into a Big Red Blob standing for "inflation." Just where the blob came from is never explained, though readers might just as well assume that, like Superman's nemesis Jax-Ur, it came from the planet Krypton.[14]

In view of the actual extent of inflation since 1914, the Fed might at least appear justified in claiming credit for avoiding *deflation*. Yet even that claim is misleading. It overlooks, first of all, the fact that several of the most notorious instances of deflation—including those of 1920–21, 1930–33, 1937–38, and 2008–09 (the last of which was severe relative to the then-established trend of steadily rising prices)—took place *after* 1914. The claim also rests on the assumption, itself common in Fed publications, that deflation is necessarily a bad thing. "At first glance," the San Francisco Fed's "Dr. Econ" (FRBSF 2006) observes,

> deflation might sound like a good thing—who would not like a world where things consumers buy get cheaper over time? However . . . in addition to falling prices of goods and services, other prices would be falling too. For instance, falling wages are likely to accompany falling prices (since wages are the price of labor). Should wages fail to adjust . . . then jobs could be lost as employers struggle to keep up with falling revenues.

Elsewhere, Dr. Econ (FRBSF 1999b) observes that "Periods of deflation typically are associated with downturns in the economy," quoting, with obvious approval, Paul Samuelson and William Nordhaus's (1998) assertion that occasions "in which prices fall steadily over a period of several years, are associated with depressions."

The trouble with this perspective is that it fails to recognize the existence of two very different sorts of deflation. "Bad" deflation happens when an insufficient level or growth rate of aggregate demand leads to a decline in equilibrium prices unconnected to any improvement in an economy's productivity. "Good" deflation, on the other hand, reflects productivity improvements. Because good deflation, unlike the bad sort, goes hand in hand with falling unit production costs, it generally doesn't entail falling profits, wage rates, or employment (Selgin 1997; Stern 2003).

In equating deflation with depression, Fed spokesmen ignore the possibility of good deflation, and so treat all deflation as demand driven. In one of his George Washington University lectures, Ben Bernanke (2012a; compare Bernanke 2002a) observes:

> The sources of deflation are not a mystery. Deflation is in almost all cases a side effect of a collapse of aggregate demand—a drop in spending so severe that producers must cut prices on an ongoing basis in order to find buyers. Likewise, the economic effects of a deflationary episode, for the most part, are similar to those of any other sharp decline in aggregate spending—namely, recession, rising unemployment, and financial stress.

In fact, the broader historical record shows that, far from being exceptional, supply-driven deflation was once far more common than the demand-driven sort (Atkeson and Kehoe 2004; Bordo and Filardo 2005b). In particular, for most of the last quarter of the 19th century, prices throughout the gold-standard bloc declined at a rate roughly reflecting declining real costs of production. Yet far from being symptomatic of a "long" or "great" depression, and notwithstanding occasional financial panics and the ululations of greenbackers and silverites, the deflation went hand in hand with robust long-term economic growth. Indeed, instead of inspiring still more rapid growth, as the Fed's pronouncements might lead one to expect, the inflation that followed new gold discoveries of the 1890s brought a slowdown.

The Fed's refusal to admit that deflation can be a good thing has had practical consequences beyond that of misleading the public. By preventing not only good (that is, productivity-driven) deflation, but good *disinflation*, in recent years, it may well have encouraged business cycles, particularly by contributing to the recent housing boom (Selgin et al. 2015). According to Alan Greenspan (2010), when the Fed decided, in 2003, to maintain a very low federal funds rate, "the probability of getting deflation . . . was less than fifty-fifty. But had it occurred, the impact would have been much too difficult to deal with." That the source of deflation (or disinflation) "risk" was not a slackening of demand but surging productivity apparently didn't matter. But it ought to have, for it meant that, instead of preventing a recession, the Fed's decision fueled a boom.

FINANCIAL PANICS

As the Fed's own accounts make clear, it was founded mainly for the purpose of putting an end to financial panics like those of 1893 and 1907. Those accounts are, however, not to be trusted when it comes to either understanding the nature of pre-Fed panics or assessing the Fed's success in preventing others like them.

As we've seen, Fed sources routinely overlook the role that misguided regulations played in causing or at least aggravating pre-Fed crises, blaming them instead on random outbreaks of unwarranted fear. "Occasionally," the Dallas Fed says (FRBD 2006: 8),

> the public feared that banks would not or could not honor the promise to redeem [their] notes, which led to bank runs. Believing that a particular bank's ability to pay was questionable, a large number of people in a single day would demand to have their banknotes exchanged for gold or silver. These bank runs created fear that often spread, causing runs on other banks and general financial panic. . . . Financial panics such as these occurred frequently during the 1800s and early 1900s.

In his opening George Washington University lecture, Ben Bernanke (2012a) likewise speaks of panic spreading, like a cold, from one bank to the rest. "[I]f one bank is having problems," he says, people "might begin to worry about problems in their bank. And so, a bank run can lead to widespread bank runs or a banking panic, more broadly." To illustrate the point, Bernanke refers to the run on Jimmy Stewart's (that is, George Bailey's) perfectly solvent bank in *It's a Wonderful Life*. Had the Federal Reserve been on the job, he says, Bailey wouldn't have had to depend on the generosity of the good citizens of Bedford Falls.[15]

But the sort of financial panic that Bernanke's "Frank Capra" theory describes happens *only* on TV (where, admittedly, it happens with alarming regularity, every December). Even in the pre-Fed United States, which had more than its fair share of crises, bank-run "contagions" were not common, and those outbreaks that did occur were narrowly confined (Calomiris and Gorton 1991; Kaufman 1994; Temzelides 1997). Instead of causing banks to fail, runs tended to be staged against banks that were already on the brink of failure. Nor were the systemwide runs that began in late February 1933 an exception, for those runs were due, not to indiscriminate panic but to a well-justified fear that Franklin Roosevelt, upon assuming office, would devalue the dollar (Wigmore 1987).

Fed sources also give the impression that, because the Fed was *supposed* to put a stop to panics, it largely succeeded in doing so, whereas in truth, panics were more common during the Fed's first two decades than they'd been during the previous four (Wicker 1996, 2000; Jalil 2009). And though panics did disappear for a while after 1933, credit for that belongs, not to the Fed, but to the Reconstruction Finance Corporation and, after it, the Federal Deposit Insurance Corporation (FDIC) and the Federal Savings and Loan Insurance Corporation.

That deposit insurance was itself no panacea was made clear both by the savings and loan crisis of the 1980s, to which the Federal Savings and Loan Insurance Corporation succumbed, and by the more recent subprime crisis. The Fed, therefore, continues to bear some responsibility for avoiding or containing panics. According to various official Fed sources, the responsible way for it to do so is by heeding the advice Walter Bagehot (1873) gives in *Lombard Street*. Bagehot, Bernanke (2012a) explains, "said that during a panic, [the] central bank should lend freely . . . against good assets." The "good assets" rule is supposed to limit last-resort lending to solvent institutions, so as to avoid propping up insolvent ones. Bagehot also wanted borrowers to be charged "high" rates, to discourage them from borrowing simply for the sake of relending at a profit, and also (since he wrote in the days of the international gold standard) to attract gold from abroad.

Intriguingly, Bagehot had nothing to say about what we now know as the "moral hazard" problem—the problem of firms, and their creditors, taking greater risks because they anticipate being rescued. He didn't have to say anything because, when he wrote, the Bank of England, to which his strictures were aimed, was still a private firm with no inclination to lend to anyone of doubtful solvency. It was all Bagehot could do to try and get the profit-oriented Bank to lend to indisputably *solvent* firms just because they were desperately illiquid.

The Fed today is, of course, a horse of a very different color. Despite being nominally privately owned and paying dividends to its owners, its purpose isn't to turn a profit, and its managers are rewarded not according to how profitable it is, but according to their perceived success in promoting price stability and high employment, among other goals.[16] Bureaucratic incentives, therefore, incline Fed officials, not to deny last-resort aid to firms that (according to Bagehot's rules) qualify for such, but to make last-resort loans to firms that *don't* qualify rather than risk being blamed for allowing a crisis to unfold. The moral hazard problem is, therefore, more than capable of rearing its ugly head.

And so it has, thanks to the Fed's having lent money repeatedly, throughout the 1980s, to banks that were, in fact, insolvent (Schwartz 1992), and especially thanks to its having, with its rescue of Continental Illinois in 1984, officially embraced the notion that some financial institutions, solvent or not, are simply too big to fail.[17] The Rubicon had been crossed. After that, creditors could hardly be blamed for assuming that, so long as a bank was sufficiently large or "systematically important," it might qualify for last-resort aid. Official Fed paeans to Bagehot thus came to be read as if there were an asterisk attached to them: "To get credit from us," the Fed was now widely understood to say, "you must *either* have good collateral *or* be strategically important." The risks inherent in this revision of Bagehot's rules were to become all too evident in the course of the next major crisis.

THE SUBPRIME CRISIS

The most recent financial crisis has allowed the Fed to achieve one of its most impressive public relations feats, to wit: convincing the public that the crisis, instead of supplying more proof of its inadequacy, shows that it's now working better than ever. To accomplish this, the Fed has had to argue that, had it not been for its interventions, the outcome would have been much worse. Typical of this spin is San Francisco Fed President John C. Williams's (2012) observation that, at the end of 2008, the U.S. economy was

> teetering on the edge of an abyss. If the panic had been left unchecked, we could well have seen an economic cataclysm as bad as the Great Depression, when 25 percent of the workforce was out of work. . . . Why then didn't we fall into that abyss in 2008 and 2009? The answer is that a financial collapse was not—I repeat, not—left unchecked. The Federal Reserve did what it was supposed to do.

But did the Fed really do everything "it was supposed to do" to contain the crisis? Is it even certain that its interventions made the crisis no *worse* than it would have been otherwise? There are good reasons for believing that the correct answer to both questions is "no."

The Fed was, first of all, "supposed" to command such superior information as ought to have allowed it to see the crisis, or at least *some* trouble, brewing. After all, according to the San Francisco Fed's "Dr. Econ" (FRBSF 2001), "Federal Reserve operations and structure provide the System with some unique insights into the health of the financial system and the economy," providing it "with firsthand knowledge of the conditions of financial institutions." In fact, Fed officials never saw what hit them. As the Federal Open Market Committee's (FOMC) 2006 transcripts make clear, that committee was convinced at that late date both that a housing market downturn was unlikely and that, if such a downturn occurred, it would not do much damage to the rest of the economy. New York Fed President Timothy Geithner, for example, observed that "we just don't see troubling signs yet of collateral damage, and we are not expecting much," while Janet Yellen did not hesitate to congratulate outgoing Fed Chairman Alan Greenspan for leaving "with the economy in such solid shape" (Appelbaum 2012).

Besides not realizing that the boom was leading to a bust, the Fed encouraged it, and so contributed to the severity of the collapse, by maintaining an extremely low federal funds rate target in the wake of the 2001 crash. Even Fed officials hint at this. "During the early 2000s," a Boston Fed education website (FRBB1) tells us, "low mortgage rates and expanded access to credit made homeownership possible for more people, increasing the demand for housing and driving up house prices"; while Federal Reserve Bank Vice President Jeff Fuhrer, speaking on the Philadelphia Fed video "The Federal Reserve and You" (FRBP1), observes that "when the Fed takes action to move interest rates up and down, it *almost always* has a significant effect on mortgage rates" (emphasis added).[18] It seems reasonable, in light of such claims, to conclude that the Fed did indeed stoke the boom, and that is indeed the conclusion many researchers, equipped with similar logic and corresponding evidence, have drawn.[19] Yet Fed spokesmen, instead of drawing the same conclusion, insist that what was "almost always" the case ceased to be so around 2003. According to them—and to Alan Greenspan and Ben Bernanke especially—low mortgage rates at that time were due to a "global saving glut" over which the Fed had no control.

Though it initially commanded some assent beyond the Fed, the savings glut hypothesis has since been subject to withering criticism. Among various counterarguments, perhaps the most fundamental is offered by Giancarlo Bertocco (2012), who points out that, in a monetary (as opposed to barter) context, the global savings glut hypothesis isn't an alternative to the domestic monetary policy hypothesis at all (see also Borio and Disyatat 2011). "In a world with money," Bertocco (2012: 11) observes,

> emerging economies can become savers [only by] selling goods to the developed country. . . . The origin of the mass of liquidity accumulated by emerging economies must therefore be [traced to] the decisions of the U.S. financial system which, by creating new money, financed the demand for goods which was fulfilled by emerging economies.

Home equity loans played no small part in financing the demand for imports of all kinds, and especially imports from China, thus contributing both to the U.S. trade imbalance and to the capital inflow that was that imbalance's inescapable counterpart.

Nor did the Fed do everything it was supposed to do when it came to last-resort lending. Ben Bernanke, as we've noted, insists that in making last-resort loans, the Fed abides by Bagehot's principles, the soundness of which he readily grants. In a 2012 speech, for example, he said that the recent crisis

> is best understood as a classic financial panic—differing in details but fundamentally similar to the panics described by Bagehot [who] advised central banks . . . to respond to panics by lending freely against sound collateral. Following that advice, from the beginning of the crisis, the Fed . . . provided large amounts of short-term liquidity to financial institutions, including primary dealers as well as banks, on a broad range of collateral. . . . [T]hose actions were, again, consistent with the Bagehot approach of lending against collateral to illiquid but solvent firms. (Bernanke 2012b)

Actually, Bernanke's Fed spurned Bagehot's advice in at least one crucial way. It didn't do so by granting last-resort loans to an investment bank or even to nonfinancial firms: whatever the Fed's own standard practice may have been, Bagehot himself never insisted that last-resort lending be confined to banks. Nor was it necessarily inconsistent of the Fed to have rescued Bear Stearns and AIG but not Lehman Brothers, for although Lehman was certainly insolvent, some authorities (e.g., Cline and Gagnon 2013) maintain that Bear and AIG were solvent when the Fed came to their aid.[20] Nor, finally, was it merely that the Fed made last-resort loans at below-market rates or without securing those loans adequately—though it has been charged with doing both.[21] The main problem was that even if the Fed did *intend* to confine its emergency lending to illiquid but solvent firms, as Bagehot's rule dictates, in its public pronouncements it justified its emergency lending, and its $29 billion loan in support of Bear Stearns's acquisition in particular, not on the Bagehotian grounds that, having been denied credit elsewhere but having good collateral to offer, the firms were entitled to it, but on the grounds that the firms it was aiding were too big (or "systematically important") to fail.

Explaining the Bear Stearns rescue to the Joint Economic Committee, for example, Ben Bernanke (2008a; see also Bernanke 2008b) testified:

> Normally, the market sorts out which companies survive and which fail, and that is as it should be. However, . . . Bear Stearns participated extensively in a range of critical markets. With financial conditions fragile, the sudden failure of Bear Stearns likely would have led to a chaotic unwinding of positions in those markets and could have severely shaken confidence. The company's failure could also have cast doubt on the financial positions of some of Bear Stearns' thousands of counterparties and perhaps of companies with similar businesses. Given the current exceptional pressures on the global economy and financial system, the damage caused by a default by Bear Stearns could have been severe and extremely difficult to contain. Moreover, the adverse effects would not have been confined to the financial system but would have been felt broadly in the real economy through its effects on asset values and credit availability.

Tim Geithner, who was then president of the New York Fed, likewise stressed not Bear's solvency but the fact that allowing it to fail would have led to "a greater probability of widespread insolvencies, severe and protracted damage to the financial system and, ultimately, to the economy as a whole" (Labaton 2008).

A similar admixture of Bagehotian and too-big-to-fail criteria for central bank lending also occurs in various postcrisis Fed publications. According to the Federal Reserve Bank of San Francisco (FRBSF2), for example, Bear Stearns's failure would have

> risked a domino effect that would have severely disrupted financial markets. To contain the damage, the Federal Reserve facilitated the

purchase of Bear Stearns by the bank JPMorgan Chase by providing loans backed [sic] by certain Bear Stearns assets. Several months later, however, the investment bank Lehman Brothers collapsed because no private company was willing to acquire the troubled investment bank and Lehman did not have adequate collateral to qualify for direct loans from the Federal Reserve. As a result, financial panic threatened to spread to several other key financial institutions, including the giant insurance company American International Group (AIG). AIG played a central role guaranteeing financial instruments, so its failure had the potential to lead to a cascade of failures and a meltdown of the global financial system. To contain this threat, the Federal Reserve provided secured loans to AIG.

The trouble with such a mingling of Bagehotian and too-big-to-fail lending criteria is, as we have seen, that it raises a moral hazard. Bernanke himself was fully aware of the danger. "Some particularly thorny issues," he observed after the Bear rescue,

> are raised by the existence of financial institutions that may be perceived as "too big to fail" and the moral hazard issues that may arise when governments intervene in a financial crisis. [Bear's rescue was] necessary and justified under the circumstances that prevailed at that time. However, those events also have consequences that must be addressed. In particular, if no countervailing actions are taken, what would be perceived as an implicit expansion of the safety net could exacerbate the problem of "too big to fail," possibly resulting in excessive risk-taking and yet greater systemic risk in the future. Mitigating that problem is one of the design challenges that we face as we consider the future evolution of our system. (Bernanke 2008b)

In retrospect, however, it's evident that the problem *wasn't* "mitigated," for Lehman's counterparties, who were well aware of its troubles, clearly expected it to be rescued, and so took no adequate precautions against its going bankrupt.

Nor could the Fed claim that it had effectively guarded against any such expectation by means of an unambiguous statement of its last-resort lending policy. "In its nearly 100-year history," Allan Meltzer (2012: 261) observes, "the Fed has never announced its policy as lender of last resort. From the 1970s on, it acted on the belief that some banks were too-big-to-fail. Although the FOMC discussed last resort policy at times, the Fed never committed itself to a policy rule about assistance."

Michael Lewis (2008) was among those who correctly anticipated the consequences of the Bear rescue. "Investment banks," Lewis wrote just afterwards, "now have even less pressure on them than they did before to control their risks." He continued:

> There's a new feeling in the Wall Street air: The big firms are now too big to fail. If the chaos that might ensue from Bear Stearns going bankrupt, and stiffing its counterparties on its billions of dollars of trades, is too much for the world to endure, the chaos that might be caused by Lehman Brothers Holdings Inc. or Goldman Sachs Group Inc. or Merrill Lynch & Co. or Morgan Stanley going bankrupt must also be too much to endure.
>
> Already we may have seen one of the pleasant effects of this financial order: the continued survival of Lehman. What happened to Bear Stearns might well already have happened to Lehman. Any firm that uses each \$1 of its capital to finance \$31 of risky bets is at the mercy of public opinion. . . . Throw its viability into doubt and the people who lent them the other \$30 want their money back as soon as they can get it—unless they know that, if it comes to that, the Fed will make them whole. The viability of Lehman Brothers has been thrown into serious doubt, and yet Lehman Brothers lives, a tribute to the Fed's new policy.

Unless they were somehow prevented from doing so by new regulations, Lewis (2008) went on to say, Lehman and other large investment banks would "use the implicit government guarantee to underwrite their relentless pursuit of incredible sums of money for themselves—and thus create problems for the Fed and the financial system that will make the undoing of

Bear Stearns seem trivial." For larger financial firms especially, market discipline did in fact deteriorate after the Bear Stearns bailout (Hett and Schmidt 2013). Lehman itself behaved as if its principal aim was to secure a place at the very top of the Fed's critical list.

When the inevitable reckoning came, the Fed faced a stark choice: it could either abandon "too big to fail" or set aside, more flagrantly than ever before, Bagehot's call for lending only on good collateral. To the financial industry's immense surprise, it took the former course, provoking a panic that was only compounded when Bernanke and Henry Paulson, in attempting to get $700 billion from Congress, warned that, without this assistance, the crisis "would threaten all parts of our economy" (U.S. Treasury 2008).[22]

Many Fed critics conclude that, having justified its rescue of Bear Stearns on too-big-to-fail grounds, the Fed ought also to have rescued Lehman. Others (Ayotte and Skeel 2010; Skeel 2009; Danielsson 2008), however, maintain that the Fed would have done still less harm by letting Bear itself go bankrupt, notwithstanding its having been solvent, for that would, at least, have suggested that the Fed was unwilling to take investment banks under its too-big-to-fail umbrella, and so would have given Lehman and its counterparties reason to prepare for that firm's bankruptcy.

The Fed also departed from Bagehot's advice by sterilizing its last-resort lending. Despite the rescues it undertook, it kept the total size of its balance sheet more or less unchanged, offsetting its emergency lending with corresponding sales of Treasury securities. Consequently, instead of adding to the overall supply of liquid funds, as it should have done were it following Bagehot's dicta (and as it had done, with good results, during past crises including Y2K and 9/11), the Fed chose to *redistribute* such funds from presumably solvent financial institutions to more doubtful ones (Labonte 2009: 28–29). Fed officials defend this course on the grounds that it allowed it to maintain its announced interest rate target. But the argument makes little sense, since in hindsight it seems clear that the occasion justified lowering the target. By sterilizing its emergency loans, the Fed inadvertently contributed to the collapse of aggregate spending that was to transform the financial crisis into a full-fledged recession.

According to Daniel Thornton (2012: 8–10), the Fed's conduct was actually due, not to its desire to maintain an (excessively high) rate target, but to Fed officials' belief "that the market's ability to allocate efficiently was impaired." This rationale, too, was suspect, owing both to the "pretense of knowledge" that underlay it, and to the fact that, by assuming the new role of credit allocation, the Fed exposed itself "to the temptation to politicize its selection of recipients of its credit" (Bordo 2008: 8).

Whatever the reason for it, sterilized lending was, according to Thornton (a vice president of and economic adviser to the Federal Reserve Bank of St. Louis), a serious policy error. "I find it puzzling," he writes,

> that the Fed decided not to increase the monetary base even though it was increasingly clear that the difficulties in the financial markets and the economy were intensifying and financial markets were in need of additional credit. Increasing the monetary base would not have been a panacea, but increasing the availability of credit to the market would have facilitated the adjustment process significantly. In any event, not increasing the supply of credit by sterilizing the Fed's lending . . . produced no noticeable results. Financial market and economic conditions continued to deteriorate, risk spreads remained high, and on March 14, 2008, the Fed participated in a bailout of Bear Stearns. (Thornton 2012: 8–9)

After Lehman failed, the Fed ceased to sterilize its lending, allowing the federal funds rate to approach zero. But it also welcomed two new measures that prevented its new stance from contributing to any substantial increase in overall lending and spending. These measures consisted, first, of the Treasury's Supplementary Financing Program (SFP) and, second, of legislation allowing the Fed to begin paying interest on bank reserves. Under the SFP, which began on September 17 and was supposed to be short lived, the Treasury effectively started doing the Fed's sterilizing for it, by issuing short-term "cash management bills" and parking the proceeds in special Fed bank accounts (Stella 2009). By paying interest on bank reserves, which it began doing on October 6, the Fed encouraged banks to hold on to excess reserves instead of lending them, further dampening the effect of the Fed's easing.[23]

These restrictive measures were once again defended on the grounds that they helped the Fed to implement its desired monetary policy. "Interest on reserves," the Board of Governors (2008) informed the press, "will permit the Federal Reserve to expand its balance sheet as necessary to provide the liquidity necessary to support financial stability while implementing the monetary policy that is appropriate in light of the System's macroeconomic objectives of maximum employment and price stability." More specifically, the step was made necessary, the press release goes on to say, because the Open Market Desk had "encountered difficulty achieving the operating target for the federal funds rate set by the FOMC," because of the large increase in reserve balances the Fed's various emergency lending facilities had sponsored over the course of the preceding weeks:

> Essentially, paying interest on reserves allows the Fed to place a floor on the federal funds rate, since depository institutions have little incentive to lend in the overnight interbank federal funds market at rates below the interest rate on excess reserves. This allows the Desk to keep the federal funds rate closer to the FOMC's target rate than it would have been able to otherwise.

A Federal Reserve Bank of San Francisco educational resource summed up the Fed's strategy thus: "The Fed's new authority gave policymakers another tool to use during the financial crisis. Paying interest on reserves allowed the Fed to increase the level of reserves and still maintain control of the federal funds rate" (FRBSF 2013).

Where to begin? The Fed can always "expand its balance sheet" as much as it wishes, without regard to the federal funds rate, by purchasing assets, as it has done during the various rounds of quantitative easing. And interest on reserves wasn't needed to "place a floor on the federal funds rate": it merely served to raise the floor—that is, the rate at which banks ceased to have any incentive to extend overnight credit to other banks—from zero to some positive value. As a solution to the "zero lower bound" problem, this was akin to raising the pavement around skyscrapers to their second story, so as not to have to worry about jumpers ever reaching the ground.

The Fed's decision to reward banks for not lending in the midst of a liquidity crunch was eerily reminiscent of one of its more notorious Great Depression blunders: its decision to double banks' minimum reserve requirement starting in 1936, just when a recovery was at last getting under way. According to many economists, that decision helped to trigger the "Roosevelt Recession" of 1937–38.

THE RECOVERY

The spin that Fed sources put on its conduct during the subprime crisis is matched by their misleading portrayal of its role in the postcrisis recovery. According to official accounts, thanks to the Fed's actions the economy has recovered more rapidly and more fully than it could possibly have done without the Fed's help. "Uncertainty," Cleveland Fed President Sandra Pianalto (2013) observed last spring, has

> been restraining the economy. Businesses have been hesitant to hire workers and make investments [while] lenders have also become more cautious. . . . In this environment, the Federal Reserve has taken aggressive and unconventional actions to nudge the U.S. economy back to self-sustaining health. . . . Clearly, the FOMC's policies have been beneficial in increasing economic growth.

In truth, it's far from "clear" that Fed policies have contributed much to the post-2008 recovery. Both theory and experience suggest, first of all, that thanks to adjusting prices and expectations, economies *eventually* recover from contractions brought about by reduced lending and spending even if nothing is done to actually restore spending to its former level. What's more, recoveries are usually rapid: in the course of his George Washington University lectures, Bernanke (2012a) observed that "if you look at recessions in the postwar period in the United States, you see very frequently that recoveries only take a couple of years . . . and in fact, very sharp [recessions] are typically followed by a faster recovery." What Bernanke didn't say is that, according to the latest careful studies, and setting aside the recent recession, contractions generally lasted no longer, and recoveries were no slower, during the four decades before the Fed's establishment than they have been since World War II (Romer 1999; Davis 2006). As for the generally disastrous interwar period, it also involved one relatively rapid recovery—from the sharp 1920–21 downturn—to which the Fed contributed very little, if anything at all.

The post-2008 recovery, in contrast, has been painfully slow. Moreover, by some measures at least, it is still far from complete. The Fed's attempts to take credit for it consequently bring to mind an episode of *The Beverly Hillbillies* (a 1960s TV show, in case you're under 50) in which the local doctor is impressed when Granny reveals that she's got a cure for the common cold—a potion that, she says, has worked like a charm for half a century. It's only at the end of the episode that Granny explains that, by "working like a charm," she means that all you have to do is take a swig, and in a week to 10 days you're as good as new. The difference is that, to judge by the pace of recovery alone, the potions the Fed has been administering to America's ailing economy since the fall of 2008, instead of merely doing nothing, appear to have made it sicker.

This isn't to deny that the Fed *might* have hastened the recovery if, during late 2007 and the first half of 2008, it had acted to preserve economywide liquidity instead of making sterilized loans aimed at bolstering particular firms and markets. According to Thornton (2012: 25), the Fed did provide some help through its Term Auction Facility, though it's having done so at subsidized rates—yet another violation of Bagehot's rules—was "troublesome." But not until late March 2009 did it begin expanding the monetary base aggressively, by its first round of quantitative easing. By that late date, however (Thornton observes), aggressive easing was no longer justified: financial markets had already stabilized, risk-spreads had declined considerably, and the Term Auction Facility auctions were undersubscribed. By June, according to the National Bureau of Economic Research's reckoning, the contraction had already ended (Thornton 2012: 14).

Instead of promoting recovery, Thornton claims, the Fed's aggressive but belated expansion hampered it by adding to the very uncertainty that

Cleveland Fed President Pianalto bemoans.[24] "Most economists agree," Thornton observes (2012: 18),

> that if important policymakers were to tell the public that we could be facing the next Great Depression, consumption would sink like a rock. . . . In a similar vein, I believe an "extreme" policy stance, such as the one the FOMC has pursued since late 2008 and indicates that it will continue until late 2014, generates expectations that the economy is much worse than it might otherwise appear. This expectations effect will be particularly important when the actions are taken at a time when there are significant signs that financial markets are stabilizing and the economy is improving.

Among other things, the "expectations effect" of the Fed's unorthodox policies gave banks and other firms a greater inclination than ever to hold cash rather than invest it, undermining the potential for quantitative easing to either reduce long-term rates or revive aggregate demand. Instead, the easing served merely to further redistribute credit, while dramatically enhancing the Fed's share of the total extent of financial intermediation.

Despite such criticisms, the belief that the Fed "saved us from another Great Depression" (Li 2013) is now well on its way to becoming conventional wisdom. The Fed has thus managed to achieve what is surely its greatest public relations coup of all. It has taken its most notorious lemon, and made lemonade from it.

10

LIBERTY STREET: BAGEHOTIAN PRESCRIPTIONS FOR A 21ST-CENTURY MONEY MARKET*

IN *LOMBARD STREET*, Walter Bagehot (1873) offered his famous advice for reforming the Bank of England's lending policy. The financial crisis of 1866, and other factors, had convinced Bagehot that, instead of curtailing credit to conserve the Bank's own liquidity in the face of an "internal drain" of specie and, thereby, confronting the English economy as a whole with a liquidity shortage, the Bank ought to lend freely at high rates on good collateral. Bagehot's now-famous advice has come to be known as the "classical" prescription for last-resort lending.

Largely forgotten, however, is Bagehot's belief that his prescription was but a second-best remedy for financial crises, far removed from the first-best remedy, namely, the substitution of a decentralized banking system—such as Scotland's famously stable, free-banking system—for England's centralized arrangement. Bagehot's excuse for proffering such a remedy was simply that he did not think anyone was prepared to administer the first-best alternative: "I propose to maintain this system," he wrote, "because I am quite sure it is of no manner of use proposing to alter it. . . . You might as well, or better, try to alter the English monarchy and substitute a republic" (Bagehot 1873: 329–30).

---

* Originally published in 2012 as "L Street: Bagehotian Prescriptions for a 21st Century Money Market," *Cato Journal* 32 (2): 303–32. The author thanks Bob Eisenbeis, Marvin Goodfriend, Bill Lastrapes, Jerry O'Driscoll, John Turner, Dan Thornton, and Lawrence H. White for helpful comments.

Like Bagehot, I offer here some second-best suggestions, informed by recent experience, for improving existing arrangements for dealing with financial crises. Unlike Bagehot, who merely recommended changes in the Bank of England's *conduct*, I propose changes to the Federal Reserve's *operating framework*. And though, like Bagehot, I consider my proposals mere "palliatives," I do not assume that we cannot ultimately do better. On the contrary, I doubt that any amount of mere tinkering with our existing, discretionary central banking system will suffice to protect us against future financial crises. To truly reduce the risk of such crises, we must seriously consider more radical reforms (see, e.g., Chapter 8 of this volume).

A TOP-HEAVY OPERATING SYSTEM

Both the financial crisis and the ways in which the Fed felt compelled to respond to it point to shortcomings of the Fed's traditional operating framework—a framework that relies heavily on a small number of systematically important financial firms known as "primary dealers," as well as on JPMorgan Chase and Bank of New York Mellon in their capacity as "clearing banks" for the Fed's temporary open market transactions.

In theory, these private institutions serve as efficient monetary policy agents—that is, as private middlemen or conduits through which liquidity is supplied by the Fed to the rest of the financial system. The theory breaks down, however, if the agents themselves become illiquid or insolvent, or if some agents fear being damaged by the liquidity or insolvency of others. In that case, the agents may cease to be effective monetary policy conduits. Instead, their involvement can undermine the implementation of ordinary monetary policy, denying solvent firms access to liquid assets. The Fed may for these reasons alone—and setting aside others that contribute to the agents' "systematic significance"—be compelled to bail out a monetary policy agent, further interfering with efficient credit allocation. The expectation that it will do so, in turn, enhances agents' "too big to fail" status, encouraging them to take excessive risks, and increasing the likelihood of future crises.

In what follows, I explore the drawbacks of the Fed's top-heavy operating framework, especially as revealed by the recent financial crisis. I then offer suggestions for making that framework both less top-heavy and more flexible. The suggested reforms should serve to reduce both the extent of the Fed's interference with an efficient allocation of credit and the extent of implicit guarantees in the financial system, while making it easier for the Fed to adhere to the spirit of Bagehot's classical rules for last-resort lending. More specifically, the changes I recommend seek to ground Fed operations more firmly in the rule of law—and make them less subject to the rule of men—by allowing the Fed to rely on one-and-the-same operating framework to both implement normal monetary policy and meet extraordinary liquidity needs during times of financial distress.

ORDINARY MONETARY OPERATIONS

The Fed traditionally conducts monetary policy by means of a combination of "permanent" and "temporary" open market operations. Permanent operations involve outright purchases and sales of Treasury securities. Because permanent open market sales are relatively rare, purchased securities are usually held in the Fed's System Open Market Account (SOMA) until they mature. Permanent open market purchases are mainly used to provide for secular growth in the stock of base money, and especially in the outstanding stock of paper currency.

Temporary open market operations, in contrast, are aimed at making seasonal and cyclical adjustments to the stock of base money, and are typically conducted, not by means of outright purchases and sales of Treasury securities, but by means of repurchase agreements or "repos" involving such securities. Although in name a repo is a contract providing for the sale of a security with an agreement by the seller to repurchase the same security at a specified price within a relatively short period after the initial sale, in practice repos resemble collateralized loans in which the security to be repurchased serves as collateral. The Fed, having first introduced repos to the U.S. economy in 1917, shied away from them after the massive bank failures of the 1930s. They came back into favor as monetary policy instruments following the 1951 Treasury Accord. Eventually, a private repo market developed in which repos, instead of being confined to Treasury securities, came to include a broad range of private debt instruments (Acharya and Öncü 2010: 323–30).

The self-reversing nature of repos, and the fact that the vast majority of them are overnight loans, make them especially fit for temporary open market operations, because the Fed has only to refrain from renewing its repos to absorb base money after a peak demand for it subsides. Repos come in handy, for example, during the Christmas season, when the Fed uses them to offset the decline in bank reserves that must otherwise result from heavy currency withdrawals. Repos also help the Fed to implement its federal funds rate target because, for banks, overnight Treasury repos are a relatively close substitute for borrowing in the federal funds market. Arbitrage, thus, tends to cause the federal funds rate to track the rate for such repos. The Fed is consequently able to use repos to move the federal funds rate in whatever direction it desires, and move it more assuredly than it could do using outright Treasury purchases and sales.

Both permanent and temporary open market operations have traditionally been conducted with a limited number of counterparties known as primary dealers. Although the roots of this primary dealer system trace to 1935, when the Fed was first prevented from buying bonds directly from the U.S. Treasury, the system officially got started with 18 members in 1960. By 1988 the number had climbed to 46. But on the eve of the crisis it had dwindled to just 20, including a dozen foreign bank affiliates. Today, after the failure of MF Global—one of two postcrisis additions to the list—there are 21. The Fed normally conducts its open market operations with these dealers only, arranging both outright Treasury security purchases and repos with them, and leaving it to them to channel funds to other financial firms mainly by means of private repos, with commercial banks, in turn, sharing reserves through the overnight federal funds market.

Two other private market agents also assist the Fed in implementing monetary policy. The failure of two major security dealers during the 1980s gave rise to so-called "tri-party" repos, in which repo counterparties, including the Fed, rely on third parties, known as clearing banks, to price and otherwise manage repo collateral. Today, as at the time of the crisis, there are only two such banks—JPMorgan Chase and the Bank of New York Mellon.

Besides being conduits for the Fed's open market operations, the clearing banks also play a crucial role in allocating available liquidity among primary dealers.

Ordinarily, as Donald Kohn (2009: 6) observes, the primary dealer system "allows the Federal Reserve to implement policy quite efficiently . . . with minimal interference in private credit markets." Because it relies on the private market to price and direct funds, the system avoids any risk of credit being provided at subsidized rates, and so heeds Bagehot's classical prescription. The Fed nevertheless maintains a standing facility—the discount window—for the purpose of direct lending to illiquid financial institutions, partly in recognition of the possibility that open market operations, as ordinarily conducted, may prove inadequate for meeting "serious financial strains among individual firms or specialized groups of institutions" during times of financial distress (Board of Governors 1971: 19).

Generally speaking, the presence of efficient wholesale lending markets means that banks are unlikely to turn to the discount window unless they lack the sort of good collateral that would qualify them for classical last-resort loans. The Fed, for its part, appears unable to resist lending to insolvent banks.[1] Consequently, several economists (Friedman 1960: 50–51, 1982b; Humphrey 1986; Goodfriend and King 1988; Kaufman 1991, 1999; Lacker 2004: 956ff.; Hetzel 2009b) have recommended doing away with extended discount window lending altogether and having the Fed supply liquidity solely through the open market. The crisis has, however, been regarded by some as proof that such a step would be imprudent. "A systemic event," Stephen Cecchetti and Piti Disyatat (2010: 12) observe, "almost surely requires lending at an effectively subsidized rate" secured by "collateral of suspect quality," which can be had only by direct appeal to a central bank.

Further consideration suggests, however, that the apparent need for direct lending during crises stems, not from the inadequacy of open market operations as such, but from the inadequacy of the Fed's particular rules and procedures for conducting such operations, including its reliance upon the primary dealer system.[2] In particular, the Fed, by depending upon a small set of primary dealers, and on two clearing banks, for its open market operations, risks a breakdown in the monetary transmission mechanism when these agents themselves become troubled. Consequently, the Fed may be compelled, not merely to engage in direct lending, but also to depart from Bagehot's principles by bailing out insolvent firms when their failure threatens to cause a breakdown in its operating framework. The Fed's reliance upon primary dealers and tri-party repos thus contributes to the notion of the "systemically important financial institution," official recognition of which, according to former Kansas City Fed president Thomas Hoenig (2011), poses a serious threat to the future of capitalism.

While some firms would perhaps continue to be regarded as "systemically important" no matter how monetary policy is conducted, a responsible central bank ought to avoid arrangements that contribute to the existence of such financial goliaths, to the extent that it can do so without otherwise compromising its ability to conduct monetary policy. Policymakers should, in turn, welcome new arrangements that might do away with a perceived need for ad hoc changes to the Fed's operating procedures in response to systemic events.

MONETARY OPERATIONS DURING THE SUBPRIME CRISIS

The Fed's primary dealer-based operating system takes primary dealers' financial health for granted. If the dealers themselves are in danger of failing, the system can break down.

Primary dealers are hardly likely to go broke owing to their participation in open market operations. However, the set of primary dealers "overlaps substantially" with that of major dealers in securities and over-the-counter derivatives, and such dealers "tend to finance significant fractions of their assets with short-term repurchase agreements" with counterparties consisting mainly of other dealers, money market mutual funds, and securities lenders (Duffie 2009: 9, 27–28). Hence, dealers' notoriously high leverage. When a dealer's solvency becomes suspect, its counterparties may choose not to renew their repos with it, so as to avoid risks involved in having to realize upon their collateral. The general refusal of a dealer's counterparties to renew can force the dealer into bankruptcy, while its attempts to provide for its own liquidity at short notice could threaten other dealers by contributing to a general decline in the market value of, and hence an increase in "haircuts" applied to, private security repos.

An increased perceived risk of primary dealer insolvency can short-circuit monetary policy in at least two ways. First, as just noted, an increase in perceived counterparty risk may cause prospective private lenders to cease lending to them except perhaps at very high rates. Second, highly leveraged banks, including dealers, upon realizing that adverse asset shocks have increased their own debt rollover risk, may "hoard" liquidity by refraining from lending—and especially from term lending—even to counterparties that they know to be solvent (Acharya and Skeie 2011). Consequently, instead of serving as efficient conduits for the transmission of reserves, dealers become so many liquidity traps, contributing to the drying-up of wholesale lending markets. The drying-up of liquidity, in turn, contributes to the perceived riskiness of nondealer counterparties and, hence, to more liquidity hoarding, possibly leading to a general credit freeze.

Such a freeze appears to have hampered monetary policy during the subprime crisis when, as various Federal Reserve officials have themselves acknowledged, instead of assisting the Fed in keeping financial markets liquid, the primary dealer system "blocked, or seriously undermined, the mechanisms through which monetary policy influences the economy" (Fisher and Rosenblum 2009; cf. Afonso et al. 2011). At the onset of the crisis during the third quarter of 2007, primary dealers, having been among the financial institutions faced with the largest toxic asset losses, were also "the quickest to freeze or reduce their lending activity" (Fisher and Rosenblum 2009), and so ceased to be a source of liquidity to either businesses or to other banks (Giles and Tett 2008). According to Kohn (2009: 6),

> The fact that primary dealers rather than commercial banks were the regular counterparties of the Federal Reserve in its open market operations, together with the fact that the Federal Reserve ordinarily extended only modest amounts of funding through repo agreements, meant that open market operations were not particularly useful during the crisis for directing funding to where it was most critically needed in the financial system.

In consequence, and despite the Fed's considerable lowering of its federal funds rate target, interest rates paid by business and households rose. Sound banks that, thanks to the reduced volume of wholesale lending, found themselves short of liquidity, had the option of turning to the Fed's discount window, but refrained from doing so owing to the stigma associated with discount window borrowing ever since the Fed's 1984 bailout of Continental Illinois. It was thanks to this credit "distribution bottleneck" that the Fed was driven to create "an array of mechanisms by which institutions, other than primary dealers, could properly avail of official liquidity provision" (Dunne et al. 2009: 4). These mechanisms included the Term Auction Facility (TAF)—a term repo lending facility established on December 12, 2007—designed to bypass the primary dealer system while avoiding the discount window stigma.[3]

Besides not having been able to rely on them as monetary policy conduits, the Fed felt obliged to rescue several primary dealers—and to do so at the expense of solvent banks. When Bear Stearns collapsed in March 2008, the Fed first announced a new Term Securities Lending Facility (TSLF), which would allow primary dealers to borrow securities for up to 28 days from the System Open Market Account so as to be able, in turn, to employ them as collateral for overnight repo borrowings of Fed funds made between March 2008 and February 2010 via the Primary Dealer Credit Facility (PDCF). As Robert Eisenbeis (2009: 5) observes, the TSLF served, in effect, to reallocate to primary dealers reserves "that would otherwise have been available to smaller banks or holders of Fed funds to support lending and asset acquisition, with some predictable results for the real economy and economic growth."

Having announced the TSLF, the Fed introduced what was, according to Acharya and Öncü (2010: 337), "its most radical change in monetary policy since the Great Depression," namely, the PDCF. The facility was, essentially, a new discount window for primary dealers. While the old discount window remained relatively quiescent, the new one witnessed an unprecedented volume of lending, most of which took place following Lehman Brothers' September 2008 failure, when the PDCF started to accept risky assets as collateral. According to the Fed's December 2010 disclosure, the heaviest borrowers were banks that were in the greatest peril of failing, including Merrill Lynch, Citigroup, Morgan Stanley, and Goldman Sachs. The accumulated borrowings of each ended up being in the neighborhood of $2 trillion (Sheridan 2011: 13–14), while the total accumulated lending of the PDCF fell just shy of $9 trillion, with a peak of about $150 billion in daily credits during the first week of October 2008.

Finally, starting in November 2008, the Fed began its first round of "quantitative easing," eventually making outright purchases of about $400 million of government-sponsored enterprise–guaranteed mortgage-backed securities and (through special purchase vehicles) of another $250 billion in commercial paper and various toxic assets acquired from Bear Sterns and AIG. According to Paul Volcker (2008: 2), these actions took the Fed "to the very edge of its lawful and implied powers, transcending certain long-embedded central banking principles and practices," and testing "the time honored central bank mantra in time of crisis—'lend freely at high rates on good collateral'—to the point of no return." Because the Fed sterilized most of its subprime asset purchases, by reducing its Treasury holdings by over $250 billion and by having the Treasury increase its deposits at the Fed by about $300 billion, the purchases actually reduced the availability of liquid funds to solvent banks. In short, in propping up an operating system that was supposed to help it act according to Bagehot's advice, the Fed found itself honoring that advice only in the breach.

The Fed's decision to support primary dealers was motivated, not so much by its desire to preserve them as direct agents for monetary policy, but by its fear that their failures could threaten the tri-party repo system by exposing one of the clearing banks to large losses. As Brickler and colleagues (2011) explain:

> To give dealers access to their securities during the day, the clearing banks settle all repos early each day, returning cash to cash investors [including the Fed] and collateral to dealers. Because of the delay in settlement, the clearing banks wind up extending hundreds of billions of intraday credit to the dealers until new repos are settled in the evening.

A clearing bank might, therefore, refuse to continue transacting with a troubled dealer, making it impossible for that dealer to meet its obligations. JPMorgan Chase appears to have taken this step with Lehman, refusing to process its payment instructions and in effect freezing $17 billion in Lehman's assets it held as collateral, the night before Lehman's failure (Duffie 2009: 39). The Fed then worried, not only that other primary dealers were in danger of failing, but that either of the two clearing banks might be exposed to large losses if a large broker-dealer defaulted (Tuckman 2010). The clearing banks themselves thus became "hot spots for systematic risk and taxpayer bailout" (Fricker 2011), and it was largely for their sake that primary dealers were rescued. The rescue of Bear Stearns and the subsequent establishment of the PDCF, in particular, appear to have been motivated not so much by Bear's heavy involvement in the market for mortgage-backed securities as by its status as a big player in the tri-party repo market.

Whether or not they were justified by dealers' systematic importance, the Fed's primary dealer rescues can only have contributed to surviving dealers' inclination—as well as that of the clearing banks—to take excessive risks. As Duffie (2009: 43–44) has observed, "Although the various new government facilities that appeared during the financial crisis of 2007–09 may have prevented some extremely damaging failures, some of these facilities may turn out to be costly to taxpayers and are likely to increase moral hazard in the risk taking of large dealer banks going forward, absent other measures."

THE PRESCRIPTIONS

To improve the Fed's current operating framework and reduce the chances for another financial crisis, I offer the five following prescriptions, all of which embody a Bagehotian perspective: (1) abolish the primary dealer system, (2) limit or abolish repos, (3) abandon "Treasuries only," (4) revive the Term Auction Facility, and (5) stop last-resort discount window lending.

ABOLISH THE PRIMARY DEALER SYSTEM

The most obvious operating system reform suggested by the crisis is to replace the primary dealer system with one in which numerous financial firms, and perhaps even some nonfinancial firms, take part in the Fed's open market operations.

There are good reasons for the Fed to dispense with its primary dealer system, even putting aside the dangers of relying upon it during crises. "In central banking terms," as Chris Giles and Gillian Tett (2008) observe, despite its long pedigree, the Fed's primary dealer system "is decidedly old-fashioned," having, as Eisenbeis (2009: 2) explains, "evolved prior to the advent of electronics and computerization of the bid and auction process when institutions relied upon messengers to transmit paper bids to the [System Open Market] Desk." Today, Eisenbeis goes on to observe, there's no reason why a much larger number of qualified firms "could not take part in the daily Open Market transaction process through the System's electronic bidding process." The orthodox arrangement, he adds, "is neither necessary nor in the best interest of taxpayers."

Eisenbeis's conclusion echoes that of a precrisis IMF working paper devoted to reviewing the pros and cons of primary dealers for developing countries. According to that paper's authors, Marcone Arnone and George Iden (2003: 8), "automation gives a means to handle large numbers of participants in auctions that was not previously possible," while "electronic markets can offer information on market conditions and prices" that primary dealers were once uniquely capable of supplying. Indeed, Arnone and Iden conclude that primary dealers are unnecessary, not just for monetary policy but also for direct sales of government securities, except in less developed economies with as-yet poorly developed securities markets.[4] In short, as a vehicle for the conduct of U.S. monetary policy, the primary dealer system is, at best, an anachronism.

The Shadow Financial Regulatory Committee, of which Eisenbeis is a member, has recommended that the Fed take advantage of modern technology to adopt an approach similar to that of the ECB, which routinely conducts open market operations "with more than 500 counterparties throughout the Euro Zone," and which might deal with more than twice as many. Doing so, the committee maintains, "would increase the efficiency of the SOMA transaction process, lower costs, reduce dependence upon a geographically concentrated set of counter parties, and enhance the monetary policy transmission process"

(Shadow Financial Regulatory Committee 2009). Electronic trading could also preserve the anonymity of firms seeking funds from the Fed.[5] Such improvements, it bears noting, would supply a rationale for doing away with the primary dealer system even if primary dealers' soundness were never in doubt.

So far as outright open market purchases are concerned, there is no reason at all for the Fed to restrict the number of its counterparties, even by limiting participation in open market operations to financial firms, since it doesn't expose itself to counterparty risk in making outright purchases. The only risk it takes on is that connected with depreciation of the securities it acquires, which is of course a function, not of the counterparties it deals with, but of the securities it chooses to buy.

Insofar as they rely upon repos rather than outright security purchases and sales, temporary open market operations pose a somewhat greater challenge, in part because repos, being in effect securitized loans, do expose the Fed to counterparty risk, and so warrant its taking measures to guard against such risk. But the view that relying exclusively upon primary dealers is itself such a measure, based as it is on the assumption that primary dealers are "the soundest of sound" financial institutions, is no longer tenable.[6] Instead, the opaque nature of broker-dealers' undertakings, their high leverage, and the fact that they aren't subject to Fed oversight make such firms particularly risky ones for the Fed to contract with.

Rather than pretend to limit its exposure to the risk of a counterparty's failure by severely limiting the number of counterparties it deals with, the Fed can achieve a genuine reduction in risk by doing just the opposite: diversifying its counterparties so as to greatly reduce its exposure to losses in the event of any single counterparty's failure. A simple way to accomplish that end, while further limiting the Fed's risk exposure and guarding against adverse selection, would be to open participation to any financial institution with a CAMEL score of 1 or 2.[7] Such a broadening of Fed counterparties would, as Hoenig (2011: 9) observes, also "enable nearly all banks to play a role in the conduct of monetary policy," leveling the credit-allocation playing field while simultaneously making the largest banks considerably less systematically important. Since the crisis, the Fed has agreed to have several new counterparties, including a number of money market funds, take part in reverse repos that it eventually intends to employ in mopping up excess base money; but it has not otherwise departed from its traditional primary-dealer-based operating framework.[8]

Although counterparty diversification might itself limit clearing banks' exposure to risk in connection with the Fed's repo operations, the clearing banks would still be heavily exposed to any primary dealer failure, and could consequently remain "hotspots for systemic risk" and for potential Fed operating system failure, through their involvement in the private repo market (Tuckman 2010). Here, Ben Bernanke himself has suggested a solution, consisting of replacing the present private clearing-bank duopoly with a centralized clearing platform or "utility" (Bernanke 2008b; see also Singh 2011 and Penney 2011). According to a Financial Economist Roundtable report, the present arrangement

> lacks transparency, has virtually no federal regulatory oversight, raises potential issues of conflicts of interest by virtue of the duopoly's unique access to information on counterparty transactions and ability to meet capital requirements, and poses systemic risks should either of these institutions experience financial distress in their other operations. . . . If ever there was a question of what firms might be determined too-big-to-fail, the operators of the tri-party repo market fit the bill. (Financial Economists Roundtable 2010: 9)

"Policymakers," the report continues, "should explore policies to encourage the movement of tri-party repo transactions to organized exchanges and centralized clearing and settlement systems to eliminate the potential conflicts of interest and systemic risk associated with the present arrangement. . . . The objective should be to avoid the transfer of risk from either of these institutions to the broader market" (Financial Economists Roundtable 2010: 9).

LIMIT OR ABOLISH REPOS

A more radical way for the Fed to avoid exposing its operations to repo-related risk would be for it to substantially reduce its use of repos, or even, as Milton Friedman (1982b) once proposed, dispense with them altogether.

Repos are convenient devices for conducting temporary open market operations, but they are hardly necessary. Having invented them in 1917, the Fed, as we have seen, largely managed without them until after 1951; and although the Bank of Canada has also been using repos since the 1950s, it was not until the 1990s that other major central banks—including those of England, Japan, Germany, Sweden, and Switzerland—began making routine use of them (Federal Reserve System Study Group 2002: 30). In the United States just prior to the crisis, although repos were the mainstay of the Fed's daily open market operations, they accounted for just 3 percent of the Fed's assets, almost 90 percent of which consisted of outright holdings of U.S. Treasury debt.

The larger the market for the securities in which open market operations are conducted, and the greater the range of maturities available, the more practical it becomes for a central bank to dispense with repos, because a sufficiently deep market allows it to do so without causing unwanted price distortions (Cheun et al. 2009: 11), and because astute management of the SOMA portfolio can provide for a substantial degree of automatic accommodation of seasonal changes in reserve demand without resort to outright sales. The breadth and depth of the market for U.S. Treasuries of all maturities, therefore, makes the Fed a prime candidate for dispensing with repos.

According to Stephen Axilrod (1997: 14), the chief advantage of repos (and reverse repos) compared to outright purchases and sales is that they "tend to enhance liquidity in the underlying securities, helping to develop a more active secondary market" while "encouraging participants to develop as many alternative sources of short-term lending and borrowing as possible." It is hard to resist concluding that, in the United States at least, this advantage is no longer relevant. The market for Treasuries is quite liquid and thick enough, though very large Fed purchases and sales will admittedly still affect their prices, and there is surely no need to further encourage private market participants to take advantage of repos for short-term lending and borrowing.

On the contrary, in introducing repos to the U.S. market, the Fed inadvertently encouraged private-market innovations that played a central role in the unfolding of the crisis. "The notion of a repurchase agreement," Henry Liu (2005: 10) trenchantly observed before the crisis,

> was a fiction dreamed up to minimize the impact of such transactions on bank and broker-dealer capital requirements. If these transactions had been called loans, then banks (and broker-dealers) would be required to set aside cash (or perhaps other capital, if a broker-dealer) against such loans. By inventing the fiction of calling what is actually a loan by some other name, banks and other broker-dealers were able to bypass banking regulation and reserve less cash/capital against such activities. . . . Repos obviously increase systemic risk in the banking system as well as in the monetary system, particularly when the daily repos volume has grown to $5 trillion and is rising by the week.

In developing repos, in short, the Fed played a Frankenstein-like part, inadvertently transforming primary dealers into so many over-leveraged financial industry monsters.

As we have seen, repos do make it easier for the Fed to target interest rates. But this hardly makes them indispensable. On the contrary, it supplies further grounds for reconsidering the Fed's reliance upon a monetary policy instrument that itself appears, in light of recent experience, to be seriously flawed (see Sumner 2011).

ABANDON "TREASURIES ONLY"

Although the proposals so far might be undertaken without altering the Fed's Treasuries-only policy for open market operations, there are good reasons for combining them with a broadening of the set of securities used in its temporary, if not in its permanent, open market operations.[9] In particular, there are good reasons for having the Fed engage in temporary purchases of some of the private-market securities it has traditionally accepted as collateral for discount window loans, provided that it subjects those securities to haircuts sufficient to protect it against potential credit risk while otherwise adhering to the classical rule of supplying credit only on relatively stiff terms.[10]

Conducting open market operations in a variety of securities, and not just in Treasuries, would increase the ability of such operations to take the place of both discount window lending and emergency credit facilities during financial crises. It would, therefore, allow the Fed to perform its last-resort lending duties during such crises without departing substantially from "business as usual," and especially without allowing the performance of those duties to interfere with the conduct of ordinary monetary policy. An expanded list of securities would also allow the Fed to spread its tri-party repo settlement risk across more than two clearing institutions (Board of Governors 2002, Sec. 2: 3–4). Finally, security diversification would be a natural complement to counterparty diversification. Taken together, the two innovations would allow the Fed to satisfy, in a straightforward manner, Bagehot's requirement that central banks supply liquid funds *freely*, on *any* good collateral—a requirement which (as we have seen) isn't necessarily satisfied by channeling funds through a handful of privileged firms only, and only in exchange for Treasuries.[11]

Here again, the ECB supplies a useful counterexample, for it does not normally distinguish between collateral eligible for last-resort (standing facility) lending and collateral eligible for use in its temporary open market operations (Cheun et al. 2009: 18).[12] Partly for this reason, the European system was able to meet the exceptional liquidity needs of the first year of the financial crisis "with relatively few adjustments" to its standard operating framework. The Fed, in contrast, was compelled to introduce new collateralized lending programs (including the TAF, TSLF, and PDCF) that served, in effect, to temporarily modify its operating framework so as to make it functionally more akin to the ECB's (Cheun at al. 2009: 23–25; Duffie 2009: 41).[13]

The Fed's Treasuries-only policy distinguishes it, not only from most major central banks, but also from its own former self. As David Marshall (2002: 45, 49) observes, at the time of the Fed's establishment its designers equated the purchasing of government debt with "lending to the crown," which they feared would undermine the Fed's independence and open the door to inflation. Consequently, they sought to confine the Fed's credit-granting activities to the discounting of commercial paper.[14] Despite this intent, the Fed soon found itself playing handmaiden to the Treasury, until formally released from the obligation to do so by the 1951 Treasury Accord.[15]

One argument against open market operations using private securities is that such purchases are risky. Although outright purchases would not expose the Fed to counterparty risk, even these would expose it to the risk of security issuers' default. It is partly because losses from such defaults ultimately translate into reduced Treasury revenues that Marvin Goodfriend (2010: 6), among others, claims that the Fed should stick to holding risk-free Treasuries. But the argument isn't entirely compelling. With respect to repos, the risk can be kept negligible by means of sufficient haircuts; and if last-resort lending is desirable at all—if it is a genuine public good—there's no reason taxpayers shouldn't shoulder some of the potential cost of providing it, just as they shoulder the cost of supplying emergency assistance to victims of natural disasters. Indeed, the argument for having taxpayers cover losses connected to last-resort lending is the stronger of the two, insofar as such lending may avert a systemic crisis that could end up having financial costs exceeding those of almost any earthquake.

A second, related argument against Fed purchases of private securities is that such purchases will distort credit markets by favoring certain securities over others. "If the Fed purchases private securities," David Marshall (2002: 52) observes, "it might be seen as selectively approving those obligors whose paper it purchases." It was owing to this concern that the Fed made its final transition to a Treasuries-only policy, between 1977 and 1984, by gradually phasing out purchases of bankers' acceptances.

But a Treasuries-only policy seems neither necessary nor sufficient for the avoidance of Fed favoritism. It isn't necessary because the Fed, rather than arbitrarily favoring certain securities or issuers, might (once again following the ECB's lead—and to some extent, that of its own discount window facility) demarcate a set of eligible securities using various objective criteria, such as issuers' (risk-adjusted) capital and private-agency security ratings. It isn't sufficient because, by dealing with Treasuries only, the Fed plays favorites with the U.S. Treasury.[16]

Here, my prescription resembles, and is partly inspired by, Willem Buiter and Anne Sibert's (2008) suggestion that central banks serve as "market makers of last resort," by either buying outright or accepting as repo collateral "systematically important" private financial instruments that have become illiquid, perhaps ceasing to have any market price at all, owing to a breakdown of the markets in which such instruments usually trade. In particular, Buiter (2008b) proposes that, during financial market disruptions, the Bank of England (and other central banks, presumably) should offer to purchase or accept as repo collateral "a slightly extended version of what the ECB currently accepts," to wit, any security "rated at least in the single A category." To discover the value of illiquid instruments, and avoid subsidizing their sellers, the Bank can purchase them by means of a "reverse Dutch auction," in which an initial, minimum purchase price is raised progressively until either no buyers are left or the predetermined purchase amount is met (see also Buiter 2007, 2008a).

Buiter and Sibert's proposal has come under criticism for assuming that central banks can, by means of appropriately designed auctions, determine efficient prices even for heterogeneous financial instruments, such as mortgage-backed securities, that lack deep markets and so may not assure multiple auction offers (Smith 2007). My proposal differs both in limiting auctions to such private securities as do not pose the difficulty just mentioned, and in being intended to inform the conduct of open market operations both during crises and in ordinary times, so as to eliminate any need for "emergency" rule changes.

The procedure I have in mind, if only in the crudest of outlines, involves simultaneous reverse (single price) auctions for a set of different securities.[17] The Fed would first have to decide what security types are eligible, favoring those for which holdings are sufficiently dispersed to provide for competitive bidding, and (to further discourage adverse selection) indicating maximum values of total and individual security purchases that it is prepared to make from a single participant.[18] The list of such securities could be compiled, and regularly updated, using reports regularly submitted by prospective counterparties as one requirement for eligibility. Next the Fed would announce the total value of an intended purchase, along with reference prices (reflecting risk-based "valuation haircuts") for particular securities. It would then hold simultaneous reverse auctions, with descending prices *expressed as reference-price percentages*, for each security type, allowing individual counterparties to take part in any or all auctions. The auction would continue, through descending-price rounds, until the total nominal value of securities offered at an announced price equals the intended aggregate purchase.

Although this auction procedure may seem cumbersome, thanks to modern technology, developing the necessary software to implement it should be well within the Fed's capabilities. Its virtues, as I indicated, are twofold. First, because it pits bidders offering different securities against each other, it can assist in establishing appropriate prices for, and hence enhance the liquidity of, similar securities that might not themselves qualify for direct Fed purchases. Second, and more importantly, it allows the *composition* of open market purchases to adjust automatically with changing market conditions, with few if any central bank purchases of relatively high-risk and long-maturity instruments taking place in normal times, and more such purchases—perhaps substantially more—occurring during times of financial distress. To assure this outcome and, thereby, make a single set of open market rules suffice to consistently conform to Bagehot's rule—while still guarding against adverse selection—the Fed need only take care to set sufficiently low reference prices.[19]

These prescriptions, taken together, might be summarized by paraphrasing Bagehot as follows: the Fed should at all times be prepared to buy good securities freely, outright or subject to repurchase, at competitively determined prices that reflect, but are generally lower than, the values those securities would normally command in the private marketplace.

REVIVE THE TERM AUCTION FACILITY

A revived TAF, like the one established by the Fed on December 12, 2007, in response to commercial banks' apparent reluctance to borrow from its discount window, and considerably expanded in March 2009, could also serve as a ready-made means for the Fed to implement several of the prescriptions suggested above. Using the TAF, the Fed auctioned off predetermined amounts of credit to depository institutions, for terms of either 28 or 84 days, against the same collateral accepted at its discount window, financing the sales by selling Treasury securities. Banks with surplus reserves that were reluctant (owing to perceived counterparty risk) to lend them in the federal funds market could use the funds to buy the Treasury securities that the Fed sold, while banks that were short of reserves, but unwilling to borrow from the discount window, could bid for TAF funds. So long as the interest the Fed earned on TAF credit exceeded the interest on Treasuries it sold, the program did not expose the Fed to any significant risk, although it did expose taxpayers to potential losses (Goodfriend 2010: 8–9).[20]

Although not, strictly speaking, a vehicle for open market operations, the TAF was something of a cross between such operations and discount window lending. On the one hand, like the former, it had counterparties taking part in the auctioning of new reserves; thus, it allowed borrowers to avoid the stigma connected to discount window borrowing, while letting the Fed maintain control of the total stock of bank reserves and limiting its involvement in the allocation of credit. On the other hand, the TAF lent on the same relatively generous collateral accepted by the discount window, and was open to depository institutions other than primary dealers.

A shortcoming of the original TAF was that it appeared to violate Bagehot's principles by extending credit at subsidy rather than penalty rates. According to Daniel Thornton (2008), whereas the Fed set its discount window primary credit rate at 100 basis points above its target federal funds rate, its lending rate under the TAF—the so-called stop-out rate that sufficed to exhaust whatever amount of funds it placed on auction—was often below its primary credit rate. Since the primary credit rate is itself often a subsidy rather than penalty rate, TAF lending was effectively subsidized. For that reason, the TAF cannot be said to have functioned solely as a vehicle for last-resort lending. To avoid this shortcoming, a revived TAF might maintain a penalty minimum bid rate, while retaining the option to increase the frequency or size of its auctions when stop-out rates substantially exceed the minimum. Although the presence of such a minimum acceptable bid might prevent the facility from making its announced maximum advance, any difference could be made up by the open market desk, which would in any case have to coordinate its operations with those of the TAF.[21]

STOP LAST-RESORT DISCOUNT WINDOW LENDING

It may seem paradoxical to conclude a list of purportedly "Bagehotian" prescriptions by recommending that the Fed altogether cease to engage in direct last-resort lending. But Bagehot wrote at a time when private securities markets were as yet undeveloped, and when central banks made no use at all of open market operations as these are presently understood. Consequently, in his day, it was only by means of direct lending that the Bank of England could be expected to supply credit "freely" in exchange for good (but mostly unmarketable) collateral.

Today, of course, all this has changed. Though a "Bagehotian" case can still be made for occasional direct Fed lending so long as the Fed's open market operations are confined, not only to a small number of counterparties, but also to a small subset of "good" securities, that case would no longer be valid were the scope of such operations expanded in the manner suggested above. Instead, under such an expanded open market framework, direct extended-term lending (as opposed to "adjustment" and seasonal lending) would be more likely than ever to violate Bagehot's rule because it would be unlikely to serve any purpose other than to supply credit to individual banks (and perhaps to other firms) that lack good securities of any sort, and are therefore almost certainly insolvent. As Olivier Armantier and colleagues (2011: 27) observe, even under the Fed's present, constrained open market framework, banks' discount window visits carry a stigma severe enough to render discount window lending almost useless as a means for preserving liquidity during financial crises. "One may," they conclude, "question the ability [sic] of the [discount window] as a channel to supply liquidity simultaneously to a broad set of banks."[22]

CONCLUSION

In 1873, Bagehot confessed:

> I know it will be said that in this work I have pointed out a deep malady, and only suggested a superficial remedy. I have tediously insisted that the natural system of banking is that of many banks keeping their own

> cash reserve, with the penalty of failure before them if they neglect it. I have shown that our system is that of a single bank keeping the whole reserve under no effectual penalty of failure. And yet I propose to maintain that system, and only attempt to mend and palliate it. (Bagehot 1873: 329)

Today, so might I confess. But while Bagehot saw his remedy as an alternative to radical reform, I see mine as a step toward such reform: by reducing the need for ad hoc changes to the Fed's operating framework, the prescriptions offered here should make it easier to base monetary policy, including last-resort lending, on strict rules, paving the way in turn toward further, more fundamental reforms that might eventually render the Federal Open Market Committee (and hence the Fed itself, understood as an agency exercising *discretion* over U.S. monetary conditions) obsolete.

Notes

CHAPTER 1

1. Selgin and White (1994) survey relevant historical and theoretical literature.
2. A divergence between the preferences of fiscal authorities and citizen-consumers implies that political "markets" do not strongly tend to weed out policies that diminish aggregate wealth. On the contrast between "Chicago" and "Virginia" views on this broad question, see Lott (1997).
3. Margaret Levi (1988) offers a modern exposition of Puviani's fiscal-predation thesis. An alternative "predatory" hypothesis is private rent seeking: government serves special interests by restricting competition. This hypothesis certainly helps explain a number of legal restrictions on private banks. But it can hardly explain the *exclusion* of private mints and banks of issue from the market in favor of a state-run monopoly.
4. On the (conjectural) evolution of private-market monetary arrangements in the absence of government intervention, see Selgin and White (1987).
5. The budget constraint for a government that issues fiat money is $\mathcal{G} = \mathcal{T} + dD + dH$, where $\mathcal{G}$ is government spending (including debt service), $\mathcal{T}$ is tax revenue, dD is the change in interest-bearing debt held by the nongovernment public, and dH is seigniorage—the change in non-interest-bearing debt (fiat base money) held by the public. For a textbook introduction to seigniorage, see J. Huston McCulloch (1982). McCulloch notes that the term "seigniorage," from the French *seigneur* or lord, reflects the feudal lord's practice of profiting from monopoly production of debased coins that his subjects were compelled to accept at face value.
6. Lorena Alcazar (1994) briefly surveys empirical work on whether actual seigniorage rates conform to the implications of the optimal-tax model. In most countries, they do not.
7. Note that medieval coins typically displayed no numbers, only graphical identifying devices.
8. The many brands of private coins minted from California gold in the 1850s were all denominated in the established gold dollar unit. Assays "invariably found" that the coins' gold content was very close to the precise legal standard, and most coins apparently erred on the side of exceeding the standard (Kagin 1981: 239–42).
9. Transportation costs, and penalties connected to legal tender laws (which were most readily enforced in local transactions), made it normally uneconomical to import better small-denomination foreign coin for domestic use. Legal tender laws compelling the acceptance of domestic coin at face value were less readily evaded for small denomination coins, because weighing coins was less worthwhile for small transactions.
10. The fact that politically influential aristocrats were the principal users of high-value coins (Cipolla 1956: 26) supplied a separate public-choice reason for rulers to refrain from debasing these coins as extensively as petty coins.
11. The government realizes a capital gain even if it does not sell off its monetary gold stock. (The central bank's balance sheet typically disguises this gain by counting fiat money as "liabilities" of the central bank, as though central bank notes were still redeemable.) Still, the failure of central banks to liquidate their gold stocks even decades after the demise of the Bretton Woods system is puzzling from a purely fiscal perspective.

12. Federal Reserve officials have recently been scrutinizing electronic payments media that amount to the reintroduction of private currency. In an unusually candid statement of the authorities' concern for seigniorage, Greenspan (1997: 49–50) worries that the result of new electronic currency substitutes may be "simply a diversion of seigniorage from the government to the private sector." Lawrence White and Donald Boudreaux (1998) argue that (nonprice) competition to "divert" seigniorage is efficient, while nationalization of currency for the sake of seigniorage implies inefficiently low quality.
13. A number of American states experimented with state-run commercial banks in the decades before 1860. Most of the banks were so incompetently run as to incur financial losses despite their monopoly privileges.
14. Glasner (1997: 39) notes that "recognition of the time-consistency problem may help rationalize the seemingly irrational attachment to the gold standard" of pre-1930 governments.
15. Information on regime types is taken from J. Denis Derbyshire and Ian Derbyshire (1996). Cukierman's 1992 survey excludes most communist countries, which had relatively dependent central banks.
16. Although Hong Kong (two private note issuers before the mainland takeover), Scotland (two), and Northern Ireland (four) retain private note issue even today, the base money is fiat (dollars or sterling) in each of the three systems. We expect that private bank notes will be phased out in Hong Kong now that it has come under mainland Chinese rule. In Scotland and Northern Ireland, seigniorage is extracted by a 100 percent marginal reserve requirement (in noninterest-bearing Bank of England liabilities) against notes.
17. There were episodes of temporary suspension (e.g., the Napoleonic Wars in Britain, the Civil War in the United States), but notes that were (correctly) expected to become redeemable in the future were not fiat money. Unlike a fiat note, a temporarily suspended note has a lower bound to its current value set by the discounted expected value of its future redemption media. The government is constrained to (re)accumulate a sufficient inventory of redemption media. If the "ancient and honorable parity" is to be reestablished, then the government's potential capital gain is limited to the interest it might earn (or loan interest it might avoid) by lending out or spending from its reserves during the suspension.
18. John Chown (1994: 201) documents this observation.
19. Earlier suspensions—the Bank of England during the Napoleonic wars, the U.S. national banks during the Civil War—were also associated with fiscal emergencies but were eventually followed by full resumption at the prewar parity.

CHAPTER 2

1. The Bank of France website, for instance, says that Napoleon established the bank "to foster renewed economic growth in the wake of the deep recession of the Revolutionary Period"! For a review of the origins of central banking in Western Europe and the United States, see Vera Smith (1936).
2. Strictly speaking, a free-banking system, to use the expression in its European sense, is one in which banks are generally free from restrictive regulations, not simply free to issue their own notes. It is, however, mainly the implications of free and competitive note issue that concern us here.
3. For details, see Selgin (1988: 37–85; 1994; and 2001), the last of which considers the possibility of a coordinated overexpansion.

4. The thoughtless extension of the Bank Charter (Peel's) Act to Scotland in 1845 began a process of currency centralization there that is as yet still incomplete. On the Scottish system in its free-banking heyday, see Lawrence White (2009).
5. Among other forms of interference, the most notorious consisted of state governments' erection of barriers to branch banking, which, by generally preventing branching both within and across state lines, gave rise to an exceedingly decentralized, undercapitalized, and underdiversified banking industry and forced "country" banks to rely on correspondents for access to the New York money market. This arrangement caused specie reserves to become concentrated in New York, much as they tended to be concentrated in privileged banks of issue elsewhere, with a similar tendency toward the excessive "pyramiding" of credit on available specie reserves during booms and corresponding disruptive contraction during busts.
6. For details, see Roeliff Breckenridge (1895). Although numerous legislative attempts were made, mainly between 1893 and 1907, to reform the U.S. currency system along Canadian ("asset currency") lines, all of them failed, owing in large part to reformers' (well-founded) belief that asset currency would have to be combined with branch banking if it was to be sufficiently "elastic." Established unit bankers for this reason aggressively and successfully opposed these proposals. It was only following the failed efforts to deregulate the U.S. currency system that reformers began to champion a "central reserve bank" alternative.

CHAPTER 3

1. According to James Barth and Robert Keleher (1984: 16), "to function as a lender of last resort [a central bank] must have authority to create money, i.e., provide *unlimited* liquidity on demand" (emphasis added).
2. Minsky (1982: 16) even tries to rule potential criticisms of his "financial-instability hypothesis" out-of-court by declaring that "No theory of the behavior of a capitalist economy has merit if it explains instability as the result either of exogenous policy mistakes or of institutional flaws that can be readily corrected."
3. Canada turned to central banking in 1935, for reasons that had little to do with securing financial stability. See Michael Bordo and Angela Redish (1987).
4. Relative freedom of note issue and activity diversification also contributed to the greater strength of Canadian banking.
5. Although the Riegle-Neal Interstate Banking and Branching Efficiency Act of 1994 eliminated most of the then-remaining barriers to branching, more than 5,000 independent commercial banks still operate today (2016).
6. That, at least, would certainly be true in the absence of deposit insurance, which by subsidizing risk taking may encourage banks to diversify in ways that would increase their overall exposure to risk (Litan 1987: 84, 103–4). This implies that deposit insurance itself may have to be reformed or repealed *before* all portfolio restrictions (except those that concern clear conflicts of interest) can safely be lifted.
7. Thus, the problems Glass-Steagall and Regulation Q were supposed to prevent can exist in the presence of federal deposit insurance.
8. This contradicts a statement in Guttentag and Herring (1983: 6). Depositors may also switch into high-powered money despite their continuing confidence in banks, because their payments plans demand greater use of hand-to-hand money. As will be shown, such behavior would not pose any threat to a fully deregulated banking system.

9. Goodhart (1987: 85) reaches the same conclusion with respect to recent runs in the United Kingdom.
10. O'Driscoll (1988: 672) observes that these failed banks "were more like the typical U.S. rather than the typical Canadian bank. Neither . . . was widely branched, and they were specialized energy banks."
11. Reasons for this are given below.
12. Recent changes in the law, including the Garn–St. Germain Act of 1982, provide for only limited relaxation of branching restrictions in the absence of similar reforms of state laws.
13. Even Lloyd Mints (1950: 186)—one of the original proponents of this "inherent instability" thesis—admits that it "is due in part to a wholly unnecessary legal restriction," namely, restrictions against note issue. He goes on to say that, to be consistent, "the defenders of fractional-reserve banking should propose [to give banks] the privilege of note issue with the same required reserve ratio for notes and deposits" (p. 188).
14. On the functioning of the secondary note market in the United States prior to 1845, see Jane Knodell (1988).
15. For an account of how and why this happens, see Selgin (1988: 16–34).
16. That deposits would still lack a distinct secondary market (or virtual secondary market) of their own does not matter if they are backed by the same general assets as notes are. This has always been the case for unregulated banks, though it was not true for the banks of the so-called "free-banking" era in the United States or for national banks afterwards. For this and other reasons, these banks were subject to information externalities despite being able to issue notes. See Selgin (1988: 138–39).
17. See Selgin (1988: 48–49).
18. Thomas Humphrey and Robert Keleher (1984: 279) observe: "Crisis situations involving the LLR [lender of last resort] frequently followed excessive credit expansions. Such credit expansions often were large and prolonged enough to produce outflows of specie and to foster doubts about the ability of commercial banks to redeem their paper in gold."
19. For critical remarks on these alleged causes of monetary overexpansion, see Selgin (1988: 70–85, 129–33).
20. It is worth noting that not a single Scottish bank failed or felt the need to apply to the Bank of England for assistance during the 1825 crisis. See White (1984: 47).
21. There are, of course, many criticisms of competitive note issue—including the claim that it is inconsistent with a generally well-behaved money supply—which I am not able to consider here. For a fairly comprehensive discussion, see Selgin (1988).
22. For many years, the Bank itself did not feel compelled to establish branches for the issue and redemption of its notes beyond the city. An 1826 campaign led by Thomas Joplin resulted in a new law allowing the establishment of joint-stock banks outside of London; but the law did not permit the new joint-stock banks to issue notes, and it encumbered them with a variety of "irksome" restrictions. Although many of the latter were eventually removed, the prohibition against joint-stock bank-note issues remained in place. See Nevin and Davis (1970: 59–60).
23. It is not clear whether Parnell borrowed this expression from Lord Liverpool or vice versa.
24. This practice was officially sanctioned by the Bank Act of 1833, which made Bank of England notes legal tender for payments among other banks.
25. Kindleberger (1978: 164) even declares that Bagehot "thought it proper that the Bank of England, and not the banks themselves, should hold the reserves necessary to get the country through a panic"—the exact opposite of the truth. A well-known British economist who shared Bagehot's critical views on central banking was Sir Robert Giffen (1905: 175–76).

26. Enforcement of the law was another matter. There are plenty of stories, including ones that are probably true, about note brokers and private individuals being "run out of town" both in Scotland and in the United States for daring to request cash in exchange for notes. Ideally, the law should allow banks to engage freely in all manner of contractual agreements with their customers, enforcing those agreements as written. In practice, the law did neither.
27. Although it is true that suspension of payment by national banks could not be based upon prior, contractual consent of their customers, Gorton (1985: 177) observes that "neither banks, depositors, nor the courts opposed it at any time."
28. Diamond and Dybvig (1983) claim that contingent-convertibility contracts may be inferior to deposit insurance because suspension under the former will harm the interests of depositors who wish to withdraw high-powered money for the purpose of increasing their consumption expenditures even as it safeguards the interests of depositors who "panic." This argument neglects the fact that high-powered money is not needed for normal expenditures, particularly if bank notes can be issued freely. A suspension of payments, unlike a bank holiday, need not interfere with depositors continuing to make purchases by check or bank note. Historically, banks (and hence the public generally) have frequently agreed to accept notes and checks of suspended (even failed) rivals at par.

CHAPTER 4

1. Although a bank note's quality can be assessed in numerous ways, I generally follow the 19th-century practice of gauging a note's quality by its capacity to circulate at its nominal (specie) value.
2. Sherman's source of information was almost certainly one of the many "bank note reporters" available at the time. As Rockoff (1975: 23) observes, these reporters "listed all counterfeits . . . even if the notes had been removed from circulation years before."
3. Later changed to August.
4. The 10 percent tax, first offered as an amendment to the Revenue Act of 1865 by Rep. James F. Wilson (R-IA), managed to squeak its way through the House of Representatives only because one of its bitterest opponents, Rep. James Brooks (D-NY), voted for it in order to move a reconsideration—and then had his motion tabled. According to Horace White (1894: 206), if Brooks "had voted in the first instance as he had fought," the 10 percent tax amendment would have failed by one vote. In the Senate, the Committee on Finance reported adversely on the tax, but was overruled by a majority of two. Republicans tended to favor the tax as a needed component of the Union's financial strategy, but Democrats tended to oppose it, partly on the grounds that it constituted an illegitimate attack on states' rights. The measure would certainly have been rejected by a peacetime Congress.

   In enacting the 10 percent tax, Congress rendered moot the Supreme Court's 1837 *Briscoe v. The Bank of Kentucky* decision affirming the constitutionality of state bank notes—a decision that relied on a distinction between the issuance of "bills of credit" by state governments themselves (which the Constitution expressly forbade) and the issuance of notes by state-licensed firms.

   The Supreme Court would eventually uphold the constitutionality of the 10 percent tax with its 1869 decision in *Veazie Bank v. Fenno.* Reading that opinion was none other than Salmon P. Chase, the former secretary of the treasury and fervent supporter of the tax, who had recently been appointed chief justice.
5. Because only 855 national banks had been established by March 3, 1865, no more than 261 state bank conversions can have occurred between November 1864 and March 3, 1865. Lack of more detailed data on the progress of state bank conversions prevents me from providing a more precise figure.

6. The Revenue Act of June 1864 had placed a tax of 1/12 percent per month on state banks' outstanding circulation plus an additional 1/6 percent per month on circulation exceeding 90 percent of a bank's capital.
7. Andrew Economopoulos (1994) as well as Rolnick and Weber (1988) provide empirical evidence of antebellum consumers' ability to discriminate between "good" and "bad" bank notes. Stephen Williamson (1992) relies on the opposite assumption. In their textbook, Xavier Freixas and Jean-Charles Rochet (1997: 40–45) purport to show how competitive note issuance tends to be undermined by free rider and "lemon" problems, resulting in a Gresham's law outcome. Their model assumes, however, that banks do not offer to redeem their own notes at a preannounced price. The model is therefore irrelevant to antebellum banking in the United States and to most other historical instances of competitive note issue.
8. Late in 1863, the New York Clearing House banks resolved to treat all national bank notes as "uncurrent" money unless a national bank had arranged to redeem its notes at par through a Clearing House member bank (Redlich 1951: 107). It seems, however, that the Clearing House never carried out this threat.
9. David Gische (1979) draws attention to a special sort of network problem that hindered the development of the national banking system. By the early 1860s, many interior banks kept balances with New York City correspondents. An interior *national* bank could apply such balances toward its legal reserve requirements only if the balances were held by another national bank. The establishment of national banks in New York may therefore have been a prerequisite for the voluntary conversion of state banks elsewhere. This particular network problem was, however, overcome well before March 1865: by March 1864, New York City already had 11 national banks (all new institutions) possessing over $20 million of paid-in capital.

   Gische argues that it was the resolution of the above-mentioned network problem, rather than the 10 percent tax, that sealed the fate of state banks of issue. His argument is unpersuasive, however, both because it makes the tax appear gratuitous and because it cannot explain the fact that most state bankers did not seek national charters until after March 3, 1865.
10. For more details on losses to free-bank noteholders, see Rolnick and Weber (1983) and Gerald Dwyer (1996). The sheer volume of recent writings on the U.S. free-banking experience might be responsible for an exaggerated view of the importance of free banking relative to other antebellum banking arrangements. In 1860, when free banking was as popular as ever, only one-third of all U.S. banks were free banks—good, bad, or indifferent—and free banks supplied only about one-quarter of the U.S. currency stock.
11. Although the Suffolk Bank disavowed responsibility for overseeing the centralized redemption of New England bank notes after the Bank of Mutual Redemption began operations in 1858, the system continued to function—and continued to be referred to as "the Suffolk system"—until the advent of the 10 percent tax.
12. Although notes from the Confederacy were generally unmarketable in Northern markets after the outbreak of the war, prior to the war the modal discount rate on these notes was 2 percent.
13. The lack of data for bank-note-market transactions *volume* stands in the way of any accurate estimate of actual losses from dealings in discounted notes. However, it seems reasonable to assume that the volume of transactions involving discounted notes declined, perhaps substantially, following the appearance of greenbacks and national bank notes.
14. Indeed, the public sometimes demonstrated a positive preference for certain state bank notes (for example, those of New England banks) over greenbacks. This preference was due in part to the belief that state banks were more likely than the federal government was to eventually

redeem their notes in specie (U.S. Treasury, *Annual Statement*, 1863: 3–39; Harter 1893: 563).

In Scotland and Northern Ireland today, the nonlegal tender notes of commercial banks remain popular—and are still outstanding in amounts equal to the limits set by Peel's Act of 1845—despite the legal-tender status and wider acceptability of Bank of England currency.

15. Rep. Michael D. Harter (D-OH) also believed that the 10 percent tax—which he called "the most arbitrary commercial law ever passed by Congress"—was resorted to only because state bank notes had been "in such high favor with the people" (1893: 562).
16. The data employed in the preceding paragraph are from Milton Friedman and Anna Schwartz (1963: 704, 735, 774) and U.S. Census Bureau (1975: 624–30, 648–49).
17. Wesley Mitchell (1903: 145–48) explains that state banks were first forced to contract their issues in response to speculative withdrawals of gold, then expanded as they were given permission to redeem their liabilities in legal tender, and finally contracted their issues again—partly in response to the 2 percent tax on state bank notes imposed by the Revenue Act of 1864.
18. Indeed, because state bankers held significant quantities of federal government securities at the outbreak of the war, the tax actually served to *reduce* the market for federal bonds compared to the extreme alternative of chartering new national banks only without allowing state banks to convert.
19. According to an 1874 estimate, cited in Redlich (1951: 119), at least 50 percent of all rural payments were being made in currency, as compared to only 5 percent in New York City.
20. Howard Bodenhorn and Hugh Rockoff (1992) show that Southern interest rates were much closer to rates in the rest of the country prior to the Civil War than afterward.
21. According to Warren E. Weber (personal communication), some national banks (e.g., those of New York State) did find it worthwhile to make seasonal changes to their note circulation. Assuming, however, that seasonal influences on currency demand were qualitatively similar in all states, the aggregate evidence suggests that such cases were exceptional.
22. Writing sometime during the 1880s, former comptroller of the currency John Jay Knox (1900: 522) observed that because many antebellum Southern banks had "issued a currency that was not only ample in volume, but entirely safe, it is quite natural that there should be a strong sentiment favorable to the issue of such circulation [by state banks] at the present day."

CHAPTER 5

1. One of the few authors to notice the reformers' emphasis, Fritz Redlich (1951: 114–16) dismisses redemption reform as an "infatuation." Lloyd Mints (1945: 230–31) observes that "the paramount importance of 'contractility' of note issues, as well as of expansionability, was repeatedly emphasized" by reformers, and that "adequate redemption facilities . . . were generally insisted upon" as a means of providing contractability; but he does not discuss redemption reform in any further detail.
2. Selgin and White (1992) discuss in more detail the quasi-high-powered status of national bank notes and the consequences. The remainder of this section draws heavily on that work.
3. The original ceiling was $300 million.
4. The second Independent Treasury Act (1846) had established subtreasuries at New York, Boston, Charleston, St. Louis, New Orleans, and Philadelphia; subsequent legislation during the National Banking period removed Charleston and added Baltimore, Cincinnati, San Francisco, and Chicago.
5. Other determinants of New York banks' excess reserves were, in order of significance: (1) movements of gold and greenbacks between banks and the public; (2) movements between the banks

and the New York subtreasury; and (3) international gold flows (Scott 1908: 273–98). From 1902 to 1907, Treasury Secretary Leslie Shaw actively intervened in the New York market by shifting funds from the subtreasury to the banks in the fall and back in spring, in an effort to reduce the seasonal fluctuations in banks' reserves and loan rates. See Richard Timberlake (1978: ch. 12) and Andrew Allen (1986: 253–68).

6. Taking the differences between averages of end-of-quarter interest rates reported by George Rich (1988: 49–50), for the period 1902–13, Montreal call loan rates varied only 30 basis points between mid-year and year-end (5.3 percent vs. 5.6 percent), whereas New York rates varied 470 basis points (2.5 percent vs. 7.5 percent), and Boston rates varied 260 basis points (3.3 percent vs. 5.9 percent). Consistent with the international arbitrage opportunities seemingly available, Rich (p. 178) observes that "in the fourth quarter . . . Canada typically acted as a lender to the New York money market." But he notes that before 1914 risks and information costs apparently prevented arbitrage from equalizing Canadian and U.S. interest rates, or even rates within the two countries (p. 151). Citing the variations in Montreal call loan rates, both over time and across banks, Rich (pp. 48–51) argues against the view that the Canadian loan rates were fixed by collusive agreements (though deposit rates may have been thus fixed).
7. Redlich (1951: 114) dismisses "the fact that National Bank notes were not at par in New York" as the result of an arbitrary clearinghouse policy. In fact, the policy reflected the costliness to the banks of redeeming or otherwise discharging unwanted notes. In Chicago, where by contrast national bank notes appear not to have accumulated, the national banks agreed in April 1864 to accept all national bank notes at par (James 1938: 357–61).
8. The 17 cities were New York, Boston, Philadelphia, St. Louis, Chicago, New Orleans, Cincinnati, Baltimore, Louisville, Detroit, Cleveland, Pittsburgh, Milwaukee, Albany, Leavenworth, San Francisco, and Washington. The first eight cities listed continued from the 1863 act; Providence, in the 1863 list, was omitted in 1864.
9. In 1837, New York city banks had resisted a similar state proposal to compel their par acceptance of upstate notes on the grounds that it would allow the country notes to "engross the circulation in New York"; see Davis Dewey (1910: 97). It is not clear why New York should have been expected to run a persistent balance of trade surplus with the rest of the state or country.
10. The plan is reproduced in *Bankers Magazine* (Sept. 1865: 198–200).
11. The views of one country banker are set forth in a letter appearing in the *Bankers Magazine* (Dec. 1865: 460–65).
12. It is reprinted in the *Commercial and Financial Chronicle* (Oct. 14, 1865: 489).
13. Clarke had resigned in mid-1866 in the wake of policy disputes with both McCulloch and Hulburd.
14. For contemporary account, see J. Laurence Laughlin (1898: 211); *Commercial and Financial Chronicle* (April 3, 1865: 422); and *Hunt's Merchants Magazine* (Oct. 1867: 289; Apr. 1869: 247).
15. The $300 million ceiling on the aggregate issue of national bank notes had been raised to $354 million by the act of July 12, 1870.
16. One possible explanation for this otherwise curious provision of the act is that the banks, in rent-seeking fashion, wished to restrict costly interbank competition for circulation shares. Providing more redemption points could be a means of competing on note quality.
17. Phillip Cagan and Anna Schwartz (1991) point out, citing 1894 testimony by Treasury Secretary John G. Carlisle (and contradicting Bell 1912: 38–60), that in practice the subtreasuries in New York and eight other major cities redeemed national bank notes. The subtreasuries shipped the

redeemed notes to Washington, where they were counted and sorted together along with the relatively few notes that banks themselves shipped directly to Washington. Fit notes, and notes for replacing unfit notes, were then returned to their issuers.

18. This and all related figures are from U.S. Treasury annual reports.
19. For comparisons of the redemption facilities of the National Banking System with those of the Canadian, Scottish, and Suffolk systems, see Selgin and White (1992). Circulation and Treasury redemption figures are shown in charts 1 and 2 of that paper.
20. Frank Lautz (1877) gives a detailed description of the new facilities and assortment process.
21. For a contrary view, see Bruce Champ and others (1993), who argue that the collateral restriction on note issue was not binding, and that national banks must have faced significant liquidity costs from redemption of notes.
22. Phillip Cagan (1963: 21–22) dismisses the elastic currency idea as a specious offspring of the real-bills doctrine, though he elsewhere acknowledges (pp. 25–27, 38) the disturbance caused by unaccommodated changes in the public's relative demand for currency. In our view, the basic aim of the proponents of an elastic currency was simply to avoid such disturbances. Though the real-bills doctrine can also be found in some of their writings, the case for an elastic currency does not depend on it.
23. See, for example, the testimony of James H. Eckels, comptroller of the currency, in U.S. Congress (1897: 235).
24. See Laughlin (1894: 104–5); *Commercial and Financial Chronicle* (Dec. 15, 1894: 1033); and U.S. Congress (1897: 409).
25. See also Redlich (1951: 116).
26. Legislation enacted in 1890 required all Canadian banks to provide par redemption at a specific city in each of the seven provinces.
27. Walker's bill was H.R. 171, 54th Cong. The others were bills written or endorsed by John Dewitt Warner (H.R. 5595, 53rd Cong.), Theodore Gilman (H.R. 3338, 54th Cong.), Samuel Hill and Charles N. Fowler (H.R. 10289, 55th Cong.), and Fowler (H.R. 13363, 57th Cong.).
28. On country bankers' opposition to branch banking, see James Livingston (1986), Richard McCulley (1992: 96–97), and Eugene N. White (1983: 83–90). Livingston appreciates the importance assigned to branch banking by proponents of asset currency, but he suggests that they wanted branching mainly as a device for centralizing reserves. By contrast, we believe that they wanted it as a device for active redemption and thereby regulation of the currency stock.
29. The Gold Standard Act allowed national banks to issue notes up to 100 percent of the par value of the bond collateral.
30. Quoted in Livingston (1986: 168). It should be noted that the New York currency committee, unlike the ABA commission, favored a government central bank as the best way to achieve an elastic currency (*Currency* 1906: 9–11). In its final report, the committee chose not to advocate that solution only because they considered it politically unrealistic (see Livingston 1986: 259–63).
31. Mints (1945: 240–44) argues on somewhat different grounds that a tax on notes was unlikely to have given the note circulation the desired degree of elasticity.
32. For such work, see White (1984); Selgin (1988, 1994).

CHAPTER 6

1. The House measure is H.R. 2912; its Senate companion is S. 1786. The House passed H.R. 3189, in which much of H.R. 2912 is incorporated as Sec. 16, in November 2015.
2. The present effort is, in fact, the second to be so inspired. In 1949, the Senate referred a bill (S. 1559) calling for the establishment of an 18-member National Monetary Commission with

authority to undertake studies to determine "what changes are necessary or desirable to the banking and monetary system of the United States, or in the laws relating to banking and currency, by reason of domestic or international considerations or both," to its Committee on Banking and Currency (U.S. Congress 1949). Although that committee reported favorably on the measure, the House recommended against it.

One notable difference between the 1949 measure and the present effort, besides the composition of the proposed commission, was the fact that Federal Reserve officials themselves had long urged the former's establishment.

3. I review the history of the gold standard in the United States in Chapter 7 of this volume.
4. See Chapter 4 of this volume.
5. Kevin Dowd (1992) gathers studies reviewing some of the more successful competitive currency systems, including a survey of the history of plural note-issue systems by Kurt Schuler.
6. See Roeliff Breckenridge (1910) and Joseph Johnson (1910).
7. That is, against a proposed reopening of the U.S. mints to unlimited coinage of silver, which threatened to undermine the gold standard.
8. McCulley (1992: 42–75) gives a detailed account of the fate of pre-1900 asset currency reform efforts.
9. Economist Horace White (1903: 50) assailed this last step as a "needless and costly extension of the national debt," while accusing the Republicans of resorting to it solely "to spare themselves the trouble of dealing with the whole bank question in a rational manner."
10. The other three were the National Park Bank, the Hanover Bank, and Chase National Bank.
11. The "unquestioned leader" of the country bankers in their effort to oppose asset currency generally, and branch banking especially, was Wisconsinite Andrew J. Frame, "a tenacious and ill-informed man who could not accept the twentieth century" (Wiebe 1962: 63).
12. Fowler himself deserves part of the blame for his first effort's failure. According to Willis (1903: 122), his "bill was so skillfully worded as to incur the hostility of nearly every group of men who would be affected by currency legislation." The bill especially suffered from attempting to achieve too many reforms at once. Besides providing for some asset-backed currency and for branch banking, it also called for "a change in the status of gold certificates, a readjustment of the basis for greenbacks, and the reorganization of the clearing-house system." Consequently, it became all too easy "for men who disliked some special feature of the bill to condemn the whole on that ground alone."
13. On the bond-backing requirements of antebellum "free-banking" laws and their contribution to bank failures and wildcat banking, see Gerald P. Dwyer Jr. (1996) and sources cited therein.
14. "Even most bankers," Lowenstein (2015: 74) observes, remained "fixated on an asset currency." In fact there was nothing unreasonable about the bankers' preference, unless by "unreasonable" one means "inconsistent with the direction events would ultimately take."
15. Outstanding Aldrich-Vreeland emergency currency notes were subject to a 5 percent tax for the first month after they were placed into circulation and to a tax of 1 percent every month thereafter.
16. Five years after the act had passed only 21 Aldrich-Vreeland currency associations had been organized, comprising 325 national banks. However, during August and September 1914, over 2,000 national banks formed 44 associations, 41 of which issued emergency notes (Wicker 2005: 46). According to Milton Friedman and Anna Schwartz (1963: 172), had the Aldrich-Vreeland provisions remained in place in 1930, they would have been more effective than the Fed turned out to be in averting that year's banking crisis. For further details see Silber (2007).

17. In all, four different bills calling for the establishment of a "Banking and Currency" or "National Currency" commission, including two introduced by Charles Fowler, were referred to the House Committee on Banking and Currency between December 1907 and April 21, 1908. The one that actually made it into the Aldrich-Vreeland bill was introduced by Rep. William Lovering (R-MA) on January 30, 1908.
18. Text of the Aldrich-Vreeland Act of May 30, 1908, as quoted in A. Piatt Andrew (1912: 3).
19. Then spelled "Jekyl." The current (and correct) spelling became official in 1929.
20. Morgan had personally recommended Davison's services to Aldrich, his intent—revealed in an unguarded cable sent to Morgan by George Perkins, another Morgan partner—having been to make sure the firm's interests were properly represented (Lowenstein 2015: 80). In August 1909, Davison arranged to have Aldrich acquire $50,000 worth of Bankers Trust stock for just $40,000, presumably to further encourage Aldrich to assign adequate weight to his advice (p. 96).
21. Although in his memoirs Vanderlip (1935: 213) claims that Strong was present, other sources do not confirm this. Because Vanderlip's recollections are quite vivid—he refers to Strong's horseback riding, among other details—I'm inclined to believe that Strong was indeed there, and that others present at the event refrained from disclosing Strong's presence owing to the fact that Stephenson himself did not disclose it. Alas, that still leaves a mystery regarding why Stephenson himself failed either to disclose or to discover that Strong was present.
22. Although Charles Calomiris and Stephen Haber (2014: 184) have claimed that the Commission "clearly understood that the unit-banking system was the core problem" and that it only refrained from recommending any reform of "the basic structure of the U.S. banking system" because it held such reform to be "politically infeasible," these claims appear unfounded. Instead, the decision to not tamper with unit banking reflected a positive preference on the Commission's part.
23. The presumption on the part of Aldrich and his advisers that central banking was an ideal arrangement even in these countries was itself far from being well justified. For a review of the origins of central banking in England, Germany, and France, including the arguments of those who opposed that development, see Vera Smith (1936).
24. Besides 16 volumes concerning the United States and the ones devoted to England, France, Germany, and Canada, the Commission published studies of the currency and banking systems of Holland, Japan, Sweden, Mexico, Austria-Hungary, Russia, and Switzerland. Of these, Switzerland had only recently abandoned decentralized note issue, establishing the Swiss national Bank on June 30, 1907, and calling for its 36 cantonal banks to retire their notes within three years of that date.
25. Unlike Warburg, who knew little about banking and currency systems apart from those of the major European powers, Charles Fowler was familiar with numerous banking and currency systems around the world, as well as with those of the antebellum United States. Yet, while Fowler paid generous tribute to Warburg during Fowler's testimony on the Federal Reserve Act, stating that he had "contributed more substantially to the advancement of [the currency] question than any other one man in the country," Warburg (1912) dismissed Fowler contemptuously: "Fowler has never been a banker, and never been successful, and I am astonished by his courage to advocate a new and untried scheme approved by no practical bankers, against a plan which has been carefully developed on the well-established European principles by the combined banking and business brains of the country." Besides being unkind, Warburg's description is a calumny: Fowler was a banker both before and after serving in Congress, and his reform proposals, while unsuccessful, were endorsed by many bankers as well as by other authorities.
26. Gabriel Kolko (1963: 244–47) summarizes the two measures' other differences.

27. Laughlin resigned his leadership of the National Citizens' League in April 1913. The extent to which he directly contributed to the drafting of the Federal Reserve Act remains a matter of some dispute. See Kolko (1963: 222–25, 242–47).
28. On the influence of the real-bills doctrine on both the Fed's original design and its subsequent conduct, see Richard Timberlake (1993: 224–25, 259–60; 2007).
29. Although some proponents of decentralized asset currency also subscribed to the real-bills doctrine, the importance that most asset currency proposals assigned to active note redemption supports James Livingston's (1986: 187) opinion that asset currency advocates' understanding of the forces limiting currency expansion in their preferred arrangement was no different from the conventional understanding, both then and now, of the forces that limited banks' creation of checkable deposits.
30. On the role of the concentration of bankers' balances in New York City in the crisis of the early 1930s, see Kris Mitchener and Gary Richardson (2016).
31. Concerning the Federal Reserve's status quo bias, see Edward Kane (1980, 1990).
32. Centennial Monetary Commission Act, H.R. 2912, 114th Cong. § 5(a)(3)(B) (2015).

CHAPTER 7

1. See, for example, Charles Morgan-Webb (1934: 5). Whether price level movements under the gold standard did in fact make it inferior to alternative standards is, nevertheless, a valid question. I consider that question briefly in Selgin (1997).
2. On instances of private gold coinage in the United States, see Brian Summers (1976) and Richard Timberlake (1993).
3. On bimetallism as a solution to the "small change" problem, see Neil Carothers (1930), Angela Redish (2000), and Thomas Sargent and François Velde (2003).
4. An 1837 amendment to the 1834 act made the ratio almost exactly 16:1 by raising the content of the gold dollar to 23.22 grains of pure gold.
5. This outcome, far from having been inadvertent, was an intentional component of the Jacksonians' assault upon the Bank of the United States, aimed at both providing convenient metallic substitutes for the bank's notes while simultaneously interfering with its ability to make change for them. See Paul O'Leary (1937).
6. According to Albert Bolles (1886: 37), had Chase, instead of heeding his own bullionist instincts, followed the bankers' advice, the government's resort to greenbacks "would certainly have been delayed . . . and the evil effects flowing therefrom would have been far less than those which followed."
7. The world market ratio increased from 16.4 in 1873 to 18.4 in 1879 (Friedman 1992: 67). According to Friedman (p. 72), had the increase been unaffected by the U.S. decision to demonetize silver, then its failure to do so would have meant that, instead of resuming on a gold basis in 1879, the country would have found itself on a de facto silver standard by 1876. Friedman speculates (pp. 73–74) that U.S. retention of the 16:1 bimetallic ratio would itself have served to stabilize the world market ratio enough to spare the United States from the "continual shifting between silver and gold," but not enough to prevent it from resuming on a silver, rather than a gold, basis.
8. On the generally superior credibility of commercial bank redemption commitments compared to those of central banks, see Selgin and White (2005).
9. See Selgin (1997) and sources cited therein. On the absence of any strict correlation of deflation with depression or recession, see Andrew Atkeson and Patrick Kehoe (2004).

10. See William Silber (2007). The success of the Aldrich-Vreeland plan in its only trial is significant both because of the contrast of that success with the Fed's subsequent failure to avert monetary collapse in the early 1930s, and because the plan was to a large extent a mere formalization of previous, ad hoc "emergency currency" measures undertaken by private clearinghouse associations, themselves designed to sidestep legal restrictions on bank-note issuance dating from the Civil War.
11. See, for example, Douglas Irwin (2010) and H. Clark Johnson (1997).
12. It was on this occasion that the governor of the Chicago Federal Reserve Bank at first refused to lower that bank's discount rate in accordance with Strong's recommendation, but was overridden by the Federal Reserve Board in a step that, for all practical purposes, marked the end of independent regional bank policymaking.
13. See Timberlake (1993). Elmus Wicker (1996) finds that gold outflows played only a minor role in the banking panics that were the proximate cause of the monetary collapse prior to 1933.
14. To say that the Fed was not constrained by a lack of gold is not to claim that it did not consider itself constrained in *some* fashion. In fact, it was constrained, not by a lack of gold, but by Board members' adherence to the real-bills doctrine. The problem was thus neither an absolute lack of gold nor a shortage of gold relative to the minimum 40 percent gold-backing requirement for outstanding Federal Reserve notes. Instead, the problem was the requirement—inspired by the real-bills doctrine—calling for the Fed to back the other 60 percent of its notes with either gold or "commercial paper." It was this artificial constraint on the Fed's nongold assets that was chiefly responsible for its having stood by while the U.S. money stock collapsed. Although the Federal Reserve Act's commercial paper requirement was relaxed somewhat by Glass-Steagall Act of February 27, 1932, which made U.S. bonds substitutable for gold, the Fed failed to take full advantage of the legislation. See Timberlake (2007).
15. See Gregory (1935: 119). Later Fed and Treasury actions, however, more than offset the boost devaluation had given to the U.S. money stock, helping to bring about the "recession within the Depression" of 1937–38 (Timberlake 1993: 288–99).
16. The change in Great Britain's status from creditor to debtor nation, the loss of its empire, and its more general postwar economic decline greatly limited sterling's anticipated role as a reserve or "key" currency. After Great Britain devalued the pound in November 1967, it effectively ceased to be an important reserve currency.
17. See Bordo (1993: 39, Chart 1.10). The claim of several authorities (cited in Bordo 1993: 68) that "the growth of the monetary gold stock was insufficient to finance the growth of world output and trade," rather than that the quantity of dollars had been allowed to grow excessively, is belied by the behavior of U.S. and other dollar-area annual inflation rates and Federal Reserve liabilities. Rates remained positive throughout the (convertible) Bretton Woods era, and approximately doubled during the 1960s. Federal Reserve liabilities grew at a rapidly accelerated rate, partly as a response to fiscal pressures connected to the escalation of the Vietnam War (pp. 74–76). The fact that the monetary gold stock did shrink after 1960 was mainly a reflection of the public's increased tendency to hoard gold in anticipation of the system's impending breakdown.
18. See also Lawrence H. Officer (n.d.).
19. It did not help that three Federal Reserve governors sat on the commission, where "their primary concern was to limit discussion touching on" the Fed's performance, and where they insisted "that the subjects of inflation and monetary policy were not a proper concern of the Commission." How the relative merits of gold versus paper were supposed to be discussed and evaluated without reference to the actual performance of the latter was, apparently, not a matter of great

concern to them, or to the two Joint Economic Committee House members who supported their position. See Anna Schwartz (1987: 17–32, 323).

20. Of course, circumstances aren't normal at present, owing to banks' extraordinarily high excess reserve holdings since 2008. Consequently, steps might first have to be taken to reduce the excess before gold payments could be successfully restored.
21. The alternative of establishing a "parallel" gold standard, instead of restoring the gold convertibility of the current dollar, would be less disruptive, but it is unlikely—barring a substantial increase in inflation—to lead to any substantial substitution away from the fiat dollar. See White (2012: 413).

CHAPTER 8

1. Although Martin Feldstein (2010: 134) recognizes that "[t]he recent financial crisis, the widespread losses of personal wealth, and the severe economic downturn have raised questions about the appropriate powers of the Federal Reserve and its ability to exercise those powers effectively," and goes on to ask whether and in what ways the Fed's powers ought to be altered, his conclusion that the Fed "should remain the primary public institution in the financial sector" (p. 135) rests, not on an actual review of the Fed's overall record, but on his unsubstantiated belief that, although the Fed "has made many mistakes in the near century since its creation in 1913, . . . it has learned from its past mistakes and contributed to the ongoing strength of the American economy."
2. Alan Blinder (2010) argues that, *given* the premise that the Fed as presently constituted will continue to be responsible for conducting U.S. monetary policy, it ought also to have its role as a supervisor of "systematically important" financial institutions preserved and even strengthened. Charles Goodhart and Dirk Schoenmaker (1995) review various arguments for and against divorcing bank regulation from monetary control.
3. Because these were episodes not merely of inflation but of stagflation, they are frequently said to have depended crucially on adverse aggregate supply shocks triggered by OPEC oil price increases. This "traditional" explanation has, however, been cogently challenged by Robert Barsky and Lutz Kilian (2001: 180), who conclude "that in substantial part the Great Stagflation of the 1970s could have been avoided, had the Fed not permitted major monetary expansions in the early 1970s" (see also Ireland 1999; Chappell and McGregor 2004). Blinder and Jeremy Rudd (2008) have, in turn, written in defense of the "traditional" perspective.
4. World War II was also a period of substantial inflation, though this fact is somewhat obscured by standard (Bureau of Labor Statistics) statistics, which do not fully correct for the presence of price controls. Friedman (1982a: 106) places the cumulative distortion in the wartime net national product deflator at 9.4 percent, while Geofrey Mills and Hugh Rockoff (1987: 201–3) place it between that value and 4.8 percent.
5. Robert Lucas (2000), in contrast, put the annual real income gain from reducing inflation from 10 percent to zero at slightly *below* 1 percent of GNP. The difference stems from Lucas's having considered inflation's effect on money demand only, while overlooking its influence on effective tax rates, which play an important part in Feldstein's analysis. Axel Leijonhufvud (1981) and Steven Horwitz (2003) discuss costs of inflation, including those of "coping" with high inflation environments and those connected to inflation's tendency to distort relative prices, that elude measurement and are for that reason overlooked by both Feldstein and Lucas.
6. These findings are based on Nathan Balke and Robert Gordon's (1986) quarterly GNP deflator estimates spliced to the Department of Commerce deflator series in the fourth quarter of 1946.

Christopher Hanes (1999) argues that pre-Fed deflator estimates understate somewhat the serial correlation of pre-Fed inflation, while overstating the volatility of pre-Fed inflation, owing to their disproportionate reliance upon (relatively pro-cyclical) prices of "less-processed" goods.

7. The coefficient on the ARCH(1) term for the pre-Fed period is not significantly different from zero. In the event that it is indeed zero, the GARCH(1) coefficient is not identified. Although Timothy Cogley and Thomas Sargent (2002) as well as several other researchers reported a decline in the persistence of inflation coinciding with the beginning of the Great Moderation, Frederic Pivetta and Ricardo Reis (2007: 1354), using a more flexible, nonlinear Bayesian model of inflation dynamics and several different measures of persistence, find "no evidence of a change in [inflation] persistence in the United States" since 1965, save for "a possible short-lived change during the 1982–1983 period."
8. Concerning the difficulty of forecasting inflation in recent years especially, see James Stock and Mark Watson (2007).
9. For more recent and international evidence of the negative effect of inflation on firm debt maturity, see Asli Demirgüç-Kunt and Vojislav Maksimovic (1999). As one might expect, the post-1983 "Great Moderation" (discussed further below) revitalized some previously moribund markets for very long-term corporate debt. Thus, Disney's 1993 "Sleeping Beauty Bonds" became the first 100-year bonds to be issued since 1954. The more recent decline in U.S. Treasury bond yields has also added to the attractiveness of very long-term corporate debt. Indeed, on August 24, 2010, Norfolk Southern managed to sell $250 million worth of century bonds bearing a record low yield of just 5.95 percent, despite the risks involved. Still, many investors remained skeptical. As one portfolio manager opined (Bullock 2010). "You are giving a company money for a long period of time with no ability to foresee the conditions in that period of time and for a very low interest rate."
10. Selgin (1997) presents informal arguments for permitting benign (productivity-driven) deflation, while Rochelle Edge and colleagues (2007), Stephanie Schmitt-Grohé and Martín Uribe (2007), and Niloufar Entekhabi (2008) offer formal arguments. For the history of thought regarding benign deflation, see Selgin (1996b).
11. The predominance of benign over harmful deflation appears to have been still more marked in the United Kingdom and Germany, owing perhaps to those countries' less crisis-prone banking systems (Bordo et al. 2003).
12. On the volatility of macroeconomic series during the interwar period, see especially Jeff Miron (1988: 2), who, comparing the quarter centuries before and after the Fed's founding, finds that stock prices, inflation, and the growth rate of output all became considerably more volatile, while average growth declined; he concludes that "the deterioration in the performance of the economy after 1914 can be attributed directly to the actions of the Fed."
13. By looking at standard deviations of output after applying the Hodrick-Prescott filter, rather than simply looking at the standard deviation of the growth rate of output, we allow for gradual changes in the sustainable or "potential" growth rate of real output and, thereby, hope to come closer to isolating fluctuations in output traceable to monetary disturbances. Concerning the general merits of the Hodrick-Prescott filter relative to other devices for isolating the cyclical component of GNP and GDP time series, see Marianne Baxter and Robert King (1999).
14. Although Zarnowitz (1992: 78) agrees that, because they are based on "cyclically sensitive" series, the standard (Kuznets-Kendricks) GNP estimates "exaggerate the fluctuations in the economy at large," he claims that, in deriving her own estimates by "simply imposing recent patterns on the old data," Romer "precludes any possibility of stabilization, thus making her conclusion inevitable and prejudging the issue in question." Paul Rhode and Richard Sutch (2006: 15) repeat

the same criticism. But Romer's method does not rule out the possibility of stabilization any more than that used in deriving the standard series does: both approaches take for granted a constant ratio of commodity output volatility to general output volatility. The difference is that, while Romer estimates the constant, Kuznets implicitly assumed a value of one. That Romer's estimate necessarily reflects postwar structural relationships hardly renders her approach more restrictive than, much less inferior to, Kuznets's.

15. The findings are, as one might expect, robust to the exclusion of nominal time series from the study.
16. For details, see Lastrapes and Selgin (2010). Numerous other studies, employing a variety of identification schemes, also find that demand shocks have been of overwhelming importance during the post–World War II period. See, for example, Olivier Blanchard and Mark Watson (1986), Blanchard and Quah (1989), Peter Hartley and Joseph Whitt (2003), Peter Ireland (2004), and James Cover and colleagues (2006). A notable exception is Jordi Gali (1992), who, using a combination of short- and long-run identifying restrictions, finds that supply shocks were more important. None of these studies examines the pre-Fed period.
17. While government size is generally negatively correlated with the volatility of output growth, it also appears to be negatively correlated with output growth itself. Thus, António Afonso and Davide Furceri (2008) find, based on estimates for the period 1970–2004, that for the OECD countries a 1 percentage point increase in the share of government expenditure to total GDP was associated with a 0.12 percentage point decline in real per capita growth. To this extent, at least, automatic stabilizers appear to be a poor substitute for a well-working monetary regime.
18. See also Richard Clarida and colleagues (2000).
19. Bernanke himself offered his thesis as a plausible conjecture only, without attempting to test it against alternatives.
20. See, among many other works on the topic, Margaret McConnell and Gabriel Perez-Quiros (2000), Shaghil Ahmed et al. (2004), Francisco Alcala and Israel Sancho (2004), F. Owen Irvine and Scott Schuh (2005), Karen Dynan et al. (2006), Christopher Sims and Tao Zha (2006), Andres Arias et al. (2007), Sylvain Leduc and Keith Sill (2007), Steven Davis and James Kahn (2008), Nir Jaimovich and Henry Siu (2009), Zheng Liu et al. (2009), Jesús Fernández-Villaverde et al. (2010), and Alessio Moro (2010). Besides attributing the Great Moderation to a "fantastic concatenation of [positive output] shocks" rather than to improved policy, the last of these studies reaches the more startling conclusions that "there is not much evidence of a difference in monetary policy among Burns, Miller, and Greenspan," and that, had Greenspan been in command in the 1970s, a somewhat *greater* rate of inflation would have been observed (Moro 2010: 4, 33).
21. According to Thomas King and James Morley's (2007) estimates, the natural rate of unemployment, having peaked at over 9 percent in 1983, fell to less than half that level by 2000. Earlier estimates of the natural rate show a similar pattern, though with smaller amplitude. The argument summarized here is complemented by those of Athanasios Orphanides and John Williams (2005) and Giorgio Primiceri (2006) to the effect that a combination of a heavy emphasis on activist employment stabilization and mistakenly low estimates of the natural rate of unemployment informed monetary policy decisions that led to double digit inflation in the 1970s and early 1980s. In the later 1980s, in contrast, the natural unemployment rate was overestimated or at least no longer underestimated. See also Paolo Surico (2008). Of course, these arguments do not by themselves rule out the possibility of negative *cyclical* movements in inflation that are independent of changes to the natural rate of unemployment, such as are likely to accompany a financial crisis like the recent one.

22. Decades before Romer, George Cloos (1963: 14) observed, in the course of a considerably more trenchant evaluation of the NBER's business cycle dating methods, "that the gross national product and the Federal Reserve Board's industrial production index are usable measures of general business activity and that peaks and troughs in these series are to be preferred to the Bureau's peaks and troughs."
23. Some experts go even further than the NBER in confusing deflation with depression. For example, Dallas Fed President Richard Fisher refers during a February 2009 CSPAN interview to the "long depression" of 1873–96 (c-span.org/Watch/watch.aspx?Programid=Economy-A-40471). Concerning the myth of a "Great Depression" of 1873–96, see Roger Shields (1969) and, for Great Britain, Samuel Saul (1969).
24. According to Robert Higgs (2009), despite the gold inflows of the 1930s and unprecedented wartime government expenditures, the U.S. private economy did not fully recover from the Great Depression until after World War II.
25. In particular, the 1930s Fed has been faulted for having regarded low nominal interest rates and high bank excess reserves as proof that money was sufficiently easy (Wheelock 1989). Scott Sumner (2009) argues that the Fed repeated the same mistake in 2008.
26. Having been obliged to borrow $3 million from the Fed to meet their legal reserve requirements in February 1932, the Fed's member banks afterwards equipped themselves with ample excess reserves. Even on the eve of the national bank holiday, they held reserves equal to 112.8 percent of requirements (Fuller 2009: 540).
27. The precise figures are: average percentage decline in output, 12.3 percent for recessions involving major panics, 4.5 percent otherwise; average length of recovery, 2.7 years for recessions involving major panics, 1 year otherwise. The length of recovery is the interval from the trough of the recession to recovery of the predownturn peak.
28. Kryzanowski and Roberts (1993) claim that 9 out of Canada's 10 banks were insolvent on a market-value basis for most of the 1930s. John Wagster (2009), in contrast, concludes on the basis of a different approach that they were insolvent only during 1932 and 1933.
29. The Bank of Canada was established in 1935, not in response to the prior crisis but, according to Bordo and Redish (1987), to appease an increasingly powerful inflationist lobby. Canadian banks' relative freedom from restrictions on their ability to issue bank notes also contributed to their capacity to accommodate exceptional demands for currency. In the United States, in contrast, national banks were unable to issue notes at all after 1935, and were severely limited in their ability to do so before the onset of the Great Depression. State bank notes had been subject to a prohibitive tax since 1866. Concerning the politics behind the decision to suppress state bank notes, and the economic consequences of that decision, see Chapter 4 of this volume.
30. Why, then, did Bagehot recommend that the Bank of England serve as a LOLR instead of recommending removal of its monopoly privileges? Because, as he put it at the close of *Lombard Street* (1873: 329), "I am quite sure that it is of no manner of use proposing to alter [the Bank of England's constitution]. . . . You might as well, or better, try to alter the English monarchy and substitute a republic."
31. Some would add the New York Fed's rescue of the Bank of New York following its November 1985 computer glitch. We instead classify this as overnight "adjustment" lending, reserving the term "last resort" for more extended lending. Concerning the Fed's last-resort lending operations after 9/11, Jeffrey Lacker (2004: 956) notes that, while they generally conformed to classical requirements, the Fed extended discount window credit at below market rates.

32. The insolvent firms included Citigroup and AIG. The way was paved toward the recent departures from Bagehot's "sound security" requirement for last-resort lending by a 1999 change in section 16 of the Federal Reserve Act, which allowed the Fed to receive as collateral any assets it deemed "satisfactory." The change was originally intended to provide for emergency lending in connection with Y2K, for which it proved unnecessary.
33. Todd Keister and James McAndrews (2009: 2) concede that both the unprecedented growth in banks' excess reserve holdings and the related collapse of the money multiplier were consequences of the Fed's October 2008 "policy initiatives," including its decision to begin paying interest on reserves. But they also insist that "concerns about high levels of reserves are largely unwarranted" on the grounds that the reserve buildup "says little or nothing about the programs' effects on bank lending or on the economy more broadly." Perhaps: but bank lending and nominal GDP data *do* say something about the programs' broader effects, and what they say is that, taken together, the programs were, in fact, severely contractionary.
34. In the Penn Central case, the Fed was prepared to supply discount window loans if necessary, and even invoked the 1932 clause allowing it to lend to nonbank institutions so as to be able to lend to Penn Central itself. But it did not actually make any last-resort loans (Calomiris 1994). In the case of the 9/11 attacks, the Fed supplied $38 billion in overnight credit to banks on the day of the attacks because the Fed had not anticipated any need for open market operations. In subsequent days, the open market desk made up the deficiency, and discount window borrowing returned to more-or-less normal levels (Lacker 2004).
35. Strictly speaking, the Fed's open market policy has been one of "Treasuries and gold and foreign exchange only." As David Marshall (2002) explains, Fed officials at one time preferred to confine open market operations to private securities, including bankers' and trade acceptances and private bills of exchange, owing in part to their fear that extensive government debt holdings would compromise the Fed's independence. In fact, the Fed first began purchasing substantial quantities of Treasury securities on the open market in response to pressure from the Treasury following U.S. entry into World War I. The Treasuries-only policy dates from the 1930s. For further details, see Marshall (2002) as well as David Small and James Clouse (2005).
36. According to Buiter (2008a), private security purchases conducted by means of reverse Dutch auctions would guarantee purchase prices reflecting illiquid securities' fundamental values but sufficiently "punitive" to guard against both moral hazard and excessive Fed exposure to credit risk. Cecchetti and Disyatat (2010), in contrast, claim that "liquidity support will often be, and probably should be, provided at a subsidized rate when it involves a liquid asset where a market price cannot be found."
37. Continental Illinois failed with $40 billion in assets, equivalent to $85 billion in 2008 dollars, as compared to the $307 billion in assets of Washington Mutual and $812 billion of Wachovia when those firms were resolved. Likewise, Drexel Burnham Lambert had $3.5 billion in assets in 1990, or the equivalent of $6 billion in 2008 dollars, while the assets of Lehman Brothers at the time of its failure amounted to $639 billion.
38. As David Tarr (2009: 5) notes, the same conclusion was reached by the international Senior Supervisory Group (SSG), which reported as well that the failures of Fannie May and Freddie Mac "were managed in an orderly fashion, with no major operational disruptions or liquidity problems." On the success of chapter 11 as a means for resolving Lehman Brothers, see Christopher Whalen (2009).
39. According to Naohiko Baba and colleagues (2009: 76), although they benefited from neither the U.S. Treasury guarantee or the Fed's money market fund liquidity facility established on the same

day, "European-domiciled dollar [money market funds] generally experienced runs not much worse than those on similar U.S. prime institutions with the same manager."

40. Wallison (2009: 3) writes that although Goldman Sachs was AIG's largest CDS counterparty, with contracts valued at $12.9 billion, a spokesman for Goldman declared that, had AIG been allowed to fail, the consequences for Goldman "would have been negligible."
41. As of April 2009, the combined value of Treasury, FDIC, and Fed capital infusions and guarantees extended in connection with the subprime crisis was $4 trillion (Tarr 2009: 3).
42. See also Elijah Brewer and Julapa Jagtiani (2009). The FDIC Improvement Act of 1991 endeavored to limit the problem of excessive guarantees, including excessive Fed lending to insolvent banks, by amending the Federal Reserve Act through inclusion of a new rule (10B) penalizing the Fed for making all save very short-term loans to undercapitalized banks. However, an exception was made for banks judged too big to fail. In mid-2008, however, banks being operated by the FDIC were exempted from the rule, largely defeating its purpose.
43. In suggesting alternatives to the Fed that "merit consideration," we deliberately exclude proposals that would merely transfer powers of discretionary monetary control from the Fed to Congress. Like Blinder (2010: 126) and many others, we believe that an independent central bank is likely to produce superior macroeconomic performance than one under congressional influence. We disagree, on the other hand, with Professor Blinder's suggestion that, because he wants to "End the Fed," Rep. Ron Paul (R-TX) must not appreciate the advantages of an independent central bank over a dependent one.
44. We forgo the opportunity to discuss proposals for multicommodity standards, which have the disadvantage of being untried and less well understood.
45. As one Bank of England official (H. R. Siepmann) observed in a 1927 memorandum, referring obliquely to the Bank of France's policies: "If one country decides to revert to the [classical] Gold Standard, it may lay claim to more gold than there is any reason to expect the gold centre to have held in reserve against legitimate Gold Exchange Standard demands. What is then endangered is not merely the working of the Gold Exchange Standard, but the Gold Standard itself. Such a violent contraction may be provoked that gold will be brought into disrepute as a standard of value" (Johnson 1997: 133). This is, in fact, precisely what happened.
46. Although prospects for any such revival can only be judged remote, World Bank president Robert Zoellick (2010) prompted renewed discussion of the merits of such a move by arguing that proponents of a new Bretton Woods–type world monetary system ("Bretton Woods II") should consider using the price of gold "as an international reference point of market expectations about inflation, deflation and future currency values." Zoellick added that "Although textbooks may view gold as the old money, markets are using gold as an alternative monetary asset today."
47. The option of suspending payments can also be a contractual feature of banking contracts, as it was in the case of early Scottish bank notes bearing a so-called option-clause. Concerning those, see James Gherity (1995) and Selgin and White (1997). On the potential incentive-compatibility of contractual suspension arrangements—that is, their ability to rule out panic-based runs—see Gary Gorton (1985). In Douglas Diamond and Philip Dybvig's (1983) model and later studies based on it, including Huberto Ennis and Todd Keister (2009), suspension is suboptimal because it entails some disruption of optimal consumption; but that conclusion depends on the unrealistic assumption that people cannot shop using (suspended) bank liabilities (Selgin 1993).
48. See also Rafael Repullo (2000) and commentators.

CHAPTER 9

1. On the tremendous growth in the Fed's size and overall role in the U.S. financial system during the first year of the recent financial crises, see Peter Stella (2009).
2. To save space in citing sources, I refer to particular Federal Reserve Banks as "FRBX," where "X" is the initial of the particular Fed bank: A = Atlanta; B = Boston; Ch = Chicago; C = Cleveland; D = Dallas; K = Kansas City; M = Minnesota; NY = New York; P = Philadelphia; R = Richmond; SF = San Francisco; SL = St. Louis. Where I draw upon more than one undated online source from the same Fed Bank, I refer to each by its order of appearance among the undated references (e.g., "FRBP1"; "FRBP2," etc.).
3. My coauthors and I review the Fed's performance for most of its first century in Chapter 8 of this volume.
4. Such statements must be distinguished from research by Fed-employed economists aimed at other researchers, which despite being vetted by the Board of Governors reflects individual Fed economist's idiosyncratic opinions. Indeed, I frequently rely on such research in identifying misinformation in works by other Fed staff and officials that are intended for general readers.
5. See, for example, Board of Governors (2013a, 2013b) and FRBP (2009).
6. The writer seems to be under the impression that any currency-issuing institution qualifies as a "central bank."
7. Hammond served for some time as the Board of Governors' assistant secretary.
8. This loss, it bears noting, is lower than that routinely incurred today by merchants who accept credit cards and by persons who draw cash from ATMs other than those belonging to their own bank.
9. According to Selgin and White (1994), this Procrustean means for achieving a uniform currency turned national bank notes into "quasi-high-powered" money, undermining the routine clearing and redemption of rival bank notes that normally constrains overissue of notes in a competitive note-issue arrangement.
10. "The Federal Reserve System," Gabriel Kolko (1963: 253) observes, "stabilized the financial power of New York within the economy, reversing the longer term trend toward decentralization by the utilization of political means of control over the central money market." See also Charles Calomiris and Stephen Haber (2014), Eugene White (1983), and Stephen Williamson (1989).
11. "We should be under no illusions," Martin told the governors prior to the vote; "a decision to move now can lead to an important revamping of the Federal Reserve System, including its structure and operating methods. This is a real possibility and I have been turning it over in my mind for months" (Board of Governors, minutes, December 3, 1965).
12. Some steps taken during the subprime crisis have also tended to further undermine the Fed's already far-from-complete independence. In particular, the Supplementary Financing Program (SFP) set up by the Treasury in December 2007 to assist the Fed in sterilizing emergency loans it was then making, threatened, in the words of one commentator "to blur operational responsibility for monetary policy" (Stella 2009: 23). Despite its having been rendered redundant when the Fed gained the power to pay interest on bank reserves, the program still exists, although it is now officially "suspended." For more concerning how the Fed's conduct during the recent crisis compromised its already-limited independence, see Michael Bordo (2010) and John Cochrane (2012).
13. On the substantial increase in price-level uncertainly since the Fed's establishment, see Chapter 8 of this volume (pp. 211–61).
14. In claiming to have done a good job combating inflation, the Fed in recent years has also taken advantage of the widespread treatment, which it has done much to encourage, of 2 percent inflation as "the new zero."

15. In fact, because the Bailey Building and Loan Association was a thrift rather than a bank, the Fed would not have had permission to lend to it until the summer of 1934, and even once it had that authority, it could not have accepted the association's mortgages as collateral for a discount window loan.
16. Nor would anyone want things to be otherwise: because the Federal Reserve's "liabilities," unlike the Bank of England's in 1873, aren't redeemable in gold (or in anything else), were it to maximize profits, the result would be considerably greater inflation than the United States has actually experienced.
17. Subsequent investigations revealed that Continental Illinois' failure would actually have had only minor systemic consequences (Bédard 2012: 358–59).
18. Bernanke (2012a) likewise observed that "by raising the overnight interest rate, known as the federal funds rate, higher interest rates feed through the system and help to slow the economy by raising the cost of borrowing, of buying a house, of buying a car."
19. See Axel Leijonhufvud (2009) and John Taylor (2007, 2013).
20. That opinion is, however, controversial. "If Bear Stearns had been viewed as solvent by the financial community," the more common understanding has it, "JPMorgan may not have insisted on such a large government cushion to acquire the firm" (Sanati 2010). In justifying Bear's rescue to the Financial Inquiry Commission, Treasury Secretary Paulson himself insisted that Bear was insolvent. "We were told Thursday night that Bear was going to file for bankruptcy Friday morning if we didn't act. So how does a solvent company file for bankruptcy?" (Sanati 2010)
21. See Thomas Hogan and colleagues (2015), Thomas Humphrey (2010), and Marc Labonte (2009). According to the last source, had the Fed's support of Bear Stearns's acquisition "been crafted as a typical discount window loan directly to JPMorgan Chase," rather than as an indirect loan through the Fed-created Limited Liability Corporation Maiden Lane I, "JPMorgan Chase would have been required to pay back the principal and interest, and it (rather than the Fed) would have borne the full risk of any depreciation of Bear Stearn assets" (Labonte 2009:19). By taking on risk connected to Bear's acquisition, the Fed violated Bagehot's rule calling for last-resort loans to be fully secured. The same criticism can be made of its support of Citigroup and Bank of America (pp. 20–25).
22. According to John Taylor (2008: 15–17), it appears to have been this testimony *rather than* Lehman's failure itself that caused the crisis to deepen during the ensuing month. The FDIC's decision, on October 28, to spare Washington Mutual's uninsured depositors at the expense of its secured creditors also appears to have contributed more than Lehman's failure did to the late-October freeze-up of the wholesale credit market (Allison 2013: 75–7).

    The direct collateral damage from Lehman's bankruptcy proved far less extensive than government authorities claimed it would be. Instead of triggering the failure of thousands of counterparties, it led to the embarrassment of only one, when the Reserve Primary (money market) Fund, which held a large amount of Lehman's securities, "broke the buck." Other funds that held Lehman's paper were able to cover their losses by drawing upon their parent companies.
23. That the interest rate payments were modest does not mean that dampening was trivial. According to Peter Ireland (2012), even a small increase in the interest rate paid on bank reserves could result in a large increase in banks' demand for excess reserves.
24. Fed (and FDIC) regulators also contributed to what Pianalto (2013) refers to as bankers' "more cautious" approach to lending. According to John Allison (2013: 138), the former CEO of BB&T, ever since the crisis, the Fed's examiners, in a classic case of slamming the barn door shut after the horses have bolted, have been "making it more difficult for banks to extend new loans and to work

with existing business borrowers who are struggling, especially any business with debt related to real estate."

CHAPTER 10

1. According to a congressional study of discount window lending during the late 1980s, of 418 banks that received discount window loans, nearly all had CAMEL scores of 5, indicating effective insolvency, at the time; and about 90 percent of them subsequently failed (Kaufman 1999: 4; see also Schwartz 1992).
2. Even considered with regard to the Fed's traditional open market procedures, Cecchetti and Disyatat's claim appears too strong: open market operations have sufficed to preserve market liquidity during several past "systemic events," including the failure of Penn Central, the October 1987 stock market crash, Y2K, and 9/11.
3. According to Olivier Armantier and colleagues (2011), the stigma was such that, after Lehman's failure, banks were willing to pay a premium of at least 150 basis points to acquire funds from the TAF rather than from the discount window.
4. A few years earlier, Robin McConnachie (1996), observing that there were then no formally designated primary dealers in Australia, Japan, Netherlands, and New Zealand, reached the same conclusion.
5. "The central bank should take the lead . . . in encouraging market practices conducive to competitive trading. It could, for instance, encourage a computerized system of bids and offers for securities that protects anonymity" (Axilrod 1997).
6. The failure of MF Global, one of two February 2011 additions to the Fed's primary dealer list, ought to settle any remaining doubts concerning the truth of this declaration. It's worth noting how, even at the time of its admission to the primary dealers club, MF Global was known for being very highly leveraged, and how the Fed waited until October 31, the date on which MF Global filed for Chapter 11 bankruptcy protection, to terminate its primary dealer status.
7. Since the Fed need never advertise its list of banks participating in its open market operations, the procedure need not undermine the confidential nature of CAMEL ratings. On the general reliability of CAMEL ratings as indicators of banks' soundness, see Rebel Cole and Lawrence White (2012).

   Counterparty diversification along the lines suggested here seems far preferable to the alternative favored by Hoenig (2011: 8), among others, of restoring Glass-Steagall-like provisions to the extent of preventing primary dealers from having commercial bank affiliates. "It is not necessary," Hoenig observes, "that primary dealers be affiliated with banks. It is only necessary that they be institutions that deal in U.S. Treasuries and participate in auctions of U.S. government debt." Hoenig's solution might prevent primary dealers from exploiting genuine economies of scope. Moreover, it was not dealers' involvement in commercial banking, but their other undertakings, that got them in hot water. Neither Lehman Brothers nor Bear Stearns had commercial bank affiliates when they failed.

   A less draconian way, also recommended by Hoenig, to limit risk-taking by the Fed's prospective counterparties, and by broker-dealers in particular, consists of "rolling back the bankruptcy law for repo collateral to the pre-2005 rules" so as to "discourage the use of mortgage-related assets as [private-market] repo collateral and reduce the potential for repo runs." According to Viral Acharya and T. Sabri Öncü (2010: 336), had mortgage-backed securities–based repos been subject to automatic stay, as they would have been under pre-2005 rules, "the Bear Stearns funds could have filed for bankruptcy and the forced fire sale of their assets could have been avoided."

As Enrico Perottti (2010: 4) observes, "bankruptcy exceptions lead to a surrendering of public control over the money supply, which becomes endogenous to the private sector's short-term funding preferences (as *any private security* may be funded with repo). This highlights the urgency of measures to contain the private creation of liquidity risk."

8. In its December 14, 2009, report, the Shadow Financial Regulatory Committee criticizes the Fed's move to expand the list of reverse-repo counterparties to include some money market mutual funds, noting that this move "continues [the Fed's] dependence upon a small number of institutions and risks creating a two tiered set of money market mutual funds—those that are and those that are not eligible to deal with the desk and potentially eligible for financial support and special treatment during times of financial stress" (Eisenbeis 2009: 2).
9. Although the Fed has long been legally authorized to purchase securities issued or guaranteed by various U.S. government agencies (including the Tennessee Valley Authority, the Small Business Administration, and the U.S. Postal Service), it made little use of this authority until December 2008, when it began acquiring substantial quantities of housing-agency debt—as well as much larger quantities of housing-agency mortgage-backed securities.
10. For the relative merits of various private securities for open market operations, see Board of Governors (2002: Sec. 2). Although the Fed offers its desire to avoid credit risk among reasons for adhering to a Treasuries-only rule, the precise threat such risk poses to it is of a vague sort, since central banks need not be particularly concerned about adverse shocks to their capital and might even operate temporarily with negative capital (compare Bindseil et al. 2004). On the other hand, Benn Steil (2011) points out the limits of a central bank's ability to function with negative capital without risking hyperinflation.
11. During the late 1990s and early 2000s, the possibility of having the Fed deal in non-Treasury securities was broached in response to the fear that continuing surpluses might render such securities too scarce for the Fed's needs. Although that particular prospect is, unhappily, no longer present, the fact that it might eventually arise again is yet another reason for reconsidering Treasuries only.
12. The ECB ordinarily accepts a variety of euro-denominated private securities, including corporate and bank bonds and mortgage-backed securities, with rating of A– or better, as collateral for both its repos and its standing facility loans. However, in the aftermath of Lehman's failure, it lowered the minimum rating to BBB–.
13. In contrast, the Fed's later Commercial Paper Funding Facility and Term Asset-Backed Securities Loan Facility programs went "beyond the scope of the Eurosystem's measures," by having the Fed engage in primary-market purchases of commercial paper and by having it take part in what amounted to outright purchases of asset-backed securities (Cheun et al. 2009: 38).
14. The Fed's founders themselves erred, on the other hand, in adhering to the "real-bills doctrine"—a doctrine that, besides limiting the sorts of private collateral upon which the Fed was willing to extend credit, caused it to surrender control of monetary policy to a badly programmed "automatic pilot."
15. The scale of the Fed's recent outright Treasury security purchases has, however, revived fears of renewed Fed financing of deficit spending, prompting the Fed and the Treasury to release a March 23, 2009, joint statement reaffirming the Fed's independence.
16. In this respect, the "pet securities" argument for Treasuries only reminds one of the similarly question-begging "pet banks" charge leveled at Andrew Jackson when he transferred the government's deposits from the Second Bank of the United States to various state banks.
17. Some countries, including France, routinely make use of multiple security auctions for primary market issues of government securities.

18. Under the TAF, bidding by individual participants was limited to 10 percent of total amounts being auctioned.
19. After sketching out my auction plan, I discovered much more carefully thought-out proposals in the same spirit by Lawrence Ausubel and Peter Cramton (2008) (for implementing the Troubled Asset Relief Program) and Paul Klemperer (2010) (to assist the Bank of England in combating the post-Northern-Rock credit crunch). In particular, the Ausubel and Cramton proposal goes beyond mine in including enhancements designed to allow for open market purchases of securities for which efficient reference prices are initially unascertainable. In soliciting the Klemperer proposal, the Bank of England asked that the design be one that it could also employ in normal times; in fact, it has been using the procedure regularly since the crisis. For further discussion of the challenges involved in designing multiple-security central bank auctions, see François Koulischer and Daan Struyven (2011).
20. Just how effective the TAF was is controversial. John Taylor and John Williams (2008), Stephen Cecchetti (2009), and Abdullah Mamun and colleagues (2010) claim the TAF was ineffective. James McAndrews and colleagues (2008), Jens Christensen and colleagues (2009), and Tao Wu (2011) offer more positive appraisals. At least some of the TAF's apparent ineffectiveness appears to stem from the fact that the Fed chose to sterilize TAF lending, financing it, in effect, by selling Treasury securities to prospective lenders in the federal funds market. Consequently, rather than increase the overall supply of liquidity to financial institutions, prior to Lehman's failure, the Fed merely forced a reallocation of liquidity to institutions that took advantage of the TAF and PDCF (Thornton 2009a, 2009b). According to Daniel Thornton (2009b: 2), if instead the Fed had "pursued a policy of increasing the total supply of credit (the monetary base)," that is, had it engaged in quantitative easing before September 2008, "financial market participants would have been better able to adjust to a decline in house prices." Thus, the failures of Bear Stearns, Lehman Brothers, and AIG—as well as the need for the Troubled Asset Relief Program—might have been avoided.
21. For further details concerning how a revived TAF or similar auction credit facility might operate, see Board of Governors (2002, Sec. 3: 3–7 and 35–39).
22. For an intriguing, contrary perspective, see Ulrich Bindseil and Flemming Würtz (2007), who claim that open market operations are dispensable, and that monetary policy might better be implemented by means of standing-facility lending. Besides overlooking the stigma problem connected to standing-facility lending, that argument assumes a lack, not only of last-resort standing-facility credits, but also of overnight ("adjustment") and seasonal credits. The need for the latter types of discount window lending is, moreover, largely a consequence of legal restrictions, including statutory reserve requirements and the Fed's monopoly of paper currency. Concerning the role of reserve requirements, see Bert Ely (1997), who observes that the volatility of the federal funds rate is mainly due to "the biweekly scramble of banks . . . to meet their reserve requirements for the just-ended two-week reserve computation period." Concerning currency monopoly as a cause of seasonal credit market pressures in the absence of accommodative central bank policies, see Selgin (1986).

References

Abrams, B. A. (2006) "How Richard Nixon Pressured Arthur Burns: Evidence from the Nixon Tapes." *Journal of Economic Perspectives* 20 (4): 177–88.

Acharya, V. V., and Öncü, T. S. (2010) "The Repurchase Agreement (Repo) Market." In V. V. Acharya, T. F. Cooley, M. P. Richardson, and I. Walter (eds.), *Regulating Wall Street*, 319–50. Hoboken, N.J.: Wiley (for the New York University Stern School of Business).

Acharya, V. V., and Skeie, D. (2011) "A Model of Liquidity Hoarding and Term Premia in Inter-Bank Markets." Federal Reserve Bank of New York Staff Report No. 498 (May).

Afonso, A., and Furceri, D. (2008) "Government Size, Composition, Volatility, and Economic Growth." Working Paper Series No. 849 (January). Frankfurt am Main, Germany: European Central Bank.

Afonso, G.; Kovner, A.; and Schoar, A. (2011) "Stressed, Not Frozen: The Federal Funds Market in the Financial Crisis." Federal Reserve Bank of New York Staff Report No. 437 (May).

Aharony, J., and Swary, I. (1983) "Contagion Effects of Bank Failures: Evidence from Capital Markets." *Journal of Business* 56: 305–22.

Ahmed, S.; Levin, A.; and Wilson, B. A. (2004) "Recent U.S. Macroeconomic Stability: Good Policies, Good Practices, or Good Luck?" *Review of Economics and Statistics* 83 (3): 824–32.

Alcala, F., and Sancho, I. (2004) "Output Composition and the U.S. Output Volatility Decline." *Economics Letters* 82 (1): 115–20.

Alcazar, L. (1994) "Political Constraints and the Use of Seigniorage: Empirical Evidence from a Cross-Country Analysis." Manuscript, Washington University, St. Louis, Mo.

Aldrich, N. W. (1910) "The Work of the National Monetary Commission." Address before the Economic Club of New York. Washington: Government Printing Office.

Allen, A. T. (1986) "Private Sector Response to Stabilization Policy: A Case Study." *Explorations in Economic History* 23 (3): 253–68.

Allison, J. A. (2013) *The Financial Crisis and the Free Market Cure*. New York: McGraw-Hill.

American Bankers' Association (various dates) "Proceedings of the Annual Convention of the American Bankers' Association." New York: American Bankers' Association.

Anderson, B. M. (1949) *Economics and the Public Welfare: A Financial and Economic History of the United States, 1914–1946*. Princeton, N.J.: D. Van Nostrand.

Anderson, G. L. (1933) "The National Banking System, 1865–1875: A Sectional Institution." Ph.D. Dissertation, University of Illinois, Urbana.

Andres, J.; Domenech, R.; and Fatas, A. (2008) "The Stabilizing Role of Government Size." *Journal of Economic Dynamics and Control* 32 (2): 571–93.

Andrew, A. P. (1909) "The Work of the National Monetary Commission." *American Economic Association Quarterly*, 3rd series, 10 (1): 377–83.

——— (1912) "Letter from the Secretary of the National Monetary Commission Transmitting, Pursuant to Law, the Report of the Commission." Washington: Government Printing Office.

Appelbaum, B. (2012) "Inside the Fed in 2006: A Coming Crisis, and Banter." *New York Times* (January 12).

Ardant, G. (1975) "Financial Policy and Economic Infrastructure of Modern States and Nations." In C. Tilly (ed.), *The Formation of National States in Western Europe*, 164–242. Princeton, N.J.: Princeton University Press.

Arias, A.; Hansen, G. D.; and Ohanian, L. E. (2007) "Why Have Business Cycle Fluctuations Become Less Volatile?" *Economic Theory* 32 (1): 43–58.

Armantier, O.; Ghysels, E.; Sarkar, A.; and Shrader, J. (2011) "Stigma in Financial Markets: Evidence from Liquidity Auctions and Discount Window Borrowing during the Crisis." Federal Reserve Bank of New York Staff Report No. 483 (January).

Arnone, M., and Iden, G. (2003) "Primary Dealers in Government Securities: Policy Issues and Selected Countries' Experience." IMF Working Paper No. 03/45 (March). Washington: International Monetary Fund.

Atkeson, A., and Kehoe, P. J. (2004) "Deflation and Depression: Is There an Empirical Link?" *American Economic Review* 94 (2): 99–103.

Ausubel, L. M., and Cramton, P. (2008) "A Troubled Asset Reverse Auction." Working Paper, University of Maryland (October 5).

Axilrod, S. H. (1997) "Transformations to Open Market Operations: Developing Economies and Emerging Markets." International Monetary Fund *Economic Issues* 5 (January).

Ayotte, K., and Skeel, D. A. Jr. (2010) "Bankruptcy or Bailouts?" *Journal of Comparative Law* 33 (5): 469–98.

Baba, N.; McCauley, R. N.; and Ramaswamy, S. (2009) "U.S. Dollar Money Market Funds and Non-U.S. Banks." *BIS Quarterly Review* (March): 65–81.

Bagehot, W. (1873) *Lombard Street: A Description of the Money Market*. London: Henry S. King.

Baily, M. N. (1978) "Stabilization Policy and Private Economic Behavior." *Brookings Papers on Economic Activity* 1: 11–50.

Balke, N. S., and Gordon, R. J. (1986) "Appendix B: Historical Data." In R. J. Gordon (ed.), *The American Business Cycle: Continuity and Change*. Chicago: University of Chicago Press and National Bureau of Economic Research.

——— (1989) "The Estimation of Prewar Gross National Product: Methodology and New Evidence." *Journal of Political Economy* 97 (1): 38–92.

Baltensperger, E. (1980) "Alternative Approaches to the Theory of the Banking Firm." *Journal of Monetary Economics* 6 (1): 1–37.

Banaian, K.; McClure, J. H.; and Willett, T. D. (1994) "The Inflation Tax Is Likely to Be Inefficient at Any Level." *Kredit und Kapital* 27 (1): 30–41.

Bankers Magazine (various dates) New York: The Bankers Publishing Company.

Barro, R. J., and Gordon, D. B. (1983) "A Positive Theory of Monetary Policy in a Natural Rate Model." *Journal of Political Economy* 91 (4): 589–610.

Barsky, R. B. (1987) "The Fisher Hypothesis and the Forecastability and Persistence of Inflation." *Journal of Monetary Economics* 19 (1): 3–24.

Barsky, R. B., and Kilian, L. (2001) "Do We Really Know That Oil Caused the Great Stagflation? A Monetary Alternative." *NBER Macroeconomics Annual* 16: 137–83.

Barth, J. R., and Keleher, R. E. (1984) "Financial Crises and the Role of the Lender of Last Resort." Federal Reserve Bank of Atlanta *Economic Review* 69 (1): 58–67.

Baxter, M., and King, R. G. (1999) "Measuring Business Cycles: Approximate Band-Pass Filters for Economic Time Series." *Review of Economics and Statistics* 81 (4): 575–93.

Beckhart, B. H., and Smith, J. G. (1932) *The New York Money Market, Vol. II: Sources and Movements of Funds*. New York: Columbia University Press.

Beckworth, D. (2007) "The Postbellum Deflation and Its Lessons for Today." *North American Journal of Economics and Finance* 18 (2): 195–214.

Bédard, M. (2012) "Are Dominoes a Good Metaphor for Systemic Risk in Banking?" *International Journal of Business* 17 (4): 352–64.

Bell, S. (1912) "Profit on National Bank Notes." *American Economic Review* 2 (1): 38–60.

Benston, G. J., and Kaufman, G. G. (1995) "Is the Banking and Payments System Fragile?" *Journal of Financial Services Research* 9 (3/4): 209–40.

Benston, G. J.; Eisenbeis, R. A.; Horvitz, P. A.; Kane, E. J.; and Kaufman, G. G. (1986) *Perspectives on Safe and Sound Banking*. Cambridge, Mass.: MIT Press.

Bernanke, B. S. (2002a) "Deflation: Making Sure 'It' Doesn't Happen Here." Speech at the National Economists Club, Washington (November 1).

——— (2002b) "On Milton Friedman's Ninetieth Birthday." Remarks at the Conference to Honor Milton Friedman, University of Chicago, Ill. (November 8).

——— (2004) "The Great Moderation." Speech at the Eastern Economic Association Meetings, Washington (February 20).

——— (2006) "The Benefits of Price Stability." Lecture at the Center for Economic Policy Studies, Princeton University, Princeton, N.J. (February 24).

——— (2008a) "The Economic Outlook." Testimony before the Joint Economic Committee, U.S. Congress (April 2).

——— (2008b) "Reducing Systemic Risk." Federal Reserve Bank of Kansas City Economic Policy Symposium, Jackson Hole, Wyo. (August 22).

——— (2009) Testimony on Oversight of the Government's Intervention at American International Group before the House Committee on Financial Services, U.S. Congress (March 24).

——— (2012a) "The Federal Reserve and the Financial Crisis." Lecture series, George Washington University School of Business, Washington (March 20, 22, 27, 29).

——— (2012b) "Some Reflections on the Crisis and the Policy Response." Speech at the Conference on "Rethinking Finance," Russell Sage Foundation and the Century Foundation, New York (April 13).

Bertocco, G. (2012) "Global Saving Glut and Housing Bubble: A Critical Analysis." Focaltà di Economia, Università dell'Insubria, Varese, Italy.

Bindseil, U., and Würtz, F. (2007) "Open Market Operations: Their Role and Specification Today." In D. G. Myers and J. Toporowski (eds.), *Open Market Operations and Financial Markets*, 54–79. London: Routledge.

Bindseil, U.; Camba-Méndez, G.; Hirsch, A.; and Weller, B. (2004) "Excess Reserves and Implementation of Monetary Policy of the ECB." Working Paper Series No. 361 (May). Frankfurt am Main, Germany: European Central Bank.

Bisson, T. (1979) *Conservation of Coinage*. Oxford: The Clarendon Press.

Blair, R. D., and Heggestad, A. A. (1978) "Bank Portfolio Regulation and the Probability of Bank Failure." *Journal of Money, Credit, and Banking* 10 (1): 88–93.

Blanchard, O. J., and Quah, D. (1989) "The Dynamic Effects of Aggregate Demand and Supply Disturbances." *American Economic Review* 79 (4): 655–73.

Blanchard, O. J., and Watson, M. W. (1986) "Are American Business Cycles All Alike?" In R. J. Gordon (ed.), *The American Business Cycle: Continuity and Change*, 123–56. Chicago: University of Chicago Press and National Bureau of Economic Research.

Blinder, A. S. (1997) "What Central Bankers Could Learn from Academics—and Vice Versa." *Journal of Economic Perspectives* 11 (2): 3–19.

——— (1998) *Central Banking in Theory and Practice*. Cambridge, Mass.: MIT Press.

——— (2010) "How Central Should the Central Bank Be?" *Journal of Economic Literature* 48 (1): 123–33.

Blinder, A. S., and Rudd, J. B. (2008) "The Supply-Shock Explanation of the Great Stagflation Revisited." NBER Working Paper No. 14563 (December). Cambridge, Mass.: National Bureau of Economic Research.

Board of Governors of the Federal Reserve System (1943) *Banking and Monetary Statistics, 1914–1941*. Washington: Board of Governors.

——— (1959) *All Bank Statistics, United States, 1896–1955*. Washington: Board of Governors.

——— (1971) "Reappraisal of the Federal Reserve Discount Mechanism." Washington: Board of Governors.

——— (1999) "Using Subordinated Debt as an Instrument of Market Discipline." Staff Study 172 (December). Washington: Board of Governors.

——— (2002) "Alternative Instruments for Open Market and Discount Window Operations." Washington: Board of Governors.

——— (2008) "Press Release" (October 6): https://www.federalreserve.gov/monetarypolicy/20081006a.htm.

——— (2009) "Monetary Policy Report to Congress." Washington: Board of Governors (February 24).

——— (2013a) "The Structure of the Federal Reserve System." https://www.federalreserve.gov/pubs/frseries/frseri.htm.

——— (2013b) "What Does It Mean that the Federal Reserve Is 'Independent within the Government?'" In *Current FAQs: Informing the Public about the Federal Reserve*: https://www.federalreserve.gov/faqs/about_12799.htm.

——— (various dates) "Minutes of the Federal Open Market Committee." Washington: Board of Governors.

Bodenhorn, H., and Rockoff, H. (1992) "Regional Interest Rates in Antebellum America." In C. Golding and H. Rockoff (eds.), *Strategic Factors in Nineteenth Century American Economic History*, 159–87. Chicago: University of Chicago Press.

Bolles, A. S. (1886) *The Financial History of the United States, from 1861 to 1885*. New York: D. Appleton and Company.

Bordo, M. D. (1986) "Financial Crises, Banking Crises, Stock Market Crashes and the Money Supply: Some International Evidence, 1870–1933." In F. Capie and G. E. Wood (eds.), *Financial Crises and the World Banking System*, 190–248. London: MacMillan.

——— (1993) "The Bretton Woods International Monetary System: A Historical Overview." In M. D. Bordo and B. Eichengreen (eds.), *A Retrospective on the Bretton Woods System: Lessons for International Monetary Reform*. Chicago: University of Chicago Press and National Bureau of Economic Research.

——— (2008) "Comment on Charles Calomiris' 'The Subprime Turmoil: What's Old, What's New, and What's Next?'" Federal Reserve Bank of Kansas City Symposium, *Maintaining Stability in a Changing Financial System*, Jackson Hole, Wyo. (August 21–23).

——— (2009) "Commentary: The Subprime Turmoil: What's Old, What's New and What's Next?" In *Maintaining Stability in a Changing Financial System*, 111–20. Federal Reserve Bank of Kansas City.

——— (2010) "The Federal Reserve: Independence Gained, Independence Lost." Shadow Open Market Committee Symposium, New York (26 March).

Bordo, M. D., and Filardo, A. (2005a) "Deflation and Monetary Policy in Historical Perspective: Remembering the Past or Being Condemned to Repeat It?" *Economic Policy* 20 (44): 799–844.

——— (2005b) "Deflation in a Historical Perspective." BIS Working Paper No. 186 (November). Basel, Switzerland: Bank for International Settlements.

Bordo, M. D., and Redish, A. (1987) "Why Did the Bank of Canada Emerge in 1935?" *Journal of Economic History* 47 (2): 405–17.

——— (2004) "Is Deflation Depressing? Evidence from the Classical Gold Standard." In R. C. K. Burdekin and P. L. Siklos (eds.), *Deflation: Current and Historical Perspectives*. New York: Cambridge University Press.

Bordo, M. D., and Roberds, W., eds. (2013) *The Origins, History, and Future of the Federal Reserve: A Return to Jekyll Island*. Cambridge: Cambridge University Press.

Bordo, M. D., and Wheelock, D. C. (2013) "The Promise of the Federal Reserve as a Lender of Last Resort, 1914–1933." In M. D. Bordo and W. Roberds (eds.), *The Origins, History, and Future of the Federal Reserve: A Return to Jekyll Island*, 59–98. Cambridge: Cambridge University Press.

Bordo, M. D.; Choudhri, E. U.; and Schwartz, A. J. (2002) "Was Expansionary Monetary Policy Feasible during the Great Contraction? An Examination of the Gold Standard Constraint." *Explorations in Economic History* 39 (1): 1–28.

Bordo, M. D.; Landon Lane, J.; and Redish, A. (2003) "Good versus Bad Deflation: Lessons from the Gold Standard Era." NBER Working Paper No. 10329 (February). Cambridge, Mass.: National Bureau of Economic Research.

Bordo, M. D.; Redish, A.; and Rockoff, H. (1996) "A Comparison of the Stability and Efficiency of the Canadian and American Banking Systems, 1870–1925." *Financial History Review* 3 (1): 49–68.

Borio, C., and Disyatat, P. (2011) "Global Imbalances and the Financial Crisis: Link or No Link?" BIS Working Paper No. 346 (May). Basel, Switzerland: Bank for International Settlements.

Bowen, F. (1866) "The National Banking System." *Bankers Magazine* (April): 773.

Boyer-Xambeu, M.-T.; Deleplace, G.; and Gillard, L. (1994) *Private Money and Public Currencies: the 16th Century Challenge*. Armonk, N.Y.: M. E. Sharpe.

Brady, K. P. (2014) "The Case for a Centennial Monetary Commission." *Cato Journal* 34 (8): 389–94.

Breckenridge, R. M. (1895) *The Banking System of Canada 1817–1890*. New York: Macmillan.

——— (1910) *The History of Banking in Canada*. Washington: Government Printing Office.

Brewer, E., and Jagtiani, J. (2009) "How Much Did Banks Pay to Become Too-Big-To-Fail and to Become Systematically Important?" Federal Reserve Bank of Philadelphia Working Paper 09–34 (December).

Brickler, L.; Copeland, A.; and Martin, A. (2011) "Everything You Wanted to Know about the Tri-Party Repo Market, but Didn't Know to Ask." Liberty Street Economics (April 11):

http://libertystreeteconomics.newyorkfed.org/2011/04/everything-you-wanted-to-know-about-the-tri-party-repo-market-but-didnt-know-to-ask.html.

Bryan, W. J. (1907) "The Asset Currency Scheme." *The Commoner* 7 (43).

Bryant, J. (1981) "Bank Collapse and Depression." *Journal of Money, Credit, and Banking* 13 (4): 454–64.

Buchanan, J. M. (1960) "'La Scienza delle Finanze': The Italian Tradition in Fiscal Theory." In *Fiscal Theory and Political Economy: Selected Essays*, 24–74. Chapel Hill: University of North Carolina Press.

Buiter, W. H. (2007) "Where the Bank of England Went Wrong, and How to Prevent a Recurrence." Willem Buiter's Maverecon (November 17): http://blogs.ft.com/maverecon/2007/11.

——— (2008a) "Central Banks and Financial Crises." Financial Markets Group Discussion Paper No. 619 (August). London: London School of Economics.

——— (2008b) "Wanted: Tough Love from the Central Bank." Willem Buiter's Maverecon (March 22): http://blogs.ft.com/maverecon/2008/03.

Buiter, W. H., and Sibert, A. (2008) "The Central Bank as the Market-Maker of Last Resort: From Lender of Last Resort to Market-Maker of Last Resort." In A. Felton and C. Reinhart (eds.), *The First Global Financial Crisis of the 21st Century*, 171–78. London: Centre for Economic Policy Research.

Bullock, N. (2010) "Norfolk Southern in 100-Year Issue." *Financial Times*, August 24.

Burns, A. F. (1960) "Progress towards Economic Stability." *American Economic Review* 50 (1): 1–19.

Burns, A. R. (1965) *Money and Monetary Policy in Early Times*. New York: Augustus M. Kelley.

Cagan, P. (1963) "The First Fifty Years of the National Banking System—An Historical Appraisal." In D. Carson (ed.), *Banking and Monetary Studies*, 15–42. Homewood, Ill.: Richard D. Irwin.

Cagan, P., and Schwartz, A. J. (1991) "The National Bank Note Puzzle Reinterpreted." *Journal of Money, Credit, and Banking* 23 (3): 293–307.

Calomiris, C. W. (1994) "Is the Discount Window Necessary? A Penn Central Perspective." Federal Reserve Bank of St. Louis *Review* 76 (3): 31–55.

——— (2000) *U.S. Bank Deregulation in Historical Perspective*. New York: Cambridge University Press.

——— (2009a) "Banking Crises and the Rules of the Game." NBER Working Paper No. 15403 (September). Cambridge, Mass.: National Bureau of Economic Research.

——— (2009b) "Financial Innovation, Regulation, Reform." *Cato Journal* 29 (1): 65–91.

Calomiris, C. W., and Gorton, G. (1991) "The Origins of Bank Panics: Models, Facts, and Bank Regulation." In G. Hubbard (ed.), *Financial Markets and Financial Crises*. Chicago: University of Chicago Press and National Bureau of Economic Research.

Calomiris, C. W., and Haber, S. H. (2014) *Fragile by Design: The Political Origins of Banking Crises and Scarce Credit*. Princeton, N.J.: Princeton University Press.

Calomiris, C. W.; Jaremski, M.; Park, H.; and Richardson, G. (2015) "Liquidity Risk, Bank Networks, and the Value of Joining the Federal Reserve System." Office of Financial Research Working Paper No. 15-05 (April). Washington: U.S. Department of the Treasury.

Canarella, G.; Fang, W. S.; Miller, S. M.; and Pollard, S. K. (2010) "Is the Great Moderation Ending? U.K. and U.S. Evidence." *Modern Economy* 1 (1): 17–42.

Cargill, T. F., and O'Driscoll, G. P. Jr. (2013) "Federal Reserve Independence: Reality or Myth?" *Cato Journal* 33 (3): 417–35.

Carothers, N. (1930) *Fractional Money*. New York: John Wiley & Sons.

Carter, S. B.; Gartner, S. S.; Haines, M. R.; Olmstead, A. L.; Sutch, R.; and Wright, G., eds. (2006) *Historical Statistics of the United States*, Millennial Edition Online. Cambridge: Cambridge University Press: http://hsus.cambridge.org/HSUSWeb/HSUSEntryServlet.

Caskey, J. P., and St. Laurent, S. (1994) "The Susan B. Anthony Dollar and the Theory of Coin/Note Substitution." *Journal of Money, Credit, and Banking* 26 (3): 495–510.

Cecchetti, S. G. (2009) "Crisis and Responses: The Federal Reserve in the Early Stages of the Financial Crisis." *Journal of Economic Perspectives* 23 (1): 51–75.

Cecchetti, S. G., and Disyatat, P. (2010) "Central Bank Tools and Liquidity Shortages." Federal Reserve Bank of New York *Economic Policy Review* 16 (1): 29–42.

Champ, B. A. (1990) "The Underissuance of National Banknotes during the Period 1875–1913." Ph.D. Dissertation, University of Minnesota.

Champ, B. A.; Wallace, N.; and Weber, W. E. (1993) "Interest Rates under the U.S. National Banking System." Federal Reserve Bank of Minneapolis Research Department Staff Report No. 161.

Chappell, H. W., and McGregor, R. R. (2004) "Did Time Inconsistency Contribute to the Great Inflation? Evidence from FOMC Transcripts." *Economics and Politics* 16 (3): 233–51.

Cheun, S.; Köppen-Mertes, I.; and Weller, B. (2009) "The Collateral Frameworks of the Eurosystem, the Federal Reserve System and the Bank of England and the Financial Market Turmoil." Occasional Paper Series No. 107 (December). Frankfurt am Main, Germany: European Central Bank.

Chicago Bank Note List (various dates) Chicago: J. A. Ellis and Company.

Chown, J. F. (1994) *A History of Money from AD 800*. New York: Routledge.

Christensen, J. H.; Lopez, J. A.; and Rudebusch, G. D. (2009) "Do Central Bank Liquidity Facilities Affect Interbank Lending Rates?" Federal Reserve Bank of San Francisco Working Paper No. 2009–13.

Christiano, L.; Motto, R.; and Rostagno, M. (2003) "The Great Depression and the Friedman-Schwartz Hypothesis." *Journal of Money, Credit, and Banking* 35 (6): 1119–98.

Cipolla, C. (1956) *Money, Prices and Civilization in the Mediterranean World*. Princeton, N.J.: Princeton University Press.

Claflin, J.; Vanderlip, F. A.; Straus, I.; Clarke, D.; Conant, C. A.; and Johnson, J. F. (1906) "The Currency." Report by the Special Committee of the Chamber of Commerce of the State of New York.

Clarida, R.; Gali, J.; and Gertler, M. (2000) "Monetary Policy Rules and Macroeconomic Stability: Evidence and Some Theory." *Quarterly Journal of Economics* 115 (1): 147–80.

Clark, L. E. (1935) *Central Banking Under the Federal Reserve System*. New York: Macmillan.

Clark, T. E. (2009) "Is the Great Moderation Over?" Federal Reserve Bank of Kansas City *Economic Review* 94 (4): 5–39.

Cline, W. R., and Gagnon, J. E. (2013) "Lehman Died, Bagehot Lives: Why Did the Fed and Treasury Let a Major Wall Street Bank Fail?" Peterson Institute for International Economics *Policy Brief* 13-21 (September).

Cloos, G. W. (1963) "How Good Are the National Bureau's Reference Dates?" *Journal of Business* 36 (1): 14–32.

Cochrane, J. (2012) "Fed Independence 2025." The Grumpy Economist (19 February): http://johnhcochrane.blogspot.com/2012/02/fed-independence-2025.html.

Coen, R. M. (1973) "Labor Force and Unemployment in the 1920's and 1930's: A Re-Examination Based on Post-War Experience." *Review of Economics and Statistics* 55 (1): 46–55.

Cogley, T., and Sargent, T. J. (2002) "Evolving Post–World War II U.S. Inflation Dynamics." *NBER Macroeconomics Annual* 16: 332–88.

Cole, R. A., and White, L. J. (2012) "Déjà Vu All Over Again: The Causes of U.S. Commercial Bank Failures *This* Time Around." *Journal of Financial Services Research* 42 (1): 5–29.

Coletta, P. E. (1964) "William Jennings Bryan and Currency and Banking Reform." *Nebraska History* 45: 31–58.

Commercial and Financial Chronicle (various dates) New York: William B. Dana Company.

Commissioner of Internal Revenue (1864) "Abstract of the Reports of the Banks, Associations, Corporations, and Individuals Doing a Banking Business." Senate Executive Document No. 50, 38th Congress, 1st Session. Washington: Government Printing Office.

Comptroller of the Currency (1870) "Banking Facilities." House Miscellaneous Document No. 140, 41st Congress, 2nd Session. Washington: Government Printing Office.

——— (various dates) *Annual Report*. Washington: Office of the Comptroller of the Currency.

Congressional Globe (various dates): https://memory.loc.gov/ammem/amlaw/lwcg.html.

Congressional Record (various dates) Washington: Government Printing Office.

Correia, I., and Teles, P. (1996) "Is the Friedman Rule Optimal When Money Is an Intermediate Good?" *Journal of Monetary Economics* 38 (2): 223–44.

Cothren, R. (1987) "Asymmetric Information and Optimal Bank Reserves." *Journal of Money, Credit, and Banking* 19 (1): 68–77.

Cover, J.; Enders, W.; and Hueng, J. C. (2006) "Using the Aggregate Demand–Aggregate Supply Model to Identify Structural Demand-Side and Supply-Side Shocks: Results Using a Bivariate VAR." *Journal of Money, Credit, and Banking* 38 (3): 777–90.

Cowen, T., and Kroszner, R. (1989) "Scottish Banking before 1844: A Model for Laissez-Faire?" *Journal of Money, Credit, and Banking* 21 (2): 221–31.

Crabbe, L. (1989) "The International Gold Standard and U.S. Monetary Policy from World War I to the New Deal." *Federal Reserve Bulletin* (June).

Crozier, A. O. (1912) *U.S. Money vs. Corporation Currency*. Cincinnati: The Magnet Company.

Cukierman, A. (1992) *Central Bank Strategy, Credibility, and Independence: Theory and Evidence*. Cambridge, Mass.: MIT Press.

Cukierman, A.; Edwards, S.; and Tabellini, G. (1992) "Seigniorage and Political Instability." *American Economic Review* 82 (3): 537–55.

Curtis, C. A. (1931) "Banking Statistics in Canada." In *Statistical Contributions to Canadian Economic History*, 1–93. Toronto: Macmillan.

Danielsson, J. (2008) "The Bankruptcy of Bear Stearns Would Have Been a Good Lesson." *The Telegraph* (March 25).

Davis, J. H. (2004) "An Annual Index of U.S. Industrial Production, 1790–1915." *Quarterly Journal of Economics* 119 (4): 1177–215.

——— (2006) "An Improved Chronology of U.S. Business Cycles since the 1790s." *Journal of Economic History* 66 (1): 103–21.

Davis, J. H.; Hanes, C.; and Rhode, P. W. (2009) "Harvests and Business Cycles in Nineteenth-Century America." *Quarterly Journal of Economics* (November): 1675–727.

Davis, S. J., and Kahn, J. A. (2008) "Interpreting the Great Moderation: Changes in the Volatility of Economic Activity at the Macro and Micro Levels." *Journal of Economic Perspectives* 22 (4): 155–80.

Day, S. A. (2013) "Arthur Burns." In D. A. Dieterle (ed.), *Economic Thinkers: A Biographical Encyclopedia*, 37–39. Santa Barbara, Calif.: Greenwood.

De Cecco, M. (1975) *Money and Empire: The International Gold Standard, 1890–1914*. Totowa, N.J.: Rowman and Littlefield.

DeLong, J. B., and Summers, L. H. (1986) "The Changing Cyclical Variability of Economic Activity in the United States." In R. J. Gordon (ed.), *The American Business Cycle: Continuity and Change*, 679–734. Chicago: University of Chicago Press.

Demirgüç-Kunt, A., and Maksimovic, V. (1999) "Institutions, Financial Markets, and Firm Debt Maturity." *Journal of Financial Economics* 54 (3): 295–336.

Dennis, R. (2003) "Time-Inconsistent Monetary Policies: Recent Research." Federal Reserve Bank of San Francisco *Economic Letter* 2003-10 (April).

Dennis, R., and Söderström, U. (2006) "How Important Is Precommitment for Monetary Policy?" *Journal of Money, Credit, and Banking* 38 (4): 847–72.

Derbyshire, J. D., and Derbyshire, I. (1996) *Political Systems of the World*. New York: St. Martin's.

Dewald, W. G. (1972) "The National Monetary Commission: A Look Back." *Journal of Money, Credit, and Banking* 4 (4): 930–56.

Dewey, D. R. (1910) "State Banking before the Civil War." Washington: Government Printing Office.

Diamond, D. W., and Dybvig, P. H. (1983) "Bank Runs, Deposit Insurance, and Liquidity." *Journal of Political Economy* 91 (3): 401–19.

Dick, T. J. O., and Floyd, J. E. (1992) *Canada and the Gold Standard: Balance-of-Payments Adjustment, 1871–1913*. Cambridge: Cambridge University Press.

Diebold, F. X., and Rudebusch, G. D. (1992) "Have Postwar Economic Fluctuations Been Stabilized?" *American Economic Review* 62 (4): 993–1005.

Dodsworth, W. (1895) "Our Paper Currency. As It Is and As It Should Be." *Sound Currency* 2 (9): 189–203.

Donaldson, R. G. (1992) "The Sources of Panics: Evidence from Weekly Data." *Journal of Monetary Economics* 30 (2): 277–305.

Dowd, K. (1988) "Option Clauses and the Stability of a Laisser Faire Monetary System." *Journal of Financial Services Research* 1 (4): 319–33.

——— (1989) *The State and the Monetary System*. Oxford: Philip Allan.

——— (1992) *The Experience of Free Banking*. London: Routledge.

——— (1995) "A Rule to Stabilize the Price Level." *Cato Journal* 15 (1): 39–64.

Duffie, D. (2009) "The Failure Mechanics of Dealer Banks." Working Paper, Stanford University (June 22).

Dunbar, C. F. (1892) "The Bank-Note Question." *Quarterly Journal of Economics* 7 (1): 55–77.

——— (1904) *Economic Essays*. New York: Macmillan.

——— (1922) *The Theory and History of Banking*, 4th ed. New York: G. P. Putnam's Sons.

Dunne, G. T. (1964) "A Christmas Present for the President." Federal Reserve Bank of St. Louis.

Dunne, P. G.; Fleming, M.; and Zholos, A. (2009) "Repo Market Microstructure in Unusual Monetary Policy Conditions." Working Paper (December 16).

Dwyer, G. P. Jr. (1996) "Wildcat Banking, Banking Panics, and Free Banking in the United States." Federal Reserve Bank of Atlanta *Economic Review* 81 (1): 1–20.

Dwyer, G. P. Jr., and Gilbert, A. R. (1989) "Bank Runs and Private Remedies." Federal Reserve Bank of St. Louis *Economic Review* (May/June): 43–61.

Dwyer, G. P. Jr., and Saving, T. R. (1986) "Government Revenue from Money Creation with Government and Private Money." *Journal of Monetary Economics* 17 (2): 239–49.

Dynan, K. E.; Elmendorf, D. W.; and Sichel, D. E. (2006) "Can Financial Innovation Help to Explain the Reduced Volatility of Economic Activity?" *Journal of Monetary Economics* 53 (1): 123–50.

Economopoulos, A. (1994) "A Discriminating Taste for Money: An Examination of the New York Antebellum Banking Market." In J. L. DiGaetani (ed.), *Money: Lure, Lore, and Literature*, 87–99. Westport, Conn.: Greenwood Press.

Edge, R. M.; Laubach, T.; and Williams, J. C. (2007) "Learning and Shifts in Long-Run Productivity Growth." *Journal of Monetary Economics* 54 (8): 2421–38.

Ehrich, L. R. (1903) "Assets Currency." *Sound Currency* 9 (1): 13–15.

Eichengreen, B. J. (1992) *Golden Fetters: The Gold Standard and the Great Depression, 1919–1939*. New York: Oxford University Press.

Eichengreen, B. J., and Temin, P. (2000) "The Gold Standard and the Great Depression." *Contemporary European History* 9 (2): 183–207.

Eisenbeis, R. A. (2009) "The Financial Crisis: Miss-Diagnosis and Reactionary Responses." Financial Institutions Center Working Paper No. 10-14. Philadelphia: Wharton School, University of Pennsylvania.

Elwell, C. K. (2011) "Brief History of the Gold Standard in the United States." CRS Report for Congress R41887 (June). Washington: Congressional Research Service.

Ely, B. (1997) "Time to Abolish Reserve Requirements." The Golembe Report No. 7 (August 27).

Ennis, H. M., and Keister, T. (2009) "Bank Runs and Institutions: The Perils of Intervention." *American Economic Review* 99 (4): 1588–607.

Entekhabi, N. (2008) "Technical Change, Wage and Price Dispersion, and the Optimal Rate of Inflation." Working Paper: http//:papers.ssrn.com/sol3/papers.cfm?abstract_id=1218078.

Falkner, R. P. (1900) "The Currency Law of 1900." *Annals of the American Academy of Political and Social Sciences* 16: 34–55.

Fatás, A., and Mihov, I. (2001) "Government Size and Automatic Stabilizers: International and Intranational Evidence." *Journal of International Economics* 55 (1): 3–28.

Feaveryear, A. (1963) *The Pound Sterling: A History of English Money*, 2nd ed. Oxford: The Clarendon Press.

Federal Reserve Bank of Atlanta (1) "The Fed Explains Inflation." http://frbatlanta.org/about/fed-explained/2012/inflation.aspx.

——— (2) "The Fed Explains Good versus Bad Standards." http://frbatlanta.org/about/fed-explained/2013/measurements.aspx.

——— (3) "Standards for Teaching about FRS." http://web.archive.org/web/20121019051621/http://www.frbatlanta.org/edresources/standards/teachingfrs/.

Federal Reserve Bank of Boston (1) "History of the Federal Reserve." http://federalreserveeducation.org/about-the-fed/history.

Federal Reserve Bank of Dallas (1) "The Fed Today." Text archived at http://archive.org/stream/ERIC_ED458167/ERIC_ED458167_djvu.txt.

——— (2) "Understanding the Fed." http://dallasfed.org/fed/understand.cfm.

——— (2006) "The Fed: The Federal Reserve, Monetary Policy, and the Economy." http://web.archive.org/web/20130808165805/http://www.dallasfed.org/assets/documents/educate/everyday/ev4.pdf.

Federal Reserve Bank of New York (1) "The Founding of the Fed." http://newyorkfed.org/aboutthefed/history_article.html.

——— (1999) "The Story of Monetary Policy." http://ia800500.us.archive.org/30/items/gov.frb.ny.comic.monetary/gov.frb.ny.comic.monetary.pdf.

Federal Reserve Bank of Philadelphia (1) "The Federal Reserve and You." http://phil.frb.org/education/federal-reserve-and-you.

——— (2) "The Fed Today." http://philadelphiafed.org/publications/economic-education/fed-today/fed-today_lesson-2.pdf.

——— (2009) "Out of Many . . . One: 2009 Annual Report." http://philadelphiafed.org/publications/annual-report/2009/structure-and-governance.cfm.

Federal Reserve Bank of San Francisco (1) "What Is the Fed: History." http://frbsf.org/education/teacher-resources/what-is-the-fed/history.

——— (2) "What Did the Fed Do to Combat the Financial Crisis?" http://sffed-education.org/econanswers/response_q1more.htm.

——— (1999a) "U.S. Monetary Policy: An Introduction." *Economic Letter* 1999-01 (January).

——— (1999b) "What Is Deflation and How Is It Different from Disinflation?" Dr. Econ (September).

——— (2001) "Does a Central Bank Have More Information about the Economy than the Government, and, If So, What Type of Information?" Dr. Econ (December).

——— (2006) "What Are the Costs of Deflation?" Dr. Econ (February).

——— (2013) "Why Did the Federal Reserve Start Paying Interest on Reserve Balances Held on Deposit at the Fed? Does the Fed Pay Interest on Required Reserves, Excess Reserves, or Both? What Interest Rate Does the Fed Pay?" Dr. Econ (March).

Federal Reserve System Study Group (2002) "Alternative Instruments for Open Market and Discount Window Operations." Washington: Board of Governors.

Feldstein, M. (1997) "The Costs and Benefits of Going from Low Inflation to Price Stability." In C. D. Romer and D. H. Romer (eds.), *Reducing Inflation: Motivation and Strategy*, 123–56. Chicago: University of Chicago Press and National Bureau of Economic Research.

——— (2010) "What Powers for the Federal Reserve?" *Journal of Economic Literature* 48 (1): 134–45.

Fernández-Villaverde, J.; Guerrón-Quintana, P. A.; and Rubio-Ramirez, J. (2010) "Reading the Recent Monetary History of the U.S., 1959–2007." NBER Working Paper No. 15929 (April). Cambridge, Mass.: National Bureau of Economic Research.

Financial Economists Roundtable (2010) "How to Manage and Help to Avoid Systemic Liquidity Risk." Philadelphia: Wharton Financial Institutions Center, University of Pennsylvania.

Fishe, R. P. H. (1991) "The Federal Reserve Amendments of 1917: The Beginning of a Seasonal Note Issue Policy." *Journal of Money, Credit, and Banking* 23 (3): 308–26.

Fisher, R. W., and Rosenblum, H. (2009) "The Blob That Ate Monetary Policy." *Wall Street Journal* (September 27).

Flannery, M. J. (2009) "Stabilizing Large Financial Institutions with Contingent Capital Certificates." Working Paper: http://papers.ssrn.com/sol3/papers.cfm?abstract_id=1485689.

Flannery, M. J., and Kaufman, G. G. (1996) "Financial Crises, Payment System Problems, and Discount Window Lending." *Journal of Money, Credit, and Banking* 28 (4): 804–24.

Flint, W. (1863) *Some Strictures on an Act to Provide a National Currency.* Boston: John Wilson and Son.

Forgan, J. B. (1903) "Letter to the Texas Bankers Association." *Sound Currency* 10 (2): 67–72.

Fowler, C. N. (1902) "The Fowler Financial and Currency Bill." Speech in the House of Representatives (June 26).

Freixas, X., and Rochet, J.-C. (1997) *Microeconomics of Banking.* Cambridge, Mass.: MIT Press.

Fricker, M. (2011) "Let's Get Going on the Real Story of the Financial Crisis: Securitized Banking." Society of American Business Editors and Writers (31 May): http://sabew.org/2011/05/let's-get-going-on-the-real-story-of-the-financial-crisis-securitized-banking.

Friedman, M. (1953) "Commodity Reserve Currency." In *Essays in Positive Economics*, 204–50. Chicago: University of Chicago Press.

——— (1960) *A Program for Monetary Stability.* New York: Fordham University Press.

——— (1961a) "Real and Pseudo Gold Standards." *Journal of Law and Economics* 4: 66–79.

——— (1961b) "The Lag in Effect of Monetary Policy." *Journal of Political Economy* 69 (5): 447–66.

——— (1982a) *Monetary Trends in the United States and the United Kingdom.* Chicago: University of Chicago Press.

——— (1982b) "Monetary Policy: Theory and Practice." *Journal of Money, Credit, and Banking* 14 (3): 98–118.

——— (1984) "Monetary Policy for the 1980s." In J. H. Moore (ed.), *To Promote Prosperity: U.S. Domestic Policy in the Mid-1980s.* Stanford, Calif.: Hoover Institution Press.

——— (1988) "The Fed Has No Clothes." *Wall Street Journal* (April 15).

——— (1992) *Money Mischief: Episodes in Monetary History.* New York: Harcourt Brace Jovanovich.

Friedman, M., and Schwartz, A. J. (1963) *A Monetary History of the United States, 1867–1960.* Princeton, N.J.: Princeton University Press and National Bureau of Economic Research.

Fry, M. J. (1988) *Money, Interest, and Banking in Economic Development.* Baltimore, Md.: Johns Hopkins University Press.

Fuller, R. L. (2009) *Drifting toward Mayhem: The Bank Crisis in the United States, 1930–1933.* Privately printed.

Gali, J. (1992) "How Well Does the IS-LM Model Fit Postwar U.S. Data?" *Quarterly Journal of Economics* 107 (2): 709–38.

——— (1994) "Government Size and Macroeconomic Stability." *European Economic Review* 38 (1): 117–32.

Gali, J., and Gambetti, L. (2009) "On the Sources of the Great Moderation." *American Economic Journal: Macroeconomics* 1 (1): 26–57.

Gallarotti, G. M. (1995) *The Anatomy of an International Monetary Regime: The Classical Gold Standard, 1880–1914.* New York: Oxford University Press.

Gallatin, J. (1864) *The National Debt, Taxation, Currency, and Banking System of the United States.* New York: Hosford & Ketchum.

Garcia, G., and Plautz, E. (1988) *The Federal Reserve: Lender of Last Resort.* Cambridge, Mass.: Ballinger.

Gherity, J. A. (1995) "The Option Clause in Scottish Banking." *Journal of Money, Credit, and Banking* 27 (3): 713–26.

Giffen, R. (1905) "Fancy Monetary Standards." In *Economic Inquiries and Studies*, 186–77. London: George Bell and Sons.

Giles, C., and Tett, G. (2008) "Lessons of the Credit Crunch." *Financial Times* (February 11).

Giovanni, A., and de Melo, M. (1993) "Government Revenue from Financial Repression." *American Economic Review* 83 (4): 953–63.

Gische, D. M. (1979) "The New York City Banks and the Development of the National Banking System, 1860–1870." *American Journal of Legal History* 23 (1): 21–67.

Glasner, D. (1989) *Free Banking and Monetary Reform*. New York: Cambridge University Press.

——— (1997) "An Evolutionary Theory of the State Monopoly over Money." In K. Dowd and R. H. Timberlake Jr. (eds.), *Money and the Nation State*, 21–45. New Brunswick, N.J.: Transaction Publishers.

Goodfriend, M. (2010) "Central Banking in the Credit Turmoil: An Assessment of Federal Reserve Practice." Working Paper (April). Pittsburgh, Pa.: Carnegie Mellon University.

Goodfriend, M., and King, R. G. (1988) "Financial Deregulation, Monetary Policy, and Central Banking." Federal Reserve Bank of Richmond *Economic Review* (May/June): 3–22.

Goodhart, C.A.E. (1987) "Why Do Banks Need a Central Bank?" *Oxford Economic Papers* 39 (1): 75–89.

——— (1988) *The Evolution of Central Banks*. Cambridge: MIT Press.

Goodhart, C. A. E., and Schoenmaker, D. (1995) "Should the Functions of Monetary Policy and Banking Supervision Be Separated?" *Oxford Economic Papers* 47 (4): 539–60.

Gorton, G. (1985) "Bank Suspension of Convertibility." *Journal of Monetary Economics* 15 (2): 177–93.

——— (1987) "Incomplete Markets and the Endogeneity of Central Banking." Manuscript.

——— (1988) "Banking Panics and Business Cycles." *Oxford Economic Papers* 40 (4): 751–81.

——— (1996) "Reputation Formation in Early Bank Note Markets." *Journal of Political Economy* 104 (2): 346–97.

Gorton, G., and Mullineaux, D. J. (1987) "The Joint Production of Confidence: Endogenous Regulation and 19th Century Commercial-Bank Clearinghouses." *Journal of Money, Credit, and Banking* 19 (4): 457–68.

Grant, J. (2014) *The Forgotten Depression: 1921: The Crash That Cured Itself.* New York: Simon & Schuster.

Graves, E. O. (1903) "The Need of an Elastic Currency." *Sound Currency* 10 (3): 82–94.

Gray, A. (1971) "Who Killed the Aldrich Plan?" *The Bankers' Magazine* 54: 62–74.

Greenspan, A. (1997) "Fostering Financial Innovation: The Role of Government." In J. A. Dorn (ed.), *The Future of Money in the Information Age*, 45–50. Washington: Cato Institute.

——— (2010) "The Crisis." *Brookings Papers in Economic Activity* 41 (1): 201–46.

Gregory, T. E. (1935) *The Gold Standard and Its Future*, 3rd (rev.) ed. New York: E. P. Dutton.

Guttentag, J., and Herring, R. (1983) "The Lender-of-Last-Resort Function in an International Context." Princeton University Essays in International Finance No. 151 (May). Princeton, N.J.

Hamilton, J. D. (1988) "Role of the International Gold Standard in Propagating the Great Depression." *Contemporary Economic Policy* 6 (2): 67–89.

——— (2005) "The Gold Standard and the Great Depression." Econbrowser (December 12): http://econbrowser.com/archives/2005/12/the_gold_standa.

Hammond, B. (1957) *Banks and Politics in America from the Revolution to the Civil War*. Princeton, N.J.: Princeton University Press.

Hanes, C. (1999) "Degrees of Processing and Changes in the Cyclical Behavior of Prices in the United States, 1869–1990." *Journal of Money, Credit, and Banking* 31 (1): 35–53.

Harter, M. D. (1893) "American Banking and the Money Supply of the Future." *Annals of the American Academy of Political and Social Science* 3: 559–72.

Hartley, P. R., and Whitt, J. A. Jr. (2003) "Macroeconomic Fluctuations: Demand or Supply, Permanent or Temporary?" *European Economic Review* 47 (1): 61–94.

Hett, F., and Schmidt, A. (2013) "Bank Rescues and Bailout Expectations: The Erosion of Market Discipline during the Financial Crisis." SAFE Working Paper No. 36 (August) Frankfurt am Main, Germany: Sustainable Architecture for Finance in Europe.

Hetzel, R. L. (2009a) "Monetary Policy in the 2008–2009 Recession." Federal Reserve Bank of Richmond *Economic Quarterly* 95 (2): 201–33.

——— (2009b) "Government Intervention in Financial Markets: Stabilizing or Destabilizing?" Working Paper. Federal Reserve Bank of Richmond.

Higgs, R. (2009) "Wartime Prosperity? A Reassessment of the U.S. Economy in the 1940s." *Journal of Economic History* 52 (1): 41–60.

Hodges' Journal of Finance and Bank Note Reporter (various dates) New York: Edward Hodges.

Hoenig, T. M. (2011) "Do SIFIs Have a Future?" Paper presented at the Conference, "Dodd-Frank One Year On," NYU–Stern School of Business Washington (June 27).

Hogan, T. L.; Le, L.; and Salter, A. W. (2015) "Ben Bernanke and Bagehot's Rules." *Journal of Money, Credit, and Banking* 47 (2/3): 333–48.

Horwitz, S. (2003) "The Costs of Inflation Revisited." *Review of Austrian Economics* 16 (1): 71–95.

Hsieh, C.-T., and Romer, C. D. (2006) "Was the Federal Reserve Constrained by the Gold Standard during the Great Depression? Evidence from the 1932 Open Market Purchase Program." *Journal of Economic History* 66 (1): 140–76.

Hughes, J., and Cain. L. P. (1998) *American Economic History*, 2nd ed. New York: Dryden Press.

Humphrey, T. M. (1986) "The Real Bills Doctrine." In T. M. Humphrey, *Essays on Inflation*, 5th ed., 80–90. Federal Reserve Bank of Richmond.

——— (2010) "Lender of Last Resort: What It Is, Whence It Came, and Why the Fed Isn't It." *Cato Journal* 30 (2): 333–64.

Humphrey, T. M., and Keleher, R. E. (1984) "The Lender of Last Resort: A Historical Perspective." *Cato Journal* 4 (1): 275–318.

Hunt's Merchants Magazine (various dates) New York: Freeman Hunt.

Ireland, P. N. (1999) "Does the Time-Consistency Problem Explain the Behavior of Inflation in the United States?" *Journal of Monetary Economics* 44 (2): 279–91.

——— (2004) "Technology Shocks in the New Keynesian Model." *Review of Economics and Statistics* 86 (4): 923–36.

——— (2012) "The Macroeconomic Effects of Interest on Reserves." NBER Working Paper No. 18409 (September). Cambridge, Mass.: National Bureau of Economic Research.

Irvine, F. O., and Schuh, S. (2005) "Inventory Investment and Output Volatility." *International Journal of Production Economics* 93–94 (8): 75–86.

Irwin, D. A. (2010) "Did France Cause the Great Depression?" NBER Working Paper No. 16350 (September). Cambridge, Mass.: National Bureau of Economic Research.

Jackson, A. L., and Sumner, S. (2006) "Velocity Futures Markets: Does the Fed Need a Structural Model?" *Economic Inquiry* 44 (4): 716–28.

Jaimovich, N., and Siu, H. E. (2009) "The Young, the Old, and the Restless: Demographics and Business Cycle Volatility." *American Economic Review* 99 (3): 804–26.

Jalil, A. (2009) "A New History of Banking Panics in the United States, 1825–1929: Construction and Implications." Working Paper (November). Berkeley: University of California, Berkeley.

James, F. C. (1938) *The Growth of Chicago Banks*. New York: Harper.

James, J. A. (1981) "Financial Development in the Postbellum South." *Journal of Interdisciplinary History* 11 (3): 443–54.

Jensen, M. C. (1988) "Takeovers: Their Causes and Consequences." *Journal of Economic Perspectives* 2 (1): 21–48.

Johnson, H. C. (1997) *Gold, France, and the Great Depression, 1919–1932*. New Haven, Conn.: Yale University Press.

Johnson, H. G. (1973) *Further Essays in Monetary Economics*. Cambridge, Mass.: Harvard University Press.

Johnson, J. F. (1910) *The Canadian Banking System*. Washington: Government Printing Office.

Jonung, L. (1985) "The Economics of Private Money: The Experience of Private Notes in Sweden, 1831–1902." Presented at the Monetary History Group Meeting, London.

Kagin, D. H. (1981) *Private Gold Coins and Patterns of the United States*. New York: Arco Publishing.

Kane, E. J. (1980) "Politics and Fed Policymaking: The More Things Change, The More They Remain the Same." *Journal of Monetary Economics* 6 (2): 199–211.

——— (1985) *The Gathering Crisis in Federal Deposit Insurance*. Cambridge, Mass.: MIT Press.

——— (1990) "Bureaucratic Self-Interest As an Obstacle to Monetary Reform." In T. Mayer (ed.), *The Political Economy of American Monetary Policy*, 283–98. New York: Cambridge University Press.

Kareken, J. H. (1986) "Federal Bank Regulatory Policy: A Description and Some Observations." *Journal of Business* 59 (1): 3–48.

Kaufman, G. G. (1988) "The Truth about Bank Runs." In C. England and T. Huertas (eds.), *The Financial Services Revolution: Policy Directions for the Future*. Boston: Kluwer Academic Publishers.

——— (1990) "Are Some Banks Too Large to Fail? Myth and Reality." *Contemporary Policy Issues* 8 (4): 1–14.

——— (1991) "Lender of Last Resort: A Contemporary Perspective." *Journal of Financial Services Research* 5 (2): 95–110.

——— (1994) "Bank Contagion: A Review of the Theory and Evidence." *Journal of Financial Services Research* 8 (2): 123–50.

——— (1999) "Do Lender of Last Resort Operations Require Bank Regulation?" Presented at the Conference, "Is Bank Regulation Necessary?" American Enterprise Institute, Washington (October 27).

——— (2000) "Comment on Benston and Wood." *Journal of Financial Services Research* 18 (2/3): 235–39.

Keating, J. W., and Nye, J. V. (1998) "Permanent and Transitory Shocks in Real Output Estimates from Nineteenth-Century and Postwar Economics." *Journal of Money, Credit, and Banking* 30 (2): 231–51.

Keister, T., and McAndrews, J. J. (2009) "Why Are Banks Holding So Many Excess Reserves?" Federal Reserve Bank of New York *Current Issues in Economics and Finance* 15 (8): 1–10.

Kemmerer, E. W. (1910) *Seasonal Variations in the Relative Demand for Money and Capital in the United States.* Washington: Government Printing Office.

Kindleberger, C. P. (1978) *Manias, Panics, and Crashes: A History of Financial Crises.* London: Macmillan.

——— (1984) *A Financial History of Western Europe.* London: Allen & Unwin.

——— (1988) "The Financial Crises of the 1930s and the 1980s: Similarities and Differences." *Kyklos* 41 (2): 171–86.

——— (1994) "Foreword." In M. T. Boyer-Xambeu, G. Deleplace, and L. Gillard, *Private Money and Public Currencies: The 16th Century Challenge*, ix–xii. Armonk, N.Y.: M. E. Sharpe.

King, R. G. (1983) "On the Economics of Private Money." *Journal of Money, Credit, and Banking* 12 (1): 127–58.

King, T. B., and Morley, J. (2007) "In Search of the Natural Rate of Unemployment." *Journal of Monetary Economics* 54 (2): 550–64.

Klein, B. (1974) "The Competitive Supply of Money." *Journal of Money, Credit, and Banking* 6 (4): 423–53.

——— (1975) "Our New Monetary Standard: The Measurement and Effect of Price Uncertainty. 1880–1973." *Economic Inquiry* 13 (4): 461–84.

Klemperer, P. (2010) "The Product-Mixed Auction: A New Auction Design for Differentiated Goods." *Journal of the European Economic Association* 8 (2/3): 526–36.

Knodell, J. (1988) "Interregional Financial Integration and the Banknote Market: The Old Northwest, 1815–1845." *Journal of Economic History* 48 (2): 287–98.

Knox, J. J. (1900) *A History of Banking in the United States.* New York: Bradford Rhodes and Company.

Kohn, D. L. (2009) "Policy Challenges for the Federal Reserve." Speech at the Kellogg School of Management, Northwestern University, Evanston, Ill. (November 16).

Kolko, G. (1963) *The Triumph of Conservatism: A Reinterpretation of American History, 1900–1916.* New York: The Free Press.

Koulischer, F., and Struyven, D. (2011) "Central Bank Liquidity Auctions and Collateral Quality." Working Paper (October). Brussels, Belgium: Université Libre de Bruxelles.

Kroszner, R. S., and Melick, W. (2011) "The Response of the Federal Reserve to the Recent Banking and Financial Crisis." In J. Pisani-Ferry et al. (eds.), *An Ocean Apart? Comparing Transatlantic Responses to the Financial Crisis*, 148–82. Brussels: Bruegel.

Kryzanowski, L., and Roberts, G. S. (1993) "Canadian Banking Solvency, 1922–1940." *Journal of Money, Credit, and Banking* 25 (3): 361–76.

Kuttner, K. (2008) "The Federal Reserve as Lender of Last Resort during the Panic of 2008." Working Paper (December 30). Williamstown, Mass.: Williams College.

Kydland, F. E., and Wynne, M. A. (2002) "Alternative Monetary Constitutions and the Quest for Price Stability." Federal Reserve Bank of Dallas *Economic and Financial Policy Review* 1 (1): 1–19.

Kydland, F. E.; Wynne, M. A.; and Prescott, E. C. (1977) "Rules Rather than Discretion: The Inconsistency of Optimal Plans." *Journal of Political Economy* 85 (3): 473–92.

Labaton, S. (2008) "Testimony Offers Details of Bear Stearns Deal." *New York Times* (April 4).

Labonte, M. (2009) "Financial Turmoil: Federal Reserve Policy Responses." CRS Report for Congress RL34427 (July). Washington: Congressional Research Service.

Lacker, J. M. (2004) "Payment System Disruptions and the Federal Reserve Following September 11, 2001." *Journal of Monetary Economics* 51 (5): 935–65.

——— (2007) "The Role of Central Banks in Credit Markets." Remarks to the International Association of Credit Portfolio Managers, New York (November 7).

Lastrapes, W., and Selgin, G. (2010) "Sources of U.S. Macroeconomic Shocks under Gold and Fiat Regimes." Working Paper, University of Georgia.

Laughlin, J. L. (1894) "The 'Baltimore Plan' of Bank-Issues." *Journal of Political Economy* 3 (1): 101–5.

——— (1898) *Report of the Monetary Commission of the Indianapolis Convention*. Chicago: University of Chicago Press.

——— (1908) "The Aldrich-Vreeland Act." *Journal of Political Economy* 16 (8): 489–513.

Lautz, F. W. (1877) "How National Bank Notes Are Redeemed." *Galaxy* 23 (5): 647–56.

Lebergott, S. (1964) *Manpower in Economic Growth: The American Record since 1800*. New York: McGraw-Hill.

Leduc, S., and Sill, K. (2007) "Monetary Policy, Oil Shocks, and TFP: Accounting for the Decline in U.S. Volatility." *Review of Economic Dynamics* 10 (4): 595–614.

Leijonhufvud, A. (1981) "The Costs and Consequences of Inflation." In *Information and Coordination*, 227–69. New York: Oxford University Press.

——— (2009) "Out of the Corridor: Keynes and the Crisis." *Cambridge Journal of Economics* 33 (4): 741–57.

Lester, R. A. (1939) *Monetary Experiments: Early American and Recent Scandinavian*. Princeton, N.J.: Princeton University Press.

Levi, M. (1988) *Of Rule and Revenue*. Berkeley: University of California Press.

Lewis, M. (2008) "How Bernanke's Banker Rescue Spells Their Demise." Bloomberg (June 10).

Li, V. (2013) "The Right Man at the Right Time." *U.S. News & World Report* (August 19).

Litan, R. E. (1987) *What Should Banks Do?* Washington: The Brookings Institution.

Liu, H. C. K. (2005) "The Wizard of Bubbleland, Part 3: How the U.S. Money Market Really Works." *Asia Times* (October 27).

Liu, Z.; Waggoner, D. F.; and Zha, T. (2009) "Sources of the Great Moderation: Shocks, Friction, or Monetary Policy?" Federal Reserve Bank of Atlanta Working Paper 2009–3 (February).

Livingston, J. (1986) *Origins of the Federal Reserve System*. Ithaca, N.Y.: Cornell University Press.

Lott, J. R. Jr. (1997) "Does Political Reform Increase Wealth?: Or, Why the Difference Between the Chicago and Virginia Schools Is Really an Elasticity Question." *Public Choice* 91 (3–4): 219–27.

Lowenstein, R. (2015) *America's Bank: The Epic Struggle to Create the Federal Reserve*. New York: Penguin Press.

Lucas, R. E. Jr. (1976) "Econometric Policy Evaluation: A Critique." *Carnegie-Rochester Conference Series on Public Policy* 1: 19–46.

——— (2000) "Inflation and Welfare." *Econometrica* 68 (2): 247–74.

Madigan, B. F. (2009) "Bagehot's Dictum in Practice: Formulating and Implementing Policies to Combat the Financial Crisis." Speech at the Federal Reserve Bank of Kansas City's Annual Economic Symposium, Jackson Hole, Wyo. (August 21).

Mamun, A.; Hassan, M. K.; and Johnson, M. (2010) "How Did the Fed Do? An Empirical Assessment of the Fed's New Initiatives in the Financial Crisis." *Applied Financial Economics* 20 (1–2): 15–30.

Mankiw, G.; Miron, J.; and Weil, D. (1987) "The Adjustment of Expectations to a Change in Regime: A Study of the Founding of the Federal Reserve." *American Economic Review* 77 (3): 358–74.

Marshall, D. (2002) "Origins of the Use of Treasury Debt in Open Market Operations: Lessons for the Present." Federal Reserve Bank of Chicago *Economic Perspectives* 26 (1): 45–54.

Mayhew, N. J. (1992) "From Regional to Central Minting, 1158–1464." In C. E. Challis (ed.), *A New History of the Royal Mint*, 83–178. New York: Cambridge University Press.

McAndrews, J.; Sarkar, A.; and Wang, Z. (2008) "The Effect of the Term Auction Facility on the London Inter-Bank Offered Rate." Federal Reserve Bank of New York Staff Report No. 335 (July).

McCallum, B. T. (2000) "Alternative Monetary Policy Rules: A Comparison with Historical Settings for the United States, the United Kingdom, and Japan." Federal Reserve Bank of Richmond *Economic Quarterly* 86 (1): 49–79.

McConnachie, R. (1996) *Primary Dealers in Government Securities Markets.* Handbook in Central Banking No. 6. London: Bank of England Centre for Central Banking Studies.

McConnell, M. M., and Perez-Quiros, G. (2000) "Output Fluctuations in the United States: What Has Changed since the Early 1980s?" *American Economic Review* 90 (5): 1464–76.

McCulley, R. T. (1992) *Banks and Politics during the Progressive Era: The Origins of the Federal Reserve System, 1897–1913*. New York: Routledge.

McCulloch, H. (1889) *Men and Measures of Half a Century*. New York: Charles Scribner's Sons.

McCulloch, J. H. (1982) *Money and Inflation*, 2nd ed. New York: Academic Press.

——— (1986) "Bank Regulation and Deposit Insurance." *Journal of Business* 59 (1): 79–85.

Meltzer, A. H. (2003) *A History of the Federal Reserve: Vol. 1: 1913–1951*. Chicago: University of Chicago Press.

——— (2012) "Federal Reserve Policy in the Great Recession." *Cato Journal* 32 (2): 255–63.

Mills, G., and Rockoff, H. (1987) "Compliance with Price Controls in the United States and the United Kingdom during World War II." *Journal of Economic History* 47 (1): 197–213.

Mingo, J. J. (1981) "The Economic Impact of Deposit Rate Ceilings." In A. A. Heggestad (ed.), *Regulation of Consumer Financial Services*. Cambridge, Mass.: Abt Books.

Minsky, H. P. (1977) "A Theory of Systemic Fragility." In E. I. Altman and A. W. Sametz (eds.), *Financial Crises: Institutions and Markets in a Fragile Environment*. New York: John Wiley & Sons.

——— (1982) "The Financial-Instability Hypothesis: Capitalist Processes and the Behavior of the Economy." In C. P. Kindleberger and J. P. Laffargue (eds.), *Financial Crises: Theory, History, and Policy*, 13–39. New York: Cambridge University Press.

Mints, L. W. (1945) *A History of Banking Theory*. Chicago: University of Chicago Press.

——— (1950) *Monetary Policy for a Competitive Society.* New York: McGraw-Hill.

Miron, J. A. (1986) "Financial Panics, the Seasonality of the Nominal Interest Rate, and the Founding of the Fed." *American Economics Review* 76 (1): 125–40.

——— (1988) "The Founding of the Fed and the Destabilization of the Post-1914 Economy." NBER Working Paper No. 2701 (September). Cambridge, Mass.: National Bureau of Economic Research.

Miron, J. A., and Romer, C. D. (1990) "A New Monthly Index of Industrial Production, 1884–1940." *Journal of Economic History* 50 (2): 321–37.

Mitchell, W. C. (1903) *A History of the Greenbacks*. Chicago: Chicago University Press.

——— (1911) "The Publications of the National Monetary Commission." *Quarterly Journal of Economics* 25 (3): 563–93.

Mitchener, K. J., and Richardson, G. (2016) "Network Contagion and Interbank Amplification during the Great Depression." NBER Working Paper No. 22074 (March). Cambridge, Mass.: National Bureau of Economic Research.

Mohanty, M. S., and Zampolli, F. (2009) "Government Size and Macroeconomic Stability." *BIS Quarterly Review* (December): 55–68.

Morgan-Webb, C. (1934) *The Rise and Fall of the Gold Standard*. New York: Macmillan.

Moro, A. (2010) "The Structural Transformation between Manufacturing and Services and the Decline in U.S. GDP Volatility." Economics Department Working Paper 09–14 (June). Universidad Carlos III de Madrid.

Motomura, A. (1994) "The Best and Worst of Currencies: Seigniorage and Currency Policy in Spain, 1597–1650." *Journal of Economic History* 54 (1): 104–27.

Mullineaux, A.W. (1987) "Why Is the U.S. Banking System So Unstable?" *Royal Bank of Scotland Review* 153: 36–52.

Myers, M. G. (1931) *The New York Money Market, Volume 1: Origins and Development*. New York: Columbia University Press.

Nevin, E., and Davis, E. W. (1970) *The London Clearing Banks*. London: ELEK Books.

New York Chamber of Commerce (1907) *Forty-Ninth Annual Report*. New York: Press of the Chamber of Commerce.

Newcomb, S. (1865) *A Critical Examination of Our Financial Policy during the Southern Rebellion*. New York: D. Appleton and Company.

Ng, K. (1988) "Free Banking Laws and Barriers to Entry in Banking, 1838–1860." *Journal of Economic History* 48 (4): 877–89.

Nichols, D. A. (1974) "Some Principles of Inflationary Finance." *Journal of Political Economy* 82 (2): 423–30.

Niehans, J. (1978) *The Theory of Money*. Baltimore, Md.: Johns Hopkins University Press.

Noyes, A. D. (1910) *History of the National Bank Currency*. Washington: Government Printing Office.

Obstfeld, M., and Taylor, A. M. (2003) "Sovereign Risk, Credibility, and the Gold Standard: 1870–1913 versus 1920–1931." *Economic Journal* 113 (487): 241–75.

O'Driscoll, G. P. Jr. (1988) "Deposit Insurance in Theory and Practice." *Cato Journal* 7 (3): 661–75.

Officer, L. H. (n.d.) "Gold Standard." EH.Net Encyclopedia: http://eh.net/encyclopedia/gold-standard.

Officer, L. H., and Williamson, S. H. (2009) "Purchasing Power of Money in the United States from 1774 to 2008." Measuring Worth: http://measuringworth.com/ppowerus.

O'Leary, P. M. (1937) "The Coinage Legislation of 1834." *Journal of Political Economy* 45 (1): 81–94.

Orphanides, A., and Williams, J. C. (2005) "The Decline of Activist Stabilization Policy: Natural Rate Misperceptions, Learning, and Expectations." *Journal of Economic Dynamics and Control* 29 (11): 1927–50.

Owen, R. L. (1913) "The Currency Bill and Financial Panics." *The Independent* (December 25): 581.

Paul, R., and Lehrman, L. (1982) *The Case for Gold: A Minority Report of the U.S. Gold Commission*. Washington: Cato Institute.

Penney, J. (2011) "Out of the Shadows: Central Clearing of Repo, A Transparent Market Structure for Cash Borrowers and Lenders." High Line Advisors (April): https://www.tradeaqs.com/papers/20110401.pdf.

Perotti, E. (2010) "Systemic Liquidity Risk and Bankruptcy." Policy Insight No. 52 (October). London: Centre for Economic Policy Research.

Phillips, D. G. (1906) "The Treason of the Senate." *Cosmopolitan* 40 (5).

Pianalto, S. (2013) "The Federal Reserve's Role in Supporting the U.S. Economy." Speech at the International Economic Forum of the Americas, West Palm Beach, Fla. (April 8).

Pivetta, F., and Reis, R. (2007) "The Persistence of Inflation in the United States." *Journal of Economic Dynamics and Control* 31 (4): 1326–58.

Postlewaite, A., and Vives, X. (1987) "Bank Runs as an Equilibrium Phenomenon." *Journal of Political Economy* 95 (3): 485–91.

Primiceri, G. E. (2006) "Why Inflation Rose and Fell: Policymakers' Beliefs and U.S. Postwar Stabilization Policy." *Quarterly Journal of Economics* 121 (3): 867–901.

Pugsley, C. A. (1907) "Emergency Circulation." In W. H. Hull (ed.), *Practical Problems in Banking and Currency*. New York: Macmillan.

Redish, A. (1993) "Anchors Aweigh: The Transition from Commodity Money to Fiat Money in Western Economies." *Canadian Journal of Economics* 26 (4): 777–95.

——— (2000) *Bimetallism: An Economic and Historical Analysis*. New York: Cambridge University Press.

Redlich, F. (1951) *The Molding of American Banking: Men and Ideas. Part II: 1840–1910*. New York: Hafner Publishing.

Reid, M. (1982) *The Secondary Banking Crisis, 1973–75*. London: Macmillan.

Repullo, R. (2000) "Who Should Act as Lender of Last Resort: An Incomplete Contracts Model." *Journal of Money, Credit, and Banking* 32 (3): 580–605.

Rhode, P. W., and Sutch, R. (2006) "Estimates of National Product before 1929." In S. B. Carter et al. (eds.), *Historical Statistics of the United States*, Millennial Edition Online. Cambridge: Cambridge University Press.

Rich, G. (1988) *The Cross of Gold: Money and the Canadian Business Cycle, 1867–1913*. Ottawa: Carleton University Press.

Ritschl, A.; Sarferaz, S.; and Uebele, M. (2008) "The U.S. Business Cycle, 1867–1995: Dynamic Factor Analysis vs. Reconstructed National Accounts." SFB 649 Discussion Paper No. 2008–066 (November). Berlin: Collaborative Research Center: http://econstor.eu/bitstream/10419/25309/1/590225162.PDF.

Roberts, R. (2010) *Gambling with Other People's Money: How Perverted Incentives Caused the Financial Crisis*. Arlington, Va.: The Mercatus Center at George Mason University.

Robertson, R. M., and Walton, G. M. (1979) *History of the American Economy*, 4th ed. New York: Harcourt Brace Jovanovich.

Rockoff, H. (1974) "The Free Banking Era: A Reexamination." *Journal of Money, Credit, and Banking* 6 (2): 141–67.

——— (1975) *The Free Banking Era: A Re-Examination*. New York: Arno Press.

——— (1986) "Institutional Requirements for Stable Free Banking." *Cato Journal* 6 (2): 617–34.

Rolnick, A. J., and Weber, W. E. (1983) "New Evidence on the Free Banking Era." *American Economic Review* 73 (5): 1080–91.

——— (1984) "The Causes of Free Bank Failures: A Detailed Examination." *Journal of Monetary Economics* 14 (3): 267–91.

——— (1986) "Gresham's Law or Gresham's Fallacy?" *Journal of Political Economy* 94 (1): 185–99.

——— (1988) "Explaining the Demand for Free Bank Notes." *Journal of Monetary Economics* 21 (1): 47–71.

——— (1994) "Inflation and Money Growth under Alternative Monetary Standards." Federal Reserve Bank of Minneapolis Research Department Working Paper No. 528.

Romer, C. D. (1986a) "Is the Stabilization of the Postwar Economy a Figment of the Data?" *American Economic Review* 76 (3): 314–34.

——— (1986b) "Spurious Volatility in Historical Unemployment Data." *Journal of Political Economy* 94 (1): 1–37.

——— (1989) "The Prewar Business Cycle Reconsidered: New Estimates of Gross National Product, 1869–1908." *Journal of Political Economy* 97 (1): 1–37.

——— (1992) "What Ended the Great Depression?" *Journal of Economic History* 52 (4): 757–84.

——— (1994) "Remeasuring Business Cycles." *Journal of Economic History* 54 (3): 573–609.

——— (1999) "Changes in Business Cycles: Evidence and Explanations." *Journal of Economic Perspectives* 13 (2): 23–44.

——— (2009) "New Estimates of Prewar Gross National Product and Unemployment." *Journal of Economic History* 46 (2): 341–52.

Root, E. (1913) "The Banking and Currency Bill." Speech in the U.S. Senate (December 13).

Root, L. C. (1894) "Canadian Bank-Note Currency." *Sound Currency* 2 (2): 309–24.

——— (1895) "New York Bank Currency: Safety Fund vs. Bond Security." *Sound Currency* 2 (5): 285–308.

Rothbard, M. N. (1962) "The Case for a 100 Per Cent Gold Dollar." In L. B. Yeager (ed.), *In Search of a Monetary Constitution*, 94–136. Cambridge, Mass.: Harvard University Press.

——— (1988) "The Myth of Free Banking in Scotland." *Review of Austrian Economics* 2: 229–45.

Rueff, J. (1972) *The Monetary Sin of the West*. New York: Macmillan.

Samuelson, P. A., and Nordhaus, W. D. (1998) *Economics*, 16th ed. New York: McGraw-Hill.

Sanati, C. (2010) "Paulson Rejects Claim That Bear Was Solvent." *New York Times* (May 6).

Sannucci, V. (1989) "The Establishment of a Central Bank: Italy in the 19th Century." In M. de Cecco and A. Giovanini (eds.), *A European Central Bank? Perspectives on Monetary Unification after Ten Years of the EMS*, 244–80. New York: Cambridge University Press.

Sargent, T. J. (1999) *The Conquest of American Inflation*. Princeton, N.J.: Princeton University Press.

Sargent, T. J., and Velde, F. R. (2003) *The Big Problem of Small Change*. Princeton, N.J.: Princeton University Press.

Saul, S. B. (1969) *The Myth of the Great Depression, 1873–1896*. London: Macmillan.

Schmitt-Grohé, S., and Uribe, M. (2007) "Optimal Inflation Stabilization in a Medium-Scale Macroeconomic Model." In K. Schmidt-Hebbel and F. S. Mishkin (eds.), *Monetary Policy under Inflation Targeting*, 125–86. Santiago, Chile: Central Bank of Chile.

Schuler, K. (1988) "Evolution of Canadian Banking, 1867–1914." Manuscript, University of Georgia.

Schumpeter, J. A. ([1918] 1954) "The Crisis of the Tax State." *International Economic Papers* 4. London: Macmillan.

Schwartz, A. J. (1987) *Money in Historical Perspective*. Chicago: University of Chicago Press and National Bureau of Economic Research.

——— (1992) "The Misuse of the Fed's Discount Window." Federal Reserve Bank of St. Louis *Review* 74 (5): 58–69.

Schweikart, L. (1987) *Banking in the American South from the Age of Jackson to Reconstruction*. Baton Rouge: Louisiana State University Press.

Scott, W. A. (1908) "Rates on the New York Money Market, 1896–1906." *Journal of Political Economy* 16 (5): 273–98.

Sechrest, L. J. (1988) "White's Free-Banking Thesis: A Case of Mistaken Identity." *Review of Austrian Economics* 2: 247–57.

Selgin, G. (1986) "Accommodating Changes in the Relative Demand for Currency: Free Banking versus Central Banking." *Cato Journal* 6 (2): 617–34.

——— (1988) *The Theory of Free Banking: Money Supply under Competitive Note Issue*. Totowa, N.J.: Rowman and Littlefield.

——— (1993) "In Defense of Bank Suspension." *Journal of Financial Services Research* 7 (4): 347–64.

——— (1994) "Free Banking and Monetary Control." *Economic Journal* 104 (427): 1449–59.

——— (1996a) "Salvaging Gresham's Law: The Good, the Bad, and the Illegal." *Journal of Money, Credit, and Banking* 28 (4): 637–49.

——— (1996b) "The 'Productivity Norm' versus Zero Inflation in the History of Economic Thought." *History of Political Economy* 27 (4): 705–35.

——— (1997) *Less Than Zero: The Case for a Falling Price Level in a Growing Economy*. London: Institute of Economic Affairs.

——— (2001) "In-Concert Overexpansion and the Precautionary Demand for Bank Reserves." *Journal of Money, Credit, and Banking* 33 (2): 294–300.

——— (2003) "Adaptive Learning and the Transition to Fiat Money." *Economic Journal* 113 (484): 147–65.

Selgin, G., and White, L. H. (1987) "The Evolution of a Free Banking System." *Economic Inquiry* 25 (3): 439–57.

——— (1992) "National Bank Notes as a Quasi-High-Powered Money." Manuscript, University of Georgia.

——— (1994) "How Would the Invisible Hand Handle Money?" *Journal of Economic Literature* 32 (4): 1718–49.

——— (1997) "The Option Clause in Scottish Banking." *Journal of Money, Credit, and Banking* 29 (2): 270–73.

——— (2005) "Credible Currency: A Constitutional Perspective." *Constitutional Political Economy* 16 (1): 71–83.

Selgin, G.; Beckworth, D.; and Bahadir, B. (2015) "The Productivity Gap: Monetary Policy, the Subprime Boom, and the Post-2001 Productivity Surge." *Journal of Policy Modeling* 37 (2): 189–207.

Shadow Financial Regulatory Committee (2009) "Reforming the Primary Dealer Structure." Statement No. 280 (December 14).

Sheridan, B. (2011) "Lender of Last Resort: An Examination of the Federal Reserve's Primary Dealer Credit Facility." Working Paper, University of Notre Dame, Ind.

Shields, R. E. (1969) "Economic Growth and Price Deflation, 1873–1896." Dissertation, University of Virginia, Charlottesville.

Short, G. D., and Gunther, J. W. (1988) *The Texas Thrift Situation: Implications for the Texas Financial Industry*. Federal Reserve Bank of Dallas.

Shughart, W. F. II. (1988) "A Public Choice Perspective of the Banking Act of 1933." *Cato Journal* 7 (3): 595–613.

Silber, W. L. (2007) "The Great Financial Crisis of 1914: What Can We Learn from Aldrich–Vreeland Emergency Currency?" *American Economic Review* 97 (2): 285–89.

Sims, C. A., and Zha, T. (2006) "Were There Regime Switches in U.S. Monetary Policy?" *American Economic Review* 96 (1): 54–81.

Singh, M. (2011) "Making OTC Derivatives Safe: A Fresh Look." IMF Working Paper No. 11–66 (March). Washington: International Monetary Fund.

Skeel, D. (2009) "Give Bankruptcy a Chance." *The Weekly Standard* (June 29).

Small, D. H., and Clouse, J. A. (2005) "The Scope of Monetary Policy Actions Authorized under the Federal Reserve Act." *Topics in Macroeconomics* 5 (1): 1–41.

Smith, V. (1936) *The Rationale of Central Banking*. London: P. S. King & Son.

Smith, Y. (2007) "Gotcha! (Willem Buiter's Market Maker of Last Resort Edition)." Naked Capitalism (December 15): http://nakedcapitalism.com/2007/12/gotcha-willem-buiters-market-maker-of.html.

Solow, R. M. (1982) "On the Lender of Last Resort." In C. P. Kindleberger and J. P. Laffargue (eds.), *Financial Crises: Theory, History, and Policy*, 237–48. New York: Cambridge University Press.

Sprague, I. (1986) *Bailout: An Insider's Account of Bank Failures and Rescues*. New York: Basic Books.

Sprague, O. M. W. (1903) "Branch Banking in the United States." *Quarterly Journal of Economics* 17 (2): 242–60.

——— (1904) "The Distribution of Money between the Banks and the People since 1893." *Quarterly Journal of Economics* 18 (4): 513–28.

——— (1910) *History of Crises under the National Banking System*. Washington: National Monetary Commission.

Spufford, P. (1988) *Money and Its Use in Medieval Europe*. Cambridge: Cambridge University Press.

Stearns, G. L. (1864) *A Few Facts Pertaining to Currency and Banking*. Boston: A. Williams and Company.

Steil, B. (2011) "No, Brad DeLong, There Is No Draghi Claus." Forbes Online (December 8).

Stella, P. (2009) "The Federal Reserve System Balance Sheet: What Happened and Why It Matters." IMF Working Paper 09-120 (May). Washington: International Monetary Fund.

Stephenson, N. W. (1930) *Nelson Aldrich: A Leader in American Politics*. New York: Charles Scribner's Sons.

Stern, G. H. (2003) "Should We Accept the Conventional Wisdom about Deflation?" Federal Reserve Bank of Minneapolis *The Region* (September 1).

Stock, J. H., and Watson, M. W. (2002) "Has the Business Cycle Changed and Why?" *NBER Macroeconomics Annual* 17: 159–218.

——— (2005) "Understanding Changes in International Business Cycle Dynamics." *Journal of the European Economic Association* 3 (5): 968–1006.

——— (2007) "Why Has U.S. Inflation Become Harder to Forecast?" *Journal of Money, Credit, and Banking* 39 (s1): 3–33.

Summers, B. (1976) "Private Coinage in America." *The Freeman* 26 (7): 436–40.

Sumner, S. (1989) "Using Futures Instrument Prices to Target Nominal Income." *Bulletin of Economic Research* 41 (2): 147–62.

——— (2006) "Let a Thousand Models Bloom: The Advantages of Making the FOMC a Truly 'Open Market.'" *Berkeley Electronic Journal of Macroeconomics* 6 (1).

——— (2009) "The Real Problem Was Nominal." Cato Unbound (September 14): http://cato-unbound.org/2009/09/14/scott-sumner/real-problem-was-nominal.

——— (2011) "Can the Fed Learn to Speak a Non-Interest Rate Language?" The Money Illusion (October 30): http://themoneyillusion.com/?p=11586.

Sumner, W. G. (1896) *A History of Banking in the United States.* New York: The Journal of Commerce and Commercial Bulletin.

Surico, P. (2008) "Measuring the Time Inconsistency of U.S. Monetary Policy." *Economica* 75 (297): 22–38.

Sylla, R. (1972) "The United States, 1863–1913." In R. Cameron (ed.), *Banking and Economic Development*, 232–62. New York: Oxford University Press.

——— (1988) "The Autonomy of Monetary Authorities: The Case of the U.S. Federal Reserve System." In G. Toniolo (ed.), *Central Banks' Independence in Historical Perspective*, 17–38. Berlin: Walter de Gruyter.

Tallman, E. W., and Moen, J. R. (2012) "Liquidity Creation without a Central Bank: Clearing House Loan Certificates in the Banking Panic of 1907." *Journal of Financial Stability* 8 (4): 277–91.

Tarr, D. G. (2009) "Bailouts and Deficits or Haircuts: How to Restore U.S. Financial Markets' Stability." Manuscript, New Economic School, Moscow (May 14): http://papers.ssrn.com/sol3/papers.cfm?abstract_id=1401555.

——— (2010) "Lehman Brothers and Washington Mutual Show Too Big to Fail Is a Myth." Manuscript, New Economic School, Moscow (July 21): http://papers.ssrn.com/sol3/papers.cfm?abstract_id=1533522.

Taub, B. (1985) "Private Fiat Money with Many Supplies." *Journal of Monetary Economics* 16 (2): 195–208.

Taylor, F. M. (1914) "The Elasticity of Note Issue under the New Currency Law." *Journal of Political Economy* 22 (5): 453–63.

Taylor, J. B. (1986) "Improvements in Macroeconomic Stability: The Role of Wages and Prices." In R. J. Gordon (ed.), *The American Business Cycle: Continuity and Change*, 639–59. Chicago: University of Chicago Press.

——— (2007) "Housing and Monetary Policy." Federal Reserve Bank of Kansas City Economic Policy Symposium, Jackson Hole, Wyo. (September 1).

——— (2008) "The Financial Crisis and the Policy Responses: An Empirical Analysis of What Went Wrong." In *A Festschrift in Honour of David Dodge*, 1–18. Ottawa: Bank of Canada.

——— (2009a) *Getting Off Track: How Government Actions and Interventions Caused, Prolonged, and Worsened the Financial Crisis*. Stanford: The Hoover Institution.

——— (2009b) "Systemic Risk and the Role of Government." Speech at the Conference on Financial Innovation and Crises, Federal Reserve Bank of Atlanta, Jekyll Island, Ga. (May 12).

——— (2013) "Reviewing the 'Too Low for Too Long' Evidence." Economics One (October 19): http://economicsone.com/2013/10/19/reviewing-the-too-low-for-too-long-evidence.

Taylor, J. B., and Williams, J. C. (2008) "A Black Swan in the Money Market." Federal Reserve Bank of San Francisco Working Paper 2008–04.

Temzelides, T. (1997) "Are Bank Runs Contagious?" Federal Reserve Bank of Philadelphia *Business Review* (November/December): 3–14.

Thomas, S. E. (1934) *The Rise and Growth of Joint-Stock Banking*. London: I. Pitman & Sons.

Thornton, D. L. (2008) "Walter Bagehot, the Discount Window, and TAF." Federal Reserve Bank of St. Louis *Economic Synopses* No. 27 (October).

——— (2009a) "The Fed, Liquidity, and Credit Allocation." Federal Reserve Bank of St. Louis *Review* 91 (1): 13–21.

——— (2009b) "Would Quantitative Easing Sooner Have Tempered the Financial Crisis and Economic Recession?" Federal Reserve Bank of St. Louis *Economic Synopses* No. 37 (August).

——— (2012) "The Federal Reserve's Response to the Financial Crisis: What It Did and What It Should Have Done." Federal Reserve Bank of St. Louis Working Paper (October).

Thornton, J. L.; Hubbard, G.; and Scott, H. (2009) "The Federal Reserve's Independence Is at Risk." *Financial Times* (August 20).

Timberlake, R. H. Jr. (1963) "Mr. Shaw and His Critics: Monetary Policy in the Golden Era Reviewed." *Quarterly Journal of Economics* 77 (1): 40–54.

——— (1978) *The Origins of Central Banking in the United States*. Cambridge, Mass.: Harvard University Press.

——— (1993) *Monetary Policy in the United States: An Intellectual and Institutional History*. Chicago: University of Chicago Press.

——— (2007) "Gold Standards and the Real Bills Doctrine in U.S. Monetary Policy." *Independent Review* 11 (3): 325–54.

——— (n.d.) "Federal Reserve System." The Concise Encyclopedia of Economics: http://econlib.org/library/Enc/FederalReserveSystem.html.

Tuckman, B. (2010) "Systemic Risk and the Tri-Party Repo Clearing Banks." CFS Policy Paper (February). New York: Center for Financial Stability.

U.S. Census Bureau (1870) *Compendium of the Ninth Census*. Washington: Government Printing Office.

——— (1975) *Historical Statistics of the United States*. Washington: Government Printing Office.

U.S. Congress (1895) "Hearings before the House Committee on Banking and Currency begun September 29, 1893." Washington: Government Printing Office.

——— (1897) "Hearings and Arguments, 1896–97." Committee on Banking and Currency, House of Representatives. Washington: Government Printing Office.

——— (1898) "Hearings and Arguments, 1897–98." Committee on Banking and Currency, House of Representatives. Washington: Government Printing Office.

——— (1908) "Hearings and Arguments on H.R. 20835." Committee on Banking and Currency, House of Representatives. Washington: Government Printing Office.

——— (1911) "Hearings on House Resolution No. 314." Committee on Rules, House of Representatives. Washington: Government Printing Office.

——— (1913) "Hearings on S. 2639 [the Federal Reserve Act]." Committee on Banking and Currency, House of Representatives. Washington: Government Printing Office.

——— (1949) "For the Establishment of the National Monetary Commission." Report to Accompany S. 1559. Committee on Banking and Currency, Senate. Washington: Government Printing Office.

——— (1991) "An Analysis of Federal Reserve Discount Window Lending to Failed Institutions." Staff Report, Committee on Banking, Finance, and Urban Affairs, House of Representatives. Washington: Government Printing Office.

U.S. Treasury (2008) "Testimony by Secretary Henry M. Paulson, Jr. before the Senate Banking Committee on Turmoil in US Credit Markets." Press Release (September 23): https://www.treasury.gov/press-center/press-releases/Pages/hp1153.aspx.

——— (various dates) *Annual Report of the Secretary of the Treasury on the State of the Finances*. Washington: Government Printing Office.

——— (various dates) *Annual Statement on the Condition of Banks in the United States*. Washington: Government Printing Office.

Vanderlip, F. A. (1935) *From Farm Boy to Financier*. New York: Appleton-Century.

Vernon, J. R. (1994) "Unemployment Rates in Postbellum America, 1869–1899." *Journal of Macroeconomics* 16 (4): 701–14.

Volcker, P. (2008) Speech before the Economic Club of New York (April 8).

Wagster, J. D. (2009) "Canadian-Bank Stability in the Great Depression: The Role of Capital, Implicit Government Support and Diversification." Manuscript, Wayne State University.

Waldo, D. G. (1985) "Bank Runs, the Deposit-Currency Ratio and the Interest Rate." *Journal of Monetary Economics* 15 (3): 269–77.

Walker, A. (1863) "The New Currency of the United States." *The Bankers' Magazine* 12 (11): 833–43.

Wallison, P. J. (2009) "Regulation without Reason: The Group of Thirty Report." American Enterprise Institute *Financial Services Outlook* (January).

Walter, J. R., and Weinberg, J. A. (2002) "How Large Is the Federal Financial Safety Net?" *Cato Journal* 21 (3): 369–93.

Warburg, P. M. (1911) "A United Reserve Bank of the United States." *Proceedings of the Academy of Political Science in the City of New York* 1 (2): 302–42.

——— (1912) "Letter to Prof. J. Laurence Laughlin, 22 April 1912." In the Paul Moritz Warburg Papers, Yale University.

——— (1930) *The Federal Reserve System: Its Origin and Growth*, Vol. 1. New York: Macmillan.

Warner, J. D. (1895) "The Currency Famine of 1893." *Sound Currency* 2 (6): 337–56.

Watkins, L. L. (1929) *Bankers' Balances: A Study of the Effects of the Federal Reserve System on Banking Relationships*. Chicago: A. W. Shaw.

Watson, M. W. (1994) "Business-Cycle Durations and Postwar Stabilization of the U.S. Economy." *American Economic Review* 84 (1): 24–46.

Weber, E. J. (1988) "Currency Competition in Switzerland, 1826–1850." *Kyklos* 41 (3): 459–78.

Weintraub, R. E. (1978) "Congressional Supervision of Monetary Policy." *Journal of Monetary Economics* 4 (2): 341–62.

West, R. C. (1977) *Banking Reform and the Federal Reserve, 1863–1923*. Ithaca, N.Y.: Cornell University Press.

Whalen, C. (2009) "Too Big to Bail: Lehman Brothers Is the Model for Fixing the Zombie Banks." Seeking Alpha (February 19): http://seekingalpha.com/article/121448-too-big-to-bail-lehman-brothers-is-the-model-for-fixing-the-zombie-banks.

Wheelock, D. (1989) "The Strategy, Effectiveness, and Consistency of Federal Reserve Monetary Policy, 1924–1933." *Explorations in Economic History* 26 (4): 453–76.

——— (2010) "Lessons Learned? Comparing the Federal Reserve's Responses to the Crises of 1929–1933 and 2007–2009." Federal Reserve Bank of St. Louis *Review* 92 (2): 89–107.

White, E. N. (1983) *The Regulation and Reform of the American Banking System, 1900–1929.* Princeton, N.J.: Princeton University Press.

White, H. (1894) "National and State Banks." *Sound Currency* 2 (1): 205–20.

——— (1903) "The Currency Question." *Sound Currency* 10 (2): 49–59.

White, L. H. (1984) *Free Banking in Britain: Theory, Experience, and Debate, 1800–45.* Cambridge: Cambridge University Press.

——— (1986) "Regulatory Sources of Instability in Banking." *Cato Journal* 5 (3): 891–97.

——— (1999) *The Theory of Monetary Institutions.* Oxford: Blackwell.

——— (2004) "Will the Gold in Fort Knox Be Enough?" American Institute for Economic Research *Economic Education Bulletin* 44 (9): 23–32.

——— (2005) "The Federal Reserve System's Influence on Research in Monetary Economics." *Econ Journal Watch* 2 (2): 325–54.

——— (2008) "Is the Gold Standard Still the Gold Standard among Monetary Systems?" Cato Institute Briefing Paper No. 100 (February).

——— (2009) *Free Banking in Britain: Theory, Experience, and Debate 1800–1845*, 2nd ed. London: Institute of Economic Affairs.

——— (2010) "The Rule of Law or the Rule of Central Bankers?" *Cato Journal* 30 (3): 451–63.

——— (2012) "Making the Transition to a New Gold Standard." *Cato Journal* 32 (2): 411–21.

White, L. H., and Boudreaux, D. J. (1998) "Is Non-Price Competition in Currency Inefficient?" *Journal of Money, Credit, and Banking* 30 (2): 252–60.

Wicker, E. (1980) "A Reconsideration of the Causes of the Banking Panic of 1930." *Journal of Economic History* 40 (3): 571–83.

——— (1996) *The Banking Panics of the Great Depression.* Cambridge: Cambridge University Press.

——— (2000) *Banking Panics of the Gilded Age.* Cambridge: Cambridge University Press.

——— (2005) *The Great Debate on Banking Reform: Nelson Aldrich and the Origins of the Fed.* Columbus, Ohio: Ohio State University Press.

Wiebe, R. H. (1962) *Businessmen and Reform: A Study of the Progressive Movement.* Chicago: Quadrangle Books.

Wigmore, B. A. (1987) "Was the Bank Holiday of 1933 Caused by a Run on the Dollar?" *Journal of Economic History* 47 (3): 739–55.

Williams, J. C. (2012) "The Federal Reserve and the Economic Recovery." Federal Reserve Bank of San Francisco *Economic Letter* (January 17).

Williams, J. E., and Everitt, J. L. (1863) *Report of a Committee on the National Bank Currency Act, Its Defects and Effects.* New York: C. S. Westcott.

Williamson, S. D. (1989) "Bank Failures, Financial Restrictions, and Aggregate Fluctuations: Canada and the United States, 1870–1913." Federal Reserve Bank of Minneapolis *Quarterly Review* 13 (3): 20–40.

——— (1992) "Laissez-Faire Banking and Circulating Media of Exchange." *Journal of Financial Intermediation* 2 (2): 134–64.

Willis, H. P. (1903) "The Status of the Currency Reform Movement." *Sound Currency* 10 (4): 117–46.

Wojnilower, A. M. (1980) "The Central Role of Credit Crunches in Recent Financial History." *Brookings Papers on Economic Activity* 2: 277–326.

Wu, T. (2011) "The U.S. Money Market and the Term Auction Facility in the Financial Crisis of 2007–2009." *Review of Economics and Statistics* 93 (2): 617–31.

Zarnowitz, V. (1992) *Business Cycles: Theory, History, Indicators, and Forecasting*. Chicago: University of Chicago Press.

——— (1996) *Business Cycles*. Chicago: University of Chicago Press.

Zoellick, R. (2010) "The G20 must look beyond Bretton Woods II." *Financial Times* (November 7).

Index

Note: Information in figures and tables is indicated by *f* and *t*; *n* designates a numbered note.

ABOUT THE AUTHOR

George Selgin directs the Cato Institute's Center for Monetary and Financial Alternatives and is Professor Emeritus of Economics at the University of Georgia. His previous books include *The Theory of Free Banking, Bank Deregulation and Monetary Order, Less Than Zero,* and *Good Money*.

About the Cato Institute and Its Center for Monetary and Financial Alternatives

Founded in 1977, the Cato Institute is a public policy research foundation dedicated to broadening the parameters of policy debate to allow consideration of more options that are consistent with the principles of limited government, individual liberty, and peace.

The Institute is named for *Cato's Letters*, libertarian pamphlets that were widely read in the American Colonies in the early 18th century and played a major role in laying the philosophical foundation for the American Revolution.

The Cato Institute undertakes an extensive publications program on the complete spectrum of policy issues. Books, monographs, and shorter studies are commissioned to examine the federal budget, Social Security, regulation, military spending, international trade, and myriad other issues. Major policy conferences are held throughout the year.

The Cato Institute's Center for Monetary and Financial Alternatives was founded in 2014 to assess the shortcomings of existing monetary and financial regulatory arrangements, and to discover and promote more stable and efficient alternatives.

In order to maintain its independence, the Cato Institute accepts no government funding. Contributions are received from foundations, corporations, and individuals, and other revenue is generated from the sale of publications. The Institute is a nonprofit, tax-exempt, educational foundation under Section 501(c)3 of the Internal Revenue Code.

CATO INSTITUTE
1000 Massachusetts Avenue, N.W.
Washington, D.C. 20001
www.cato.org